Introduction to Windows Azure

An Introduction to Cloud Computing Using Microsoft Windows Azure

Henry Li

Apress®

Introduction to Windows Azure

ISBN-13 (pbk): 978-1-4302-2469-3

ISBN-13 (electronic): 978-1-4302-2470-9

Printed and bound in the United States of America 9 8 7 6 5 4 3 2 1

President and Publisher: Paul Manning
Lead Editor: Matthew Moodie
Technical Reviewer: Bing Long
Editorial Board: Clay Andres, Steve Anglin, Mark Beckner, Ewan Buckingham, Gary Cornell, Jonathan Gennick, Michelle Lowman, Matthew Moodie, Jeffrey Pepper, Frank Pohlmann, Douglas Pundick, Ben Renow-Clarke, Dominic Shakeshaft, Matt Wade, Tom Welsh
Project Manager: Anita Castro
Copy Editor: Hastings Hart
Compositor: Tricia Bronkella
Indexer: Potomac Indexers
Artist: April Milne
Cover Designer: Anna Ishchenko

Distributed to the book trade worldwide by Springer-Verlag New York, Inc., 233 Spring Street, 6th Floor, New York, NY 10013. Phone 1-800-SPRINGER, fax 201-348-4505, e-mail `orders-ny@springer-sbm.com`, or visit `http://www.springeronline.com`.

For information on translations, please e-mail `info@apress.com`, or visit `http://www.apress.com`.

Apress and friends of ED books may be purchased in bulk for academic, corporate, or promotional use. eBook versions and licenses are also available for most titles. For more information, reference our Special Bulk Sales–eBook Licensing web page at `http://www.apress.com/info/bulksales`.

The source code for this book is available to readers at `http://www.apress.com`. You will need to answer questions pertaining to this book in order to successfully download the code.

This book is dedicated to my dear father, math Professor Rondong Li, who is always my source of spiritual encouragement, and my mother, who was my first math teacher at primary school.

Contents at a Glance

Contents

Foreword

Forget the buzzword-compliant prognostications of the IT pundits and forget the fevered predictions of open vs. proprietary, because everything is changing and changing fast. Maybe everything is changing so fast that some folks still see cloud computing as a discussion about the future, when in fact it is real, with many popular applications currently running in cloud environments. Cloud computing is just a term for what has been slowly brewing on the back burner for many years. It is the natural evolution of technology.

The evolution timeline goes something like this. In the beginning there was the mainframe. The mainframe cost a lot and used a lot of power, so it made sense to sell slices of time to companies needing computing power. After a while, computers became smaller and less expensive and businesses and consumers began buying their own. But then networks began to form, and the eventually ubiquitous Internet was born. This led the way to the idea of the application service provider (ASP). Ah, those were the days.

Well, everyone forgot about all that stuff for a few years as the technology sector went through a reality adjustment. But as always, business keeps moving forward. In that time a few companies began, or shall I say fell into, the idea of the cloud more by necessity than anything else. Salesforce.com and Amazon were so popular and successful that they sought to expand their businesses by providing platforms that would allow developers to not only configure their applications (what used to be called ASPs and are now called software as a service) but also customize them. But it was almost natural for these well-architected platforms to start spawning new applications that didn't have anything to do with the original application, and thus we now have what is currently called cloud computing.

There is no doubt it will take years for the majority of companies to adopt cloud computing, especially for their more mission-critical, enterprise, highly secure, or financial applications. But that is okay, because there will be a lot of time for the companies and applications that are a perfect fit to work out the bugs. They will pave the way for every company to take part. Because of competitive pressures and the efficiency associated with cloud computing, it will be inevitable that most if not all companies will use the cloud in some way.

The cost of hosting applications has traditionally been quite expensive. The first high-availability web applications required that a company either maintain its own data center with redundant hardware and 24-hour or on-call staff. The alternative was to pay managed services data centers thousands of dollars per month to maintain a dedicated hosting environment. IT managers had to forecast the processing power needed to run their applications, and often this led to an over-purchase of hardware and software. This paradigm has led to vast data centers wasting huge amounts of power with many thousands of servers humming along nicely with no more than two or three percent utilization. But in the last decade, as virtual servers have evolved in both hosted and on-premise data centers, it was only a matter of time before the technology allowed companies and applications to share processors with little risk of one errant application affecting another.

The evolution of technology may have come full circle with utility computing (remember the mainframe?), but it looks very different than anyone could have imagined. The inevitability of the virtual future has played its hand in the convergence of process, platform, tools, architectures, and services, and it is how we are currently building applications.

So let's take a moment to explore why cloud computing will be hard to ignore in the coming years. First of all, cloud computing by definition is inherently scalable and as reliable as any high-end managed hosting service. We are accustomed to paying several thousand dollars a month for a handful of servers in a traditional managed hosting environment. This has been the standard for mission-critical applications for quite some time now. A similar entry-level cost of a fully scalable and redundant system can cost hundreds instead of thousands often quoted by the enterprise managed hosting companies. But probably the most important point when talking about the scalability of cloud computing is its ability to scale up and scale down quickly, which will be very important for companies that might need to acquire a substantial amount of processing power for a short amount of time. Now they can do so without any long-term commitments or substantial capital expenditures.

The second benefit of cloud computing is reduced time to market for new applications. Managed hosting companies or corporate data centers often needed weeks to months of lead time to acquire hardware and install operating systems and database software required for most applications. Cloud computing accounts can often be provisioned with applications deployed and made live within hours.

Last but certainly not one of the least benefits of cloud computing is that it is in line with green IT initiatives, which are quickly becoming an integral part of corporate strategies. By sharing resources with other organizations, we no longer have acres of server farms consuming huge amounts of power while sitting nearly idle waiting for the peak load at some time in the future. The fact is that that peak load will almost never happen as IT managers always err on the side of caution and purchase multiples of the processing power they will ever actually use.

This book is an introduction to Windows Azure, Microsoft's offering for cloud computing. Windows Azure is not just a virtual hosting solution that infinitely scales. Nor is it just a few editing and deployment tools tacked onto a virtual hosting solution. Windows Azure is a cloud application platform that enables companies to build and run applications that scale in a reliable, available, and fault-tolerant manner by providing the fundamental services every application needs. It is a suite of hosting services, development environment, and development tools combined with a set of robust services. Some of these services .NET developers have been working with for the last several years, and some are fairly new.

Developers who have worked on other cloud platforms will quickly notice that in terms of comprehensive services and features, this platform is leaps and bounds beyond any other cloud computing platform on the market today, which is saying a lot given that Amazon and Salesforce.com have been building and perfecting their solutions for the better part of the past decade. Microsoft has also gone one step further and built its platforms and services in a manner that can be utilized by open development technologies including Python, Ruby, PHP, and open protocols and standards, including REST, SOAP, and XML.

This book will walk you through the development process with a detailed set of exercises. With the many screenshots and code samples included, you can expect to be developing full-blown Windows Azure applications that use almost every service and feature currently offered.

Your first steps in learning the Windows Azure platform will be to understand and utilize the cloud table, queue, and blob storage services. You will walk through the process of integration using Windows Communication Foundation (WCF) and Windows Workflow Foundation (WF). Next you will explore the Windows .NET Access Control Service, the Service Bus, and workflows that allow you to coordinate services and build distributed connected applications. You will explore SQL Data Services in depth, and the final chapter explains how to deploy your applications into a production environment.

As with any new development technology introduced by Microsoft, there will be a steep learning curve and lots of new terminology and concepts to understand. On the bright side, just as with the introduction of .NET, Window Presentation Foundation, or Windows Communication Foundation, you will not be alone in your quest. You will have lots of great resources to help you along the way, and

Henry's book is certainly a great place to start. This will be another big programming paradigm shift for programmers, so fully understanding the contents of this book will be a big start in the process of learning this new and relevant technology.

I wish you all the best in your new adventures of developing applications for the Windows Azure platform.

Bruce Wilson, CTO, Planned Marketing Solutions International

About the Author

Henry Li is a technical consultant, specializing in enterprise application integration and distributed system automation solutions. He runs his own consulting firm SoftnetSolutions Consulting, Inc., based in Hillsboro, Oregon, delivering business solutions for large-scale enterprises, government agencies, and small businesses.

He has been engaged in numerous large-scale middleware infrastructures, front-end and back-end architecture designs, and implementations based upon Microsoft .NET and BizTalk technologies. He has served clients across the United States, including diverse enterprise organizations, government agencies, semiconductor manufacturers, and industry equipment facility manufacturers. He also has intensive experience designing data-driven, event-driven industry automation solutions using XML and design patterns. He strongly believes that object-oriented programming is not only a software development technology but also a philosophy that should be applied to any analysis of business solution architecture design.

Henry Li resides with his wife, Wenyan, and lovely daughter, Emma, who is an all-A-qualified swimmer of the USA Swimming Society, in the beautiful Portland metro area of Oregon. He can be contacted at `yinghong@softnetsolution.net` with any questions regarding this book and his most-interested-in areas, SOA (service-oriented architecture), AOP (aspect-oriented programming), and XML data-driven solutions.

About the Technical Reviewer

Bing Long, Ph.D. in mathematics, lives in Seattle, WA. He is an IT consultant, with extensive enterprise software design/development and system integration, across platforms and languages. His e-mail is `bing_long@yahoo.com`.

Acknowledgments

I would like to thank the following individuals for their contributions to my professional life:

- Ronald Phaneuf, who provided me an opportunity to use Visual Basic 1.0 to program the fantastic data acquisition user interface for the Electron Synchrotron Research project.
- Mark Beckner, who provided me with a road map of how to become a professional solution architect and technical writer.
- Wesley Yong, who brought me to join the Microsoft BizTalk project and to learn how Microsoft designs and develops software.
- Brandon Gross, Larry Smith, and Dan Alworth, who provided me with the opportunity of designing and developing Microsoft award-winning BizTalk solutions at EMC Microsoft Practice.
- Tom Wu, Mike Johnson, and Paul McKelvey, who provided me with an opportunity to demonstrate my talent to design and build large-scale data-driven enterprise SOA solutions for shop floor automation.
- Mike Cole, who brought me into a commercial software development team to learn how to be a professional C++ developer.
- Yimin Zhu, who provided me with an opportunity to apply XML data-driven design concepts to design and implement the Florida Department of Transportation Road User Cost application.

A great deal of gratitude is owed to the ever-widening network of friends and coworkers who are bound for incredible successes, including the people from the Microsoft BizTalk group, the Shopping Intel development group at the Intel marketing department, Timberline Software (Sage Software), EMC's Microsoft Practice, and Siltronic Co.

Special thanks goes to my wife, Wenyan. This book would not be able to come to the reader's bookshelf on schedule without her cooking and housekeeping for our family.

Introduction

The cloud platform is getting more and more attractive to the computing world. Today, service-oriented architecture (SOA) and aspect-oriented programming (AOP) techniques are widely used in enterprise solutions. A question an IT management team or a software development team may ask is, what is the next trend going to be? Cloud computing seems to be the right answer. Different names are used for this kind of platform, including utility computing, on-demand platform, and platform as a service. A set of new buzzwords has been widely used in relation to cloud computing, such as Program as a Service (PaaS), Software as a Service (SaaS), and anything you can think of as a service (XaaS).

For any enterprise business solution, the cost to build, deploy, host, and maintain infrastructures and applications is always challenging for the administrative and development teams in an organization. The cloud platform aims to take away the cost of building, deploying, updating, and maintaining.

Applications used in organizations today are called on-premises applications. In this case, infrastructure and storage facilities, as well as the applications, are hosted within an organization. By contrast, both storage and application services provided by the cloud platform are hosted externally (they can also be hosted within an organization for a local cloud environment) through the Internet. Microsoft offers such services to host both storage and applications from its data centers via its Windows Azure cloud platform.

Windows Azure Essentials

Azure is a new cloud system from Microsoft that allows applications to run from a remote connected system, hosted in a Microsoft data center, and store data in the cloud.

Figure 1 shows the Windows Azure architecture. The platform consists of three parts:

- *Development runtime*: Simulates the Azure runtime allowing you to test, debug, and tune your application in a local development environment before deploying it to the cloud.
- *Azure runtime*: Includes the Azure fabric, Azure storage service, and Windows Azure OS.
- *Applications*: Applications are run from the Azure runtime. A set of Internet-based services work as building blocks for you to build your applications. The services package includes .NET Services (formerly BizTalk Services), SQL Azure, and Live Services.

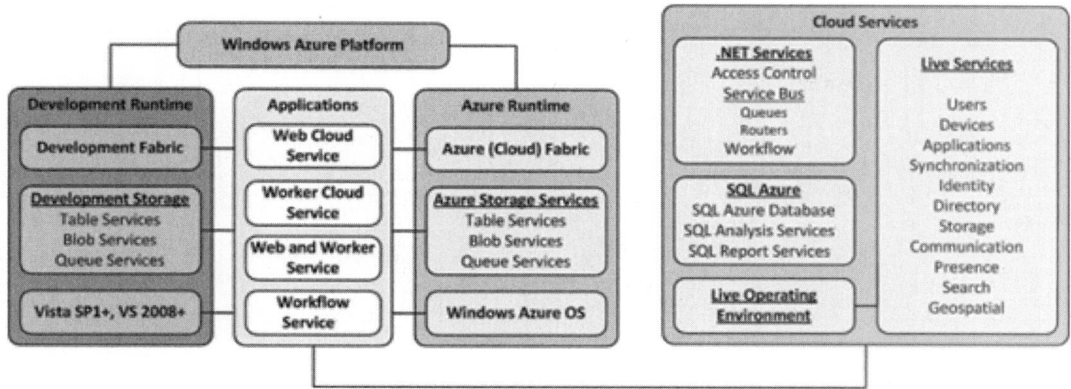

Figure 1. *Windows Azure architecture*

Figure 2 describes the concept of the Azure platform. Any on-premises type of application built in an organization could also leverage the services provided by Azure through the Internet. However, to host and run applications from the Azure cloud platform, the applications must be developed by using the .NET Framework. Both Azure applications and on-premises applications can access the Azure storage service using a representational state transfer (RESTful) approach. Cloud storage no longer relies on the relational model in order to meet the requirements of Internet scalability, which we'll look at in this book. There are three types of storage available from the Azure platform: blob storage, queue storage, and table storage, all covered in later chapters.

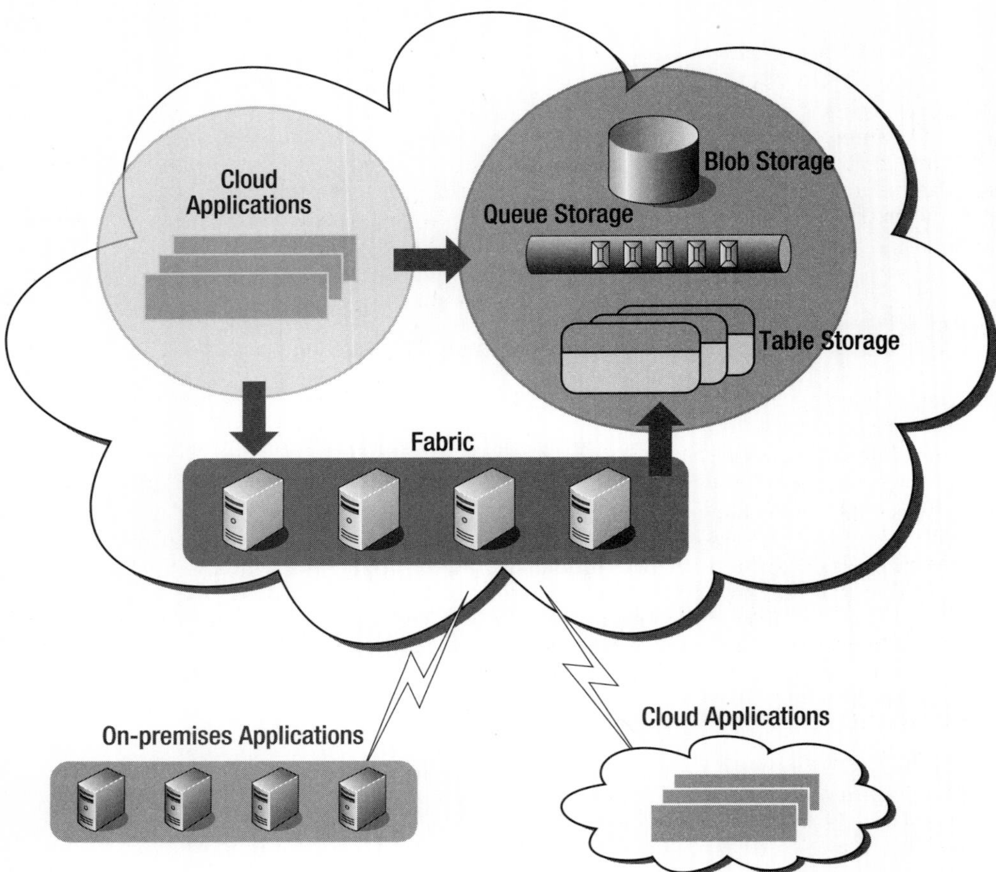

Figure 2. Infrastructure of the Azure cloud platform

It is obvious that the features that Azure offers are tremendously beneficial to organizations. Instead of spending a lot of money to build their own infrastructure, organizations can build their infrastructure from the cloud and use it as a utility and never worry about maintenance and upgrade issues.

Figure 2 shows that Azure does at least two things:

- Host and run applications from a remote connected system at a Microsoft data center
- Provide data storage using a remote connected system at a Microsoft data center

An application running from the Azure platform may have multiple instances; each instance runs in its own virtual machine supported by a 64-bit operating system. An application instance may have either a web role or worker role or both.

Web Role

Each web role instance accepts incoming HTTP/HTTPS requests through Internet Information Services (IIS) 7. A web role can be implemented using ASP.NET, Windows Communication Foundation (WCF), or another .NET Framework technology that works with IIS.

At runtime, all web role instances work spread across connected infrastructures hosted from the Microsoft data center. Azure provides built-in load balancing to spread requests across web role instances that are part of the same application. We are going to provide more information in detail later in this book.

Worker Role

In contrast, a worker role instance cannot accept requests directly from the outside world. A worker role is not allowed to have any incoming network connections, nor is IIS running in its virtual machine.

A worker role gets input from a web role instance, typically via a queue in Azure storage. However, the output results of a worker role can be written to Azure storage: blob storage, table storage, or queue storage. But they can also be sent to the outside world directly; outgoing network connections are not prohibited for a worker role.

In practice, a worker role takes a batch job and can run indefinitely, pretty much close to the behavior of a regular Windows service. To send the results from a worker role to the outside world directly, a worker role needs to create a handler to deal with the incoming HTTP request from a web role and close the handler up when the request has been processed. A worker role can be implemented using any .NET technology.

Azure Fabric

As noted, the major difference between a web role and worker role is that only the web role can communicate via the Internet and take HTTP messages, whereas the worker role does not. A worker role typically is a batched process and can communicate to the web role via a cloud queue or WCF services. Both web roles and worker roles are run from the Azure fabric. The fabric is an innovative technology and can be understood as the Azure runtime context. The concept of an Azure application is shown in Figure 3. To reach the goal of Internet scalability, each web role instance and worker role instance has its dedicated processor core. The default number of instances is configured to one when a cloud application is created from Visual Studio. It can be increased by the account owner via the `Web.config` configuration file even after deployment.

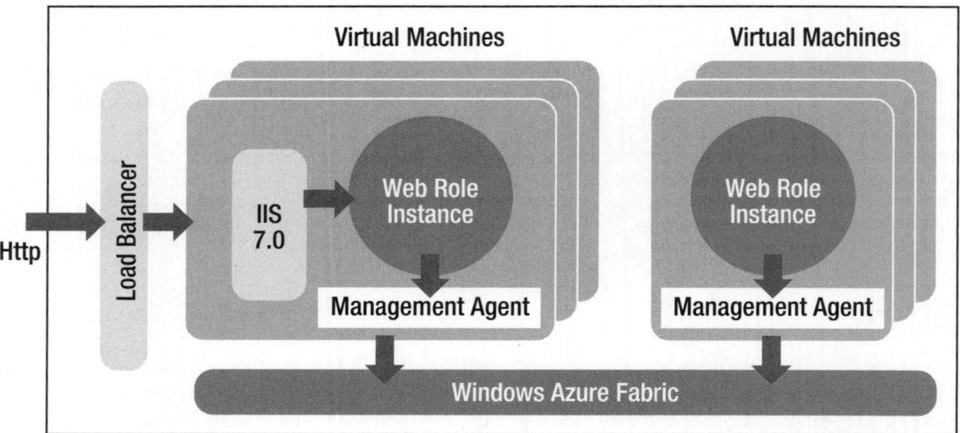

Figure 3. *Concept of Azure applications running in the cloud*

The Azure framework also provides a local fabric simulation environment to simulate the environment of the cloud. This allows you to debug, test, and tune your application locally before deploying to production. The local fabric can be started manually. The details will be covered later in this book.

The functions of the fabric are summarized in the following list:

- *Monitor the application's state*: Each Azure application has an owner. The owner account is authenticated using Microsoft Live ID. The owner can control some aspects of the application's behavior by changing the configuration of the application to govern security and scalability (the number of instances). The Azure fabric monitors the status of the application settings to fulfill the requests from applications at runtime.
- *Log and trace*: When an application has been deployed to the cloud, the only way to log runtime information and send alerts or notification to the application owner is through the fabric.
- *Ensure the performance of applications*: A cloud application runs in a cloud virtual machine (VM), and Azure maintains a one-to-one relationship between a VM and a physical processor core. If an application makes a request to increase the number of instances, the fabric will allocate new VM resources from the cloud and assign these VMs to the cores.
- *Failover handling*: The fabric monitors the application's runtime state. When one instance fails, the fabric will start a new instance from a new VM resource.

You'll find no difference between developing Azure applications from any .NET Windows or ASP.NET applications.

Who This Book Is For

To shift to cloud computing, you need to understand the similarities and differences between the on-premises platform and the cloud platform. This book assumes that you fully understand object-oriented programming, the basic concepts of SOA, and distributed application systems. A major change from an on-premises platform to a cloud platform is that the services for both storage and application will communicate across the Internet. For this reason, the cloud platform must support Internet-scale usage. Any service within the cloud platform may be concurrently requested by a massive number of clients.

This book uses the Windows Azure Platform and Windows Azure SDK as the foundation to help you across the bridge between the on-premises platform and the cloud platform. The basic methodology used by this book is to expose the differences and similarities between these two kinds of platforms.

The readers of this book are those who need to shift from SOA to the cloud platform using Azure. This book allows you to learn the fundamental concepts and essential skills by studying selected exercise examples from the real world. This book also reveals undocumented information and practical solutions to the challenges that you may encounter. Each exercise example is followed by a conclusion section to discuss extended topics.

This book also provides useful tools, such as the `LargeDataToBlobStorage` tool from Chapter 3, for you to be more efficient during your Azure development.

Prerequisites

This book uses examples to help you shorten your learning curve and get hands-on experience to build and deploy cloud platform solutions.

Before you start to read this book you need to establish your Azure account. To get a free evaluation account:

1. Get your Windows Live ID if you don't have one yet at `https://accountservices.passport.net/ppnetworkhome.srf?vv=650&lc=1033`, since Azure uses your Windows Live ID as your global secure access ID.

2. Go to the Azure portal page at `http://www.microsoft.com/azure/windowsazure.mspx`. Here you can request a new Azure account and download all the necessary SDKs for Azure development. Microsoft did a great job to simplify the lives of Azure developers by integrating a lot of important client-side APIs into the SDKs.

3. After you submit the request for an Azure evaluation account Microsoft will send you an e-mail with an invitation code. When you receive the invitation code go to the portal page and use the Windows Live ID to log in. You can use the secure web site at `https://lx.azure.microsoft.com`.

4. Redeem your invitation code and carry out the initialization work to finalize your participation. The web site will guide you step by step through the process smoothly.

Later in the book, I'm going to provide guidance for special cases related to particular services, such as SQL Azure in Chapter 8.

To run examples provided by this book or by other resources, the following features need to be available in your local environment:

- Windows Vista SP1 (or Windows Server 2008) or later
- .NET Framework 3.5 SP1 or later
- Microsoft Visual Studio 2008 or later
- IIS 7.0 (with ASP.NET and WCF HTTP Activation)
- Microsoft SQL Server Express 2005 or Microsoft SQL Server Express 2008

To set up the environment to run all the exercises provided in this book, the following packages need to be installed from a local development machine:

- `WindowsAzureSDK-x86.msi`
- `VSCloudService.msi`
- `silverlight_chainer.exe`
- `sdsSDK.msi`
- `Microsoft .NET Services SDK Setup.exe`
- `LiveFrameworkTools.exe`
- `LiveFrameworkSDK.MSI`
- `LiveFrameworkClient.msi`

Note All these packages can be downloaded from Microsoft.

How This Book Is Structured

There is no requirement to read the chapters sequentially. You can select any topic to read. This book contains three parts. Part 1, from Chapter 1 to Chapter 3, covers Windows Azure Storage. Part 2, from Chapter 4 to Chapter 8, covers .NET Services, including hosting WCF and WF services in the cloud, .NET Services Access Control, .NET Service Bus Queue, and SQL Azure. Part 3 contains contains Chapter 9, which covers the topic of how to deploy and manage cloud applications. Each exercise mentioned in this section has a corresponding code bundle in the code download for this book.

Chapter 1: Create Cloud Table Storage

It is one of the most costly tasks for any development team to build and maintain infrastructure for data storage. One of the most attractive advantages of Windows Azure is giving this tough task to Microsoft. There is no need to worry about scalability, software upgrades, security patching, and so on, at all. They are all the responsibilities of Microsoft. Windows Azure amazingly simplifies the data storage layer's design and implementation. The Windows Azure SDK development environment hides the complexity of the transformation between data entity objects. Windows Azure allows a developer to focus on the data modeling; the storage database, including all relational data tables, will be analyzed and automatically generated by the SDK at design time. There is no data schema definition, data-access stored procedure customizing, or data mapping required to build the data storage. They will all be taken care of by the services provided by Windows Azure.

This chapter provides a simple example showing you how to create cloud data storage. This chapter also provides an example of how to resolve the non-portable custom defined data type problem.

- Exercise 1-1: Creates cloud data storage with a simple data structure.
- Exercise 1-2: Creates cloud data storage with a relational data structure.

Chapter 2: Access Cloud Table Storage

Azure uses LINQ for data access. All data I/O functions are encapsulated into the Windows Azure SDK as services. This chapter demonstrates the services provided by the Azure SDK for inserting, querying, updating, and deleting cloud storage data.

- Exercise 2-1: Accesses a single cloud data storage table.
- Exercise 2-1: Deletes and updates an entity in a single cloud data storage table.
- Exercise 2-3: Handles relational cloud data storage tables.

Chapter 3: Working with Cloud Queue and Blob Storage

This chapter presents four exercise projects to walk you through how to create and use cloud queue and blob storage.

- Exercise 3-1: Creates a message queue, puts messages into a queue, and queries messages from the queue. This exercise also demonstrates how to poll a queue and create an event handler to handle the queue polling event.
- Exercise 3-2: Introduces the fundamental steps to create blob storage, and upload, query, and delete data from blob storage. This exercise also provides an example of how to use the REST API to query blob data.
- Exercise 3-3: Uses both queue and blob storage to create a template for a loosely coupled event-driven system using a web role and worker role in a cloud application.
- Exercise 3-4: Presents a solution using a .NET background worker and asynchronous mechanisms to upload and delete large amounts of data from blob storage.

Chapter 4: Windows Azure Application Integration Using WCF

This chapter covers Windows Azure integration using Windows Communication Foundation.

- Exercise 4-1: Presents an example of how to build a cloud service to host WCF services.

Chapter 5: Windows Azure .NET Services—Access Control

This chapter covers access control in Azure applications.

- Exercise 5-1: Builds your first cloud application using .NET Services Access Control.
- Exercise 5-2: Explores using CardSpace in Azure.

Chapter 6: Windows Azure .NET Services—Service Bus

This chapter covers .NET Service Bus.

- Exercise 6-1: Creates a console-based .NET service host to host a WCF service using relay bindings.
- Exercise 6-2: Demonstrates how two applications can run behind firewalls and be connected directly through the cloud using relay hybrid connection mode.
- Exercise 6-3: Uses .NET Service Bus to create an event-driven distributed Windows application system. A controller Windows application posts relay events to control another Windows application.
- Exercise 6-4: Builds a .NET Service Bus `QueueClient` wrapper class, that provides an easy way for you to integrate the .NET Service Bus queue access in applications.

Chapter 7: Windows Azure .NET Services—Workflows

As you'd expect, Windows Azure works with workflows, which I examine in this chapter.

- Exercise 7-1: Hosts a workflow service in the Azure cloud environment.
- Exercise 7-2: Coordinates workflow services using `HttpWebRequest`.

Chapter 8: SQL Azure

As this book was nearing completion, Microsoft replaced SQL Data Services with SQL Azure.

- Exercise 8-1: Creates a data-driven, XML application to work with the SQL Azure database services.

Chapter 9: Deploy Windows Azure Applications to Production

This chapter does not contain any exercises but covers how to deploy and manage your applications to the cloud.

Appendix

The appendix contains the specification Windows Azure blob storage and details of the Azure Services Management Tools.

Downloading the Code

The source code for this book is available at `http://www.apress.com` or `http://www.softnetsolution.net/Apress/SourceCodeDownLoad/`.

Note All code used in this book is designed for proof of concept and could potentially be used. However, the code has to be optimized and fine-tuned before you can use it in an application. It is especially important to add data-validation and error-handling code.

Contacting the Author

Henry Li can be contacted via e-mail at `yinghong@softnetsolution.net` or via regular mail at SoftnetSolutions, Inc., 192 NE 74th Ave., Hillsboro, OR 97124.

You can visit the web site of SoftnetSolutions at `http://www.softnetsolution.net`. All your comments and feedback are appreciated.

CHAPTER 1

■ ■ ■

Create Cloud Table Storage

An application, either on-premises or cloud-based, should use a kind of storage. For on-premises applications, the storage can be either local or remote. Storage on the cloud platform comes in a different style. It is hard to require a development team or an organization to provide generic, reusable data schemas for remote storage. The following list contains some items to pay attention to when switching from traditional relational data structure design to cloud table storage.

- The data structure for cloud remote storage should be as simple as possible. The data model exposed to the outside world must be straightforward. The objects generally should be a set of binary bytes stored as buckets in clouds. Applications create, read, and delete objects in buckets. If an object needs to be updated, delete it and replace it with an object with updated values. This is how the cloud platform service changed to meet the Internet's scalability requirements. The simpler the data structure, the better the performance will be for multiple Internet instances to access cloud data storage concurrently. Since storage in the remote cloud is so cheap, for an organization to scale up will be not an issue at all. The organization needs to simply increase the instance number from the configuration file.
- You should be aware when migrating from on-premises storage to the cloud platform that if you have a relational data structure, then you will be responsible for managing the constraints between the data storage entities, because the cloud storage tables are not relational. This may be a challenge and the price you have to pay for using cloud storage. This is a new topic that .NET developers to have to face.

In the cloud, the application can access its data from anywhere at any time and store any amount of data for any length of time. Azure storage provides a rich set of data abstractions in the following three aspects:

- Blob storage, usually used to store data of large size.
- Table storage that provides structured storage for applications. However, table storage is not relational data storage. Since table storage is in the cloud environment, a relational structure is not allowed.
- Queue storage that provides asynchronous work dispatch to enable service communication.

Azure Table is the structured storage provided by the Azure platform. It supports massively scalable tables in the cloud, with capability to support up to billions of entities and terabytes of data. Depending upon the traffic demand, the storage will efficiently scale up by automatically spreading to thousands of servers.

Azure table storage supports the Language Integrated Query (LINQ) extensions for .NET 3.0 or later versions, ADO.NET Data Services, and representational state transfer (REST), which allows applications developed using non-.NET languages to access table storage via the Internet. There is no limit on the number of tables and entities or on the table size. There is no need for table storage developers to handle the data access transactions, optimistic concurrency for updates, and deletes. Also, there is no need for developers to worry about performance, since cloud storage is highly scalable. Especially for long queries or queries that encounter a time-out, partial results will be returned and the unfinished queries can be continued with a return continuation token.

In this chapter we are going to look at cloud data storage in detail. We'll cover

- The table storage specification
- Azure development storage, which allows us to test cloud storage on the local machine
- Creating cloud data storage and all the issues surrounding moving your data into the cloud

The Table Storage Specification

To access Azure storage you must use a valid account. When a new Azure storage account is created using the Windows Azure portal web interface, a 256-bit public shared key will be sent to you via e-mail. Usually it takes about couple of days for processing. The secret key must be passed as one of the parameters when initializing storage table access. The access will be authenticated based on the secret key. Authentication is required for each request to table storage. When REST is used to access table storage, the account name is part of the host name in the URL string. The URL is constructed with the format of `http://<accountName>.table.core.windows.net`. An example of an account can be found from `DevelopmentStorage.exe.config` of the Windows Azure SDK.

The following are the key parts of the specification:

- *Table*: A table contains a set of entities. Table names are associated to the account. There is no limit on how many tables an application may create within a storage account.
- *Entity*: An entity can be understood as a row in cloud table storage, which is the basic data item stored in a table. An entity has a set of properties.
- *Property*: A property can be understood as a value being held in an entity. The name for a property is case-sensitive. A rich type set is supported for property values, as Table 1-1 shows.

Table 1-1. *Value Types Supported by Cloud Table Entity Properties*

Property Type	Details
`Binary`	An array of bytes up to 64 KB
`Bool`	A Boolean value
`DateTime`	A 64-bit value expressed as UTC time; range is 1/1/1600 to 12/31/9999
`Double`	A 64-bit floating point value
`GUID`	A 128-bit globally unique identifier
`Int`	A 32-bit integer
`Int64`	A 64-bit integer
`String`	A UTF-16-encoded value; may be up to 64 KB

- *PartitionKey*: Every table has a special property called `PartitionKey`. Since the actual data of table storage is physically distributed to many storage nodes, which may cross many storage servers running in the cloud, the cloud storage system uses this key to manage the storage nodes' distribution.
- *RowKey*: `RowKey` is the second key property defined for each table storage. This is the unique ID of the entity, and an entity can be identified using the combination of the `PartitionKey` and `RowKey` in a table.
- *Timestamp*: The `Timestamp` indicates the time a table is created.
- *Partition*: The `Partition` is a logical set of entities defined in a table with the same `PartitionKey` value.
- *Sort Order*: A single index is provided for all entities in a table. Data entities are sorted by `PartitionKey` and then `RowKey`. This makes queries specifying these keys more efficient.

A Closer Look at Entities

It's worth having a closer look at entities before we go any further:

- *Number of properties*: The maximum number of properties an entity can define is 255, including `PartitionKey`, `RowKey`, and `Timestamp`.
- *Type*: `PartitionKey` and `RowKey` are of string type.
- *Timestamp*: `Timestamp` is a read-only property.

- *Schema*: There is no schema stored in Windows Azure tables. The data storage model for properties is a name and typed value pair. A table can not have two entities with the same name, but it may have two properties with the same name because they belong to different parent entities.
- *Size of an entity*: The size limit for an entity is 1 MB. This size is the summation of the size of the property, the property values or their types, and the two mandatory key properties, `PartitionKey` and `RowKey`.

Now that we know a little about Azure's table storage, we should look at development storage, which allows us to test our Azure applications on our local machine.

Azure Development Storage

The Windows Azure SDK development environment includes out-of-the-box development storage, a utility that simulates the storage services available in the cloud. The Azure SDK provides the development storage services to allow developers to create, debug, and unit test the cloud data service on a local machine before they deploy their application to production.

By default, development storage relies on a SQL Server Express database, either the 2005 edition or the 2008 edition, to simulate the storage environment in the cloud. It's possible to use the full SQL Server as we'll see next, but to use SQL Server Express, you must have it installed. You also need to install SQL Server Management Studio to manage SQL Server Express. Development storage connects to SQL Server Express by using Windows authentication.

To switch from SQL Server Express to SQL Server 2005 or 2008, you need to modify the configuration file, `DevelopmentStorage.exe.config`, and one line in the `DevtableGen.exe.config` file, as shown in Listing 1-1 and Listing 1-2. These configuration files are located in the `bin` directory of Windows Azure as shown in Figure 1-1.

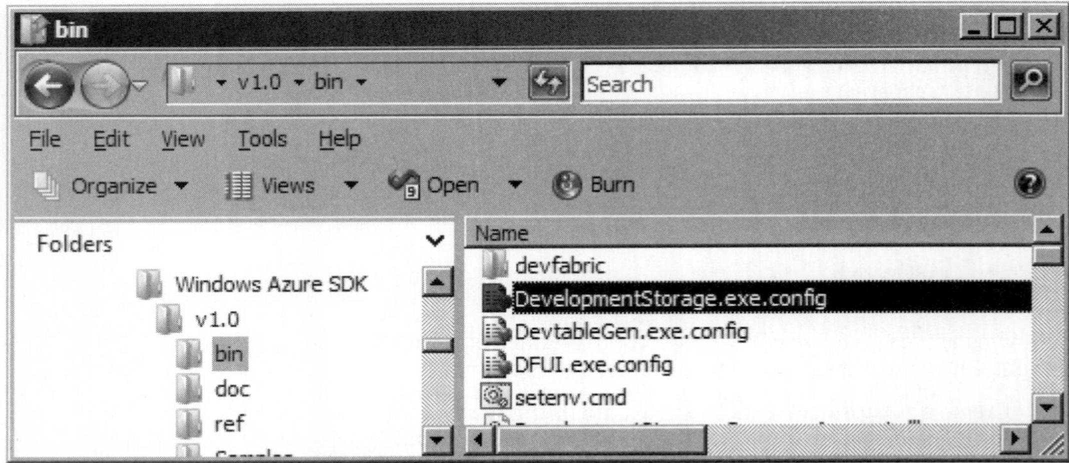

Figure 1-1. *Azure SDK `DevelopmentStorage.exe.config` and `DevtableGen.exe.config` configuration files*

Listing 1-1. The `DevelopmentStorage.exe.config` *SQL Storage Service*

```
  <connectionStrings>
    <add name="DevelopmentStorageDbConnectionString"
         connectionString="Data Source=.\SQLEXPRESS;Initial Catalog=DevelopmentStorageDb;
Integrated Security=True"
         providerName="System.Data.SqlClient" />
  </connectionStrings>

  <appSettings>
    <add key="ClientSettingsProvider.ServiceUri" value="" />
  </appSettings>

  <developmentStorageConfig>
    <services>
      <service name="Blob"
               url="http://127.0.0.1:10000/"/>
      <service name="Queue"
               url="http://127.0.0.1:10001/"/>
      <service name="Table"
               url="http://127.0.0.1:10002/"
         dbServer="localhost\SQLExpress"/>
    </services>
```

Replace the data source configuration with the local machine name in two places in this configuration file.

Listing 1-2. The `DevtableGen.exe.config` *for SQL Table Service*

```
<?xml version="1.0" encoding="utf-8" ?>
<configuration>
  <appSettings>
    <add key="DefaultSQLInstance" value=".\SQLExpress"/>
  </appSettings>
</configuration>
```

The first exercise in this chapter uses development storage to create cloud data storage with a simple data structure.

Create Cloud Data Storage with a Simple Data Structure

In the following exercise, we are going to create a data table in the local cloud development environment. The code is available in the Exercise 1-1 code bundle.

1. Create a new project from Visual Studio, using the Worker Cloud Service template from the Add New Project dialog panel as Figure 1-2 shows. The path to find the template is the Visual C# ➤ Cloud Service. Enter the name `CreateDataStorage` for the solution.

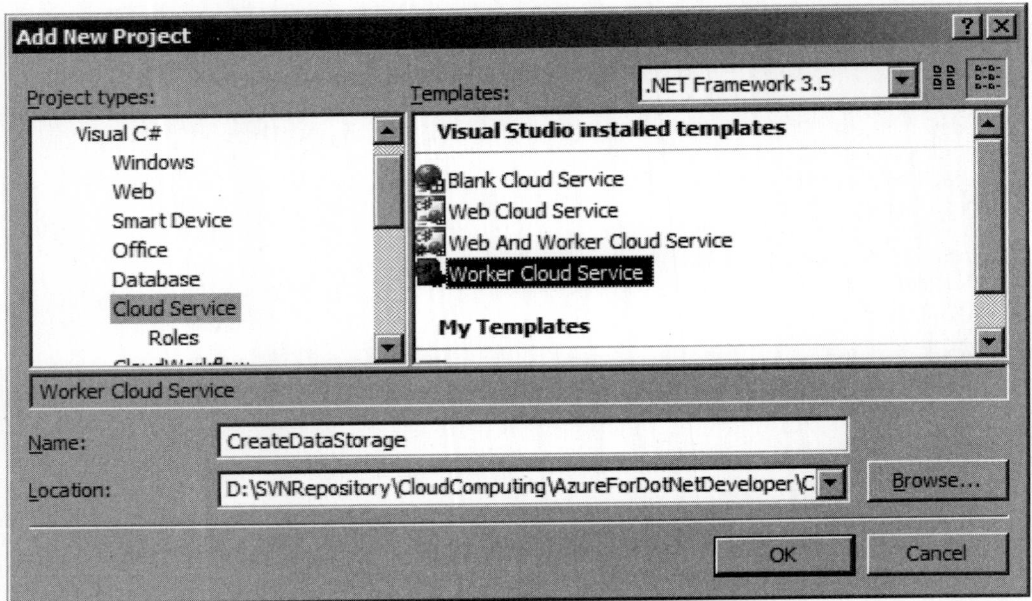

Figure 1-2. Visual Studio Worker Cloud Service template

2. Visual Studio will generate two projects for this solution by default. Add a reference to `StorageClient.dll` to the project. This assembly can be found from the bin directory where the Azure SDK was installed, for example, `C:\Program Files\Windows Azure SDK\v1.0\Samples\StorageClient\Lib\bin\Debug` as Figure 1-3 shows.

■ **Note** You may need to load the sample project into Visual Studio after you have installed the SDK (as discussed in the Introduction) and recompile it. After installation, a ZIP file named `samples.zip` will be generated under the install target folder. For example, if the install folder is `C:\Program Files` then the full path to find this file is `C:\Program Files\Windows Azure SDK\v1.0\samples.zip`. This ZIP file contains a set of sample projects. Unzip this file and find the solution folder called `CloudDrive`. Load that solution into Visual Studio and recompile it (this requires you to run Visual Studio under a login account with Administrator privilege), and the assembly file `StorageClient.dll` will be generated as Figure 1-3 shows.

Figure 1-3. *Azure SDK assembly* `StorageClient.dll` *location*

3. Add a new C# library project, `CloudData.Models`, to the solution. In this project, define a very simple data entity class, `Address`, which must inherit from a SDK base class, `Microsoft.Samples.ServiceHosting.StorageClient.TableStorageEntity`. Listing 1-3 shows that this class simply has a group of attributes of address information and no method functions but the class constructors.

Listing 1-3. *Class* `Address` *Definition*

```
public class Address : TableStorageEntity
{
    private State? _state;

    public string Address1 { get; set; }
    public string Address2 { get; set; }
    public string City { get; set; }
    public int? State { get { return (int)_state; } set { _state = (State)value; } }
    public string Zip { get; set; }
    public string County { get; set; }
    public string Country { get; set; }

    public Address():this(Guid.NewGuid())
    {
    }

    public Address(Guid internalID)
: base(ConfigurationManager.AppSettings["PartitionKey"], internalID.ToString())
    { }
    public Address(string address1,
                   string address2,
                   string city,
                   State state,
                   string zip,
                   string county,
                   string country,
                   Guid internalID)
        :this(internalID)
    {
        Address1 = address1;
        Address2 = address2;
```

```
            City = city;
            State = (int)state;
            Zip = zip;
            County = county;
            Country = country;
        }
    }
```

4. In the same project, create a folder called CloudDataService. Add three interface definitions—IDataTableService, IHasDependencyTableService, and INoDependencyTableService—to this folder. The interface IDataTableService exposes three basic data table access functions: Insert, Update, and Delete. All these functions accept a parameter of type TableStorageEntity defined in the Microsoft.Samples.ServiceHosting.StorageClient namespace. The two other interfaces are derived from the interface IDataTableService. The interface IHasDependencyTableService exposes one method, UpdateDependencyTable(), which also accepts a parameter of type TableStorageEntity. The third interface, INoDependency, does not expose any methods but provides a type definition used for marking a class as having no logical dependency data object.

5. Add two classes into the folder CloudDataServices—DataTableService and AddressTableService. Mark the first class as an abstract class. The AddressTableService class is a derived class from the DataTableService class and implements the interface INoDependencyTableService. In the base class DataTableService, all three basic data I/O methods—Insert, Update, and Delete—are implemented. The Insert and Delete methods are marked as virtual, allowing concrete classes derived from this base class to override them. The implementation for all interfaces and classes is shown in Listing 1-4.

Listing 1-4. *Implementation for All Interfaces and Classes Defined in the Folder* `CloudDataServices`

```
using System;
using System.Collections.Generic;
using System.Linq;
using System.Text;

namespace CreateDataStorage.Models.CloudDataServices
{
    using Microsoft.Samples.ServiceHosting.StorageClient;

    public interface IDataTableService
    {
        bool Insert(TableStorageEntity entity);
        bool Update(TableStorageEntity entity);
        bool Delete(TableStorageEntity entity);
    }

    public interface IHasDependencyTableService : IDataTableService
    {
        bool UpdateDependencyTable(TableStorageEntity entity);
    }
```

```
    public interface INoDependencyTableService : IDataTableService
    {
    }
}

using System;
using System.Collections.Generic;
using System.Linq;
using System.Text;

namespace CreateDataStorage.Models.CloudDataServices
{
    using Microsoft.Samples.ServiceHosting.StorageClient;
    using CreateDataStorage.Models.CloudDataContext;

    abstract public class DataTableService
    {
        protected UserDataContext _userDataContext = null;
        protected string _Table { get; set; }

        public DataTableService()
        {
            _userDataContext = new UserDataContext();
        }

        public UserDataContext DataContext() { return _userDataContext; }

        virtual public bool Insert(TableStorageEntity entity)
        {
            bool success = false;

            try
            {
                if (this is IHasDependencyTableService)
                {
                    (this as IHasDependencyTableService).UpdateDependencyTable(entity);
                }
                _userDataContext.AddObject(_Table, entity);
                _userDataContext.SaveChanges();
                success = true;
            }
            catch { }

            return success;
        }

        public bool Update(TableStorageEntity entity)
        {
            bool success = false;

            try
```

```
            {
                if (Delete(entity))
                {
                    success = Insert(entity);
                }
            }
            catch { }

            return success;
        }

        virtual public bool Delete(TableStorageEntity entity)
        {
            bool success = false;

            try
            {
                if (this is IHasDependencyTableService)
                {
                    (this as IHasDependencyTableService).UpdateDependencyTable(entity);
                }
                _userDataContext.DeleteObject(entity);
                _userDataContext.SaveChanges();
                success = true;
            }
            catch { }

            return success;
        }
    }
}

using System;
using System.Collections.Generic;
using System.Linq;
using System.Text;
using System.Configuration;

namespace CreateDataStorage.Models.CloudDataServices
{
    using Microsoft.Samples.ServiceHosting.StorageClient;
    using CreateDataStorage.Models.CloudData;

    public class AddressTableService : DataTableService, INoDependencyTableService
    {
        public AddressTableService()
        {
            _Table = ConfigurationManager.AppSettings["AddressTable"];
        }
    }
}
```

6. In the same project, add the class UserDataContext, derived from the Azure SDK base class TableStorageDataServiceContext. This class encapsulates a cloud storage query function as Listing 1-5 shows.

Listing 1-5. Class UserDataContext Definition

```
    public class UserDataContext : TableStorageDataServiceContext
    {
        public DataServiceQuery<Address> AddressTable
        {
            get
            {
                return
CreateQuery<Address>(ConfigurationManager.AppSettings["AddressTable"]);
            }
        }

    }
```

7. Right-click on the CreateDataStorage project node in the Solution Explorer panel to bring up the Property dialog box. Select Development in the left pane. Enter the database name, AzureForDotNetDeveloper, into the dialog box, as Figure 1-4 shows.

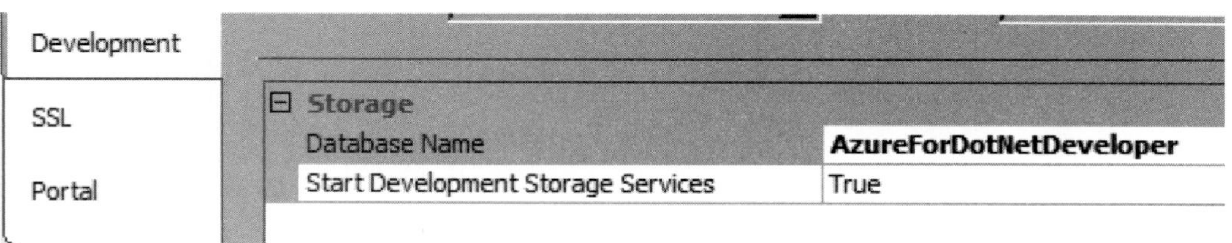

Figure 1-4. Enter data table name

8. Add a reference to CloudData.Models.dll to the CloudStorageService_WorkerRole project.

9. Right-click on the CreateDataStorage project and select Create Test Storage Table as Figure 1-5 shows. The compiler will analyze the code and generate a table for the database. The generated table in the database is shown in Figure 1-6.

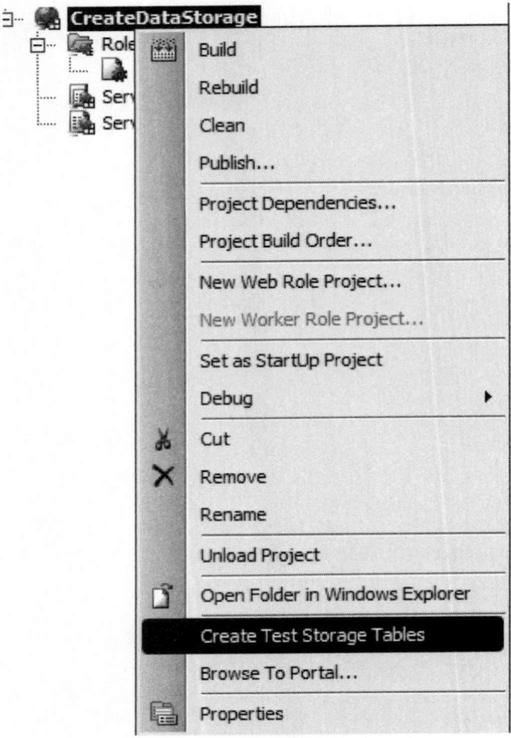

Figure 1-5. Generate SQL storage

Figure 1-6. Data table has been generated in local SQL database

When development storage is created the first time, message boxes will be popped up as shown in Figure 1-7 and Figure 1-8. The local development storage and development fabric can be manually started from the Windows Start menu as Figure 1-9 shows. Figure 1-10 and Figure 1-11 show the results of these services having been successfully started from the local development environment.

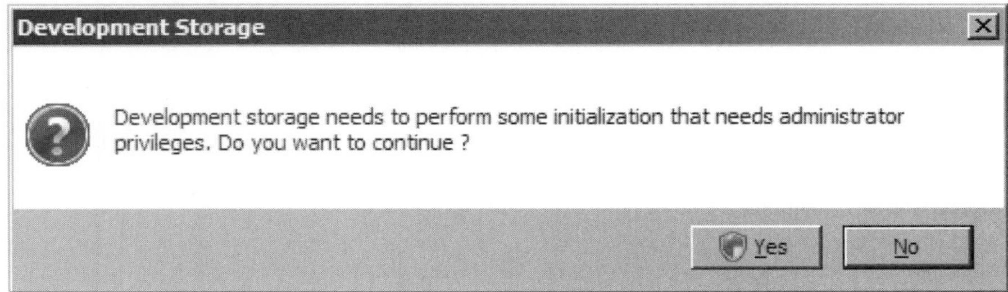

Figure 1-7. Dialog message to confirm installation of development storage

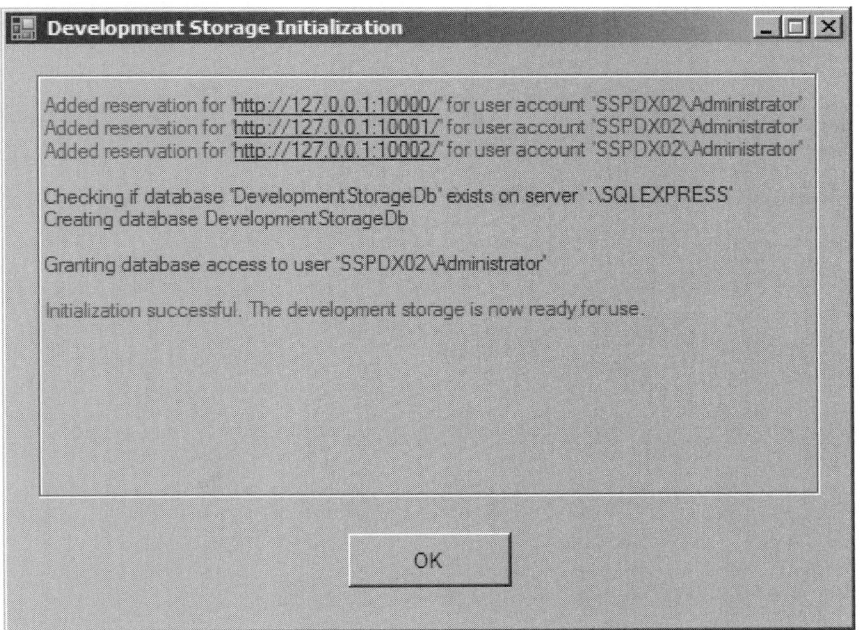

Figure 1-8. Confirming the settings using the default endpoint address for development storage the first time local development storage is used

Figure 1-9. Manually starting local development storage and development fabric

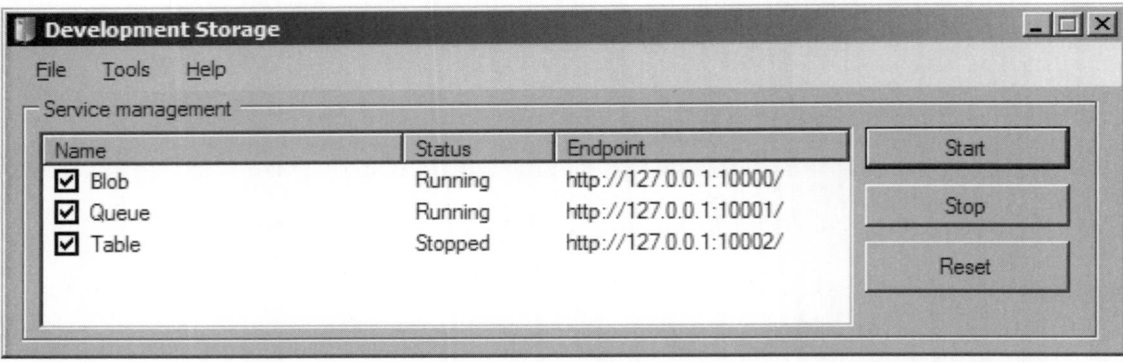

Figure 1-10. Opening the information window to verify current status of the development fabric

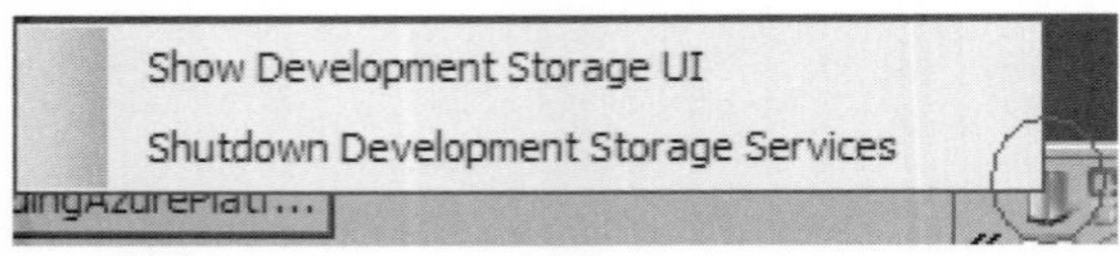

Figure 1-11. Right-clicking on the development storage icon to shut down the development fabric

This exercise demonstrates the basic steps to create a cloud data storage table using Windows Azure SDK development storage table service. In principle, the approach is fairly straightforward. However, in practice, since storage usage in a cloud environment is quite different from that in the regular on-premises environment, we should follow some rules and best practices.

Using Portable Data Types for Data Columns

Essentially, the data type of a data column should be portable to a SQL data type, or be able to be understood as a system-defined basic data type.

Using Data Tables Generated by Windows Azure Development Tool

Use the Azure development tool provided by the Azure development SDK to invoke the development storage service from Visual Studio to generate the data storage database and data tables. The development tool analyzes the data objects of all projects across the cloud application solution to generate the data structure for you. The number of data tables equals the number of data entity classes that derive from the `TableStorageEntity` class. The number of columns in a generated data table equals the number of public access properties defined in that data entity class.

Solutions to Non-Portable Data Types

If the data type is a custom-defined type, the SDK development tools will fail to invoke `DevelopmentStorage.exe` and `DevtableGen.exe`. The following example illustrates how to solve this problem if we have to use a data column in a data table with a custom-defined type, generally an embedded class of the parent, which is the type not portable to a SQL database.

In this example, we need to define two data object classes, the `State` and the `Address`. The `State` is the enumeration type with total of 59 members representing the states used by United States Postal Service. Each `Address` class has an attribute member with this custom-defined `State` type as shown in Listing 1-6.

***Listing 1-6.** An `Address` Class with an Attribute Member Using a Non-portable Custom-defined Type `State`*

```
public enum State
{
    AL,AK,AS,AZ,AR,CA,CO,CT,DE,DC,FM,FL,GA,GU,HI,
    ID,IL,IN,IA,KS,KY,LA,ME,MH,MD,MA,MI,MN,MS,MO,
    MT,NE,NV,NH,NJ,NM,NY,NC,ND,MP,OH,OK,OR,PW,PA,
    PR,RI,SC,SD,TN,TX,UT,VT,VI,VA,WA,WV,WI,WY
}

public class Address : TableStorageEntity
{
    ...
    public State State { get; set; }
    ...
}
```

When we invoke Create Test Storage Table from Visual Studio again as we did before, we will be asked to confirm removal of the existing storage from the database as Figure 1-12 shows.

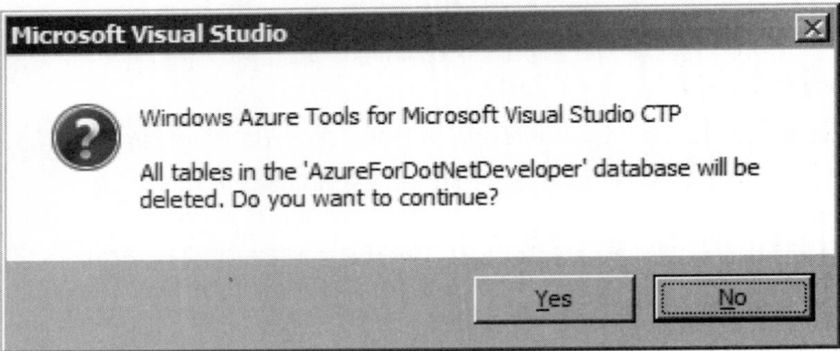

Figure 1-12. *Confirmation to remove existing table from cloud data storage dialog box when regenerating the cloud storage*

Click Yes to confirm this action. An error message pops up to show the failure of the action as Figure 1-13 shows.

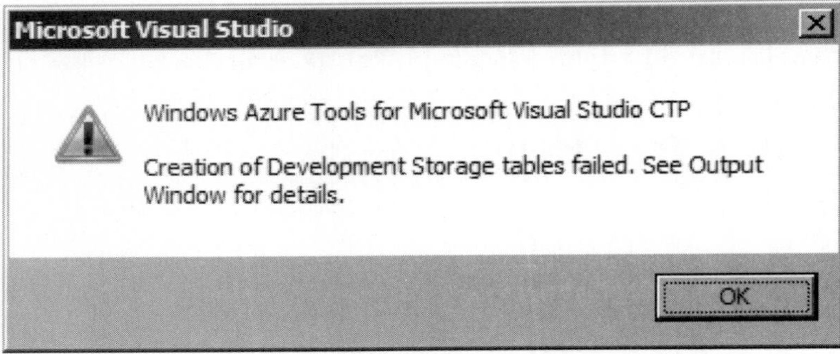

Figure 1-13. *Error message from the compiler when attempting to regenerate the storage tables if a non-portable data type is added to a cloud table*

The error message from the output window of Visual Studio is:

```
DevTableGen(0,0): error DG10: No tables were generated. Either no candidate classes were
found or they did not meet the requirements for the table storage.
```

This error message does not make much sense for troubleshooting, nor does the compiler provide any specific information on why the data table could not be created.

We can follow four steps to regenerate the table:

1. Make the `State` type inherit the type `int`, since `int` is a system-defined type and portable to a SQL database.
2. Define a member variable `_state` with the type of `State` in the `Address` class.
3. Apply the .NET nullable design pattern to this member variable.
4. Cast the type between the portable and custom-defined `enum` type from the access function.

The modified code is in boldface in Listing 1-7. After the modification, use Visual Studio to regenerate the table. The error will go away, and the table will be recreated in the local SQL database.

***Listing 1-7.** An Example of Solutions for Non-portable Data Types*

```
public enum State : int
{
    AL,AK,AS,AZ,AR,CA,CO,CT,DE,DC,FM,FL,GA,GU,HI,
    ID,IL,IN,IA,KS,KY,LA,ME,MH,MD,MA,MI,MN,MS,MO,
    MT,NE,NV,NH,NJ,NM,NY,NC,ND,MP,OH,OK,OR,PW,PA,
    PR,RI,SC,SD,TN,TX,UT,VT,VI,VA,WA,WV,WI,WY
}


public class Address : TableStorageEntity
{
    private State _state;

    public int? State
    {
        get { return (int)_state; }
        set { _state = (State)value; }
    }
}
```

Data Context Class Inheritance

In addition to the data entity class, for each data storage table, a class that inherits from the class `TableStorageDataServiceContext` must be defined with a data service query function implementation as Listing 1-8 shows.

Listing 1-8. *The Context Query Class Derived from* `TableStorageDataServiceContext` *Implemented in a Data Table Storage*

```
public class UserDataContext : TableStorageDataServiceContext
{
    ...
    public DataServiceQuery<Address> AddressTable
    {
        get
        {
            CreateQuery<Address>(ConfigurationManager.AppSettings["AddressTable"]);
        }
    }
    ...
}
```

■ **Note** The compiler does not provide detailed information about why the data storage generation failed. Hopefully, the information will be available from Microsoft in future releases.

Using PartitionKey and RowKey to Organize the Data to be Distributed

In order to support load balancing, tables and therefore entities in the cloud are partitioned across storage nodes, which may be physically located in different servers. Each partition holds a consecutive range of entities that have the same partition key value, which is how partitions are organized. As noted above, we specify the partition key as the `PartitionKey` property in a table, and it must be unique to allow for consecutive ordering into partitions. This sounds familiar, because the partition key forms part of an entity's primary key in combination with `RowKey`.

The data can be organized based on the usage of `PartitionKey` and `RowKey` for each data table entity. By design, the values for both `PartitionKey` and `RowKey` could be empty strings, whereas null values are not allowed. Table 1-2 below shows possible combinations of `PartitionKey` and `RowKey`.

Table 1-2. *Using* `PartitionKey` *and* `RowKey` *to Organize the Table Structures*

PartitionKey	RowKey	Usage Conditions
Empty string	Empty string	One partition or one row
Has value	Empty string	Multiple partitions or one row
Empty string	Has value	One partition or multiple rows per a partition
Has value	Has value	Multiple partitions of multiple rows for each partition

Create Cloud Data Storage with Relational Data Structure

Migrating existing relational data storage from an on-premises system to a cloud environment is a really interesting topic and a challenge for an organization to face. There are a variety of good answers and solutions. In this exercise, we are going to create data storage with a relational structure among data entities to provide you with a starting point. SQL Azure provides a ready-made solution for relational data storage infrastructure and is covered in Chapter 8. The rest of this chapter will provide an example exercise to handle a simple relational data structure that runs in a cloud using table storage, as you may not want the full-blown SQL Azure service.

The data structure we will build includes three data entities: `Address`, `Person`, and `User`. The `Address` data entity is the same as the one we created in the first exercise. A `Person` data entity has an encapsulated object `Address`. A `User` data entity has an encapsulated object `Person`. In terms of the XML schema, the relationship among these entities can be understood as the reference of one schema to another, such as a `User` reference to `Person` and a `Person` reference to `Address`. This is a typical example using an object-oriented approach to data modeling and schema definitions. Figure 1-14 and Figure 1-15 provide the relationship in terms of XML schemas.

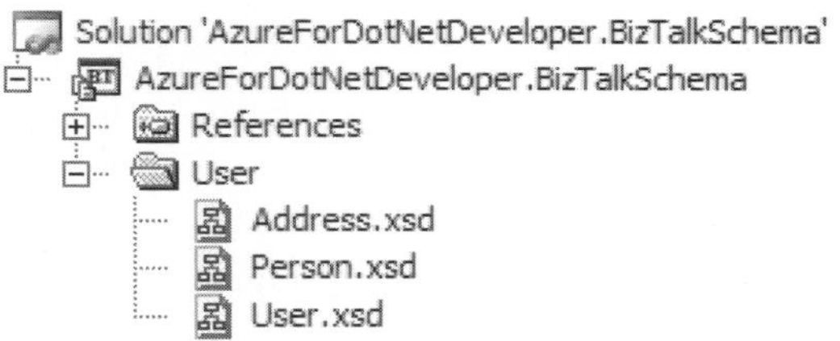

Figure 1-14. *`User` data structure schemas*

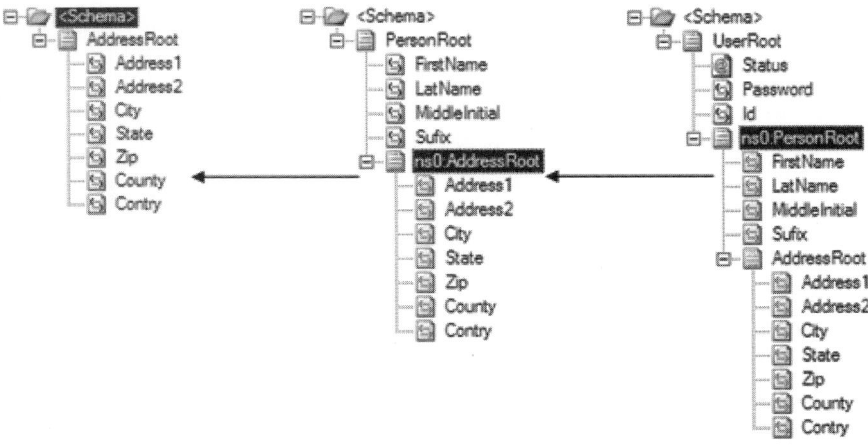

Figure 1-15. *Schema for `Address`, `Person`, and `User`*

As explained in the previous exercise, we cannot use the property access attribute to expose an embedded object from an entity class. We either have to alter the embedded object as we did previously or use methods to provide access to the internal objects. Otherwise, the data table generation fails and the compiler does not provide the specific reason. Listing 1-9 shows how to expose a custom-defined inner data entity object from a data object class using class member methods instead of member attributes.

Listing 1-9. *Using a Member Method Instead of Member Attributes to Expose Inner Data Entity Objects of a Non-portable Custom-defined Type*

```
public class Person : TableStorageEntity
{
    ...
    private Address _address = null;

    public string FirstName { get; set; }
    public string LastName { get; set; }
    public string MiddleInitial { get; set; }
    public string Suffix { get; set; }
    ...
    public Address GetAddress() { return _address; }
    ...
}
```

Following the same procedures as we had in the first exercise, we successfully generated three data tables from local cloud data storage as the screenshot shows in Figure 1-16.

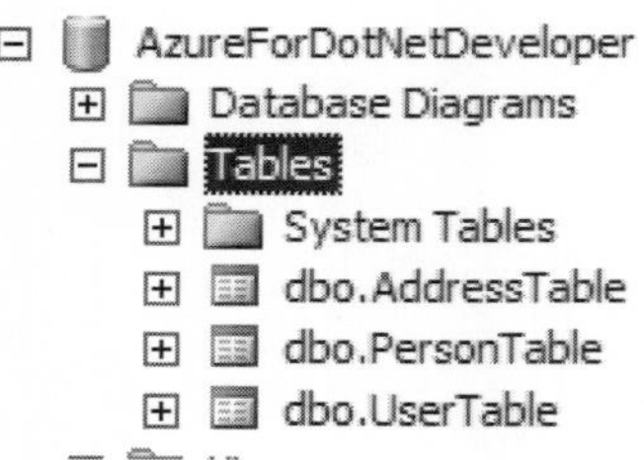

Figure 1-16. *Generated relational data storage*

From this example, we learned that data entity classes with relational structures in a cloud platform have some limitations. If an entity class has a dependency entity class, property attributes cannot be used for access. Instead, member methods should be used. It should be borne in mind that you need to refactor existing data storage for the cloud. We will discuss more refactoring issues in later chapters.

A Constraint for Data Entity Classes Contains Embedded Entity Classes

Today, a lot of existing software uses data entity classes generated from XML schemas using the .NET utility `Xsd.exe` shipped with the .NET Framework. By default, the generated data entity classes using `Xsd.exe` use a property attribute function to access the embedded data entity objects. When we refactor existing code to a cloud platform, we can simply derive these data entity classes from `TableStorageEntity`. However, all property functions used to expose embedded data object from a container or parent class must be refactored to `Get`/`Set` member method pairs instead.

Listing 1-10 shows the data entity class for `Person` generated by using `Xsd.exe`. All attribute properties such as the `AddressRoot`, as highlighted in Listing 1-9, must be reimplemented as `Get`/`Set` member method pairs.

Listing 1-10. *The `Person` Class Generated from `Xsd.exe` Using the XML Schemas*

```
    [System.CodeDom.Compiler.GeneratedCodeAttribute("xsd", "2.0.50727.3038")]
    [System.SerializableAttribute()]
    [System.Diagnostics.DebuggerStepThroughAttribute()]
    [System.ComponentModel.DesignerCategoryAttribute("code")]
    [System.Xml.Serialization.XmlTypeAttribute(AnonymousType=true,
Namespace="http://AzureForDotNetDeveloper.Schema.User.Person")]
    [System.Xml.Serialization.XmlRootAttribute
(Namespace="http://AzureForDotNetDeveloper.Schema.User.Person", IsNullable=false)]
    public partial class PersonRoot {
        private string firstNameField;
        private string latNameField;
        private string middleInitialField;
        private string suffixField;
        private AddressRoot addressRootField;
        /// <remarks/>
[System.Xml.Serialization.XmlElementAttribute
(Form=System.Xml.Schema.XmlSchemaForm.Unqualified)]
        public string FirstName {
            get {
                return this.firstNameField;
            }
            set {
                this.firstNameField = value;
            }
        }
        /// <remarks/>
        [System.Xml.Serialization.XmlElementAttribute(
Namespace="http://AzureForDotNetDeveloper.Schema.User.Address")]
        public AddressRoot AddressRoot {
            get {
                return this.addressRootField;
            }
```

```
            set {
                this.addressRootField = value;
            }
        }
    }
```

Refactoring Data Entity Classes

A solution to the constraint for data entity classes containing embedded entity classes is to refactor. To refactor the PersonRoot class for Windows Azure platform, follow these steps:

1. Add using `Microsoft.Samples.ServiceHosting.StorageClient;` into the project.
2. Make the PersonRoot class derive from the TableStorageEntity class.
3. Modify the Get/Set property pair into the GetAddress()/SetAddress() method pair. Listing 1-11 shows the results after the Person data entity class has been refactored.

Listing 1-11. *Refactoring the* Person *Class to the Azure Cloud Platform*

```
    using Microsoft.Samples.ServiceHosting.StorageClient;

    /// <remarks/>
    [System.CodeDom.Compiler.GeneratedCodeAttribute("xsd", "2.0.50727.3038")]
    [System.SerializableAttribute()]
    [System.Diagnostics.DebuggerStepThroughAttribute()]
    [System.ComponentModel.DesignerCategoryAttribute("code")]
    [System.Xml.Serialization.XmlTypeAttribute(AnonymousType=true,➥
 Namespace="http://AzureForDotNetDeveloper.Schema.User.Person")]
    [System.Xml.Serialization.XmlRootAttribute(Namespace=➥
"http://AzureForDotNetDeveloper.Schema.User.Person", IsNullable=false)]
    public partial class PersonRoot : TableStorageEntity
    {
        public AddressRoot GetAddressRoot()
        {
           return this.addressRootField;
        }

        public void SetAddressRoot(AddressRoot address)
        {
            this.addressRootField = address;
        }
    }
```

Close SQL Analysis

When creating a test cloud storage table, any active SQL query analysis running against the existing cloud storage table needs to be closed from SQL Management Studio to avoid the failure of data storage creation.

Summary

As we have learned so far, creating cloud table storage is a straightforward job. Microsoft claims that the Azure framework is a true developer-oriented framework. All the hard work should have been done and encapsulated in the SDK. Your life as a .NET developer is now a lot easier; what remains for you to do is nothing but derive your client classes from the base classes from the SDK and follow the right procedures to build your cloud applications. However, I have not presented how to access cloud table storage yet. That is the task we are going to pursue in the next chapter.

CHAPTER 2

■ ■ ■

Access Cloud Table Storage

To access Azure table storage, we must use Azure web roles, since the worker role cannot connect to or communicate with the outside world directly. A worker role is usually used on batch jobs (see the book's introduction). The Azure SDK provides a set of templates in a client service access library, `StorageClient.dll`. This chapter has three exercises. In the first section of this chapter we will walk through a process to access cloud storage step by step and see how to use these templates to insert and query data using the cloud table storages. The second exercise focuses on deleting the records from a cloud storage table. The third exercise is an example of how to manipulate data in tables with a relational structure. The cloud storage we are going to use was created in Chapter 1. From these three exercises you will learn the basic skills to deal with cloud table storage.

Essentially all cloud tables are addressable using a URI. The cloud table can be accessed by a web request via HTTP. The Azure SDK provides client-side components that implement all the base classes used to access Azure table storage. These components can be found in the `bin` folder of the SDK. You then need to create classes derived from the base classes defined in the SDK.

Accessing a Single Cloud Data Storage Table

First, let's see how to access a single cloud data storage table. Before we drill down into the details let's create a new WebRole cloud service in Visual Studio by selecting New Project ➤ Visual C# ➤ Cloud Service ➤ Web Cloud Service and name it `CloudTableStorageService`.

■ **Note** The code for this example is in the exercise 2-1 bundle from the code download.

Visual Studio will automatically generate two projects as a solution package. One project is called `CloudTableStorageService`, and another one is called `CloudTableStorageService_WebRole`. The first project is a new type of Visual Studio project introduced by the Windows Azure framework.

There are two files automatically generated in the `CloudTableStorageService` project by Visual Studio. One is `ServiceConfiguration.cscf`, a configuration XML file containing user account information. By default, all the URI addresses generated in this file point to the local development environment with a default account authentication key called `AccountSharedKey` with a base-64 encoding token key value. When a project is deployed to the remote cloud host in a Microsoft data center, all the values in the configuration need to be changed to point to your account. You will find out how to do this later in this book and get information in more detail about deploying an Azure project to a remote cloud environment from Chapter 9. Visual Studio also adds a reference to point to the second project. The second project, `CloudTableStorageService_WebRole`, is a regular ASP.NET project with a default web form file defined inside the project. Renamed it `AddressTable.aspx`.

Right-click on the second project we have just created, `CloudTableStorageService_WebRole`, and insert three new folders into that project—`CloudTableStorageDataContext`, `CloudTableStorageDataService`, and `CloudTableStorageDataEntity`. We are going to add and implement more classes in these three folders in the rest of this exercise.

■ **Note** You can delete the second web role project and create your own regular web application type project and add it back by changing the reference to your own web application project. By design there is only one web application project that can be referenced from an Azure storage service project.

---

1. As Listing 2-1 shows, create a base class `TableContext`. This class inherits from `TableStorageDataServiceContext`. This class is part of the `Microsoft.ServiceHosting.Service.dll` assembly from the Azure SDK. The constructor of the `TableContext` class takes `StorageAccountInfo` as a parameter. The `StorageAccountInfo` class instance retrieves the configuration (`DevelopmentStorage.exe.config`, shown in Listing 2-2) from the SDK install directory and reads it at runtime. There is no need to do any more work with this derived class. All necessary jobs and hard tasks have been done from the base class. This makes your life a lot easier since you do not need to know the details of how to hook up to the Azure framework runtime environment. The only thing for you to do is to provide correct authentication information.

Listing 2-1. *A Cloud Data Object Class Must Inherit from the Base Class* `TableStorageDataServiceContext`

```
abstract public class TableContext : TableStorageDataServiceContext
{
    public string TableName { get; set; }

    public TableContext(StorageAccountInfo accountInfo)
        : base(accountInfo)
    {
    }
}
```

Listing 2-2. *The Configuration File* `DevelopmentStorage.exe.config`

```
<developmentStorageConfig>
    <services>
      <service name="Blob"
               url="http://127.0.0.1:10000/"/>
      <service name="Queue"
               url="http://127.0.0.1:10001/"/>
```

```
    <service name="Table"
             url="http://127.0.0.1:10002/"
       dbServer="localhost\SQLExpress"/>
  </services>

  <accounts>
    <account name="devstoreaccount1"
             authKey="<AUTH_KEY>"
             isAdmin="false"
             contactInfo=""/>
  </accounts>
</developmentStorageConfig>
```

2. Create another class called DataTableService. This class has two member variables. One is the type of the TableContext class we have just created, and the another member variable is the StorageAccountInfo type. This class is also defined in the Microsoft.ServiceHosting.Service.dll assembly of the Azure SDK. In the body of the constructor of the DataTableService class, add a line of code to instantiate the class StorageAccountInfo and the retrieve the account configuration information from the configuration file DevelopmentStorage.exe.config as shown in Figure 2-1. Figure 2-1 shows the debug information at the breakpoint set at the constructor of the DataTableService class at runtime. The configuration information retrieved by the framework should match the configuration settings. The implementation of the TableContext class is fairly straightforward. This class only implements a query interface to the cloud table AddressTable, as Listing 2-1 and the class diagram in Figure 2-2 show.

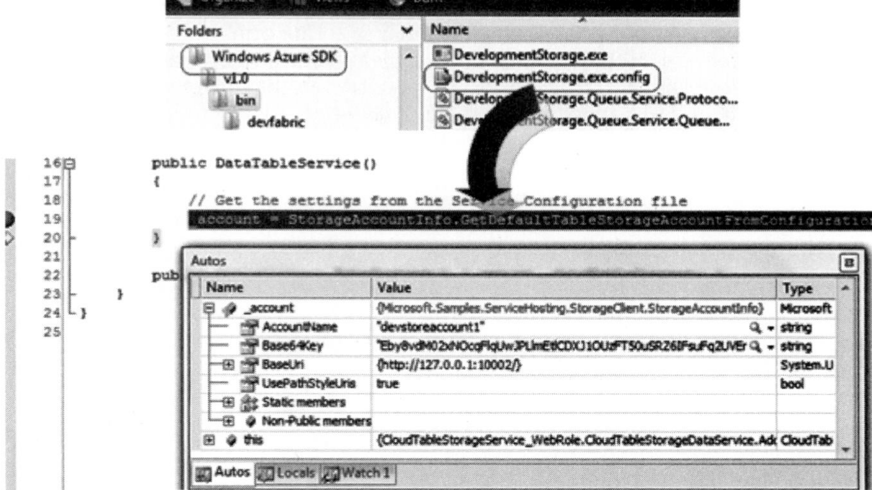

Figure 2-1. Account information is configured in DevelopmentStorage.exe.config and retrieved at runtime

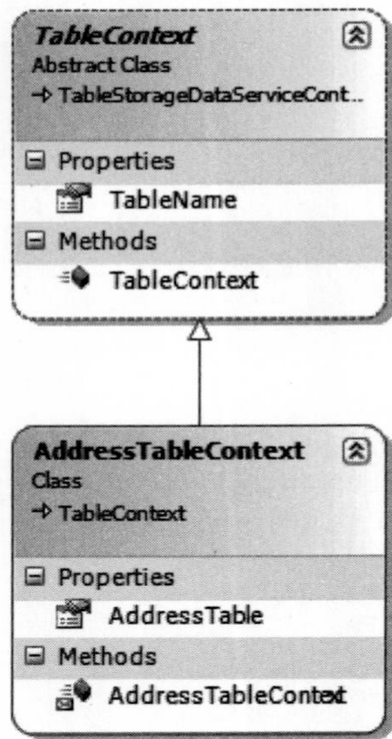

Figure 2-2. The `AddressTableContext` class diagram

3. Add a new class called `AddressTableContext` to inherit from the base class `TableContext`, as shown in Listing 2-3. The purpose of creating this class is to encapsulate the table storage interface function to a specific data table. In this exercise we only access the `Address` table, so we only need to create one derived class from `TableContext`. If there are multiple tables we need to access then we need to create more classes derived from `TableContext` in the future. Each derived class is dedicated to a specific data table. So why can't we come up with a generic table-access class, which exposes the data table access functions and returns generic types. The answer is the table name is a static string and needs to match the name of the physical data storage table. Another reason is that this allows the client code to accept the return data table type as a concerte type without transforming the generic type. This will significantly reduce unnecessary complexity. To reach that end there are three tasks that need to be done.

    1. Create a constructor to this class to accept a parameter of instance of `StorageAccountInfo`.

    2. Read the table name from the configuration settings in the body of the constructor.

    3. Add a query interface to query the `Address` table.

Listing 2-3. Implementation of Class `AddressTableContext`*, a Derived Class of* `TableContext`

```
using System;
using System.Collections.Generic;
using System.Linq;
using System.Web;
using System.Configuration;

namespace CloudTableStorageService_WebRole.CloudTableStorageDataContext
{
    using Microsoft.Samples.ServiceHosting.StorageClient;
    using CloudTableStorageService_WebRole.CloudTableStrorageDataEntity;

    internal class AddressTableContext : TableContext
    {
        internal AddressTableContext(StorageAccountInfo accountInfo)
            : base(accountInfo)
        {
            TableName = ConfigurationManager.AppSettings["AddressTable"];
        }

        public IQueryable<Address> AddressTable
        {
            get { return CreateQuery<Address>(TableName); }
        }

    }
}
```

4. In the `CloudTableStorageService_WebRole` project create a C# class called `DataTableService` and mark it as an abstract class since we are going to use it as a base class. This class implements the facade design pattern to encapsulate the `StorageAccountInfo` and `TableContext` classes. The definition of this base class is shown in Listing 2-4.

Listing 2-4. Definition of Base Class `DataTableService`

```
using System;
using System.Collections.Generic;
using System.Linq;
using System.Web;

namespace CloudTableStorageService_WebRole.CloudTableStorageDataService
{
    using Microsoft.Samples.ServiceHosting.StorageClient;
    using CloudTableStorageService_WebRole.CloudTableStorageDataContext;

    abstract public class DataTableService
    {
        protected StorageAccountInfo _account = null;
        protected TableContext _dataTableContext = null;
```

```
        public DataTableService()
        {
            // Get the settings from the Service Configuration file
            _account = StorageAccountInfo.GetDefaultTableStorageAccountFromConfiguration();
        }

        public TableContext TableContext() { return _dataTableContext; }
    }
}
```

5. Add a new C# class `AddressTableService` in the same folder. (The class diagram is shown in Figure 2-3. The implementation for the class is shown in Listing 2-5.) This class is derived from the base class `DataTableService` and provides a set of public access functions to perform basic data I/O between the table storage context and the custom-defined data entity container classes. This class must have at least the next four public methods:

    - `Select()`: The `Select()` method can include functionality to retrieve an enumerable collection of data items and to retrieve a single item. In this example we are going to implement `Select()` to retrieve the enumerable item collection from the table `AddressTable`.
    - `Insert()`: To insert an entity into a cloud storage table; in this example, to the table `AddressTable`.
    - `Update()`: To refresh changes of a data entity to a cloud storage table; in this example, to the table `AddressTable`.
    - `Delete()`: To remove a data entity from a cloud storage table; in this example, from the table `AddressTable`.

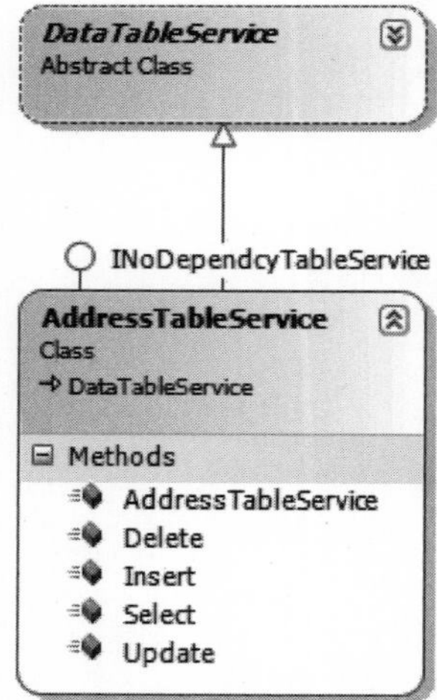

Figure 2-3. *Class `AddressTableService` provides data IO services*

Listing 2-5. Implementation of the Class AddressTableService

```
using System;
using System.Collections.Generic;
using System.Linq;
using System.Web;
using System.Data.Services.Client;
using System.Configuration;

namespace CloudTableStorageService_WebRole.CloudTableStorageDataService
{
    using Microsoft.Samples.ServiceHosting.StorageClient;
    using CloudTableStorageService_WebRole.CloudTableStrorageDataEntity;
    using CloudTableStorageService_WebRole.CloudTableStorageDataContext;

    public class AddressTableService : DataTableService
    {
        /// </summary>
        public AddressTableService()
        {
            _dataTableContext = new AddressTableContext(base._account);
            dataTableContext.RetryPolicy =
              RetryPolicies.RetryN(Convert.ToInt32(
                  ConfigurationManager.AppSettings["Retry"]),
                  TimeSpan.FromSeconds(1));
        }

        public IEnumerable<Address> Select()
        {
            if (null == _dataTableContext ||
                null == (_dataTableContext as AddressTableContext))
            {
                return null;
            }

            var results =
                from a in (_dataTableContext as AddressTableContext).AddressTable select a;

            if (0 == (results as
                DataServiceQuery<Address>).ToArray<Address>().Count<Address>())
            {
                return null;
            }

            TableStorageDataServiceQuery<Address> query =
              new TableStorageDataServiceQuery<Address>(
                                      results as DataServiceQuery<Address>);
            IEnumerable<Address> queryResults = query.ExecuteAllWithRetries();
            return queryResults;
        }
```

```
        public bool Insert(Address entity)
        {
            bool success = false;

            try
            {
                _dataTableContext.AddObject(_dataTableContext.TableName, entity);
                _dataTableContext.SaveChanges();
                success = true;
            }
            catch { }

            return success;
        }

        public bool Update(Address entity)
        {
            bool success = false;

            try
            {
                if (Delete(entity))
                {
                    success = Insert(entity);
                }
            }
            catch { }

            return success;
        }

        public bool Delete(Address entity)
        {
            bool success = false;

            try
            {
                _dataTableContext.AttachTo(_dataTableContext.TableName, entity, "*");
                _dataTableContext.DeleteObject(entity);
                _dataTableContext.SaveChanges();
                success = true;
            }
            catch { }

            return success;
        }
    }
}
```

6. Open `AddressTable.aspx` from the project in Visual Studio and insert two table objects into the body of the form as Figure 2-4 shows.

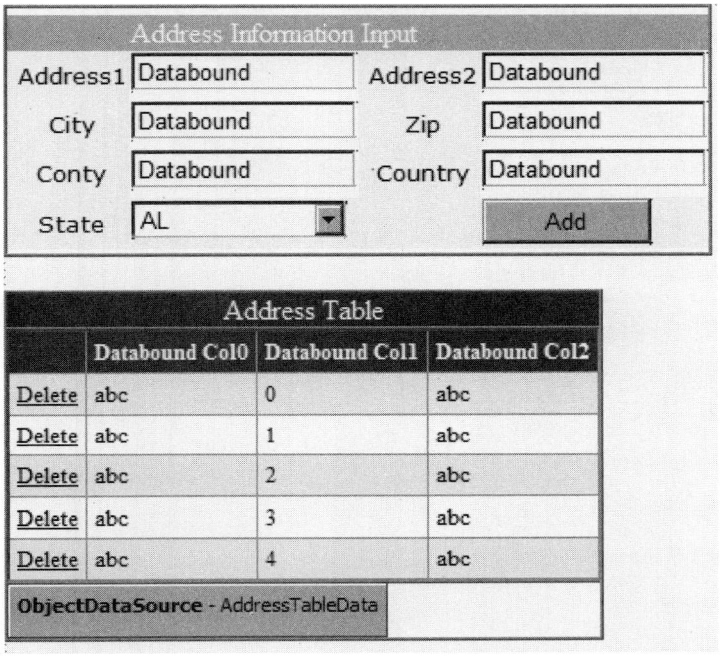

Figure 2-4. Create a web form table for input and a `GridView` on the ASPX page

7. In the first table add an ASP.NET `FormView` and implement an `InsertItemTemplate` in the body of the `FormView` as Listing 2-6 shows. Define an ASP.NET `GridView` in the second web form table as Listing 2-7 shows.

***Listing 2-6.** Implement `FormView` with `InsertItemTemplate` from the First ASP.Net Web Form Table*

```
<table cellspacing="0" cellpadding="0" border="1"
          style="width: 600; height: 145px;">
           <asp:FormView
              id="formAddAddress"
              DataSourceId="AddressTableData"
              DefaultMode="Insert"
              Runat="server"><%-- Address Table--%>
              <InsertItemTemplate>
                  <tr>
                      <td bgcolor="#FFCC00"></td>
                      <td bgcolor="#FFCC00" colspan="3">Address Information Input</td>
                  </tr>
                  <tr>
                      <td class="input_lable">Address1</td>
                      <td class="input_Text">
                          <asp:TextBox
```

```
                    ID="txtAddress1"
                    Text='<%# Bind("Address1") %>'
                    runat="server"
                    Width="125px">
                </asp:TextBox>
            </td>
            <td class="input_lable">Address2</td>
            <td class="input_Text">
                <asp:TextBox
                    ID="txtAddress2"
                    Text='<%# Bind("Address2") %>'
                    runat="server"
                    Width="125px"></asp:TextBox>
            </td>
        </tr>
        <tr>
            <td class="input_lable">City</td>
            <td class="input_Text">
                <asp:TextBox
                    ID="City"
                    Text='<%# Bind("City") %>'
                    runat="server"
                    Width="125px"></asp:TextBox>
            </td>
            <td class="style10">Zip</td>
            <td class="style11">
                <asp:TextBox
                    ID="Zip"
                    Text='<%# Bind("Zip") %>'
                    runat="server"
                    Width="125px">
                </asp:TextBox>
            </td>
        </tr>
        <tr>
            <td class="style10">County</td>
            <td class="style11">
                <asp:TextBox
                    ID="County"
                    Text='<%# Bind("County") %>'
                    runat="server"
                    Width="125px">
                </asp:TextBox>
            </td>
            <td class="style10">Country</td>
            <td class="style11">
                <asp:TextBox
                    ID="Country"
                    Text='<%# Bind("Country") %>'
                    runat="server"
                    Width="125px">
```

```
        </asp:TextBox>
    </td>
</tr>
<tr style=" background-color: #ffffbe;
        font-weight:normal;
        font-size: 10pt;
        font-family: Verdana, Geneva, Arial, Helvetica, sans-serif;
        padding: 2px 2px 2px 6px;
        text-align: center; color:Black; height:25px;">
     <td class="input_lable">State</td>
     <td class="input_Text">
         <asp:DropDownList
            ID="combState"
            runat="server"
            SelectedIndex='<%#Bind("State")%>'
            Height="23px"
            Width="119px">
             <asp:ListItem>AL</asp:ListItem>
             <asp:ListItem>AK</asp:ListItem>
             <asp:ListItem>AS</asp:ListItem>
             <asp:ListItem>AZ</asp:ListItem>
             <asp:ListItem>ZR</asp:ListItem>
             <asp:ListItem>CA</asp:ListItem>
             <asp:ListItem>CO</asp:ListItem>
             <asp:ListItem>CT</asp:ListItem>
             <asp:ListItem>DE</asp:ListItem>
             <asp:ListItem>DC</asp:ListItem>
             <asp:ListItem>FM</asp:ListItem>
             <asp:ListItem>FL</asp:ListItem>
             <asp:ListItem>GA</asp:ListItem>
             <asp:ListItem>GU</asp:ListItem>
             <asp:ListItem>HI</asp:ListItem>
             <asp:ListItem>ID</asp:ListItem>
             <asp:ListItem>IL</asp:ListItem>
             <asp:ListItem>IN</asp:ListItem>
             <asp:ListItem>IA</asp:ListItem>
             <asp:ListItem>KS</asp:ListItem>
             <asp:ListItem>KY</asp:ListItem>
             <asp:ListItem>LA</asp:ListItem>
             <asp:ListItem>ME</asp:ListItem>
             <asp:ListItem>MH</asp:ListItem>
             <asp:ListItem>MD</asp:ListItem>
             <asp:ListItem>MA</asp:ListItem>
             <asp:ListItem>MI</asp:ListItem>
             <asp:ListItem>MN</asp:ListItem>
             <asp:ListItem>MS</asp:ListItem>
             <asp:ListItem>MO</asp:ListItem>
             <asp:ListItem>MT</asp:ListItem>
             <asp:ListItem>NE</asp:ListItem>
             <asp:ListItem>NV</asp:ListItem>
             <asp:ListItem>NG</asp:ListItem>
```

```
                                <asp:ListItem>NJ</asp:ListItem>
                                <asp:ListItem>NM</asp:ListItem>
                                <asp:ListItem>NY</asp:ListItem>
                                <asp:ListItem>NC</asp:ListItem>
                                <asp:ListItem>ND</asp:ListItem>
                                <asp:ListItem>MP</asp:ListItem>
                                <asp:ListItem>OH</asp:ListItem>
                                <asp:ListItem>OK</asp:ListItem>
                                <asp:ListItem>OR</asp:ListItem>
                                <asp:ListItem>PW</asp:ListItem>
                                <asp:ListItem>PA</asp:ListItem>
                                <asp:ListItem>PR</asp:ListItem>
                                <asp:ListItem>RI</asp:ListItem>
                                <asp:ListItem>SC</asp:ListItem>
                                <asp:ListItem>SD</asp:ListItem>
                                <asp:ListItem>TN</asp:ListItem>
                                <asp:ListItem>TX</asp:ListItem>
                                <asp:ListItem>UT</asp:ListItem>
                                <asp:ListItem>VT</asp:ListItem>
                                <asp:ListItem>VI</asp:ListItem>
                                <asp:ListItem>VA</asp:ListItem>
                                <asp:ListItem>WA</asp:ListItem>
                                <asp:ListItem>WV</asp:ListItem>
                                <asp:ListItem>WI</asp:ListItem>
                                <asp:ListItem>WY</asp:ListItem>
                            </asp:DropDownList>
                       </td>
                       <td class="style10"></td>
                        <td class="style9">
                           <asp:Button
                               ID="btnAddAddress"
                               runat="server"
                               Text="Add"
                               CommandName="Insert"
                               Width="94px" />
                       </td>
                     </tr>
               </InsertItemTemplate>
               </asp:FormView>
           </table>
```

Listing 2-7. *A* `GridView` *Used to Display Query Results from Cloud Table Defined in the Second Web Form Table in* `AddressTable.aspx`

```
<asp:GridView
                id="AddressView"
                DataSourceId="AddressTableData"
                DataKeyNames="PartitionKey,RowKey"
                AllowPaging="False"
                AutoGenerateColumns="True"
```

```
            GridLines="Vertical"
            Runat="server"
            BackColor="White" ForeColor="Black"
            BorderColor="#DEDFDE" BorderStyle="None" BorderWidth="1px"
            CellPadding="4" Font-Size="Small">
        <Columns>
            <asp:CommandField ShowDeleteButton="true"  />
        </Columns>
        <RowStyle BackColor="#F7F7DE" />
        <FooterStyle BackColor="#CCCC99" />
        <PagerStyle BackColor="#F7F7DE" ForeColor="Black" HorizontalAlign="Right" />
        <SelectedRowStyle BackColor="#CE5D5A" Font-Bold="True" ForeColor="White" />
        <HeaderStyle BackColor="#6B696B" Font-Bold="True" ForeColor="White" />
        <AlternatingRowStyle BackColor="White" />
    </asp:GridView>
```

8. Insert code at the bottom of the `AddressTable.aspx` file to create an `ObjectDataSource` and then bind the `Address` data entity class to `AddressTableService` as Listing 2-8 shows.

Listing 2-8. *Insert an `ObjectDataSource` Definition into the `AddressTable.aspx` File and Bind It to the `Address` Data Entity Class*

```
<asp:ObjectDataSource
  runat="server"
  ID="AddressTableData"
  TypeName=
    "CloudTableStorageService_WebRole.CloudTableStorageDataService.AddressTableService"
  DataObjectTypeName="CloudTableStorageService_WebRole.CloudTableStrorageDataEntity.Address"
  SelectMethod="Select" DeleteMethod="Delete" InsertMethod="Insert">
</asp:ObjectDataSource>
```

■ **Note** The class object name must be fully qualified, with the combination of name space and class name.

---

9. Open `AddressTable.aspx.cs` and insert code into the `Page_Load` event handling function and implement the `AddAddress_Click` event-handling function. Since we use data binding between the `GridView` and the `ObjectDataSource` in `AddressTable.aspx` and the data binding is bidirectional, the code-behind file is extremely concise as Listing 2-9 shows.

Listing 2-9. *Code in `AddressTable.aspx.cs`*

```
using System;
using System.Collections.Generic;
using System.Linq;
using System.Web;
```

```
using System.Web.UI;
using System.Web.UI.WebControls;
using System.Threading;
using System.Data.Services.Client;

namespace CloudTableStorageService_WebRole
{
    using CloudTableStorageService_WebRole.CloudTableStorageDataService;
    using CloudTableStorageService_WebRole.CloudTableStrorageDataEntity;
    using CloudTableStorageService_WebRole.CloudTableStorageDataContext;

    public partial class WebForm1 : System.Web.UI.Page
    {
        private AddressTableService _addressTableService = null;

        protected void Page_Load(object sender, EventArgs e)
        {
            if (!Page.IsCallback)
            {
                _addressTableService = new AddressTableService();
            }
            else
            {
                _DataBinding();
            }
        }

        protected void btnAddAddress_Click(object sender, EventArgs e)
        {
            if (Page.IsValid)
            {
                _DataBinding();
            }

        }

        private void _DataBinding()
        {
            AddressView.DataBind();
        }
    }
}
```

10. Set the CloudTableStorageService project as the startup project by right-clicking on the project node in Solution Explorer; start the service from Visual Studio by pressing F5 (with debugging) or Ctrl+F5 (without debugging). Visual Studio will start the table storage service and launch the AddressTable.aspx page in the default browser as Figure 2-4 shows.

11. Before we start testing what we have achieved so far, I strongly recommend you do one more thing. The cloud storage table needs to be created in cloud storage, either locally during development or remotely after being deployed, at the time of the first data access request. To improve performance and avoid creating the table multiple times, insert a piece of code into the static function `ApplicationStartUponFirstRequest` in `Global.asax` as shown in Listing 2-10.

Listing 2-10. Call to Create Cloud Storage Table at the Time of Application Starting

```
private static void ApplicationStartUponFirstRequest(HttpContext context)
{
  StorageAccountInfo account =
    StorageAccountInfo.GetDefaultTableStorageAccountFromConfiguration();

  TableStorage.CreateTablesFromModel(typeof(AddressTableContext), account);
}
```

Now it is time to insert and query data from cloud table storage. Use the two ASP.NET web form tables we added in step 7: Address Information Input, used to accept the user input, and `AddressTable`, used to display the results as Figure 2-5 shows.

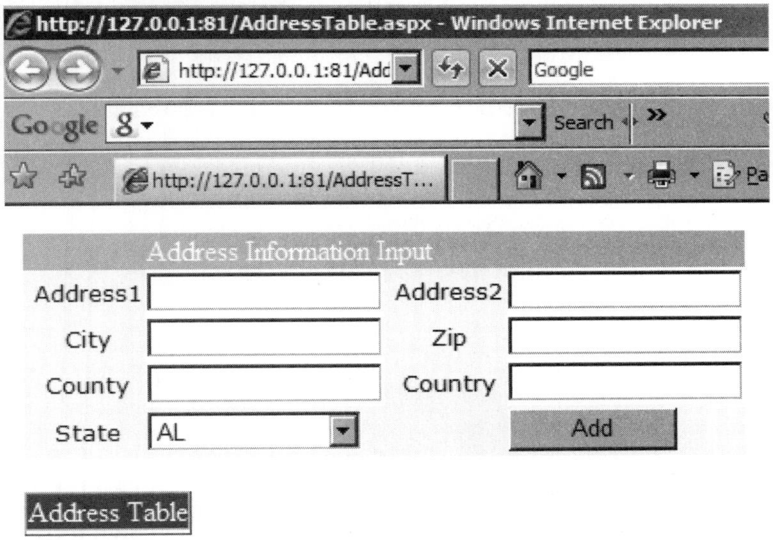

Figure 2-5. `AddressTable.aspx` has been loaded in IE, though there is no data in `AddressTable`

At this point, the development storage and development fabric services should also be launched from the local system. Their icons can be found in the system tray as shown in Figure 2-6. Right-click on development storage to open the window shown in Figure 2-7. You can find Blob, Queue, and Table services running on the local cloud platform. The current data table should be `AddressTable` in the database `AzureForDotNetDeveloper`. Figure 2-8 shows the local fabric windows where the running

WebRole service instance can be found with the debug log information showing in the black resizable windows.

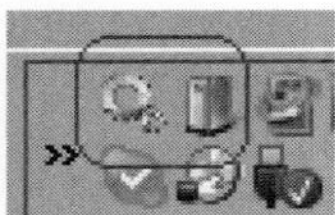

Figure 2-6. *Icons from the system tray showing that the development storage service and development fabric services have been launched from the local development environment*

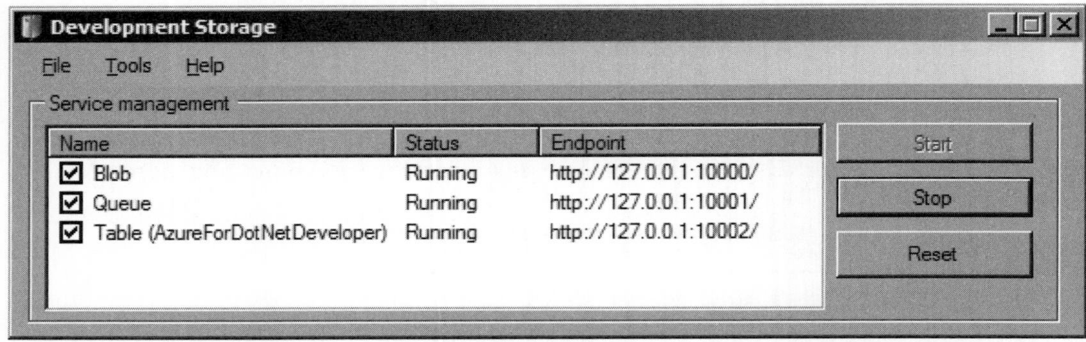

Figure 2-7. *Development storage service window showing cloud storage services running from local system*

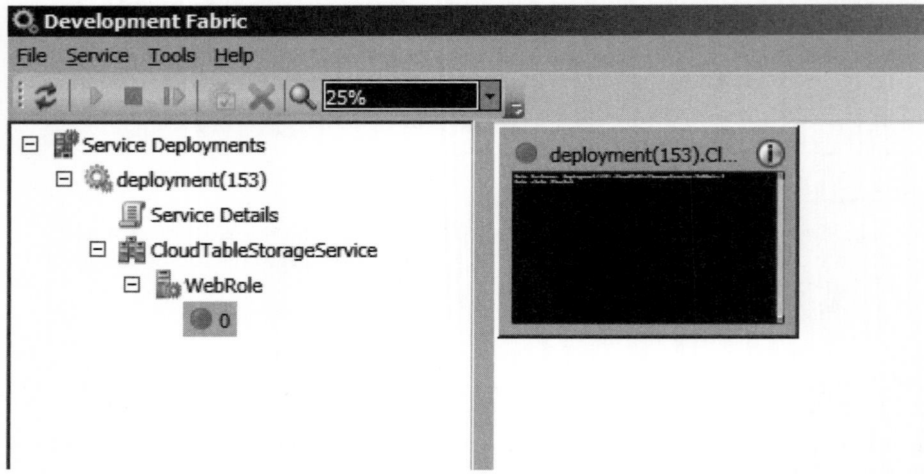

Figure 2-8. *Development fabric service window showing the instance running from local cloud system*

Enter the address information and click the Add button. The data will be persisted into the database and then retrieved back into the `GridView`. The results shown in the `GridView` match those when querying the database from SQL Server Management Studio directly. The screenshot for testing results is shown in Figure 2-9.

***Figure 2-9.** Data have been inserted into local cloud table storage*

There is a Delete link in the first column of the `GridView` used to delete the entry as Figure 2-9 shows.

So far we have successfully performed basic data I/O with local cloud table storage. If you don't see the data updating correctly after inserting a new row of data, refresh the web page from the toolbar of the web browser.

There are a few important things you should be aware of to ensure access to cloud table storage, so let's look at them now.

Data Entity Class Constructors

For any data entity container class used in a cloud storage application, if the class is derived from an Azure SDK `StorageClient` like the `Address` class used in this example, it is a must to explicitly define a non-parameterized default constructor in addition to parameterized constructors, as Listing 2-11 shows. The non-parameterized default constructor is required from the `StorageClient` component of the Azure SDK at runtime.

***Listing 2-11.** A Data Entity Class Requires a Non-parameterized Constructor to Be Explicitly Defined*

```
public Address()
    : this(Guid.NewGuid().ToString(), Guid.NewGuid().ToString())
{
}
```

```
public Address(string partitionKey, string rowKey)
    : base(partitionKey, rowKey)
{
}
```

Table Storage Keys

By default, cloud storage tables use two primary keys as a compound key, `PartitionKey` and `RowKey`. If we need to use just one primary key and set another primary, usually the partition key, as a constant value, we can specify the value from the configuration file and modify this constructor and insert a value into the configuration file for the web role as Listing 2-12 shows.

Listing 2-12. *Modify the Entity Class to Use a Constant Value as the* `PartitionKey`

```
public Address()
: this(ConfigurationManager.AppSettings["PartitionKey"],
       Guid.NewGuid().ToString())
{
}

<appSettings>
  <add key="PartitionKey" value="AzureForDotNetDeveloper"/>
  <add key="UserTable" value="UserTable"/>
  <add key="PersonTable" value="PersonTable"/>
  <add key="AddressTable" value="AddressTable"/>
  <add key="AzureForDotNetDeveloperUserRowKey"
       value="AzureForDotNetDeveloperUserRowKey"/>
  <add key="Retry" value="3"/>
</appSettings>
```

The `PartionKey` takes any valid string value including an empty string, but not `null` values.

Log Runtime Message and Event Information for Debugging

Logging support is one of the things most .NET developers are interest in. The local development fabric service provides a nice way for you to test and troubleshoot your applications or components. After an application has been deployed to the local fabric or the Azure fabric, the only way to diagnose and debug the application is using the log. Visit the MSDN documentation at `http://msdn.microsoft.com/en-us/library/dd179455.aspx` to learn about the Azure log mechanisms.

In the local development environment the simplest way to write log messages or events is using the `RoleManager` class to log messages to the local fabric service. The log information will be shown in the development fabric log window as we have seen before. You need to be aware of a limit with this way of logging messages or events. Since the `RoleManager` is not available until the services start, to log events or messages, especially exceptions that happen before a service has been started, you need to use the Azure SDK command-line tool `CSRun.exe` with the `/dumplogs` option. Information on how to get and use the Azure command-line tools can be found at `http://msdn.microsoft.com/en-us/library/dd179412.aspx`. There is a very good article published by Bruno Terkaly from Microsoft that talks about how to log messages and events in both the development fabric and the Azure fabric and provides a useful approach for handling Azure message login. His article can be found at http://blogs.msdn.com/brunoterkaly/archive/2009/01/18/windows-azure-services-exercise-2-configuration-logging-and-debugging.aspx.

Leverage the Power of Development Fabric Services

We briefly described the development fabric in the Introduction. The development fabric is a powerful feature of the Azure Framework. The development fabric simulates the Azure fabric service on a local computer environment. You can run, test, debug, and do any necessary tuning on performance or local configuration before deploying applications to production.

An Azure application can be deployed to the local fabric and run stand-alone from the local fabric as well as launching from Visual Studio if step-by-step debugging is needed. Azure applications need to be packed before being deployed to either the local fabric or the Azure fabric. The package can be generated using a command-line utility from the SDK, CSPack, with the /copyonly option. CSPack will generate a structured package, including the configuration file. The package will be automatically generated if you select Publish by right-clicking on the solution node of an application from Visual Studio. The generated configuration package and application package can be found from the project folder as shown in Figure 2-10.

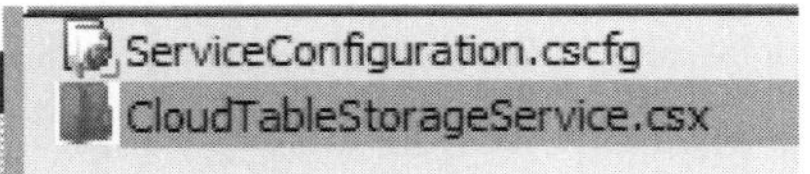

Figure 2-10. *The package used to deploy an Azure application to fabric*

The command-line utility provided by the Azure SDK, CSRun.exe, is the tool used to deploy the package to the local fabric, which can be found from the installed SDK bin directory. Detailed information to use this tool can be found from MSDN http://msdn.microsoft.com/en-us/library/dd179412.aspx. Based on my experience, in most cases Visual Studio in conjunction with the Azure Portal should handle all deployment tasks very well.

Using Fiddler 2 to Debug Cloud Storage Applications

Fiddler 2 is a very powerful web debugging tool from Microsoft and can be downloaded from http://www.fiddler2.com/fiddler2/. This tool can be used to compose, listen to, and send HTTP messages. This tool can also be used to debug and test Azure applications including cloud storage applications. Below is an example of how to use this tool to help debug a cloud storage application. In order to do the demo we need to deploy the cloud storage application we created previously to run from the remote Azure fabric.

Deploying an application to the remote Azure cloud environment is a topic covered in Chapter 9. When the application is successfully hosted in the cloud, there is an URL assigned as shown in Figure 2-11.

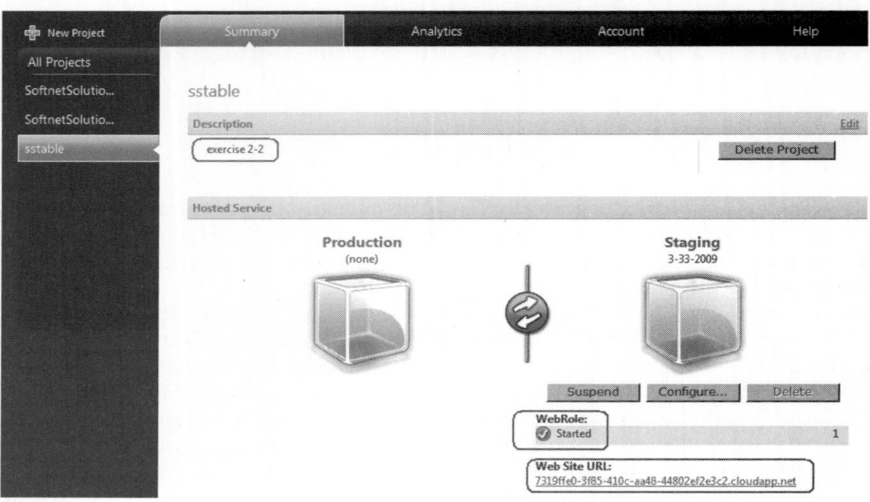

Figure 2-11. The URL is assigned after the storage web role has been deployed to Microsoft and is running from the remote cloud environment

Copy that URL in your browser and `Default.aspx` will launch the application and access the remote storage as Figure 2-12 shows. Figure 2-13 shows the debugging information captured when we click on the Add button using Microsoft Fiddler 2.

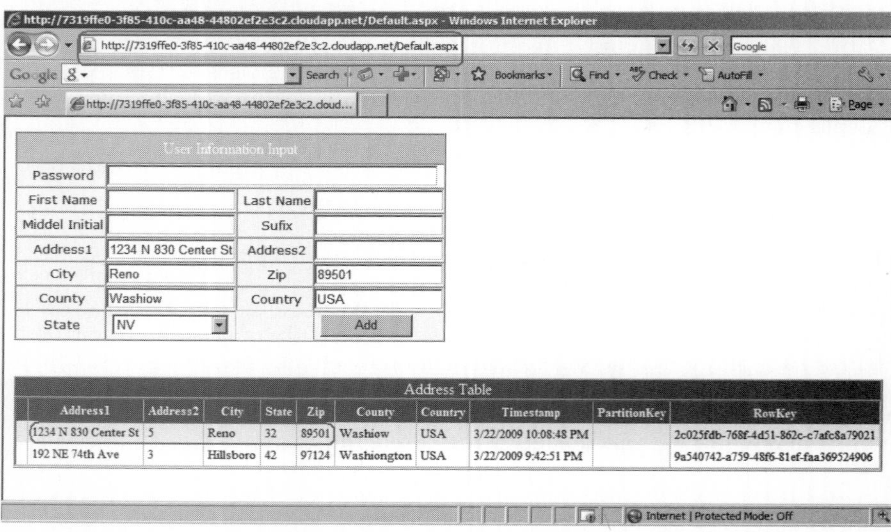

Figure 2-12. As the web role been hosted from Microsoft, using the URL as shown from Figure 2-11 to launch the `default.aspx` page and access the storage running in the cloud

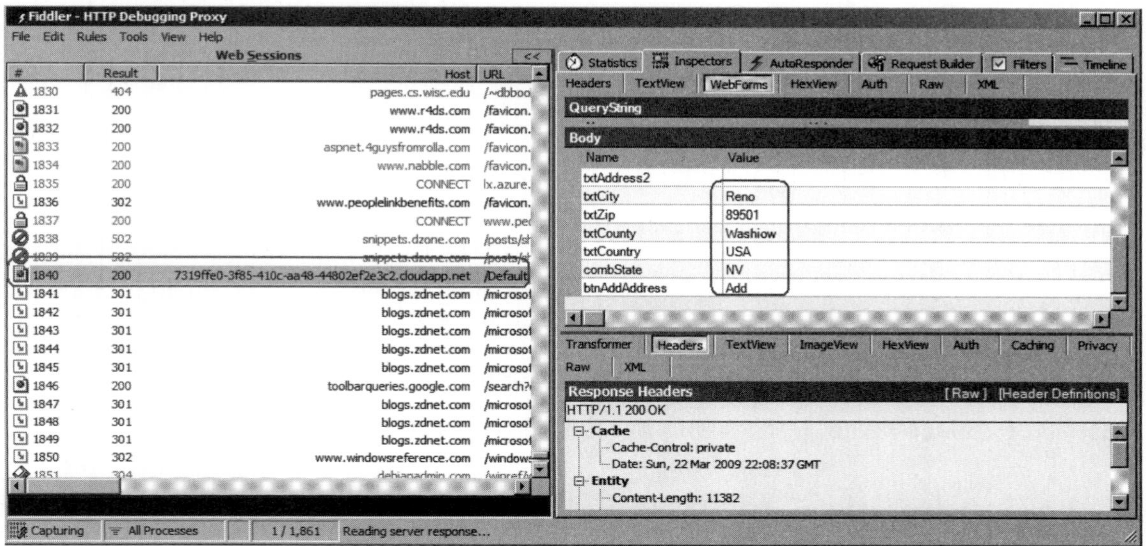

Figure 2-13. *The HTTP debugging information captured when adding data to a cloud storage table using Microsoft Fiddler2*

Leverage LINQ to Query Entities in Cloud Storage

LINQ is a feature introduced with Microsoft .NET 3.0 that provides an agile way to query cloud table entities. Listing 2-13 is an example of using LINQ to print out all RowKey values of all rows from the table Address for tracing purposes.

Listing 2-13. *Using LINQ to Query RowKey Values of All Rows from Address Table*

```
_addressTableService.TableContext().CreateQuery<Address>
(_addressTableService.TableContext().TableName).ToList<Address>().ForEach(
  x => System.Diagnostics.Trace.WriteLine(string.Format("--- Row Key = <{0}>",
  x.RowKey)));
```

An example using LINQ to return the top two entities from the Address table is shown in Listing 2-14.

Listing 2-14. *Using LINQ to Query RowKey Top N Rows from the Address Table*

```
int i = 0;
foreach( Address a in _addressTableService.TableContext()
.CreateQuery<Address>(_addressTableService.TableContext().TableNam)
.ToList<Address>().Take<Address>(2) )
{
  System.Diagnostics.Trace.WriteLine(
```

```
    string.Format("--- Row Key[{0}] = <{1}>", i, a.RowKey)
  );
  ++i;
}
```

Using HTTP REST to Query the Top N Entities

REST (Representational State Transfer) provides a powerful way to access Internet resources using HTTP and is widely used for web-related applications. It can also be used to access Azure table storage. The syntax to retrieve the top N entities from a cloud table is the following, using HTTP GET:

```
http://<TableStorageSolution>.table.core.windows.net/<TableName>()?$top=N
```

To query our Address table for the top 10 records the syntax is:

```
http://softnetsolutionstorage.table.core.windows.net/AddressTable()?$top=10
```

Using Continuation Tokens to Retrieve Paginated Data

When querying a large set of data from cloud tables, the number of entities returned in the query may be limited due to one of the following reasons:

- The number of total entities to return is greater than the maximum number of entities allowed in the response by the server (currently 1,000).
- The total size of the entities in the response is greater than the maximum size of a response, currently 4 MB including the property names but excluding the XML tags used for REST.
- The time for completing the query is more than the timeout (currently 60 seconds).

If your queries fall foul of these restrictions, you can use continuation tokens to page the data. You can consider continuation tokens to be keys used to query data sequentially, where one chunk of data follows another one. The continuation tokens can be obtained from the return header from the current query results. Listing 2-15 is sample code to peek at continuation tokens. This piece of code is a stand-alone piece and not part of the project of this exercise. We leave it to you as homework. (The class DataServiceQuery used in this piece of code is a class from the StorageClient assembly of the Azure SDK.) The highlighted code in the next listing shows how to get the continuation token programmatically from the response header. There is no continuation token returned if the query does not meet the limit conditions listed above. This function is extracted from the project in the next exercise and can be found from the code in Default.aspx.cs. We are going to talk more about the continuation tokens used in the code in the next section.

Listing 2-15. *Sample Code for Peeking at the Continuation Tokens*

```
private void _ContinuationKeyPeek()
{
  AddressTableContext tableContext =
```

```
        _addressTableService.TableContext() as AddressTableContext;
    ContinuationToken continuationToken = null;
    do
    {
      var topTenAddress =
        tableContext.CreateQuery<Address>(tableContext.TableName).Take(10);
      var query = topTenAddress as DataServiceQuery<Address>;

      if (continuationToken != null)
      {
        query = query.AddQueryOption("NextPartitionKey",
                                     continuationToken.PartitionKey);
        if (continuationToken.RowKey != null)
        {
          query = query.AddQueryOption("NextRowKey", continuationToken.RowKey);
        }
      }

      var response = query.Execute() as QueryOperationResponse;

      if (response.Headers.ContainsKey("x-ms-continuation-NextPartitionKey"))
      {
        continuationToken.PartitionKey =
          response.Headers["x-ms-continuation-NextPartitionKey"];
        if (response.Headers.ContainsKey("x-ms-continuation-NextRowKey"))
        {
          continuationToken.RowKey =
            response.Headers["x-ms-continuation-NextRowKey"];
        }
      }
      else
      {
        continuationToken = null;
      }
    } while (continuationToken != null);
}

public class ContinuationToken
{
  public string PartitionKey { get; set; }

  public string RowKey { get; set; }
}
```

There are rich technologies available to retrieve the data from cloud table storage, including the web role service offered by the Azure Framework, LINQ or REST, or tools such as Fiddler using the HTTP protocol. Next we are going to learn other basic cloud table storage data I/O actions—deleting and updating data from cloud table storage.

Deleting and Updating an Entity in a Single Cloud Data Storage Table

Below are some concepts we should be aware of before we move to the exercise for deleting and updating data from cloud table storage. Essentially, the class `DataServiceContext` plays a core role for all cloud table storage I/O, including the data retrieving action we have been using so far. If you go back to look at the project we created, the base class of `AddressTableContext` is in a hierarchical relationship with `DataServiceContext`; you can trace down like this: `AddressTableContext` ➤ `TableContext` ➤ `TableStorageDataServiceContext` ➤ `DataServiceContext`.

- For each entity table in Azure cloud table storage there is an internal property called `tracked` that is assigned when a table is created. This is for the `DataServiceContext` to track the concurrency of the data table. The options for the value for this property are `AppendOnly`, `OverwriteChanges`, `PreserveChanges`, and `NoTracking`. It is mandatory to assign a value to this property before the data I/O actions, such as updating, inserting, and deleting. How to determine the selection of this attribute should be analyzed on a case-by-case basis.
    - The default setting is `AppendOnly`. This option means the server will not load the entity instance if the instance is already presented in the caches. When this option is selected and the entity is already tracked by a previous retrieve call, the `DataServiceContext` object will not update. There is a chance the update will fail unless the application has very good information about the previous action's updating call.
    - If the `OverwriteChanges` option is selected, the `DataServiceContext` always loads the entity instance from the server and keeps it up to date and overwrites the previously tracked entity.
    - If `PreserveChanges` is selected, any property changes made to the entity object `DataServiceContext` are preserved. This should be a good choice when recovering from concurrency errors is required. Using `PreserveChanges` is the best way to ensure that the data is updated, because the server always loads the entity prior to update. The price to pay is less efficient performance.
    - If `NoTracking` is selected, the `AttachTo()` method must be called prior to updating the data.
- Use LINQ to put data into the `DataServiceContext` object, and use a C# class as a data container object to hold the values to be updated.
- Add the C# object back to the same `DataServiceContext` object for update by calling the `AttachTo()` method and use the same object to perform update actions.
- Call the method `SaveChanges()` using the instance of `DataServiceContext` class to send the update request to the server.

Next we go back to the main topic of this exercise. In order to reuse the code in the next exercise we are going to abstract our object architecture based on the previous exercise to introduce three interfaces—`ICloudEntity`, `ITableContext`, and `ICloudTableStorageService`—and three new classes—

TableContext, DataTableService, and CloudTableServiceFactory. This will allow us to reuse the code to handle multiple data entities in our future development. Figure 2-14 shows the definition of properties and methods for the three interfaces in detail.

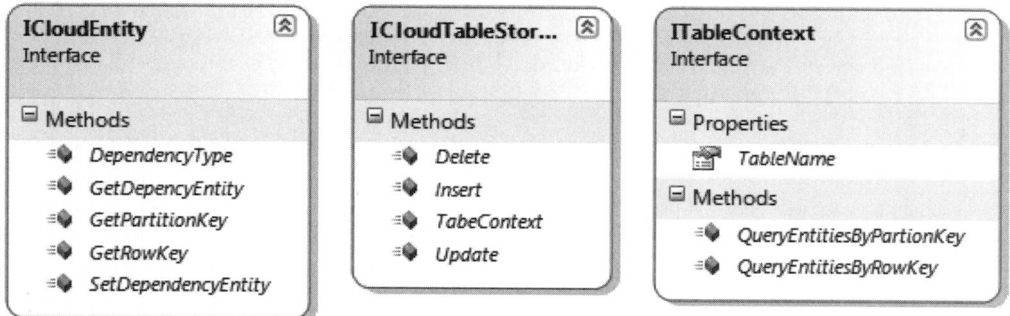

Figure 2-14. *Interfaces definition for cloud entity, cloud table storage service, and cloud table context*

■ **Note** The code for this example is in the exercise 2-2 bundle from the code download.

The interface definition for ICloudEntity is shown in Listing 2-16. This interface exposes four methods: GetPartitionKey(), GetRowKey(), GetDependencyEntity(), and SetDependencyEntity().

Listing 2-16. *Interface ICloudEntity Definition*

```
using System;
using System.Collections.Generic;
using System.Linq;
using System.Text;

namespace CloudTableStorageService_WebRole.CloudTableStrorageDataEntity
{
    using Microsoft.Samples.ServiceHosting.StorageClient;

    public interface ICloudEntity
    {
        string GetPartitionKey();
        string GetRowKey();
        ICloudEntity GetDepenencyEntity();
        void SetDependencyEntity(ICloudEntity entity);
        List<ICloudEntity> DependencyType();
    }
}
```

The interface definition for ICloudTableStorageService is shown in Listing 2-17. This interface expose four methods. One method is called TableContext() with return type of TableContext (we are going to define this new base class after the interfaces definitions), and the remaining three are basic data table I/O methods: Insert(), Update(), and Delete(). These three data table I/O functions accept the ICloudEntity type parameter. A class that implements the interface ICloudTableStorageService is used as the I/O service to expose the cloud table data. It is also responsible for resolving dependency issues (the relation between parent or child entity objects) during data table access in order to keep the integrity of the entire data structure.

Listing 2-17. *Interface ICloudTableStorageService Definition*

```
using System;
using System.Collections.Generic;
using System.Linq;
using System.Text;

namespace CloudTableStorageService_WebRole.CloudTableStorageDataService
{
    using Microsoft.Samples.ServiceHosting.StorageClient;
    using CloudTableStorageService_WebRole.CloudTableStrorageDataEntity;
    using CloudTableStorageService_WebRole.CloudTableStorageDataContext;

    public interface ICloudTableStorageService
    {
        bool Insert(ICloudEntity entity);
        bool Update(ICloudEntity entity);
        bool Delete(ICloudEntity entity);
        TableContext TableContext();
    }
}
```

The interface definition for ITableContext is shown Listing 2-18. This interface defines one property TableName with a get/set accessing pair and two methods, QueryEntitiesByPartitionKey() and QueryEntitiesByRowKey(). The return type for these two methods is ICloudEntity, and the input parameter is PartitionKey and RowKey respectively. ITableContext is the facade class of a cloud data storage table that is responsible for retrieving URL endpoint information during the table context construction. This interface defines the basic query function for retrieving the cloud storage table.

Listing 2-18. *Interface ITableContext Definition*

```
using System;
using System.Collections.Generic;
using System.Linq;
using System.Text;

namespace CloudTableStorageService_WebRole.CloudTableStorageDataContext
{
    using CloudTableStorageService_WebRole.CloudTableStrorageDataEntity;
    public interface ITableContext
    {
```

```
        string TableName { get; set; }
        ICloudEntity QueryEntitiesByPartionKey(string partitionKey);
        ICloudEntity QueryEntitiesByRowKey(string rowKey);
    }
}
```

As Listing 2-19 shows, a new abstract base class TableContext is defined to implement the interface ITableContext. This base class inherits from the class TableStorageDataServiceContext of StorageClient implemented in the Azure SDK. This class has one property access function, TableName, and two abstract methods, QueryEntitiesByPartitionKey() and QueryEntitiesByRowKey().

Listing 2-19. *Abstract Base Class*

```
using System;
using System.Collections.Generic;
using System.Linq;
using System.Web;

namespace CloudTableStorageService_WebRole.CloudTableStorageDataContext
{
    using Microsoft.Samples.ServiceHosting.StorageClient;
    using CloudTableStorageService_WebRole.CloudTableStrorageDataEntity;

    abstract public class TableContext : TableStorageDataServiceContext, ITableContext
    {
        public string TableName { get; set; }

        public TableContext(StorageAccountInfo accountInfo)
            : base(accountInfo)
        {
        }

        abstract public ICloudEntity QueryEntitiesByPartionKey(string partitionKey);
        abstract public ICloudEntity QueryEntitiesByRowKey(string rowKey);
    }
}
```

The class CloudTableServiceFactory is a utility class that implements the factory method design pattern using.NET Reflection to dynamically instantiate the concrete cloud table entity subclasses. The implementation of this class is shown in Listing 2-20.

Listing 2-20. *The Class CloudTableServiceFactory Implements the Factory Method Design Pattern Used to Dynamically Create a Concrete Cloud Table Class*

```
using System;
using System.Collections.Generic;
using System.Linq;
using System.Web;
using System.Reflection;
```

```
namespace CloudTableStorageService_WebRole.CloudTableStorageDataService
{
    using CloudTableStorageService_WebRole.CloudTableStrorageDataEntity;
    public class CloudTableServiceFactory
    {
        public CloudTableServiceFactory()
        {
        }

        public ICloudTableStorageService FactoryCloudTableService(ICloudEntity entity)
        {
            ICloudTableStorageService cloudTableStorageService = null;

            try
            {
                Assembly assembly = Assembly.GetExecutingAssembly();
                string typeName =
                    string.Format(
                        "{0}.{1}TableService", this.GetType().Namespace,
                        entity.GetType().Name);
                cloudTableStorageService =
                    Activator.CreateInstance(assembly.GetType(typeName), new object[] { })
                      as ICloudTableStorageService;
            }
            catch (Exception ex)
            {
            }

            return cloudTableStorageService;
        }
    }
}
```

As Listing 2-21 shows, we have re-engineered the class `DataTableService` to implement the interface `ICloudTableStorageService`. A new member variable with type of `CloudTableServiceFactory` is defined in this class and has been instantiated in the constructor. The major modification to the cloud table data I/O methods, such as `Insert()`, `Update()`, and `Delete()`, from the versions used in the previous exercise is looping through the dependency tables to apply the data I/O actions. The instances of the data table service for all dependency data tables are dynamically created using the class names. The dependency table collection list of a data entity table is populated in the data entity table class constructor by calling the method `_Initialization()`.

Listing 2-21. *Re-engineering the Class `DataTableService` to Implement the Interface `ICloudTableStorageService`*

```
using System;
using System.Collections.Generic;
using System.Linq;
using System.Web;
using System.Data.Services.Client;
```

```
namespace CloudTableStorageService_WebRole.CloudTableStorageDataService
{
    using Microsoft.Samples.ServiceHosting.StorageClient;
    using CloudTableStorageService_WebRole.CloudTableStorageDataContext;
    using CloudTableStorageService_WebRole.CloudTableStrorageDataEntity;

    abstract public class DataTableService : ICloudTableStorageService
    {
        protected StorageAccountInfo _account = null;
        protected TableContext _dataTableContext = null;
        protected CloudTableServiceFactory _cloudTableFactory =
            new CloudTableServiceFactory();

        public DataTableService()
        {
            // Get the settings from the Service Configuration file
            account = StorageAccountInfo.GetDefaultTableStorageAccountFromConfiguration();
            _cloudTableFactory = new CloudTableServiceFactory();
        }

        public TableContext TableContext() { return _dataTableContext; }

        virtual public bool Insert(ICloudEntity entity)
        {
            bool success = false;
            ICloudEntity dependency = null;

            try
            {
                _dataTableContext.AddObject(_dataTableContext.TableName, entity);
                _dataTableContext.SaveChanges();

                dependency = entity.GetDependencyEntity();
                while (null != dependency)
                {
                    cloudTableFactory = new CloudTableServiceFactory();
                    cloudTableFactory.FactoryCloudTableService(dependency)
                        .Insert(dependency);
                    dependency = dependency.GetDependencyEntity();
                }
                success = true;
            }
            catch { }


            return success;
        }

        virtual public bool Update(ICloudEntity entity)
        {
```

```
        bool success = false;

        if (null != entity)
        {
            _dataTableContext.MergeOption = MergeOption.PreserveChanges;

            _dataTableContext.AttachTo(_dataTableContext.TableName, entity, "*");
            _dataTableContext.UpdateObject(entity);
            _dataTableContext.SaveChanges();

            success = true;
        }

        return success;
    }

    virtual public bool Delete(ICloudEntity entity)
    {
        bool success = false;

        if (null != entity)
        {
            foreach (ICloudEntity entityType in entity.DependencyType())
            {
                ICloudEntity dependency =
                    QueryDependencyEntity(entityType,
                                          (entity as TableStorageEntity).RowKey);

                if (null != dependency)
                {
                    _cloudTableFactory.FactoryCloudTableService(dependency)
                      .Delete(dependency);
                }
            }

            try
            {
                _dataTableContext.AttachTo(_dataTableContext.TableName, entity, "*");
                _dataTableContext.DeleteObject(entity);
                _dataTableContext.SaveChanges();
                success = true;
            }
            catch (Exception ex)
            {
            }

        }

        return success;
    }
```

```
        protected ICloudEntity QueryDependencyEntity(ICloudEntity entity, string key)
        {
            ICloudEntity  dependencies = null;
            ICloudTableStorageService cloudTableservice =
                _cloudTableFactory.FactoryCloudTableService(entity);
            dependencies = cloudTableservice.TableContext().QueryEntitiesByPartionKey(key);

            return dependencies;
        }
    }
}
```

We re-engineered the Address class based upon these new definitions as Listing 2-22 shows. There is no cloud table entity upon which the Address entity depends, so the body of the overridden method `_Initialization()` is empty.

Listing 2-22. *Class `Address` Is Derived from the Base Class `TableStorageEntity`*

```
using System;
using System.Collections.Generic;
using System.Linq;
using System.Web;
using System.Configuration;

namespace CloudTableStorageService_WebRole.CloudTableStrorageDataEntity
{
    using Microsoft.Samples.ServiceHosting.StorageClient;

    public enum State : int
    {
        AL, AK, AS, AZ, AR, CA, CO, CT, DE, DC, FM, FL, GA, GU, HI,
        ID, IL, IN, IA, KS, KY, LA, ME, MH, MD, MA, MI, MN, MS, MO,
        MT, NE, NV, NH, NJ, NM, NY, NC, ND, MP, OH, OK, OR, PW, PA,
        PR, RI, SC, SD, TN, TX, UT, VT, VI, VA, WA, WV, WI, WY
    }

    public class Address : CloudTableStorageEntity
    {
       private State _state =
         CloudTableStorageService_WebRole.CloudTableStrorageDataEntity.State.OR;

        public string Address1 { get; set; }
        public string Address2 { get; set; }
        public string City { get; set; }
        public int? State { get { return (int)_state; } set { _state = (State)value; } }
        public string Zip { get; set; }
        public string County { get; set; }
        public string Country { get; set; }

        public Address()
            : this(Guid.NewGuid().ToString(), Guid.NewGuid().ToString())
```

```
        {
        }

        public Address(string partitionKey, string rowKey)
            : base(partitionKey, rowKey)
        {
        }

        public Address(string partitionKey)
            : this(partitionKey, Guid.NewGuid().ToString())
        {
        }

        public Address(string address1,
                       string address2,
                       string city,
                       State state,
                       string zip,
                       string county,
                       string country,
                       string parentRowKey)
            : this(parentRowKey, Guid.NewGuid().ToString())
        {
            Address1 = address1;
            Address2 = address2;
            City = city;
            State = (int)state;
            Zip = zip;
            County = county;
            Country = country;
        }

        override public ICloudEntity GetDependencyEntity() { return null; }
        override public void SetDependencyEntity(ICloudEntity entity) { }

        override protected void _Initialization()
        {
        }
    }
}
```

Listing 2-23 shows a code example for deleting and updating an Address. In terms of proof of concept we just simply use the default settings of the MergeOption for the DataContext object without assigning any value.

Listing 2-23. Code Example of Implementation for `Delete` *and* `Update` *an Entity from a Single Cloud Storage Table*

```
public bool Update(Address entity)
{
  bool success = false;

  try
  {
    _dataTableContext.AttachTo(_dataTableContext.TableName,  entity, "*");
    _dataTableContext.UpdateObject(entity);
    _dataTableContext.SaveChanges();
    success = true;
  }
  catch(Exception ex)
  {
  }

  return success;
}

public bool Delete(Address entity)
{
  bool success = false;

  try
  {
    _dataTableContext.AttachTo(_dataTableContext.TableName, entity, "*");
    _dataTableContext.DeleteObject(entity);
    _dataTableContext.SaveChanges();
    success = true;
  }
  catch { }

  return success;
}
```

As Listing 2-23 shows, the final update is via a `DataServiceContext` object. To dig into the technical details is out of the scope of this book, so check out the documentation.

The code example to implement the `Default.aspx` file used to test the `Address` table update is shown in Listing 2-24.

Listing 2-24. Request Update `Address` *Table from Multiple Thread Concurrently*

```
protected void btnAddAddress_Click(object sender, EventArgs e)
{
  if (Page.IsValid)
  {
    _UpdateTest();
```

```
            _DataBinding();
        }
    }

    private void _UpdateTest()
    {
        const string PREVIOUS_ENTITY = "PREVIOUS_ENTITY";
        _previousEntityAddress = Session[PREVIOUS_ENTITY] as Address;

        if (null != _previousEntityAddress)
        {
            _addressTableService.Delete(_previousEntityAddress);
        }

        Address address = new Address(txtAddress1.Text.Trim(),
                                      "0",
                                      txtCity.Text.Trim(),
                                      (State)combState.SelectedIndex,
                                      txtZip.Text.Trim(),
                                      txtCounty.Text.Trim(),
                                      txtCountry.Text.Trim(),
                                      string.Empty);

        _addressTableService.Insert(address);

        Session.Add(PREVIOUS_ENTITY, address);

        for (int i = 1; i < 4; ++i)
        {
            Thread thread = new Thread(new ParameterizedThreadStart(_Update));
            thread.Start(new object[] { i, address } as object);
            thread.Join(100);
        }

        _DataBinding();
    }

    private void _Update(object parameters)
    {
        AddressTableService addressTableService = new AddressTableService();
        TableContext tableContext = _addressTableService.TableContext();
        var currentEntity = from a
            in tableContext.CreateQuery<Address>(tableContext.TableName)
            where a.RowKey == ((parameters as object[])[1] as Address).RowKey
            select a;
        if (null != currentEntity)
        {
            ICloudEntity currentAddress = currentEntity.Single<Address>();
            int currentValue = int.Parse((currentAddress as Address).Address2.Trim());
            (currentAddress as Address).Address2 =
```

```
        Convert.ToString(currentValue +
        (int)((parameters as object[])[0] as object));
      addressTableService.Update(currentAddress);
    }
}
```

For demonstration, we are going to update only one column (Address 2) in the same record to prove the concept described above. The easiest way to reach that goal is to set all of the columns including the PartitionKey and RowKey to empty or null values. (Remember that null is a valid value to these key columns. In this way we do not have to specify the keys every time we call the updating method.)

In btnAddAddress_Click() we call the _UpdateTest() method to insert an empty entity and set the Address2 attributed value to "0". Then we create three work threads to concurrently update the entity we have just inserted. In the thread handler we create a new AddressTableService (TableContext) and use LINQ to query the entity on the server. After we retrieve the entity from the server we add the value of Address2 to the index of the thread and update the server with the new value. We should observe that value increasing. Some very nice features from LINQ have been used in this method, such as using currentEntity.Single<Address>() to extract a single object from a numeric collection. They make the code much more concise.

The test results should match the value displayed in Figure 2-15.

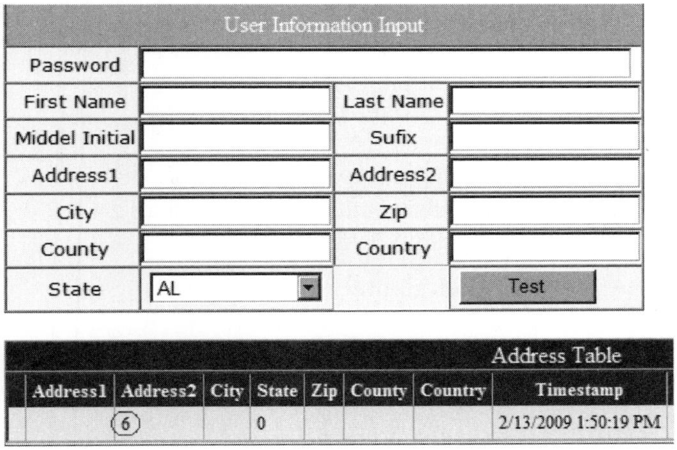

User Information Input			
Password			
First Name		Last Name	
Middel Initial		Sufix	
Address1		Address2	
City		Zip	
County		Country	
State	AL		Test

Address Table							
Address1	Address2	City	State	Zip	County	Country	Timestamp
	6		0				2/13/2009 1:50:19 PM

Figure 2-15. *Test results for update request from multiple threads*

Update Data Tables in Buckets

In Internet-based cloud table storage, the simplest way to update a single entity is to replace it with a completely new object. This means deleting it from the table and inserting a new entity object with updated values. In other words, we want to update data in buckets. The price we have to pay is that we need to make double trips for each update action. This will challenge relational cloud tables to maintain data integrity.

To meet the requirements of Internet-scaleable data storage, updating data in buckets is sensible, since cloud storage is designed to be Internet scaleable, and the cost is not a concern. To update data in buckets should tremendously simplify the effort for the development team when dealing with relational data infrastructures. As we know, with traditional database structures inserting, updating, or deleting a record from a relational database applies to the record's dependencies too. We should design and implement our data storage and data access approaches for cloud storage differently from the traditional approaches for databases we are used to. We are going to focus on the topic of how to handle relational cloud tables next.

Best Practices in Using the DataServiceContext Object

Before we discuss updating data in buckets, let us spend a little time talking about best practices in using the DataServiceContext object , since we are going to apply these rules in our example. The following are best practices recommended for using DataServiceContext.

- Make the DataServiceContext object thread-safe, since the DataServiceContext does not support thread-safe access.
- Instantiate an instance of the DataServiceContext object every time you need to use it, since there is no mechanism for a DataServiceContext instance to persist its state in a thread. For instance, using the same DataServiceContext instance across all inserts, updates, and deletes may cause a failure. Each of these actions requires invoking the SaveChanges() method to commit the changes. If the same instance is used to do all these activities, the internal trace of the instance to the actual object may be lost when the instance is used across the different actions.
- DataServiceContext has MergeOption, which is used to control how the DataServiceContext handles the tracked entities. We covered this topic in the last section.
- Call AttachTo() before calling Insert(), Update(), or Delete() as the following snippet shows. This will cause the server to track the data entity with an ETag and make sure the action is applied to the correct entity. If the MergeOption of the context object is set to the value of AppendOnly and the entity is already being tracked by a previous action with the same DataServiceContext object instance, then a failure may occur and you may get the error message saying that the data have been tracked already.

```
_dataTableContext.AttachTo(_dataTableContext.TableName, entity, "*");
```

Now it is the time for us to back to our topic of handling updating and deleting data from cloud storage in buckets.

Handling Relational Cloud Data Storage Tables

As we mentioned in Chapter 1, Azure table storage is not relational data storage. In the real world, the solution Microsoft has comes up with to handle relational data structures is SQL Azure (covered in Chapter 8).

The following example is based on an assumption that the relational data structure in the cloud environment for an application to access is relatively simple and that the number of objects in the data model is small. This example proves the concept of dealing with such types of cloud relational data structures without using SQL Azure. This approach may add value to a development team as an alternate design option.

■ **Note** The code for this example is in the exercise 2-3 bundle from the code download.

Our design will use the interfaces we have just defined from the last section. As Figure 2-16 shows, using the `PartitionKey` and `RowKey` provided by cloud table storage, we can establish the relational constraints between the cloud data entities. Our three cloud entity classes are `Address`, `Person`, and `User`. The `Address` holds a reference to the child class `Person`, and the `Person` entity has a child entity class `Address`.

Consider that there are multiple records from the `Person` table but that only one row is referenced by its parent table `Address`, where the `RowKey` matches the `PartitionKey` from the row of its parent table `Address`. In a similar way we can establish the reference relationship between a row from the `User` table and the `Person` table. Figure 2-17 shows the results after inserting the data into these tables.

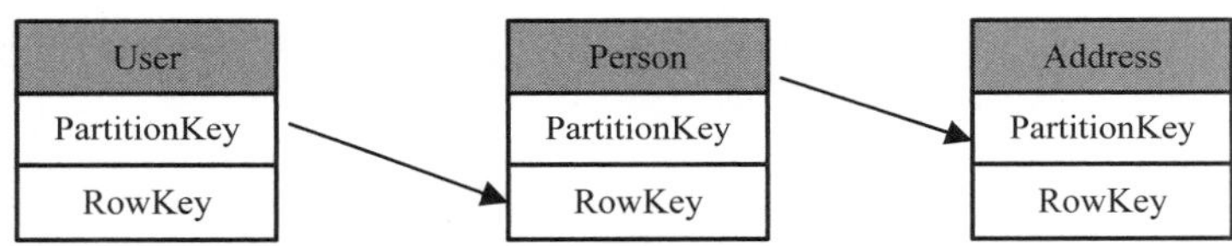

***Figure 2-16.** Using the `PartitionKey` and `RowKey` to establish constraints between relational data entities of cloud storage tables*

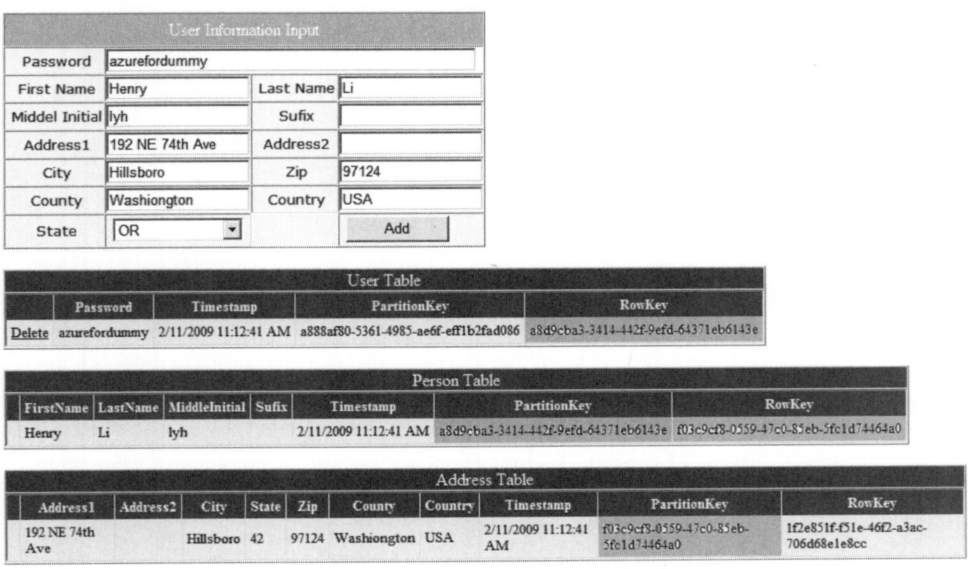

User Table

	Password	Timestamp	PartitionKey	RowKey
Delete	azurefordummy	2/11/2009 11:12:41 AM	a888af80-5361-4985-ae6f-eff1b2fad086	a8d9cba3-3414-442f-9efd-64371eb6143e

Person Table

FirstName	LastName	MiddleInitial	Sufix	Timestamp	PartitionKey	RowKey
Henry	Li	lyh		2/11/2009 11:12:41 AM	a8d9cba3-3414-442f-9efd-64371eb6143e	f03c9cf8-0559-47c0-85eb-5fc1d74464a0

Address Table

Address1	Address2	City	State	Zip	County	Country	Timestamp	PartitionKey	RowKey
192 NE 74th Ave		Hillsboro	42	97124	Washiongton	USA	2/11/2009 11:12:41 AM	f03c9cf8-0559-47c0-85eb-5fc1d74464a0	1f2e851f-f51e-46f2-a3ac-706d68e1e8cc

***Figure 2-17.** Results of inserted tables with relational relationship established using the `PartitionKeys` and `RowKeys`*

The following are tips on how to use the PartitionKeys and RowKeys to build up the relationship between cloud tables.

- A cloud table storage data entity class in a relational structure needs to provide information on which data entity is a dependency entity. This can be done in the class constructor to call the method _Initialization() to instantiate an instance for each dependent entity class and then to persist the dependency information in a protected member variable. The dependency information will be used to resolve constraints between the cloud storage table entity objects when accessing the cloud tables in a relational structure at runtime. The source code we are going to present later will show you how to get this task done in detail.
- Expose all data entities in an interface and implement a factory method to dynamically instantiate concrete table entities at runtime and return the class instance with the type of the interface. This is the typical object-oriented programming approach. The implementation of the factory method has been shown in Listing 2-20. This approach allows the data table access to be handled in a unified way.
- When inserting data to cloud storage tables, a parent entity object is responsible for instantiating an instance of an embedded entity data entity object and populating the data. This usually happens in the client-side code, as shown in Listing 2-25 and Listing 2-26. The Insert() handler method recursively finds the embedded object, dynamically.

Listing 2-25. *Parent Entity Object Instantiating the Embedded Entity Object at the Create Time*

```
private void _InsertUser()
{
  User user = new User();
  user.Password = txtPassword.Text.Trim();

  Person person = new Person(txtFirstName.Text.Trim(),
                             txtLastName.Text.Trim(),
                             txtMiddelInitial.Text.Trim(),
                             txtSufix.Text.Trim(),
                             user.GetRowKey());

  user.SetDependencyEntity(person);

  Address address = new Address(txtAddress1.Text.Trim(),
                                txtAddress2.Text.Trim(),
                                txtCity.Text.Trim(),
                                (State)combState.SelectedIndex,
                                txtZip.Text.Trim(),
                                txtCounty.Text.Trim(),
                                txtCountry.Text.Trim(),
                                person.GetRowKey());

  person.SetDependencyEntity(address);
```

```
  _userTableService.Insert(user as User);

}
```

Listing 2-26. Recursively Loop the Embedded Entity Object to Insert a Relational Data Set to Cloud Storage Tables

```
virtual public bool Insert(ICloudEntity entity)
{
  bool success = false;
  ICloudEntity dependency = null;

  try
  {
    _dataTableContext.AddObject(_dataTableContext.TableName, entity);
    _dataTableContext.SaveChanges();

    dependency = entity.GetDependencyEntity();
    while (null != dependency)
    {
      CloudTableServiceFactory cloudTableFactory =
        new CloudTableServiceFactory();
      cloudTableFactory.FactoryCloudTableService(dependency)
        .Insert(dependency);
      dependency = dependency.GetDependencyEntity();
    }
  success = true;
  }
  catch { }

  return success;
}
```

- To delete a set of relational data entities from cloud table storage, a parent entity object is responsible for passing the partition key that is the RowKey of the child record. The list of dependency entities is the one we built up when constructing each entity instance . The highlighted lines from Listing 2-27 show how to accomplish this task.

Listing 2-27. Recursively Loop the Embedded Entity Object to Delete a Relational Data Set

```
virtual public bool Delete(ICloudEntity entity)
{
  bool success = false;

  foreach (ICloudEntity entityType in entity.DependencyType())
  {
    ICloudEntity dependency =
      QueryDependencyEntity(entityType, (entity as TableStorageEntity).RowKey);
```

```
    if (null != dependency)
    {
      _cloudTableFactory.FactoryCloudTableService(dependency).Delete(dependency);
    }
  }
  try
  {
    _dataTableContext.AttachTo(_dataTableContext.TableName, entity, "*");
    _dataTableContext.DeleteObject(entity);
    _dataTableContext.SaveChanges();
      success = true;
  }
  catch {}


  return success;
}
```

- The implementation for the `Update()` method is relatively simple as shown in Listing 2-28. It is just a combination call to the `Delete()` and `Insert()` methods based upon the strategy updating cloud storage data in buckets.

Listing 2-28. *Updating Relational Entities in Buckets*

```
virtual public bool Update(ICloudEntity entity)
{
  bool success = false;

  try
  {
    if (Delete(entity))
    {
      success = Insert(entity);
    }
  }
  catch { }

  return success;
}
```

- Elaborately designed, tested, and tuned `PartitionKey` and `RowKey` are very important tasks for cloud table data modeling. To learn more about this topic from the Microsoft documentation search the web for "Azure Choosing a partition key is important for an application to be able to scale well."

If you are interested in the data center traffic characteristics you can find the Microsoft official documentation at `http://research.microsoft.com/en-us/people/mzh/wren09.pdf`.

Summary

In this chapter we covered a lot of ground; we examined quite a few aspects of cloud table storage. We saw how to access data in the cloud and worked through quite a few hints and tips to use when working with cloud table storage data access. There are many useful tools available to you, such as Fiddler 2, LINQ, and REST.

Storing your data in the cloud would be useless if you couldn't alter it or remove it, so we covered this aspect of data storage next. We saw how to update data in buckets (a useful technique with cloud storage) and covered some best practices.

Finally, we looked at relational storage in cloud table storage, which is definitely an option for some projects.

CHAPTER 3

■ ■ ■

Working with Cloud Queue and Blob Storage

Azure Queue and Blob storage services are two basic forms of storage offered by the Azure framework. Another basic cloud storage offered by the Azure framework is table storage, which we covered in the last two chapters. In this chapter we are going to focus on Queue and Blob. Azure Queue messages can be listened for via event subscription. This feature makes Azure Queue a good candidate for building an event-driven distributed system. In this chapter I'll provide the basic know-how for using these two types of storage, a description of how to use both storage types to build an event-driven distributed system, and a tool for you to load a large stream to cloud Blob storage.

The first exercise is about the basics of how to create and use the Azure Queue. The second exercise is an example of cloud Blob storage. In this exercise we will use Azure Queue as a trigger to create a blob record when the queue receives a message. The third exercise uses both Azure Queue and Blob storage services to build an event-driven distributed system.

Before we see the exercises, however, let's see what Azure Queue and Blob Storage services are.

Azure Queue

Azure Queue provides a simple and asynchronous work dispatch mechanism. This makes Azure Queue a great message delivery tool that can be used to connect different components of a cloud application into an integrated service system. The outstanding merits of Azure Queue are high availability, durability, and performance efficiency. Azure Queue guarantees message delivery and ensures that a message can be processed at least once. Azure Queue provides REST interfaces, which allow applications written in languages other than C# to access the queue at any time from anywhere across the Internet. This makes a cloud application or on-premises application very easily integrated, extendable, and scalable.

Azure Queue can be used for both cloud applications and on-premises applications for the following two purposes:

- Message communication bus
- Component or functional module decoupling

For service-oriented applications built on a front-end architecture with distributed infrastructure, the immediate advantages to be taken from Azure Queue (in conjunction with Azure Blob storage) are related to scalability:

- *Back-end traffic measurement using length of queue*: If an application is built on Azure Queue and needs to determine scalability based on back-end traffic, the application can do so by measuring the queue length. Since the queue length directly reflects the delay time of the back-end workload, a growing queue length indicates that the back-end servers cannot process the work fast enough, so increasing the back-end instances for the application would help the server to process the workload in the queue more quickly. In contrast, if the measurement of queue length is close to zero, it is an indication that the capacity of the server process may be more than is needed, and you can consider decreasing the back-end server instances to save system resources. Therefore applications can monitor the queue length to make resource usage more efficient and scale-up more smooth.
- *System module decoupling*: Applications built based on the message publish/subscribe architecture are loosely coupled, which gives applications extreme flexibility for extension and scaling up. If all modules and all components in an application use the message queue to communicate with each other either in the front end or in the back end, an application can easily replace any component independently, adjust the workflow logic, and upgrade the features without either interrupting irrelevant components (the components from presentation UI layers, business logical layers, or data storage access layers) or recompiling the code.
- *Efficient resource management*: Message-queue-based applications can manage system resource allocation more efficiently. System resources can be grouped and assigned into distinct queues according to their critical levels. For instance, components that consume large system resources, such as audio or video processing, can have their own dedicated queues for communication in order to reduce the impact on other components or processes in the system.
- *Buffering messages when traffic soars*: Queue-based system architecture allows message buffering and delayed processing without data loss if the traffic flow suddenly soars. Azure Queue has been designed to support guaranteed message delivery, which frees applications from handling data persistence due to traffic burst or other message-delivery difficulties. Traditionally, an application needs to persist the inbound message if it cannot process the message due to the volume of the message. To build data persistence at runtime is very costly. Using the message-buffering feature provided by the Azure Queue tremendously reduces the cost of application development for persisting inbound messages and for resubmitting messages if there are errors during transmission.

Usually, to use Azure Queue as a message bus an application needs to use Azure Blob storage as well in order to reduce memory usage and improve performance. The exercises provided in this chapter show examples of how to achieve that goal.

Azure Blob Storage

Blob storage can be understood as special table storage in the cloud. Basically cloud Blob storage extends table storage and targets large amounts of data. The difference between the two types of cloud storage is:

- Table storage uses `PrimaryKey` and `RowKey` to manage the tables, whereas Blob storage uses a storage container and a blob ID (GUID) to manage the storage.
- Table storage stores all portable system-defined data types, such as characters, strings, texts, integers, float numbers, and XML in storage tables. Blob storage stores data in binary format as data chunks.

Figure 3-1 shows the concepts of cloud Blob storage. Blob storage access is based on an account. An Azure account can create multiple Blob containers. A Blob container can be understood as a placeholder for a group of Blob storages. Blob storage can have metadata, which can be understood as a collection of header attributes. Blob storage can be partially updated and committed using block objects. Each Blob can own a set of metadata in `NameValueCollection` string format. The Microsoft specification for blob storage can be found in Appendix A.

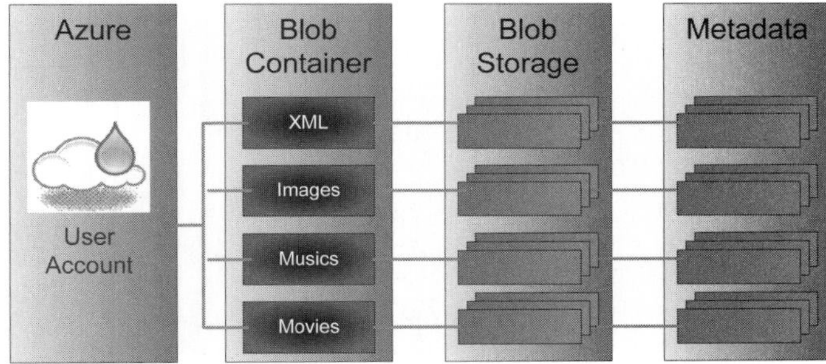

Figure 3-1. *Cloud blob storage structure concepts*

The data object model of Azure Blob storage is shown in Figure 3-2. (This data map is generated using SQL Server Management Studio against the `DevelopmentStorageDb` on a local machine. The `DevelopmentStorageDb` database will be created the first time development storage is accessed and the local development storage is initialized by the Azure framework.) This database map actually reflects the concept diagram of Figure 3-1 and the relationship among the participants of all Blob storage tables. For example, a Blob container has an ID as its primary key, which is a foreign key of the `Blob` table. As I have mentioned, the local development environment and runtime environment fabric simulate the remote cloud environment. In the Azure cloud environment a physical table may have multiple instances running from distinct remote virtual machines.

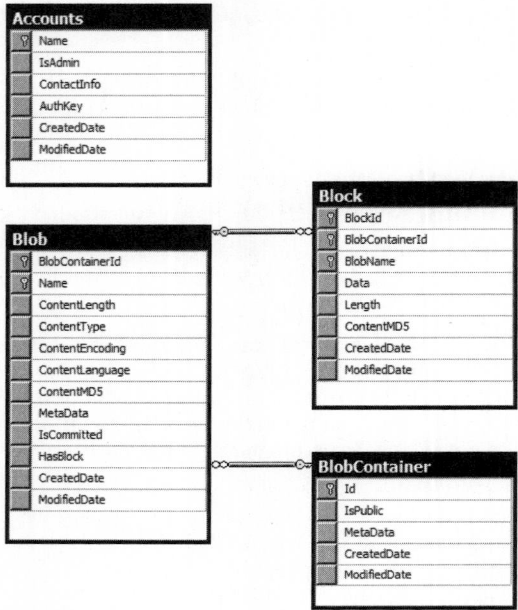

Figure 3-2. *Object models of blob storage*

Creating a Cloud Queue

This exercise shows the basic steps to create a cloud queue, and how to put messages in and retrieve messages from queues. A queue can be created from either a worker role or a web role. In order to explore the collaboration mechanism between a web role and worker role in a cloud application, this exercise creates a queue from a worker role.

■ **Note** The code for this example is in the Exercise 3-1 bundle from the code download.

Add a Worker Role in the Cloud Service Solution

Add a worker role and associate that role to the service, as Figure 3-3 shows. The purpose of this approach is to demonstrate that the queue message can be manipulated from different processes. The responsibilities of this worker role are defined as:

- Retrieve account information from the configuration.
- Create a named queue storage container from cloud storage.
- Create a named queue within the queue storage.

These responsibilities will be implemented in one function and called by the start handler of the worker role when the service application starts from the Azure fabric.

Figure 3-3. Insert a worker role for queue initialization

Create a Queue Storage Container and Create a Named Queue from the Start Handler of the Worker Role

The data object model for Azure Queue storage is shown in Figure 3-4. The `AcctQueueContainerMap` table is used to map a queue name to the unique queue ID. This ID is used as a foreign key in the `QueueContainer` table and the `Message` table. These tables will be generated using the same approach we used in Chapter 1 to create the data entity C# classes; that is, we'll use Visual Studio to generate them.

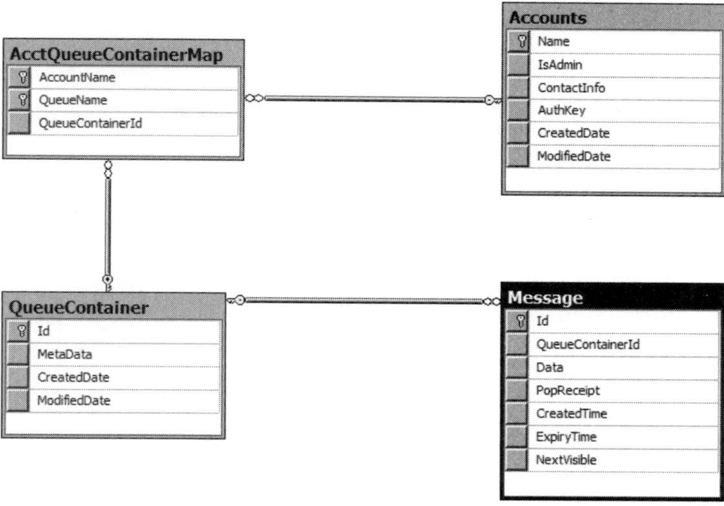

Figure 3-4. The data object model of Azure Queue

All queue names must be alphanumerical characters and are case-sensitive as well. Characters only in lowercase are accepted for a queue name.

A `QueueStorage` instance needs to be instantiated before a named queue can be created. The constructor of `QueueStorage` accepts an account information object as a parameter. As is the case when creating table storage, an account with a base-64 security key and storage end points is assigned at the time you register a storage type project on the Azure portal page. In the development environment the account information can either be hard-coded in the configuration file or entered programmatically. Listing 3-1 shows the configuration settings from the configuration file for queue storage.

Listing 3-1. *Account and HTTP Port End Point Configuration for Queue Storage in the Development Environment*

```
<appSettings>
  <add key = "AccountName" value="devstoreaccount1"/>
  <add key = "AccountSharedKey" value="<ACCOUNT_KEY>"/>
  <add key="QueueStorageEndpoint" value="http://127.0.0.1:10001" />
</appSettings>
```

Create the Queue Using Account Information from the Configuration File

Listing 3-2 is the implementation of the worker role project. The lines in bold show an example of how to create a named queue.

Listing 3-2. *Implementation of WorkerRole Shows How to Create Queue Using Configuration Files*

```
using System;
using System.Threading;
using Microsoft.ServiceHosting.ServiceRuntime;
using Microsoft.Samples.ServiceHosting.StorageClient;
using System.IO;
using System.Configuration;
using System.Net;
using System.Xml;

namespace CloudTableStorageService_WorkerRole
{
    public class WorkerRole : RoleEntryPoint
    {
        public const string XML_PAYLOAD_QUEUE_NAME = "createxmlmessagequeue";
        public const string XML_CONTAINER_NAME = "xmlpayload";

        private Stream CreateXmlStreamBlob(byte [] byteData)
        {
            return new MemoryStream(byteData);
        }

        public override void Start()
        {
            QueueStorage queueStorage =
              QueueStorage.Create(StorageAccountInfo
                .GetDefaultQueueStorageAccountFromConfiguration());
            MessageQueue queue = queueStorage.GetQueue(XML_PAYLOAD_QUEUE_NAME);
```

```
            bool containerAndQueueCreated = false;
            while (!containerAndQueueCreated)
            {
                try
                {
                    queue.CreateQueue();
                    containerAndQueueCreated = true;
                }
                catch (WebException e)
                {
                    if (e.Status == WebExceptionStatus.ConnectFailure)
                    {
                        RoleManager.WriteToLog(
                          "Error",
                          string.Format("Connect failure! The most likely reason is that
the local Development Storage tool is not running or your storage account configuration is
incorrect. " +
                          "Message: '{0}'", e.Message)
                        );
                        System.Threading.Thread.Sleep(5000);
                    }
                    else
                    {
                        throw;
                    }
                }
            }

            while (true)
            {
                try
                {
                    Message msg = queue.GetMessage();
                    if (msg != null)
                    {
                        string path = msg.ContentAsString();

                        RoleManager.WriteToLog("Information",
                                               string.Format("Done with '{0}'", path));
                    }
                    else
                    {
                        Thread.Sleep(1000);
                    }
                }
                catch (StorageException e)
                {
                    RoleManager.WriteToLog(
                      "Error",
                      string.Format("Exception when processing queue item. Message: '{0}'",
                      e.Message)
```

```
                    );
                }
            }
        }

        public override RoleStatus GetHealthStatus()
        {
            // This is a sample worker implementation. Replace with your logic.
            return RoleStatus.Healthy;
        }
    }
}
```

Create the Queue Programatically

Listing 3-3 is an example of creating a queue programatically inside a C# class instead of reading the information from a configuration file. This code snippet can be used to replace the highlighted part in Listing 3-2.

Listing 3-3. *Create the Queue Programatically*

```
string accountName = "devstoreaccount1";
string accountKey = "<ACCOUNT_KEY>";
string address = "http://127.0.0.1:10001";
StorageAccountInfo accountInfo =
  new StorageAccountInfo(new Uri(address), null, accountName, accountKey);

QueueStorage queueStorage = QueueStorage.Create(accountInfo);
MessageQueue messageQueue = queueStorage.GetQueue(XML_PAYLOAD_QUEUE_NAME);
```

Before a client can access the cloud queue one of the two initialization steps shown in the previous listing is required.

Put a Message into the Queue

There are three data types you can use as a raw queue message: stream, byte array, and string.

In this exercise we are going to use the class Address defined in Chapter 1 and Chapter 2 as a data entity class. Since XML is the most popular data exchange format, we are going to transform the data of an instance of Address into an XML string by using the .NET XmlSerialization class and put it into the queue as a message. Listing 3-4 shows the code to transform the data entity Address into an XML string and put it into the queue as a queue message.

Unlike the behavior of a regular Windows queue object, when a message is put into the cloud queue it can be read (de-queued) multiple times by applications. The message will not be removed from the queue until another service calls to delete the queue explicitly. The message body is encoded and stored in a data field of the Message table after the message has been put into the queue. Figure 3-5 shows the data query results from the local database when the message is submitted to the queue in the local development environment. The data has been encoded as you can see.

Listing 3-4. *Convert Address Data Entity Object into XML String and Put into Queue*

```
protected void btnAddAddress_Click(object sender, EventArgs e)
{
    if (Page.IsValid)
    {
        _GetXmlPayloadQueue().PutMessage(new Message(_ComposeXmlString()));
    }
}

private string _ComposeXmlString()
{
    Address address = new Address(txtAddress1.Text.Trim(),
                                  txtAddress2.Text.Trim(),
                                  txtCity.Text.Trim(),
                                  (State)combState.SelectedIndex,
                                  txtZip.Text.Trim(),
                                  txtCounty.Text.Trim(),
                                  txtCountry.Text.Trim(),
                                  string.Empty);

    XmlSerializer serializer = new XmlSerializer(address.GetType());
    StringBuilder sb = new StringBuilder();
    StringWriter writer = new StringWriter(sb);

    serializer.Serialize(writer, address);

    return writer.GetStringBuilder().ToString();
}

private BlobContainer GetXmlPayloadContainer()
{
    _Initialization();
    return _blobStorage.GetBlobContainer(WorkerRole.XML_CONTAINER_NAME);
}

private MessageQueue _GetXmlPayloadQueue()
{
    _Initialization();
    return _queueStorage.GetQueue(WorkerRole.XML_PAYLOAD_QUEUE_NAME);
}
```

```
protected void btnDelete_Click(object sender, EventArgs e)
{
    Message message = _GetXmlPayloadQueue().GetMessage(UPDATE_TIMEOUT_SEC);
    if (message != null)
    {
        _GetXmlPayloadQueue().DeleteMessage(message);
    }
}
```

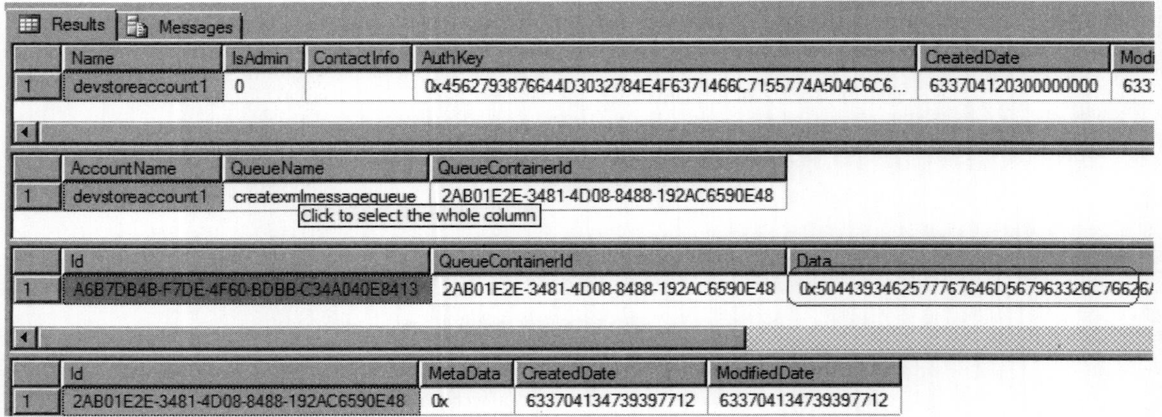

Figure 3-5. Queue message persisted in data field of Message *table and encoded*

Poll and Delete a Message from the Queue

The MessageQueue class defined in the StorageClient assembly also provides polling infrastructure under the covers and delivers the message via venting. The default poll interval setting in the MessageQueue class is 30 seconds. This polling interval value can be set during initialization of a queue instance. Listing 3-5 is the initialization handler implemented in the code behind Default.aspx.cs. To receive the queue polling events, a local event-handler function needs to be defined. The event handler function is called private void _OnMessageReceive(object sender, EventArgs args), which has the typical event-handler signature with two parameters. The first parameter is the basic object type, and the second parameter is the EventArgs type. The application can have any logic it needs in the event-polling handler. In this example, we simply print out the content of the message polled from the queue. As the highlighted part shows in Listing 3-5, the event handler is hooked up right after the queue is created. This function also uses the synchronization object _syncObj to make it thread-safe in a multi-thread environment.

■ **Note** Never call `queue.StartReceiving()` if there is no event handler such as `queue.MessageReceived += new MessageReceivedEventHandler(_OnMessageReceive)` implemented in the class. Otherwise it causes a `NullObject` reference exception to be thrown at runtime.

Listing 3-5. Polling the Queue and Handling Received Events

```
        private void _Initialization()
        {
            if (_initialized)
            {
                return;
            }

            lock (_syncObj)
            {
                try
                {
                    _queueStorage =
                      QueueStorage.Create(StorageAccountInfo
                        .GetDefaultQueueStorageAccountFromConfiguration());
                    MessageQueue queue =
                      _queueStorage.GetQueue(WorkerRole.XML_PAYLOAD_QUEUE_NAME);

                    queue.MessageReceived +=
                      new MessageReceivedEventHandler(_OnMessageReceive);
                    queue.PollInterval = 1000; // in milliseconds
                    queue.StartReceiving(); // start polling
                }
                catch (WebException ex)
                {
                    throw new WebException(
                      string.Format(
                        "---{0}:_Initialization, Azure failed to instatiate storage using
current account information. exception caught : {1}",
                        this.ToString(),
                        ex.Message
                      )
                    );
                }

                _initialized = true;
            }
        }

        private void _OnMessageReceive(object sender, EventArgs args)
        {
            Message message = (args as MessageReceivedEventArgs).Message;
```

```
            System.Diagnostics.Trace.WriteLine(
              string.Format(
                "{0}:_OnMessageReceive, message = <{1}>",
                this.ToString(),
                message.ContentAsString()
              )
            );
        }

        private MessageQueue _GetXmlPayloadQueue()
        {
             _Initialization();
             return _queueStorage.GetQueue(WorkerRole.XML_PAYLOAD_QUEUE_NAME);
        }
```

Delete a Message from the Queue

To delete a message from a queue is straightforward as Listing 3-6 shows. The method `btnDelete_Click()` is implemented in the `Default.aspx.cs` file and is the button click event handler used to delete a message from the queue.

Listing 3-6. *Listen and Delete Message from a Queue Implementation*

```
        const int UPDATE_TIMEOUT_SEC = 5;
        protected void btnDelete_Click(object sender, EventArgs e)
        {
            Message message = _GetXmlPayloadQueue().GetMessage(UPDATE_TIMEOUT_SEC);
            if (message != null)
            {
                _GetXmlPayloadQueue().DeleteMessage(message);
            }
        }
```

The reason for specifying the timeout before calling to delete a message from the queue is that having received a message that has been put into queue, that message is locked for the specified timeout. If the message is not deleted within the timeout, it is unlocked and becomes visible again to other queue readers. Microsoft designs this to prevent a queue reader trying to process a message and then dying as a result of an error or exception, leaving the message locked. This approach is known as a loose transaction, since transactions in cloud queue storage are not supported.

Parse a Message Received from the Queue

When a message has been received, we need to parse it back to the original data format. The `Message` class from the Azure SDK provides functions to parse the raw message as either an array or a string as Listing 3-7 shows.

Listing 3-7. *Parse Message Received from a Queue into String*

```
const int UPDATE_TIMEOUT_SEC = 5;
Message message = _GetXmlPayloadQueue().GetMessage(UPDATE_TIMEOUT_SEC);
if (message != null)
{
    btnDelete.Enabled = true;

    LabelMessage.Text = Server.HtmlEncode(message.ContentAsString());
}
else
{
    btnDelete.Enabled = false;
}
```

The results of Exercise 3-1 are shown in Figure 3-6. The messages put into the queue will be displayed in a loop one after another on the update panel. The automatic updating is controlled by the Ajax update manager component, which needs to be inserted in the `Default.aspx` page.

User Information Input			
Address1	192 NE 74th Ave	Address2	
City	Hillsboro	Zip	97124
County	Washiongton	Country	USA
State	OR		Add

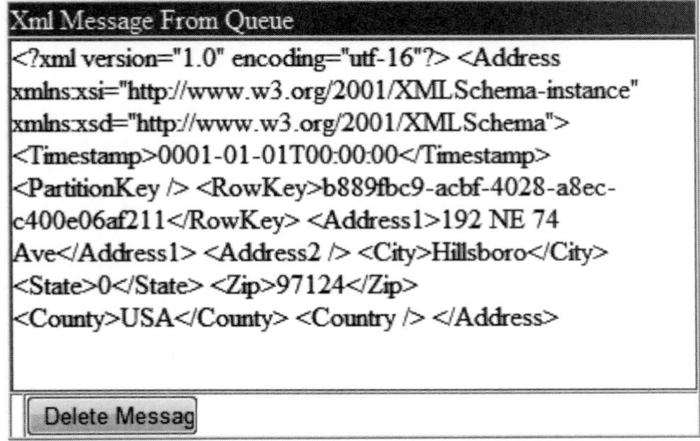

Figure 3-6. *Results of Exercise 3-1 displaying multiple data records in a loop*

Query a Queue Using HTTP REST

The syntax to use HTTP REST to query a queue is listed in Table 3-1.

Table 3-1. *Syntax Used to Query Queue Message with REST*

REST API	HTTP	Example	Description
Create Queue	PUT	`http://myaccount.queue.core.windows.net/myqueue`	
Delete Queue	DELETE	`http://myaccount.queue.core.windows.net/myqueue`	
Get Metadata	GET/HEAD	`http://127.0.0.1:10001/myaccount/myqueue?comp=metadata`	Also returns the message count; other properties are free-form name/value pairs
Set Metadata	PUT	`http://127.0.0.1:10001/myaccount/myqueue?comp=metadata`	
Get Messages	GET	`http://127.0.0.1:10001/myaccount/myqueue/messages`	
Peek Messages	GET	`http://myaccount.queue.core.windows.net/myqueue/messages?peekonly=true`	
Delete Message	DELETE	`http://127.0.0.1:10001/myaccount/myqueue/messages/messageid?popreceipt=string-value"lightweight commit"`	
Clear Messages	DELETE	`http://myaccount.queue.core.windows.net/myqueue/messages`	Deletes all the messages in the queue

Creating Cloud Blob Storage

The following exercise demonstrates how to create, query, and delete blob data. This exercise uses the data from the queue message, which we created in Exercise 3-1, and stores data in a blob.

■ **Note** The code for this example is in the Exercise 3-2 bundle from the code download.

Add blob-related member variables to the `Default.aspx` code as shown in Listing 3-8.

Listing 3-8. Blob-Storage-Related Member Variables Defined in `Default.aspx`

```
public const string BLOB_CONTAINER_NAME = "blobcontainerpayload";
private static BlobStorage _blobStorage = null;
private static BlobContainer _blobContainer = null;
const int UPDATE_TIMEOUT_SEC = 5;
const string SUFFIX = "xml";
```

Add initialization code to the `_Initialization` handler as Listing 3-9 shows. The `ContainerAccessControl` should be set to `Public` so applications can query the blob using REST APIs. By design, to change the access scope there are two `CreateContainer()` methods. The first instantiates a blob container object by passing a blob container's name (characters in the blob container's name should be all in lowercase), and is called from the instance of the blob storage. The second is just a call to an overloaded function of the blob container class. This call must use a valid instance of a blob container by passing in the enumeration value `ContainerAccessControl.Public`. This call is optional and should not override the instance itself but modify the access scope.

Listing 3-9. Initialization Code for Blob Storage Access

```
private void _Initialization()
{
    if (_initialized)
    {
        return;
    }

    lock (_syncObj)
    {
        try
        {
            _blobStorage =
              BlobStorage.Create(StorageAccountInfo
                .GetDefaultBlobStorageAccountFromConfiguration());
            _blobContainer = _blobStorage.GetBlobContainer(BLOB_CONTAINER_NAME);
            // Make the container public so that we can use REST API to query blob
            // via the URLs from the web
            _blobContainer.CreateContainer(new NameValueCollection(),
                                           ContainerAccessControl.Public);

            _queueStorage =
              QueueStorage.Create(StorageAccountInfo
                .GetDefaultQueueStorageAccountFromConfiguration());
            _queueStorage.RetryPolicy =
              RetryPolicies.RetryN(3, TimeSpan.FromSeconds(5));
            MessageQueue queue = _queueStorage.GetQueue(BLOB_PAYLOAD_QUEUE_NAME);
            queue.CreateQueue();
            queue.MessageReceived +=
              new MessageReceivedEventHandler(_OnMessageReceive);
```

```
                queue.PollInterval = 500; // in milliseconds
                queue.StartReceiving(); // start polling
            }

            catch (WebException ex)
            {
                throw new WebException(
                  string.Format(
                    "---{0}:_Initialization, Windows Azure failed to instatiate storage
using current account information. Exception caught : {1}",
                    this.ToString(),
                    ex.Message
                  )
                );
            }

            _initialized = true;
        }
    }
```

After the call to `_Initialization()`, both the blob storage and blob container have been instantiated, and a blob record can be created using the instance of the blob container. Listing 3-10 shows the code to create a blob storage record. In this exercise, the name of the blob storage is created at the time a queue message has been received.

The blob name is assigned when a blob is created. How to construct a blob's name is flexible as long as the name meets the specification, except it must be unique. The specification for the blob name convention is listed in Appendix A. It is not recommended to include the Azure user account in the name string, because the account name could be changed via a configuration file when the application is deployed to the Azure cloud.

Azure offers a service called Service Bus, which uses the end point to address a cloud component. To adapt blob storage to Azure .NET Service Bus, it is recommended that the blob name should be elaborately constructed. The following are the recommendations how to construct the blob name based upon my experience using other commercial information message buses. This makes it a lot easier not only for a cloud application but also for any REST API using the Azure .NET Service Bus to address cloud blob storage.

- Use the .NET name space convention to compose the blob name.
- Compose the blob name in a virtual hierarchy based upon the logical or relational structure of blob storages, although Azure blob storage in the cloud storage platform is not physically hierarchical.

The metadata of Azure blob storage is constructed when the `BlobProperties` object has been instantiated. The metadata object is embedded into the object instance of `BlobProperties`. As we mentioned, the metadata is used as the set of attributes of blob storage. The metadata is in the name-value pair format. The actual class for the metadata is called `NameValueCollection`, which is a .NET class. The namespace `System.Collections.Specialized` must be included before this class can be instatiated.

Blob containers take two parameters for blob storage creation, `BlobContents` and `BlobProperties`. The first parameter holds the body of the information, and the second parameter holds the attribute information. Only two data types can be used for these two parameters, `Stream` and `Byte` array. The information body must be transformed into either of these two types before instantiation of a `BlobContents` object. As Listing 3-10 shows, in this exercise we create the blob object in the message queue event handler. Figure 3-7 shows the screenshot of the `Default.aspx` page at runtime, and Figure 3-8 shows the results of using SQL Server Management Studio to query tables `Accounts`, `AcctBlobContainerMap`, `BlobContainer`, and `Blob` from the local `DevelopmentStorageDb`.

The results show the structure of the relation between these tables and how the tables reference each other as we have presented in Figure 3-1 and Figure 3-2 at the beginning of this chapter. It also shows that access scope of the blob container has been set to public (a value of 1).

Listing 3-10. *Create a Blob to Store Information from a Message Sent from a Queue*

```
private void _OnMessageReceive(object sender, EventArgs args)
{
    Message message = (args as MessageReceivedEventArgs).Message;
    System.Diagnostics.Trace.WriteLine(
      string.Format(
        "---   {0}:_OnMessageReceive, message = <{1}>",
        this.ToString(),
        message.ContentAsString()
      )
    );

    string blobName = string.Format("{0}{1}", message.Id, SUFFIX);

    if (!_blobContainer.DoesBlobExist(blobName))
    {
        BlobProperties properties = new BlobProperties(blobName);

        // Create metadata to be associated with the blob
        NameValueCollection metadata = new NameValueCollection();

        metadata["MediaID"] = message.Id;

        properties.Metadata = metadata;
        properties.ContentType = "text/xml";

        // Create the blob
        byte[] buffer =
          UTF8Encoding.UTF8
            .GetBytes(message.ContentAsString().Replace("\r\n", string.Empty));
        MemoryStream ms = new MemoryStream(buffer);

        BlobContents mediaBlob = new BlobContents(ms);
        _blobContainer.CreateBlob(properties, mediaBlob, true);
    }

    _DataBind();
}
```

Figure 3-7. *Screenshot of the blob creating results*

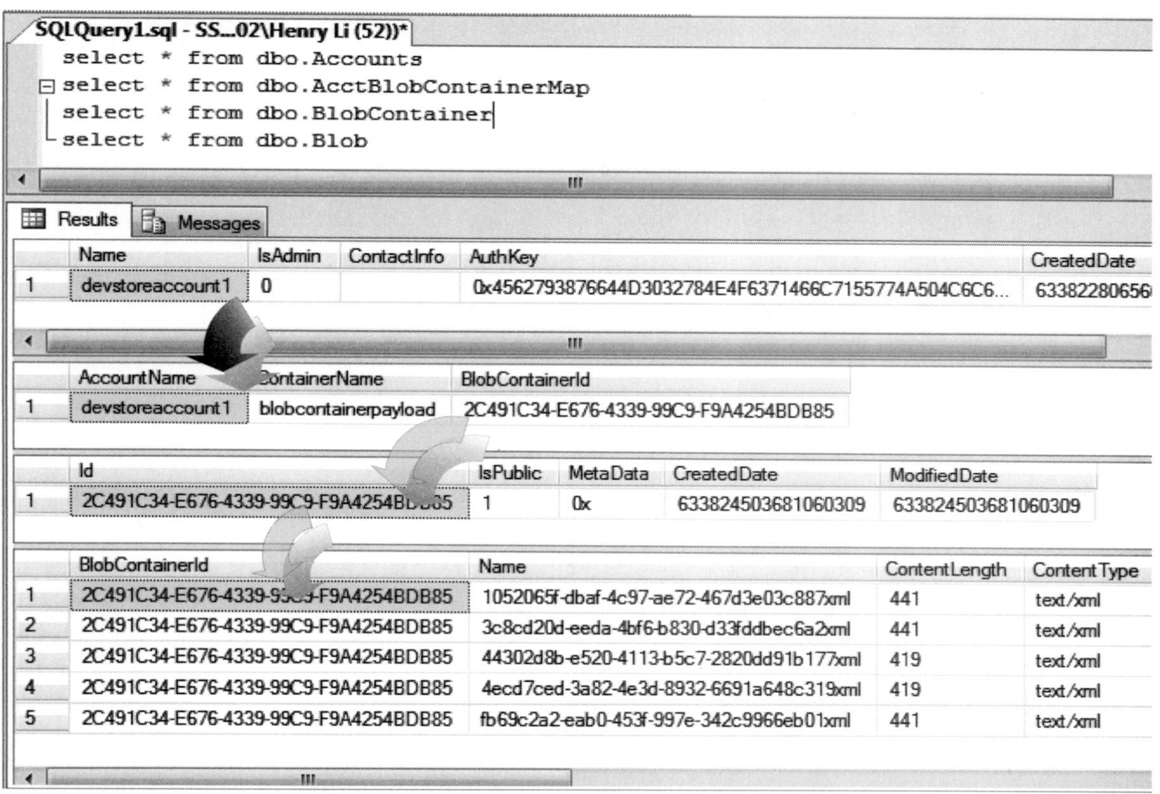

***Figure 3-8.** Quering results after blob storage records have been created*

To retrieve information stored in a blob, the `BlobContainer` class provides a set of access functions to query blobs in a blob container or the properties of a specific blob. The following are the steps to retrieve the information from a blob.

1. As Listing 3-11 shows, we create a C# container class called `MediaInfo` with three properties—`BlobName`, `MediaUri`, and `MediaID`—used to hold the information of a blob record.

2. In this exercise we define a `GridView` from the `Default.aspx` page to display the blob record as shown in the bold lines in Listing 3-12. The columns of the `GridView` bind to the properties of the `MediaInfo` class accordingly. For example, the `DataTextField` is bound to the property `MediaID`, and `DataNavigateUrlFields` is bound to `MediaUri`.

3. Use the instance `_blobContainer` to call `ListBlobs()` and pass two parameters: `prefix` (an empty string in this exercise) and a `boolean` flag, `CombineCommonPrefixs` (`false` in this exercise). This function should return an instance of the `IEnumerable` type.

4. Loop through the collection of the blob record and populate the record into a local collection instance of `mediaList` with `List<MediaInfo>` type.

5. Assign the `mediaList` as the `DataSource` of the `GridView` and call the `DataBind()` method to bind the data to the `GridView`. By design, the call to `ListBlobs()` must occur prior to the call of `GetBlobProperties()`. Otherwise the call to `GetBlobProperties()` always returns a `null` object.

Listing 3-11. Retrieving information from a blob

```
public class MediaInfo
{
    public MediaInfo(string blobName,
                     string mediaAddress,
                     string mediaID)
    {
        BlobName = blobName;
        MediaUri = mediaAddress;
        MediaID = mediaID;
    }

    public string MediaUri{get; set;}
    public string BlobName { get; set; }
    public string MediaID { get; set; }
}

    private void _DataBind()
    {
        IEnumerable<object> blobs = _blobContainer.ListBlobs(string.Empty, false);
        List<MediaInfo> mediaList= new List<MediaInfo>();

        foreach (object blob in blobs)
        {
            if ((blob as BlobProperties )!= null)
            {
                BlobProperties blobProperties =
                  _blobContainer.GetBlobProperties((blob as BlobProperties).Name);
                NameValueCollection mediaEntryProperties = blobProperties.Metadata;
                mediaList.Add(
                  new MediaInfo(
                    blobProperties.Name,
```

```
                    (blob as BlobProperties).Uri.ToString(),
                    mediaEntryProperties["MediaID"]
                )
            );
        }
    }

    BlobLinksView.DataSource = filesList;
    BlobLinksView.DataBind();
}
```

To delete a blob, the blob name needs to be passed as Listing 3-12 shows. In order to get the blob name, we need to insert a row command handler into the GridView from Default.aspx of this exercise as a linked button. To retrieve the specific blob item ID when the corresponding view item is clicked, a code behind handler RowCommandHandler should be inserted into Default.aspx.cs as Listing 3-13 shows.

Listing 3-12. *Pass Blob Name of the Blob Container Instance to Delete a Blob*

```
<asp:GridView
     id="BlobLinksView"
     DataKeyNames="BlobName"
     AllowPaging="False"
     AutoGenerateColumns="False"
     GridLines="Vertical"
     Runat="server"
     onrowcommand="RowCommandHandler"
     BackColor="#B3F2FD" ForeColor="Black"
     BorderColor="#0066FF" BorderStyle="None" BorderWidth="1px"  CellPadding="4"
     Font-Size="Small" Width="394px">
 <Columns>
     <asp:ButtonField Text="Delete" CommandName="DeleteEntry"/>
     <asp:HyperLinkField
         HeaderText="Blob ID"
         DataTextField="MediaID"
         DataNavigateUrlFields="MediaUri" />
 </Columns>
 <RowStyle BackColor="#F7F7DE" />
 <FooterStyle BackColor="#CCCC99" />
 <PagerStyle BackColor="#F7F7DE" ForeColor="Black" HorizontalAlign="Right" />
 <SelectedRowStyle BackColor="#CE5D5A" Font-Bold="True" ForeColor="White" />
 <HeaderStyle BackColor="#6B696B" Font-Bold="True" ForeColor="White" />
 <AlternatingRowStyle BackColor="White" />
</asp:GridView>

protected void RowCommandHandler(object sender, GridViewCommandEventArgs e)
{
    try
    {
```

```
            if (e.CommandName == "DeleteEntry")
            {
                int index = Convert.ToInt32(e.CommandArgument);
                string blobName = (string)BlobLinksView.DataKeys[index].Value;

                if (_blobContainer.DoesBlobExist(blobName))
                {
                    _blobContainer.DeleteBlob(blobName);
                }
            }
        }
        catch { }

        _DataBind();
    }
```

Listing 3-13. Command Handler Used to Interprete Which Blob Item Row Has Been Selected

```
    protected void RowCommandHandler(object sender, GridViewCommandEventArgs e)
    {
        try
        {
            if (e.CommandName == "DeleteEntry")
            {
                int index = Convert.ToInt32(e.CommandArgument);
                string blobName = (string)BlobLinksView.DataKeys[index].Value;

                if (_blobContainer.DoesBlobExist(blobName))
                {
                    _blobContainer.DeleteBlob(blobName);
                }
            }
        }
        catch { }

        _DataBind();
    }
```

In addition to using `ListBlobs()` to retrieve blob records in a C# class as I demonstrated, the blob record can also be retrieved using a REST query with tools or applications, such as Fiddler, that can generate web HTTP GET/POST/UPDATE requests.

Figure 3-9 shows an example of the REST query results against our blob storage. The tool used to do the REST query is Fiddler 2.

The example of syntax for the query string is as follows:

```
http://127.0.0.1:10000/devstoreaccount1/blobpayload/caa95517-3414-4bc2-8f16-0a44a6f156e1xml
```

The return code for a success REST query is 200.

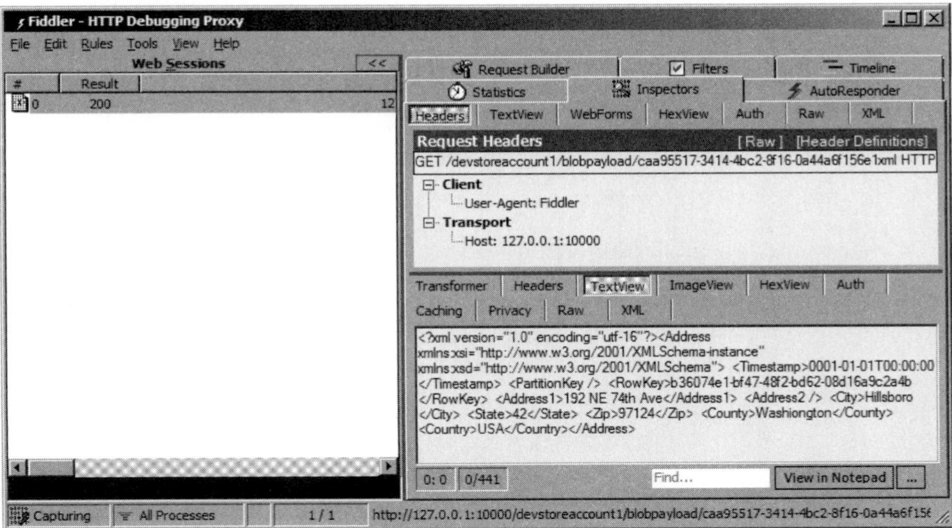

Figure 3-9. REST query results of blob data using Fiddler 2 HTTP debug tool

Creating a Loosely Coupled Event-Driven System

Using both queue and blob storage, we can easily design loosely-coupled, event-driven applications. Figure 3-10 is the case study diagram of this type of application design. The concept is very simple and straightforward as the diagram shows. The following are the highlights of the design concepts.

- Define an events listener to monitor a specific event. The event is fired at the time a message is delivered to the queue. A listener from the server side should be constructed with two components: a dedicated queue to accept a message with a specific topic (queue name) and an event handler. For example, if we need to handle actions that insert and delete data, we need to define two queues and implement two event handlers to deal with these two events respectively.
- The domain for all listeners is the blob container. The blob container is the data access layer to the under-the-hood blob storage.
- A listener queue may have no event handler if there is no need to access the data. For example, after a blob has been inserted successfully, we send a message to the results queue with the message body containing the blob name. In this case sending a response queue message is good enough. This allows us to remove the responsibility for the server sending notification to the client when a blob is inserted or deleted, and to avoid sending a big message over the Internet. A client application can implement its own event listener to monitor the result events from the results queue using a synchronized approach.

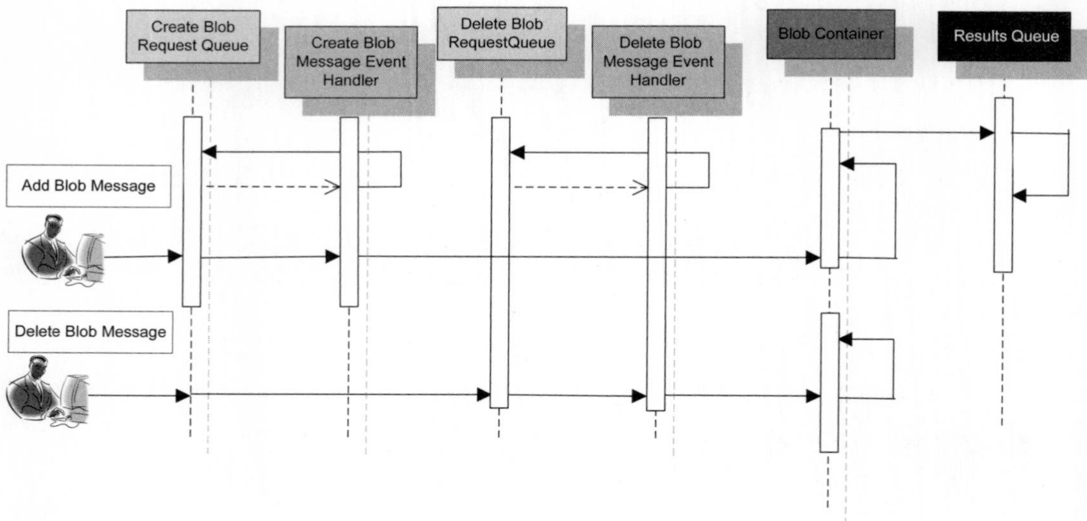

Figure 3-10. Case study diagrams for an event-driven system design, using both queue storage and blob storage

---

■ **Note** The code for this example is in the Exercise 3-3 bundle from the code download.

To reach this goal, we need to accomplish the following steps.

1. Move all code related to blob creation and deletion from the `Default.aspx.cs` code behind into the worker role as shown in Listing 3-14. In the `_Initialization()` method, we need to do the following:
    1. Instantiate an instance of `BlobContainer`.
    2. Instantiate an instance of `QueueStorage`.
    3. Use the instance of `QueueStorage` to create a dedicated queue to listen to the blob create request message and register the event handler.

4. Create a dedicated queue to deliver the results (in other words, notification that a blob name has been created). For this queue we don't need to register an event handler. Note: it is very important that you don't call the `StartReceiving()` method to start polling the queue if a queue does have an event handler registered. This will cause an `ObjectNullReference` exception at runtime, and there is no way to catch the exception or trace down the error stack, even in the development environment.

2. Delete a message from the queue after it has been processed to avoid duplicate message appearing after the locking period.

3. Use `XmlSerializer` to serialize the object into an XML string and place it in the body of the blob storage.

Listing 3-14. *Worker Role to Implement Listener Queues to Handle Blob Create and Delete Requests*

```
using System.Drawing;
using System.Configuration;
using System.NET;
using System.Xml;
using System.Xml.Serialization;
using System.Collections.Specialized;
using System.Diagnostics;

namespace CloudQueueStorageService_WorkerRole
{
    public class WorkerRole : RoleEntryPoint
    {
        public const string PAYLOAD_RESULTS_QUEUE_NAME = "resultspayloadqueue";
        public const string PAYLOAD_CREATE_REQUEST_QUEUE_NAME = "createblobrequestqueue";
        public const string PAYLOAD_DELETE_QUEUE_NAME = "deleteblobqueue";
        public const string PAYLOAD_BLOB_CONTAINER_NAME = "blobpayload";
        public const string PAYLOAD_BLOB_SUFFIX = "xml";
        public const int UPDATE_TIMEOUT_SEC = 5;

        private static BlobStorage _blobStorage = null;
        private static QueueStorage _queueStorage = null;
        private static BlobContainer _blobContainer = null;

        private static bool _initialized = false;
        private static object _syncObj = new Object();
        const int POLLING_INTERVAL = 1000;// in milliseconds

        public void LogLevel(string logStream, string logString)
        {
            if (!RoleManager.IsRoleManagerRunning)
            {
                Trace.WriteLine(logString);
            }
            else
            {
```

```
            RoleManager.WriteToLog(logStream, logString);
        }
    }

    static WorkerRole()
    {
    }

    public void Log(string logString)
    {
        LogLevel("Information", logString);
    }

    public void LogError(string logString)
    {
        LogLevel("Error", logString);
    }

    public override void Start()
    {
        while (!_initialized)
        {
            try
            {
                _Initialization();
            }
            catch (WebException e)
            {
                if (e.Status == WebExceptionStatus.ConnectFailure)
                {
                   RoleManager.WriteToLog(
                     "Error",
                     string.Format("Connect failure. Message: '{0}'", e.Message)
                   );
                   System.Threading.Thread.Sleep(5000);
                }
                else
                {
                    Throw e;
                }
            }
        }

        while (true)
        {
            Log(string.Format("---{0} heart beat ---", this.ToString()));
            Thread.Sleep(1000);
        }
    }

    public override RoleStatus GetHealthStatus()
```

```
{
    return RoleStatus.Healthy;
}

private void _Initialization()
{
    if (_initialized)
    {
        return;
    }

    lock (_syncObj)
    {
        try
        {
            //Instatiate BlobStorage
            _blobStorage =
              BlobStorage.Create(StorageAccountInfo
                 .GetDefaultBlobStorageAccountFromConfiguration());
            _blobContainer =
              _blobStorage.GetBlobContainer(WorkerRole.PAYLOAD_BLOB_CONTAINER_NAME);
            // Make the container public so that we can hit the URLs from the web
            _blobContainer.CreateContainer(new NameValueCollection(),
                                           ContainerAccessControl.Public);

            //Instatiate QueueStorage
            _queueStorage =
              QueueStorage.Create(StorageAccountInfo
                 .GetDefaultQueueStorageAccountFromConfiguration());
            _queueStorage.RetryPolicy =
              RetryPolicies.RetryN(3, TimeSpan.FromSeconds(5));

            //Create a queue to listen blob create request message
            //and register the events
            MessageQueue requstQueue =
              _queueStorage.GetQueue(PAYLOAD_CREATE_REQUEST_QUEUE_NAME);
            requstQueue.CreateQueue();
            requstQueue.MessageReceived +=
              new MessageReceivedEventHandler(_OnCreateBlobMessageReceive);
            requstQueue.PollInterval = POLLING_INTERVAL;
            requstQueue.StartReceiving();

            //Create a queue without to register any event to send the blob created
            //message with blob name to the queue
            MessageQueue resultsQueue =
              _queueStorage.GetQueue(PAYLOAD_RESULTS_QUEUE_NAME);
            resultsQueue.CreateQueue();

            //Create a queue to listen blob delete request message
            //and register the events
            MessageQueue deleteQueue =
```

```
                    _queueStorage.GetQueue(PAYLOAD_DELETE_QUEUE_NAME);
                deleteQueue.CreateQueue();
                deleteQueue.MessageReceived +=
                  new MessageReceivedEventHandler(_OnDeleteBlobMessageReceive);
                deleteQueue.PollInterval = POLLING_INTERVAL;
                deleteQueue.StartReceiving();

                _initialized = true;
            }
            catch (Exception ex)
            {
                LogError(
                  string.Format(
                    "--- {0}:_Initialization, exception caught : {1}",
                    this.ToString(),
                    ex.Message
                  )
                );
            }

            _initialized = true;
        }
    }

    private void _CreateBlob(Message message)
    {
        lock (_syncObj)
        {
            string logMessage =
              string.Format(
                "---{0}:_OnMessageReceive, message = <{1}>",
                this.ToString(),
                message.ContentAsString()
              );
            System.Diagnostics.Trace.WriteLine(logMessage);
            Log(logMessage);

            string blobName = string.Format("{0}{1}", message.Id, PAYLOAD_BLOB_SUFFIX);
            if (!_blobContainer.DoesBlobExist(blobName))
            {
                // Compose a unique blob name
                BlobProperties properties = new BlobProperties(blobName);

                // Create metadata to be associated with the blob
                NameValueCollection metadata = new NameValueCollection();

                metadata["MediaID"] = message.Id;

                properties.Metadata = metadata;
                properties.ContentType = "text/xml";
```

```
            // Create the blob
            byte[] buffer =
              UTF8Encoding.UTF8.GetBytes(
                message.ContentAsString().Replace("\r\n", string.Empty)
              );
            MemoryStream ms = new MemoryStream(buffer);

            BlobContents blobContents = new BlobContents(ms);
            _blobContainer.CreateBlob(properties, blobContents, true);

            var blob = (from m in _blobContainer.ListBlobs(string.Empty, false)
                       where (m as BlobProperties).Name == blobName
                        select m as BlobProperties).Single <BlobProperties>();
            if (null != blob )
            {
                MediaInfo mediaInfo =
                  new MediaInfo(
                    blobName,
                    (blob as BlobProperties).Uri.ToString(),
                    message.Id
                  );
                Message resultsMessage = _CreateMediaInfoMessage(mediaInfo);
                MessageQueue queue =
                  _queueStorage.GetQueue(PAYLOAD_RESULTS_QUEUE_NAME);
                queue.PutMessage(resultsMessage);
            }

        }
        _queueStorage.GetQueue(PAYLOAD_CREATE_REQUEST_QUEUE_NAME)
          .DeleteMessage(message);
    }
}

private void _OnCreateBlobMessageReceive(object sender, EventArgs args)
{
    lock (_syncObj)
    {
       _CreateBlob((args as MessageReceivedEventArgs).Message);
    }
}

private Message _CreateMediaInfoMessage(MediaInfo info)
{
    StringBuilder sb = Helper.XmlPersist(info, typeof(MediaInfo));
    return new Message(UTF8Encoding.UTF8.GetBytes(sb.ToString()));
}

private void _OnDeleteBlobMessageReceive(object sender, EventArgs args)
{
    lock (_syncObj)
    {
```

```
                Message message = (args as MessageReceivedEventArgs).Message;
                string blobName = message.ContentAsString();
                Log(
                  string.Format(
                    "---{0}:received delete blob request, blob name   = <{1}>",
                    this.ToString(),
                    blobName
                  )
                );

                if (_blobContainer.DoesBlobExist(blobName))
                {
                    Log(
                      string.Format(
                        "---{0}:delete blob request, blob name = <{1}>",
                        this.ToString(),
                        blobName
                      )
                    );
                    _blobContainer.DeleteBlob(blobName);
                }
                _queueStorage.GetQueue(PAYLOAD_DELETE_QUEUE_NAME).DeleteMessage(message); ;
            }
        }
    }
}
```

Compiling the code and running the application, we get the same results with this new architecture design as Figure 3-8 shown in the last exercise.

Through this exercise, we have actually built a template for a cloud application that can be used as a communication bus between the web roles and worker roles. This is the solution to decouple a web role from a worker role. Since a worker role cannot expose its end point, it cannot accept external HTTP requests. We can leverage the queue as the message bus to build the communication bridge between a web role and worker role. In fact Azure uses the same approach to decouple its front-end services to increase efficiency and performance.

Implementing a Client Application to Access Cloud Blob Storage

If we need to upload or delete a large amount of data from cloud blob storage in a client-side application, we should consider not only using an asynchronous approach to handle the task in a background thread, but also supporting manually interruption if something goes wrong, which may be caused by network failure or other reasons since Azure blob storage handles transactions on the server side, not on the client side.

Under the hood, the SDK client wrapper dispatches the request by calling two different overloaded handler methods based upon the size of the data. If the data size is greater than 2 MB, the data will be processed through the large data upload hander from the Azure storage client. The Azure blob storage client may contact a group of connected servers in the cloud based upon the balance of the server load.

The contents will be split into numerous data blocks and spread to multiple servers. The Azure blob storage client will call a method to commit the transaction. If any process fails or an interruption occurs, the transaction will not be committed.

This exercise provides a workaround to resolve uploading and downloading a large amount of blob data on the client side. This application may potentially be used as a utility tool for anyone who needs to transmit a large amount of data to a cloud blob. In this exercise we will walk you through creation of a Windows-based tool that can be used to upload and delete large amounts of data from cloud blob storage.

■ **Note** The code for this example is in the Exercise 3-4 bundle from the code download.

There are two technologies for handling large amounts of data, especially data transmission over the network:

- Asynchronous data transmission
- Background worker item thread

The .NET Framework provides extensive support for these two technologies, such as a thread pools and a background worker class. This exercise uses these two technologies in conjunction with other software design patterns, such as the command and facade design patterns to come up with a useful client-side tool to handle large data I/O to Azure blob storage. At the highest level, we define two modules: `AzureStorageFacade` and `BlobStorageActionStatus`. The responsibilities of these two classes are as follows.

- `AzureStorageFacade` is an abstract base class that wraps the class of the Azure storage SDK client. The responsibility of the base class is to instantiate the Azure account object, including the authentication key information. We are going create two classes called `BlobStorageFacade` and `TableStorageFacade` that will inherit from this class. `BlobStorageFacade` encapsulates the blob container and blob properties objects used to access a specific named blob storage from the cloud. This class provides an agile way to perform insert and delete actions to blob storage (update can be done by changing the `overwrite` flag to `false`). To reach this goal, the constructor of this class accepts three parameters of blob storage: `BlobContents`, `BlobProperties`, and a `boolean` flag of `overwrite`.
- `BlobStorageActionStatus` is an abstract base class. This class uses a combination of the bridge design pattern and the command design pattern (without supporting the memento pattern, because there is actually no transaction supported from the client side in the cloud platform. The constructor of this class has exactly the same structure as that of `BlobStorageFacade`. The responsibility of this class is to spawn a worker thread to handle the long-running blob storage access tasks and to provide the progress status of the data access. `BlobStorageActionStatus` has two derived classes, `CreateBlobStatus` and `DeleteBlobStatus`, which are responsible for blob storage creation and deletion respectively. All derived classes implement the `ICommand` interface, which provides an `Excuse()` function to update the progress status.

Figure 3-11 is the diagram for the class layout. As noted above, in order to make our components reusable, we define a base class called `AzureStorageFacade`, which encapsulates the account initialization function in the constructor. We subclass three classes also using the facade design pattern to wrap up all the interfaces used to access Azure basic storages, table, queue and blob, respectively. These three subclasses are `AzureStorage`, `TableStorage`, and `BlobStorage`. In this exercise we are going to use this base class to re-engineer the blob access classes from previous exercise and leave you to apply the first two classes to all existing exercises from previous chapters or use them in future development.

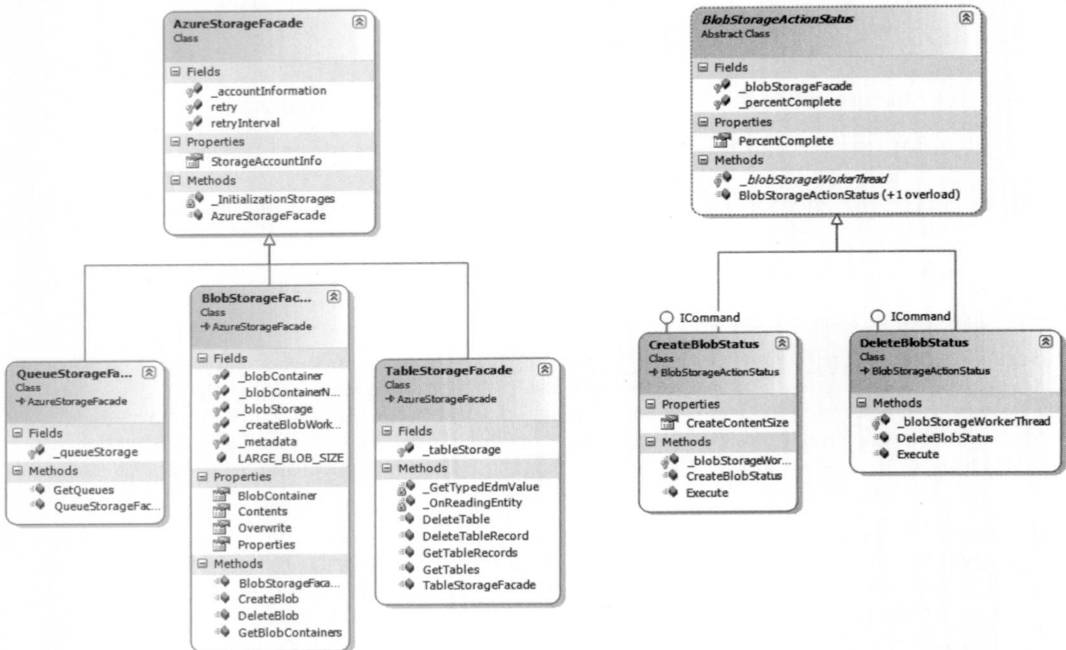

Figure 3-11. *Class diagram for large data I/O to cloud blob storage tools*

Listing 3-15 is the implementation of the base class `AzureStorageFacade`. There is only one member method `_Initialization()` defined, which is used to retrieve the account information from the configuration file.

Listing 3-15. *Implementation of the Base Class* `AzureStorageFacade`

```
using System;
using System.Configuration;

namespace AzureForDotNetDevelopers.LargeDataToBlob
{
    using Microsoft.ServiceHosting.ServiceRuntime;
    using Microsoft.Samples.ServiceHosting.StorageClient;
```

```
    public class AzureStorageFacade
    {
        protected StorageAccountInfo _accountInformation;
        protected int retry = 1;
        protected int retryInterval = 1000;

        public StorageAccountInfo StorageAccountInfo
        {
            get{ return _accountInformation; }
        }


        public AzureStorageFacade()
        {
            _InitializationStorages();
        }

        protected void _InitializationStorages()
        {
            retry = Convert.ToInt32(ConfigurationManager.AppSettings["Retry"]);
            retryInterval =
              Convert.ToInt32(ConfigurationManager.AppSettings["RetryInterval"]);
            _accountInformation =
              StorageAccountInfo.GetDefaultBlobStorageAccountFromConfiguration();
        }
    }
}
```

Listing 3-16 shows the implementation of the blob facade class, which encapsulates all blob storage access functions and attributes of blob storage needed for a client application in a more comprehensive manner than in the implementation in the previous exercise.

Listing 3-16. *Implementation of the* `BlobStorageFacade` *Class Derived from the* `AzureStorageFacade` *Class*

```
using System;
using System.Collections.Generic;
using System.Linq;
using System.Text;
using System.Configuration;
using System.Collections.Specialized;
using System.Threading;
using System.IO;

namespace AzureForDotNetDevelopers.LargeDataToBlob.CloudStorage.BlobStorage
{
    using Microsoft.ServiceHosting.ServiceRuntime;
    using Microsoft.Samples.ServiceHosting.StorageClient;

    using CSharpBuildingBlocks;
```

```
public class BlobStorageFacade : AzureStorageFacade
{
    static public long LARGE_BLOB_SIZE = 2 * 1024 * 1024;// 2 MB
    protected BlobStorage _blobStorage;
    protected BlobContainer _blobContainer;
    protected string _blobContainerName =
      ConfigurationManager.AppSettings["BlobContainerName"];
    protected NameValueCollection _metadata = null;
    protected Thread _createBlobWorkerthread = null;
    public BlobContents Contents { get; set; }
    public BlobProperties Properties { get; set; }
    public bool Overwrite { get; set; }

    public BlobStorageFacade()
    {
        _blobStorage = BlobStorage.Create(_accountInformation);
        _blobStorage.RetryPolicy =
          RetryPolicies.RetryN(retry, TimeSpan.FromMilliseconds(retryInterval));
        _blobContainer = _blobStorage.GetBlobContainer(_blobContainerName);
    }

    public BlobStorageFacade(NameValueCollection metadata):this()
    {
        _metadata = metadata;
        _blobContainer.CreateContainer(_metadata, ContainerAccessControl.Private);
    }

    public BlobStorageFacade(BlobContents blobContents,
                             BlobProperties blobProperties,
                             bool overwrite) : this(blobProperties.Metadata)
    {
        Contents = blobContents;
        Properties = blobProperties;
        Overwrite = overwrite;
    }

    public BlobContainer BlobContainer
    {
        get { return _blobContainer; }
    }

    public IEnumerable<BlobContainer> GetBlobContainers()
    {
        return _blobStorage.ListBlobContainers();
    }

    public void CreateBlob()
    {
        _blobContainer.CreateBlob(Properties,
                                  Contents,
```

```
                                            Overwrite);
        }

        public void DeleteBlob()
        {
            if (_blobContainer.DoesBlobExist(Properties.Name))
            {
                _blobContainer.DeleteBlob(Properties.Name);
            }
        }
    }
}
```

As mentioned before, we use a background worker thread and ICommand design pattern in this application. The base class implementation for these two classes comes from my existing building block collection library. The reference assemblies are called CSharpBuildingBlocks and CSharpBuildingBlocks.QueuedBackgroundWorker. These two assemblies come with the source code download and will be used several places in other chapters.

Listing 3-17 and Listing 3-18 are the implementation for CreateBlobStatus and DeleteBlobStatus. A worker thread is created at the time a message arrives for either creating or deleting a blob request. Two member functions are used to handle create or delete activities accordingly. The algorithms for progress are different in these two classes.

For blob creation, the percentage of the creation progress is determined by comparing the size of the blob to be created against the actual size of the data that has been committed to cloud blob storage. No incremented progress can be reported to the client application, because the detailed information of a newly created or deleted blob will not be updated until the transactions have been committed on the server.

Listing 3-17. *The* CreateBlobStatus *Class Derived from the* BlobStorageAction *Class*

```
using System;
using System.Collections.Generic;
using System.Linq;
using System.Text;
using System.Configuration;
using System.Collections.Specialized;
using System.Threading;

namespace AzureForDotNetDevelopers.LargeDataToBlob.CloudStorage.BlobStorage
{
    using Microsoft.ServiceHosting.ServiceRuntime;
    using Microsoft.Samples.ServiceHosting.StorageClient;
    using CSharpBuildingBlocks;

    public class CreateBlobStatus : BlobStorageActionStatus, ICommand
    {
        public long CreateContentSize { get; set; }

        public CreateBlobStatus(BlobContents blobContents,
                                BlobProperties blobProperties,
```

```
                                bool overwrite)
            : base(blobContents,
                   blobProperties,
                   overwrite)
        {
        }


        public void Execute()
        {
            try
            {
                if (_blobStorageFacade.BlobContainer
                      .DoesBlobExist(_blobStorageFacade.Properties.Name))
                {
                    var blob =
                      (from m
                       in _blobStorageFacade.BlobContainer.ListBlobs(string.Empty, false)
                       where (m as BlobProperties).Name
                         == _blobStorageFacade.Properties.Name
                       select m as BlobProperties).Single<BlobProperties>();
                    _percentComplete =
                      (float)(((blob as BlobProperties).ContentLength * 100.0) /
                               (CreateContentSize * 1.0));
                    System.Diagnostics.Trace.WriteLine(
                      string.Format(
                        "---{0}:Execute, _percentComplete = <{1}>",
                        this.ToString(),
                        _percentComplete
                      )
                    );
                }

            }
            catch (Exception ex)
            {
                System.Diagnostics.Trace.WriteLine(
                  string.Format(
                    "---{0}:Execute,exception caught <{1}>",
                    this.ToString(),
                    ex.Message
                  )
                );
            }
        }

        override protected void _blobStorageWorkerThread(object paramters)
        {
            try
            {
```

```
                (paramters as BlobStorageFacade).CreateBlob();
            }
            catch { }
        }
    }
}
```

Listing 3-18. *The* `DeleteBlobStatus` *Class Derived from the* `BlobStorageAction` *Class*

```
using System;
using System.Collections.Generic;
using System.Linq;
using System.Text;
using System.Threading;

namespace AzureForDotNetDevelopers.LargeDataToBlob.CloudStorage.BlobStorage
{
    using Microsoft.ServiceHosting.ServiceRuntime;
    using Microsoft.Samples.ServiceHosting.StorageClient;
    using CSharpBuildingBlocks;

    public class DeleteBlobStatus : BlobStorageActionStatus, ICommand
    {
        public DeleteBlobStatus(BlobContents blobContents,
                                BlobProperties blobProperties,
                                bool overwrite)
            : base(blobContents,
                   blobProperties,
                   overwrite)
        {
        }

        public void Execute()
        {
            try
            {
                if (!_blobStorageFacade.BlobContainer
                       .DoesBlobExist(_blobStorageFacade.Properties.Name))
                {
                    _percentComplete = 100.0f;
                }
            }
            catch { }
        }

        override protected void _blobStorageWorkerThread(object paramters)
        {
            try
            {
                (paramters as BlobStorageFacade).DeleteBlob();
                Thread.Sleep(2000);
```

```
            }
            catch { }
        }
    }
}
```

The CSharpBuildingBlock.QueuedBackgroundWorker assembly contains a building block component called QueuedBackgroundWorkerComponent. This component can place a worker item into a queue and run from a background thread. There are three events that can be fired up from that component, DoWork, ProgressChanged, and RunWorkerCompleted as Figure 3-12 shows. The event handlers need to be registered either at design time via the properties dialog as in Figure 3-12 or programmatically as shown in Listing 3-19. Listing 3-20 shows the event handlers for DoWork, RunWorkerCompleted, and ProgressChanged. After accomplishing these steps to create or delete blob storage with a large amount of data the rest is relatively simple and straightforward. What is left for you is instantiating CreateBlobStatus of DeleteBlobStatus as an ICommand type and passing it to QueuedBackgroundWorkerItem.

The job will run in the background without locking up the UI thread. The progress and task accomplished event will be reported to the client as we expected. The upload blob name can be automatically generated. If the size of the contents of blob is greater than 2 MB, a suffix _large is attached to the end of the name. There is no particular constraint for the blob name as long as it meets the specification illustrated in Appendix A. To interrupt ongoing processing, either for creating or deleting, a user needs to set the flag of CancelAll from QueuedBackgroundWorkerItem by clicking on the Abort button.

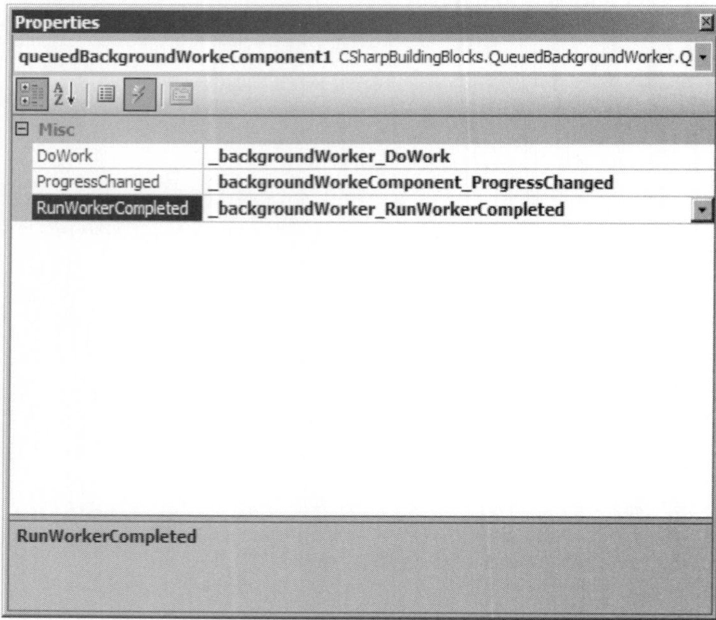

Figure 3-12. *Event bindings if using the* QueuedBackgroundWorkerComponent

The rest of this chapter, from Listing 3-19 to Listing 3-23, shows the implementation of a Windows form user interface, including the event handling, application initialization, and GUI updating. This part should be straightforward to any professional .NET developer, and we are not going to drill down to analysis in detail. You can download the source code and verify the results attached to the end of this chapter and potentially use this as an administration tool to transmit a large amount of data to blob storage as part of the infrastructure of a cloud application.

Listing 3-19. *Register Events for Background Worker Items from the Client UI Class Constructor*

```
public FormBlobAccess()
{
    InitializeComponent();

    this._backgroundWorkeComponent = new QueuedBackgroundWorkeComponent();
    this._backgroundWorkeComponent.DoWork +=
      new System.ComponentModel.DoWorkEventHandler (this._backgroundWorker_DoWork);
    this._backgroundWorkeComponent.RunWorkerCompleted +=
      new System.ComponentModel.RunWorkerCompletedEventHandler(
        this._backgroundWorker_RunWorkerCompleted
      );
    this._backgroundWorkeComponent.ProgressChanged +=
      new System.ComponentModel.ProgressChangedEventHandler(
        this._backgroundWorkeComponent_ProgressChanged
      );

    _UpdateUI();
}
```

Listing 3-20. *Event Handler for* `DoWorker`*,* `RunWorkerCompleted`*, and* `ProgressChanged`

```
        private void _backgroundWorker_DoWork(object sender, DoWorkEventArgs e)
        {

            if (e.Argument is CreateBlobStatus)
            {
                _command = (CreateBlobStatus)e.Argument;
                if (_backgroundWorkeComponent._QueuedBackgroundWorker
                      .IsCancellationPending(_command))
                {
                    e.Cancel = true;
                }
            }
            else if (e.Argument is FibGeneratorState)
            {
                _command = (FibGeneratorState)e.Argument;
            }

            if (null != _command)
            {
                while (!_backgroundWorkeComponent._QueuedBackgroundWorker
```

```
                .IsCancellationPending(_command)
              && _command.PercentComplete < 100)
        {
            _backgroundWorkeComponent._QueuedBackgroundWorker
              .ReportProgress(_command.PercentComplete, _command);
            _command.Execute();
            e.Result = _command;
            Application.DoEvents();
        }
    }
}

private void _backgroundWorker_RunWorkerCompleted(object sender,
                                              RunWorkerCompletedEventArgs e)
{
    if (null != _fileStream)
    {
        _fileStream.Close();
        toolStripProgressBar1.Visible = false;
    }

    lblTimeEnd.Text = DateTime.Now.ToString();
    if (_command is CreateBlobStatus)
    {
        toolStripStatusLabel1.Text = "Upload blob success.";
    }
    else if (_command is DeleteBlobStatus)
    {
        toolStripStatusLabel1.Text = "Delete blob success.";
    }

    _UpdateUI();
}

private void _backgroundWorkeComponent_ProgressChanged(object sender,
                                                   ProgressChangedEventArgs e)
{
    //_progressBar.Value = e.ProgressPercentage;
    Update();
    Application.DoEvents();
}
```

Listing 3-21. *Instantiate an Instance of* `CreateBlobStatus` *and Pass It to* `QueuedBackgroundWorker` *to Create a Large Blob in the Background*

```
private void btnUpload_Click(object sender, EventArgs e)
{
    toolStripProgressBar1.Visible = true;
    toolStripStatusLabel1.Text = string.Empty; ;
    btnAbort.Enabled = true;
```

```
    btnDelete.Enabled = false;
    lblTimeStart.Text = DateTime.Now.ToString();
    lblTimeEnd.Text = string.Empty;
    lblTimeElapsed.Text = string.Empty;
    timer1.Enabled = true;

    if (null == _azureStorage)
    {
        _azureStorage = new AzureStorageFacade();
    }

    _fileStream = new FileStream(_fileName.Text.ToString().Trim(),
                                 FileMode.Open,
                                 FileAccess.Read);
    if (txtBlobName.Text.ToString().Trim() == string.Empty)
    {
        btnGenerateBlobName_Click(this, null);
    }

    string blobName = txtBlobName.Text.ToString().Trim();

    BlobProperties properties = new BlobProperties(blobName);
    NameValueCollection metadata = new NameValueCollection();
    properties.Metadata = metadata;
    properties.ContentType = "byte";
    BlobContents blobContents = new BlobContents(_fileStream);

    _command = new CreateBlobStatus(blobContents,
                                    properties,
                                    true)
    {
        CreateContentSize = _fileInfo.Length
    } ;

    _backgroundWorkeComponent._QueuedBackgroundWorker.RunWorkerAsync(_command);
}
```

Listing 3-22. *Instatiate an Instance of*`DeleteBlobStatus` *and Pass It to* `QueuedBackgroundWorker` *to Delete a Large Blob from Background*

```
private void btnDelete_Click(object sender, EventArgs e)
{
    toolStripProgressBar1.Visible = true;
    toolStripStatusLabel1.Text = string.Empty;
    toolStripStatusLabel1.ForeColor = Color.Black;
    btnAbort.Enabled = true;
    lblTimeStart.Text = DateTime.Now.ToString();
    lblTimeEnd.Text = string.Empty;
    lblTimeElapsed.Text = string.Empty;
    timer1.Enabled = true;
```

```
        string blobName = combBoxBlobList.SelectedItem.ToString();
        try
        {
            BlobProperties properties = new BlobProperties(blobName);
            NameValueCollection metadata = new NameValueCollection();
            properties.Metadata = metadata;
            properties.ContentType = "byte";
            BlobContents blobContents = new BlobContents(new MemoryStream());

            _command = new DeleteBlobStatus(blobContents,
                                            properties,
                                            true);
            _backgroundWorkeComponent._QueuedBackgroundWorker.RunWorkerAsync(_command);
        }
        catch (Exception ex)
        {
            toolStripStatusLabel1.ForeColor = Color.Red;
            toolStripStatusLabel1.Text = ex.Message;
        }
    }
```

Listing 3-23. Set Flag from `QueuedBackgroundWorker` *to Interrupt Create or Delete Blob Actions*

```
    private void btnCancel_Click(object sender, EventArgs e)
    {
        timer1.Enabled = false;
        btnUpload.Enabled = true;
        btnDelete.Enabled = true;
        btnAbort.Enabled = false;
        toolStripStatusLabel1.Text = "Actiong aborted.";
        _backgroundWorkeComponent._QueuedBackgroundWorker.CancelAllAsync();
    }
```

■ **Note** To run this application from the local development environment, the development storage service and development fabric must be started first.

The following screenshots are the test results of Exercise 3-4.

First, we upload a large amount of data to blob storage. The results are shown in Figures 3-13 and 3-14.

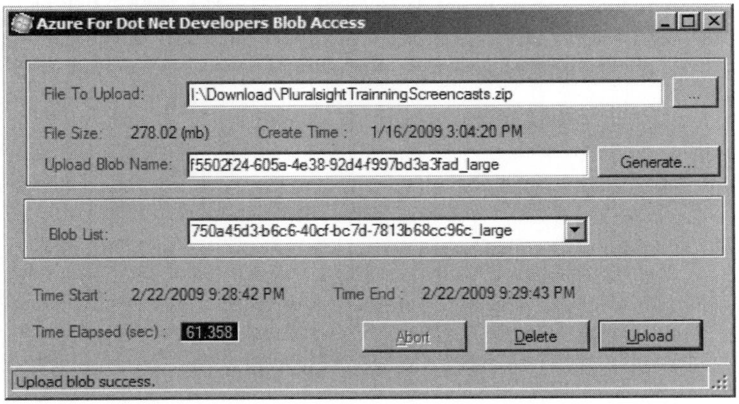

Figure 3-13. File of size 278 MB created and uploaded to blob, taking 61.358 seconds in the local development environment with the system configuration shown in Figure 3-14

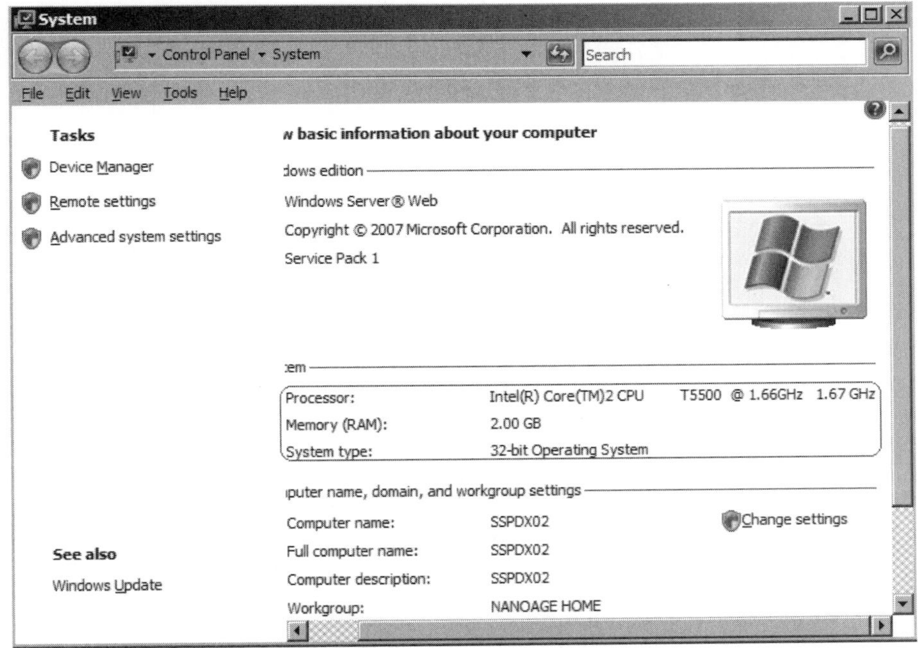

Figure 3-14. System configuration to run Exercise 3-4

We can also upload a small amount of data to blob storage.

This tool, of course, can also be used to transmit any size of data between local systems and cloud blob storage. Figure 3-15 shows an example using this tool to upload a small file to a blob storage table. Note that the file name created by the tool in this case has no suffix.

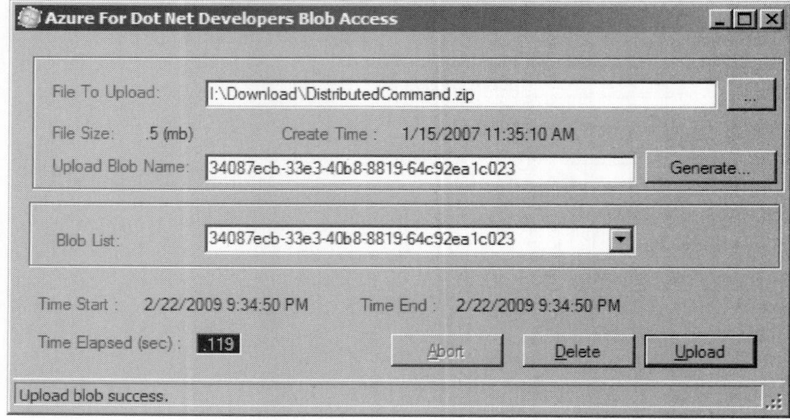

Figure 3-15. Creating a small blob

Since the job is done from a queued worker thread running in the background, aborting an action turns out to be very easy; you can simply click on the Abort button to interrupt the processing as Figure 3-16 shows.

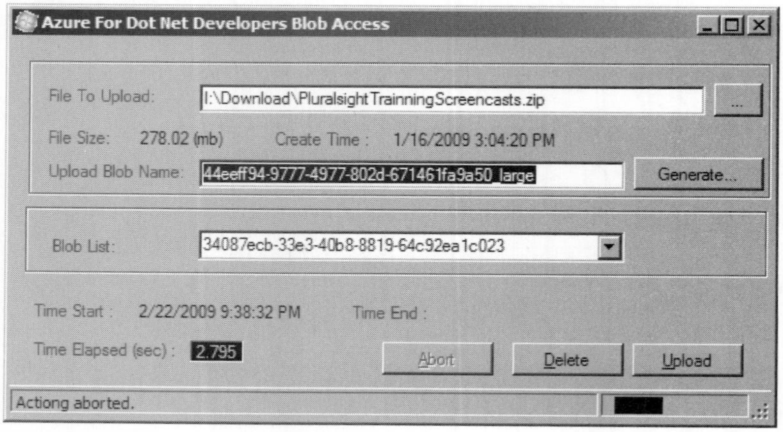

Figure 3-16. The background blob create action can easily be interrupted and aborted at any time.

To delete a record from blob storage, select an available item from the list and click the Delete button. All information retrieved by this tool is in raw data format, as shown in Figure 3-17. One enhancement would be to display the information as a human readable string or provide mapping information for the user, both of which would help to prevent accidental record deletion.

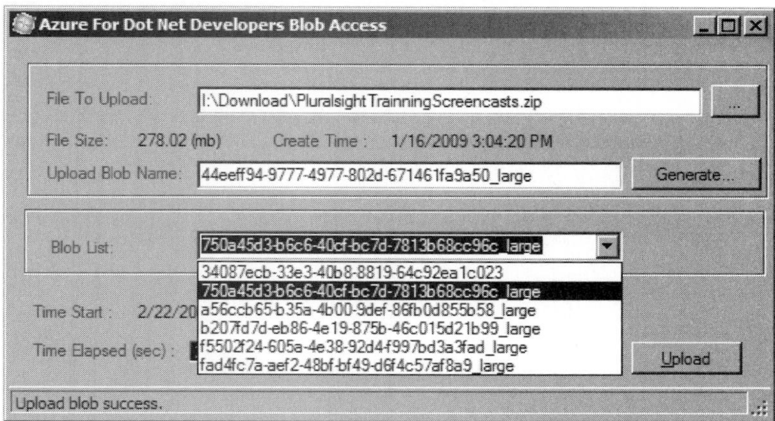

Figure 3-17. All blobs in the specified container are queried and listed in the drop-down list.

Summary

In this chapter we looked at the final two forms of basic storage provided by Azure: Blob and Queue. When they are combined, we can create some powerful, loosely coupled systems to link our applications together. I showed you how to create a cloud queue and how to poll messages from it, as well as how to remove messages when you have processed them. I followed that up by showing how to create blob storage.

The natural thing to do was combine the two into a loosely coupled, event-driven system that takes advantage of these two technologies. I provided a full example that handled events and notifications using a queue. The final example was a tool to help you work with blob storage.

CHAPTER 4

■ ■ ■

Windows Azure Application Integration Using WCF

Whenever a new technology is introduced to the computing world, it raises a lot of questions for an enterprise or organization regarding integration. How do you integrate an application built on new technology into the existing system infrastructure? What are appropriate tools to select for integration? How do you select the right candidate subsystem to migrate, refactor, or re-engineer? Although Windows Azure provides a revolutionary new platform, it is almost impossible for any organization to migrate the entire existing on-premises system and infrastructure into the cloud platform. Therefore, integration strategies are extremely important. Even subsystems, which are built with Windows Azure technology, still need to be integrated together. Microsoft has already provided cloud-computing-based services, such as .NET Services, SQL Azure, and Live Services. These services provide organizations with rich functionality and a broad range of building blocks for integration.

Windows Azure offers amazing, innovative, and attractive features. One of these features is the ability to host an application in the cloud. Not only cloud-based applications, but also the on-premises applications can leverage cloud services and applications. As I mentioned, to run an application from the cloud is far from the whole story. There is always an integration issue associated with the system architecture design. It should not be too difficult to understand why integration plays the essential role. All applications, services, and infrastructures involved in a computing system need to be coordinated in data exchange, resource sharing, status persisting, logic synchronizing, and so on. All these tasks should be done via integration.

No matter what integration strategy an organization plans to use, an essential feature of an integration platform is that it must support cross-platform communication. Microsoft BizTalk server and WCF (Windows Communication Foundation, part of .NET 3.0 or later versions of the .NET platform) should meet these criteria. In principle, Microsoft BizTalk server is designed to support any existing communication protocol in the computing world through built-in, third-party, or custom adapters. The great advantages we can take from Microsoft BizTalk server are its power to integrate and call any existing .NET components, to extend a solution with custom pipelines, data mapping functions, and dynamic data transforming and mapping. And it has sophisticated workflow control, business rules integration, and error handling via Windows BizTalk orchestrations. In contrast, the advantage we can get from WCF is that it is a web-services-based platform. WCF is built in to .NET 3.0 and later versions and can be deployed and hosted from Windows Azure. The scope of this book is limited to covering the topic of integrating Windows Azure applications with each other or with other non-cloud-based on-premises applications using Windows WCF.

Using WCF

WCF unifies all the communication models supported by web services, including message queues, .NET Remoting and distributed transactions into a general service-oriented architecture (SOA), and it also supports SOAP (with an optimized SOAP binary format). WCF also supports both JSON and REST data formats. You can flexibly consume data from Windows Azure using Ajax or .NET by simply providing URLs of the target resources. When a method is invoked against specific URLs, parameters from the URLs are automatically extracted and passed into the target method.

These features as described make WCF a great integration tool not only for on-premises applications but also for Windows Azure cloud applications, in addition to Windows BizTalk server. WCF services can be hosted from Windows API applications or from IIS. It would make WCF more attractive from the perspective of integration if WCF services could be hosted from Windows Azure.

Microsoft .NET Services, originally called BizTalk Services, was designed as a set of highly scalable developer-oriented services hosted in Microsoft data centers as part of the Windows Azure platform. These services are common building blocks or infrastructure services for cloud-based applications. As one of the core services offered by .NET Services, .NET Workflow Services allows you to define highly scalable cloud-based workflows using Workflow Foundation (WF). In addition, the .NET Workflow Service also provides management tools and web-service-based APIs for .NET Workflow Services type and instance management. Moving forward,.NET Workflow Services tightly collaborates with WCF. In this chapter, we are going to explore the fundamental steps of using WCF and WF as a cloud-based application integration platform.

Host WCF Service from Azure

In this exercise, we are going to build an example to host a WCF service from Windows Azure. Following are the steps we need to perform to reach this goal.

1. From Visual Studio, create a new cloud service web role service project called `HostWCFService` as shown in Figure 4-1.

Figure 4-1. *Create a cloud web role service,* `HostWCFService`*, from Visual Studio*

2. Create a DLL library project called `AzureForDotNetDeveloperWCFServiceLibrary`. In this project we define a WCF service contract interface, `IUserRegisterService`, and a data contract class, `User`, as Listing 4-1 shows. The service contract interface, `IUserRegisterService`, has two operation contracts defined. `AddUser()` (taking an instance of `User` as a parameter) is used to provide a service to add a user when a user registers to a cloud application. `GetUserList()` is used to retrieve the collection of users who have registered to a cloud application.

Listing 4-1. *WCF Service Contract* `IUserRegisterService` *and Data Contract* `User` *Definition*

```
using System;
using System.Collections.Generic;
using System.Linq;
using System.Text;
using System.Runtime.Serialization;
using System.ServiceModel;

namespace AzureForDotNetDeveloperWCFServiceLibrary
{
    [ServiceContract]
    public interface IUserRegisterService
    {
        [OperationContract]
        void AddUser(User user);

        [OperationContract]
        List<User> GetUserList();
    }

    [DataContract]
    public class User
    {
        [DataMember]
        public string FirstName;

        [DataMember]
        public string LastName;

        [DataMember]
        public DateTime TimeRegistered;

        [DataMember]
        public string Password;
    }
}
```

3. From the `HostWCFService_WebRole` project in the Solution Explorer panel, right-click on the project node and select Add ➤ New Item to bring up the Add New Item dialog box. Select WCF Service from the dialog window and name it `UserRegisterService.svc` as Figure 4-2 shows. Add the reference to `AzureForDotNetDeveloperWCFServiceLibrary` we have just created. There are three changes we need to make after the service component has been inserted into the project:

    - Open `UserRegisterService.svc` from Visual Studio by double-clicking on that file node and correct the string value for Service. The string in quotation marks should be the fully qualified class name with namespace:

```
AzureForDotNetDeveloperWCFServiceLibrary.UserRegisterService
```

- Delete `UserRegisterService.svc.cs` from the project because we have already defined the services contracts from `AzureForDotNetDeveloperWCFServiceLibrary`.
- Remove the following section from `UserRegisterService.svc` by double-clicking on that file node from the Solution Explorer panel of Visual Studio. The results are shown in Listing 4-2:

```
<Code behind="HostWCFService_WebRole.UserRegisterService.svc.cs"
```

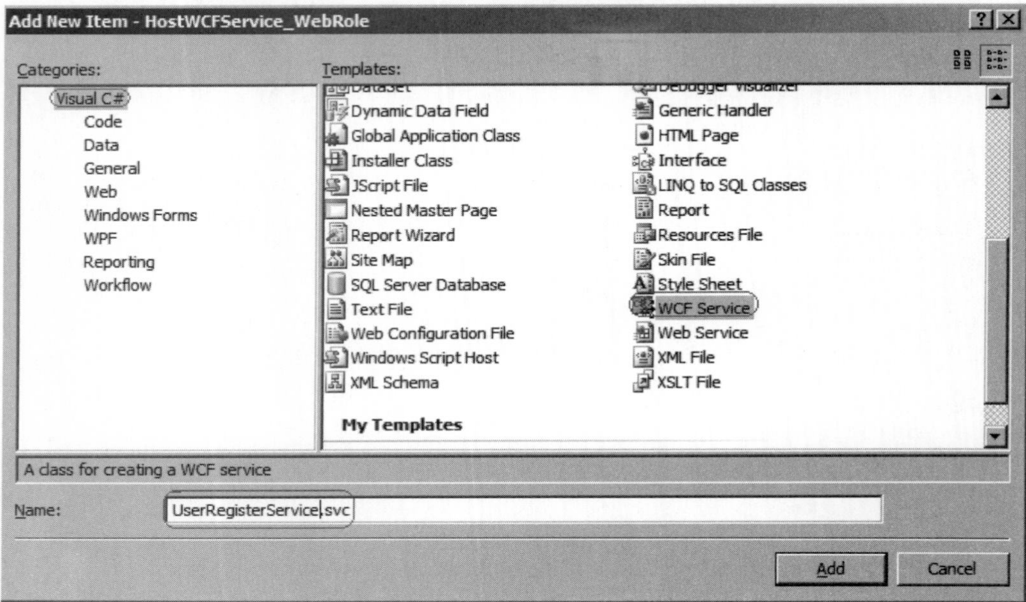

Figure 4-2. *Insert a WCF service item into the* `HostWCFService_WebRole` *project*

Listing 4-2. *Modify the File* `UserRegisterService.svc` *to Use the Correct Namespace and Remove the Code-behind Section*

```
<%@ ServiceHost Language="C#" Debug="true"
    Service="AzureForDotNetDeveloperWCFServiceLibrary.UserRegisterService" %>
```

4. From Visual Studio, select Tools ➤ WCF Configuration Editor and open the `Web.config` file of the `HostWCFService` project as shown in Figure 4-3. Use this tool to configure the WCF service endpoint and metadata endpoint. The results for `Web.config` are shown in Listing 4-3. The `Web.config` file can be edited by using any XML editor instead of using WCF Configuration Editor. However I recommend that you edit the WCF configuration file with the configuration editor. This is tedious work, and it is very easy to make mistakes.

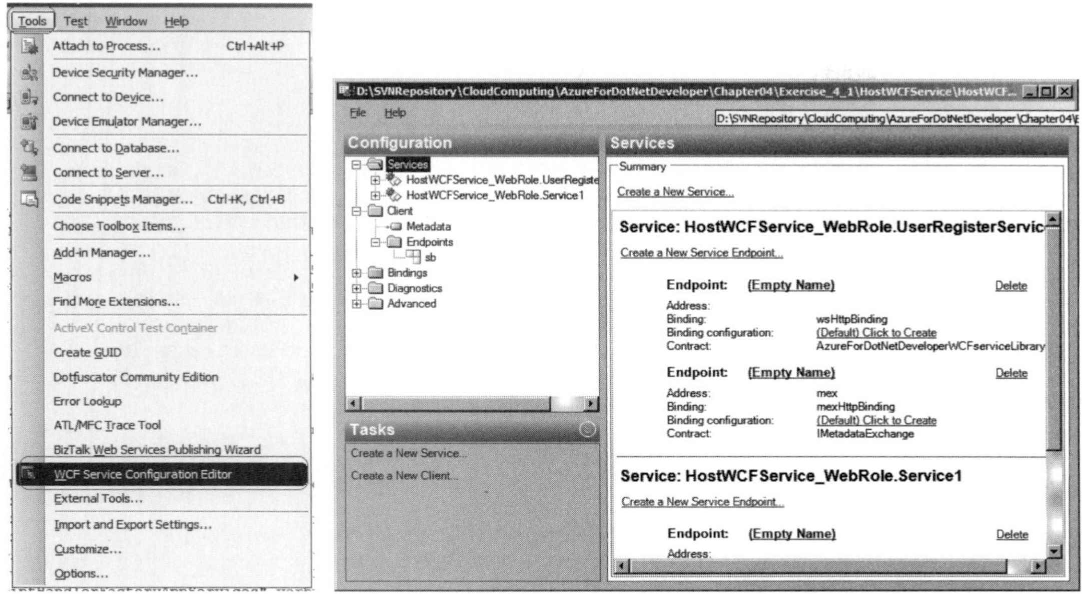

Figure 4-3. *Launch WCF Configuration Editor from Visual Studio*

Listing 4-3. *Configuration for WCF Service* `UserRegisterService.svc`

```
<?xml version="1.0"?>

<configuration>

  <appSettings>
    <add key="AccountName" value="devstoreaccount1"/>
    <add key="AccountSharedKey" value="<KEY>"/>
    <add key="BlobStorageEndpoint" value="http://127.0.0.1:10000"/>
    <add key="QueueStorageEndpoint" value="http://127.0.0.1:10001"/>
    <add key="TableStorageEndpoint" value="http://127.0.0.1:10002/"/>
  </appSettings>
  <connectionStrings/>

  <system.webServer>
      <validation validateIntegratedModeConfiguration="false"/>
      <modules>
        <remove name="ScriptModule" />
 <add name="ScriptModule" preCondition="managedHandler"
      type="System.Web.Handlers.ScriptModule, System.Web.Extensions,
           Version=3.5.0.0, Culture=neutral, PublicKeyToken=31BF3856AD364E35"/>
      </modules>
      <handlers>
```

```
        <remove name="WebServiceHandlerFactory-Integrated"/>
        <remove name="ScriptHandlerFactory" />
        <remove name="ScriptHandlerFactoryAppServices" />
        <remove name="ScriptResource" />
        <add name="ScriptHandlerFactory" verb="*" path="*.asmx"
             preCondition="integratedMode"
             type="System.Web.Script.Services.ScriptHandlerFactory, System.Web.Extensions,
                   Version=3.5.0.0, Culture=neutral, PublicKeyToken=31BF3856AD364E35"/>
        <add name="ScriptHandlerFactoryAppServices" verb="*" path="*_AppService.axd"
             preCondition="integratedMode"
             type="System.Web.Script.Services.ScriptHandlerFactory, System.Web.Extensions,
                   Version=3.5.0.0, Culture=neutral, PublicKeyToken=31BF3856AD364E35"/>
        <add name="ScriptResource" preCondition="integratedMode" verb="GET,HEAD"
             path="ScriptResource.axd" type="System.Web.Handlers.ScriptResourceHandler,
                   System.Web.Extensions, Version=3.5.0.0, Culture=neutral,
                   PublicKeyToken=31BF3856AD364E35" />
      </handlers>
    </system.webServer>
    <system.serviceModel>
        <client>
            <remove contract="IMetadataExchange" name="sb" />
            <endpoint address=""
                      binding="netTcpRelayBinding"
                      bindingConfiguration="metadataExchangeRelayBinding"
                contract="IMetadataExchange" name="sb" />
        </client>
        <behaviors>
            <serviceBehaviors>
                <behavior name="HostWCFService_WebRole.UserRegisterServiceBehavior">
                    <serviceMetadata httpGetEnabled="true" />
                    <serviceDebug includeExceptionDetailInFaults="false" />
                </behavior>
                <behavior name="HostWCFService_WebRole.Service1Behavior">
                    <serviceMetadata httpGetEnabled="true" />
                    <serviceDebug includeExceptionDetailInFaults="false" />
                </behavior>
            </serviceBehaviors>
        </behaviors>
        <services>
            <service
                behaviorConfiguration="HostWCFService_WebRole.UserRegisterServiceBehavior"
                name="HostWCFService_WebRole.UserRegisterService">
                <endpoint
                   address=""
                   binding="wsHttpBinding"
                   contract="AzureForDotNetDeveloperWCFServiceLibrary.IUserRegisterService">
                    <identity>
                        <dns value="localhost" />
                    </identity>
                </endpoint>
                <endpoint address="mex"
```

```
                        binding="mexHttpBinding"
                        contract="IMetadataExchange" />
          </service>
          <service behaviorConfiguration="HostWCFService_WebRole.Service1Behavior"
                   name="HostWCFService_WebRole.Service1">
              <endpoint address=""
                        binding="wsHttpBinding"
                        contract="HostWCFService_WebRole.IService1">
                  <identity>
                      <dns value="localhost" />
                  </identity>
              </endpoint>
              <endpoint address="mex"
                        binding="mexHttpBinding"
                        contract="IMetadataExchange" />
          </service>
      </services>
  </system.serviceModel>
</configuration>
```

5. Insert an `App.config` file to the project *AzureForDotNetDeveloperWCFServiceLibrary* and modify it as shown in Listing 4-4.

Listing 4-4. *Configuration for AzureForDotNetDeveloperWCFServiceLibrary*

```
<?xml version="1.0" encoding="utf-8" ?>
<configuration>
  <system.web>
    <compilation debug="true" />
  </system.web>
  <!-- When deploying the service library project, the content of the config
       file must be added to the host's app.config file.
       System.Configuration does not support config files for libraries. -->
  <system.serviceModel>
    <services>
      <service
        behaviorConfiguration="AzureForDotNetDeveloperWCFServiceLibrary.Service1Behavior"
        name="AzureForDotNetDeveloperWCFServiceLibrary.UserRegisterService">
        <endpoint address="" binding="wsHttpBinding"
                  contract="AzureForDotNetDeveloperWCFServiceLibrary.IUserRegisterService">
          <identity>
            <dns value="localhost" />
          </identity>
        </endpoint>
        <endpoint address="mex" binding="mexHttpBinding" contract="IMetadataExchange" />
        <host>
          <baseAddresses>
            <add baseAddress="http://localhost:8080/UserRegisterService" />
          </baseAddresses>
        </host>
```

```
      </service>
    </services>
    <behaviors>
      <serviceBehaviors>
        <behavior name="AzureForDotNetDeveloperWCFServiceLibrary.Service1Behavior">
          <!-- To avoid disclosing metadata information,
          set the value below to false and remove the metadata endpoint above
          before deployment -->
          <serviceMetadata httpGetEnabled="True"/>

          <!-- To receive exception details in faults for debugging purposes,
          set the value below to true.  Set to false before deployment
          to avoid disclosing exception information -->
          <serviceDebug includeExceptionDetailInFaults="False" />
        </behavior>
      </serviceBehaviors>
    </behaviors>
  </system.serviceModel>
</configuration>
```

6. Add a new Visual Studio Team Test project called `HostWCFServiceUnitTest` from the Solution Explorer panel.
7. Add a service reference to the client test project `HostWCFServiceUnitTest` and enter a name for that reference (the name can be changed after adding the reference) as shown in Figure 4-4.

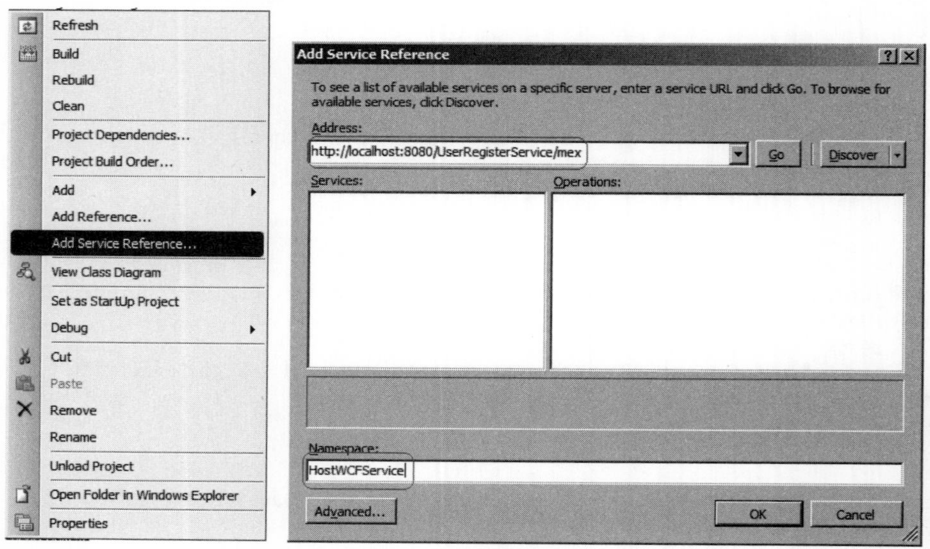

Figure 4-4. Add a service reference to the client application `HostWCFServiceUnitTest`

8. Visual Studio will generate a service client proxy. There is actually a package generated, including `service.wsdl`, the web service definition language file, and `Reference.cs`. The first file contains information of the endpoint address, service contract definition, and data object definitions. The second one is where the C# classes have been generated by Visual Studio using the WSDL file. Listing 4-5 is extracted from the generated `service.wsdl` file, and Listing 4-6 is the C# client proxy classes generated by Visual Studio. If an application, either a Windows application or a web application, is also developed using the .NET platform, the generated C# proxy classes can be directly referenced. An application built with other platforms, such as Java, can use the generated WSDL to create its own web service proxy and communicate with this service. The auto-generated proxy package should contain all service interface functions as well as the data structure container classes. To use these generated classes from client applications should be straightforward as with other regular C# classes.

Listing 4-5. *Extract from the Generated WSDL File* `service.wsdl`

```
<wsdl:service name="UserRegisterService">
  <wsdl:port name="WSHttpBinding_IUserRegisterService"
             binding="tns:WSHttpBinding_IUserRegisterService">
    <soap12:address location="http://localhost:8080/UserRegisterService" />
    <wsa10:EndpointReference>
      <wsa10:Address>http://localhost:8080/UserRegisterService</wsa10:Address>
      <Identity xmlns="http://schemas.xmlsoap.org/ws/2006/02/addressingidentity">
        <Dns>localhost</Dns>
      </Identity>
    </wsa10:EndpointReference>
  </wsdl:port>
</wsdl:service>
```

Listing 4-6. *Service Proxy Classes Generated by Visual Studio*

```
//------------------------------------------------------------------------------
// <auto-generated>
//     This code was generated by a tool.
//     Runtime Version:2.0.50727.3053
//
//     Changes to this file may cause incorrect behavior and will be lost if
//     the code is regenerated.
// </auto-generated>
//------------------------------------------------------------------------------

namespace HostWCFSrviceUnitTest.HostWCFService {
    using System.Runtime.Serialization;
    using System;

    [System.Diagnostics.DebuggerStepThroughAttribute()]
    [System.CodeDom.Compiler.GeneratedCodeAttribute("System.Runtime.Serialization",
```

```
                                                  "3.0.0.0")]
    [System.Runtime.Serialization.DataContractAttribute(
        Name="User",
        Namespace=

"http://schemas.datacontract.org/2004/07/AzureForDotNetDeveloperWCFServiceLibrary")]
    [System.SerializableAttribute()]
    public partial class User : object, System.Runtime.Serialization.IExtensibleDataObject,
      System.ComponentModel.INotifyPropertyChanged {
        [System.NonSerializedAttribute()]
        private System.Runtime.Serialization.ExtensionDataObject extensionDataField;

        [System.Runtime.Serialization.OptionalFieldAttribute()]
        private string FirstNameField;

        [System.Runtime.Serialization.OptionalFieldAttribute()]
        private string LastNameField;

        [System.Runtime.Serialization.OptionalFieldAttribute()]
        private string PasswordField;

        [System.Runtime.Serialization.OptionalFieldAttribute()]
        private System.DateTime TimeRegisteredField;

        [global::System.ComponentModel.BrowsableAttribute(false)]
        public System.Runtime.Serialization.ExtensionDataObject ExtensionData {
            get {
                return this.extensionDataField;
            }
            set {
                this.extensionDataField = value;
            }
        }

        [System.Runtime.Serialization.DataMemberAttribute()]
        public string FirstName {
            get {
                return this.FirstNameField;
            }
            set {
                if ((object.ReferenceEquals(this.FirstNameField, value) != true)) {
                    this.FirstNameField = value;
                    this.RaisePropertyChanged("FirstName");
                }
            }
        }

        [System.Runtime.Serialization.DataMemberAttribute()]
        public string LastName {
            get {
                return this.LastNameField;
```

```
            }
            set {
                if ((object.ReferenceEquals(this.LastNameField, value) != true)) {
                    this.LastNameField = value;
                    this.RaisePropertyChanged("LastName");
                }
            }
        }

        [System.Runtime.Serialization.DataMemberAttribute()]
        public string Password {
            get {
                return this.PasswordField;
            }
            set {
                if ((object.ReferenceEquals(this.PasswordField, value) != true)) {
                    this.PasswordField = value;
                    this.RaisePropertyChanged("Password");
                }
            }
        }
        [System.Runtime.Serialization.DataMemberAttribute()]
        public System.DateTime TimeRegistered {
            get {
                return this.TimeRegisteredField;
            }
           set {
                if ((this.TimeRegisteredField.Equals(value) != true)) {
                    this.TimeRegisteredField = value;
                    this.RaisePropertyChanged("TimeRegistered");
                }
            }
        }
        public event System.ComponentModel.PropertyChangedEventHandler PropertyChanged;

        protected void RaisePropertyChanged(string propertyName) {
            System.ComponentModel.PropertyChangedEventHandler propertyChanged =
              this.PropertyChanged;
            if ((propertyChanged != null)) {
                propertyChanged(
                  this,
                  new System.ComponentModel.PropertyChangedEventArgs(propertyName));
            }
        }
    }

    [System.CodeDom.Compiler.GeneratedCodeAttribute("System.ServiceModel", "3.0.0.0")]
    [System.ServiceModel.ServiceContractAttribute(
      ConfigurationName="HostWCFService.IUserRegisterService")]
    public interface IUserRegisterService {
       [System.ServiceModel.OperationContractAttribute(
```

```
            Action="http://tempuri.org/IUserRegisterService/AddUser",
            ReplyAction="http://tempuri.org/IUserRegisterService/AddUserResponse")]
         void AddUser(HostWCFSrviceUnitTest.HostWCFService.User user);
         [System.ServiceModel.OperationContractAttribute(
            Action="http://tempuri.org/IUserRegisterService/GetUserList",
            ReplyAction="http://tempuri.org/IUserRegisterService/GetUserListResponse")]
         HostWCFSrviceUnitTest.HostWCFService.User[] GetUserList();
     }

     [System.CodeDom.Compiler.GeneratedCodeAttribute("System.ServiceModel", "3.0.0.0")]
     public interface IUserRegisterServiceChannel :
       HostWCFSrviceUnitTest.HostWCFService.IUserRegisterService,
       System.ServiceModel.IClientChannel {
     }
     [System.Diagnostics.DebuggerStepThroughAttribute()]
     [System.CodeDom.Compiler.GeneratedCodeAttribute("System.ServiceModel", "3.0.0.0")]
     public partial class UserRegisterServiceClient :
       System.ServiceModel.ClientBase
         <HostWCFSrviceUnitTest.HostWCFService.IUserRegisterService>,
       HostWCFSrviceUnitTest.HostWCFService.IUserRegisterService {

         public UserRegisterServiceClient() {
         }
         public UserRegisterServiceClient(string endpointConfigurationName) :
                 base(endpointConfigurationName) {
         }
         public UserRegisterServiceClient(string endpointConfigurationName,
                                          string remoteAddress) :
                 base(endpointConfigurationName, remoteAddress) {
         }
         public UserRegisterServiceClient(string endpointConfigurationName,
                                          System.ServiceModel.EndpointAddress remoteAddress)
 :
                 base(endpointConfigurationName, remoteAddress) {
         }
         public UserRegisterServiceClient(System.ServiceModel.Channels.Binding binding,
                                          System.ServiceModel.EndpointAddress remoteAddress)
 :
                 base(binding, remoteAddress) {
         }
         public void AddUser(HostWCFSrviceUnitTest.HostWCFService.User user) {
             base.Channel.AddUser(user);
         }
         public HostWCFSrviceUnitTest.HostWCFService.User[] GetUserList() {
             return base.Channel.GetUserList();
         }
     }
 }
```

9. Compile the solution, and we are ready to test the results.

10. Add two unit test cases and test initialization code into the `HostWCFServiceUnitTest` project as in Listing 4-7.

Listing 4-7. Unit Test Cases for WCF Service Hosted in Azure

```
using System;
using System.Text;
using System.Collections.Generic;
using System.Linq;
using Microsoft.VisualStudio.TestTools.UnitTesting;

namespace HostWCFSrviceUnitTest
{
    using HostWCFService_WebRole;
    using NUnit.Framework;

    [TestFixture]
    [TestClass]
    public class HostWCFClientUnitTest
    {
        private HostWCFService.UserRegisterServiceClient _userRegisterServiceClient = null;

        public HostWCFClientUnitTest()
        {
        }

        private TestContext testContextInstance;

        public TestContext TestContext
        {
            get
            {
                return testContextInstance;
            }
            set
            {
                testContextInstance = value;
            }
        }

        #region Additional test attributes
         [TestInitialize()]
         [SetUp]
         public void MyTestInitialize()
         {
             _userRegisterServiceClient =
               new HostWCFSrviceUnitTest.HostWCFService.UserRegisterServiceClient(
                 "WSHttpBinding_IUserRegisterService"
               );
         }
```

```
        #endregion

        [TestMethod]
        [Test]
        public void TestRegisterUser()
        {
            HostWCFService.User user = new HostWCFService.User();
            user.FirstName = "Henry";
            user.LastName = "Li";
            user.Password = "Hello Azure WCF host";
            _userRegisterServiceClient.AddUser(user);
        }

        [TestMethod]
        [Test]
        public void TestGetUserList()
        {
            TestRegisterUser();
            HostWCFService.User[] users =
              (HostWCFService.User[])_userRegisterServiceClient.GetUserList();
            Assert.IsTrue(users.Count<HostWCFService.User>() > 0 );
        }
    }
}
```

11. To test a single unit test case using the Visual Studio test framework, mouse over to the context of the specific test code body in Visual Studio and set a break point for debugging purposes as Figure 4-5 shows.

```
                HostWCFService.User[] users = (HostWCFService.User[])_userRegi
                Assert.IsTrue(users.Count<HostWCFService.User>() > 0);
        }
```

Figure 4-5. *Mouse over the test code body and right-click to bring up the context menu to run a single test case from the context in Visual Studio*

12. If you want to test the entire test suite you can simply press the F5 key or select Debug ➤ Start Debugging.

The program will stop at the break point, and an icon in the system tray will indicate that the WCF service has been hosted in `HostWCFService_WebRole`, as Figure 4-6 shows. Mouse over the variable `users`, and the instance watch dialog windows should display the data we have just added via the WCF service. The data is stored in the memory and is the local instance of `List<User> userList = new List<User>()` defined in the `UserRegisterService` class.

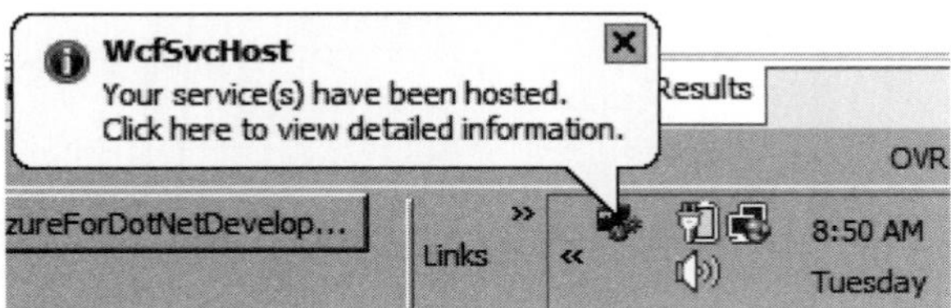

Figure 4-6. Icon from system tray shows the WCF service has been hosted from `HostWCFService_WebRole`

Verify HostWCFService from the Local Development Environment

Set `HostWCFService` as the startup project and run from Visual Studio by pressing F5. When the service host icon shows from the system tray as in Figure 4-6 and the instance is shown in the local fabric as shown in Figure 4-7, start Internet Explorer and enter `http://localhost:8080/UserRegisterService` in the address bar to retrieve the metadata from the service. The results are shown in Figure 4-8.

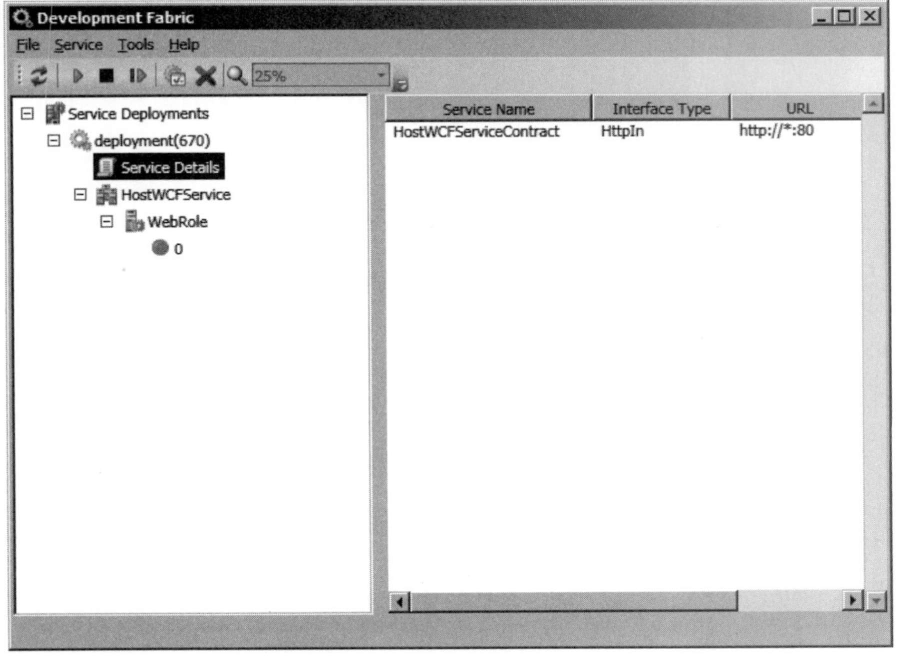

Figure 4-7. The WCF service is hosted from the local development cloud and run from the local fabric

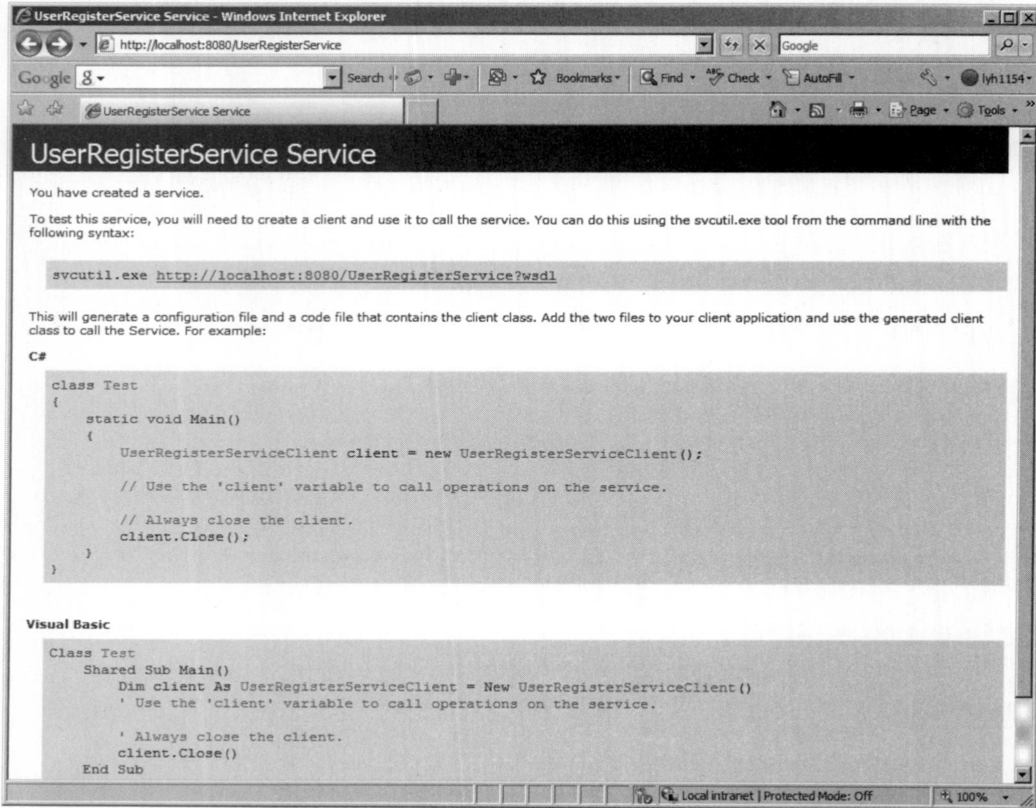

Figure 4-8. Metadata and WSDL retrieved from the WCF service

In Chapter 7 we are going to discuss hosting workflow services in cloud-based development.

Summary

In this chapter I introduced the concept of integrating applications using WCF and Windows Azure. WCF is a powerful tool for writing enterprise-class applications and makes loosely coupled applications easier to write and manage. Add to that the benefits of Windows Azure, and there are plenty of possibilities. A lot of the intricacies of WCF and Azure are beyond the scope of this book, so I simply showed you how to host a WCF service in the cloud. I demonstrated how other .NET applications (and even Java applications) will be able to take advantage of your cloud-based WCF services.

CHAPTER 5

■ ■ ■

Azure .NET Services—Access Control

Azure .NET Services contains a collection of three services: .NET Service Bus, .NET Workflow Service, and .NET Access Control Service. .NET Access Control Service is the core service, which provides the endpoint registration and access rules services for not only the other two .NET services of the service collection set but also SQL Azure (an additional cloud-based service from the Microsoft cloud-based service family, which is covered in Chapter 8), to access the cloud. To submit any application to the cloud you must go through the .NET Service Bus, and the .NET Service Bus relies on the .NET Access Control Service for securing access to cloud applications through a claims-based model. .NET Service Bus, the partner service of the Access Control Service, significantly simplifies the communication between applications and their clients. With .NET Service Bus, an application no longer needs to resolve the endpoint IP address from organizations. Instead it uses the IP address provided by the .NET Service Bus. At the time of this writing you cannot yet intuitively manage the registered endpoint address from .NET Access Control Service, meaning that you have no direct access to modify the low-level data of .NET Access Control Service yet.

.NET Access Control Service is built on the WCF services. You just need to specify the type of federation in configuration files. In this chapter, after an introduction to the .NET Access Control Service, we are going to provide exercises showing how to use WCF services in conjunction with the Azure portal, instead of the using the Azure Service Management Tools, to manage the .NET Access Control Service for cloud-based applications.

Working with the .NET Access Control Service

With the .NET Access Control Service, cloud-based applications or on-premises applications can federate authentication information and allow services to be called across the firewall. Whether the Azure application uses a security directory system, such as Active Directory or any standards-based infrastructure, the application responds as if the user's account were managed locally. Since the .NET Access Control Service supports using programming frameworks and web protocols, it offers an easy way for you to integrate an application with different platforms and architectures.

For most distributed applications, identity is a fundamental issue. The application needs information on the application's user to determine what they are allowed to do. Imagine that a single company has tens or hundreds of applications or services, and each application has its private storage for user identities, and each storage needs a particular approach to authentication. This turns out to be not only very expensive for a company to maintain but also extremely tedious work for application development and integration. The .NET Access Control Service provides an attractive approach to solve this problem. The concept uses a claims-based identity model to allow the common features of authentication and authorization to be provided by an external service. To reach that goal applications use the Security Assertion Markup Language (SAML) to claim SAML tokens. Each SAML token carries a piece of information about a user. For instance, one token contains user name information, while another token contains user role information. Tokens are generated by a program called Security Token Service (STS).

However, there is another challenge for this approach to address. A SAML token may not contain claims that the application is not expecting, and the services that generated the response token cannot be trusted by the application. A solution to this is to involve another STS in the process to ensure that all SAML tokens carry the correct claims and to perform the transformation to convert the SAML token into the application-trusted token based on the rules defined for the transformation. To ensure tokens are generated from a trusted STS, the .NET Access Control Service uses a federation mechanism to establish the trust relationship between the new STS and the one that generated the token; it runs the STS from the cloud to do the federation.

Figure 5-1 shows how the .NET Access Control Service provides claims transformation and identity federation. Figure 5-2 is the screenshot using the Azure Services Management Tool. From this screenshot we can see that two default rules have been assigned to each Azure development account. The claim name is "Action," with two associated values, "Listen" and "Send."

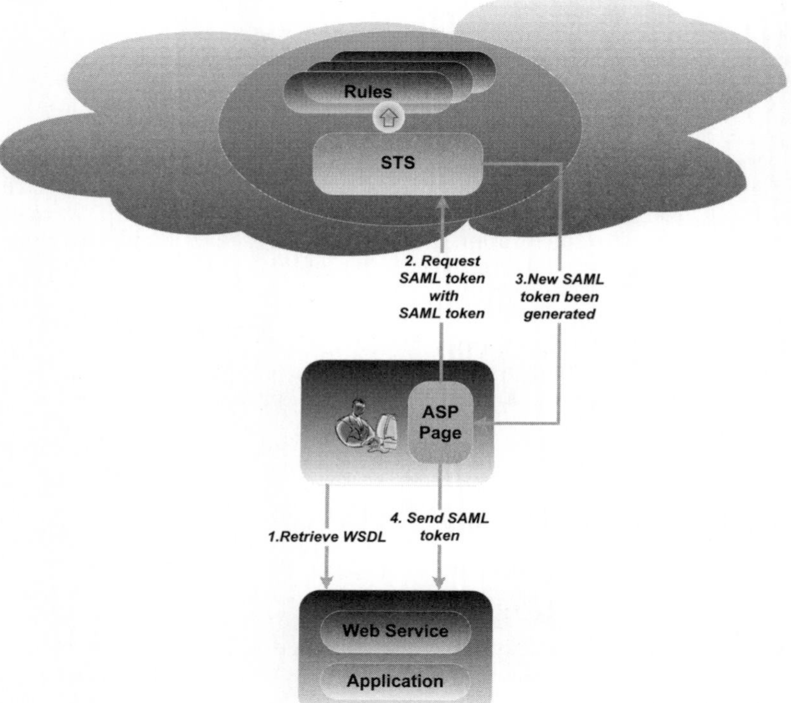

Figure 5-1. *Logic flow for the Access Control Service showing how it provides rule-based claims and identity federation*

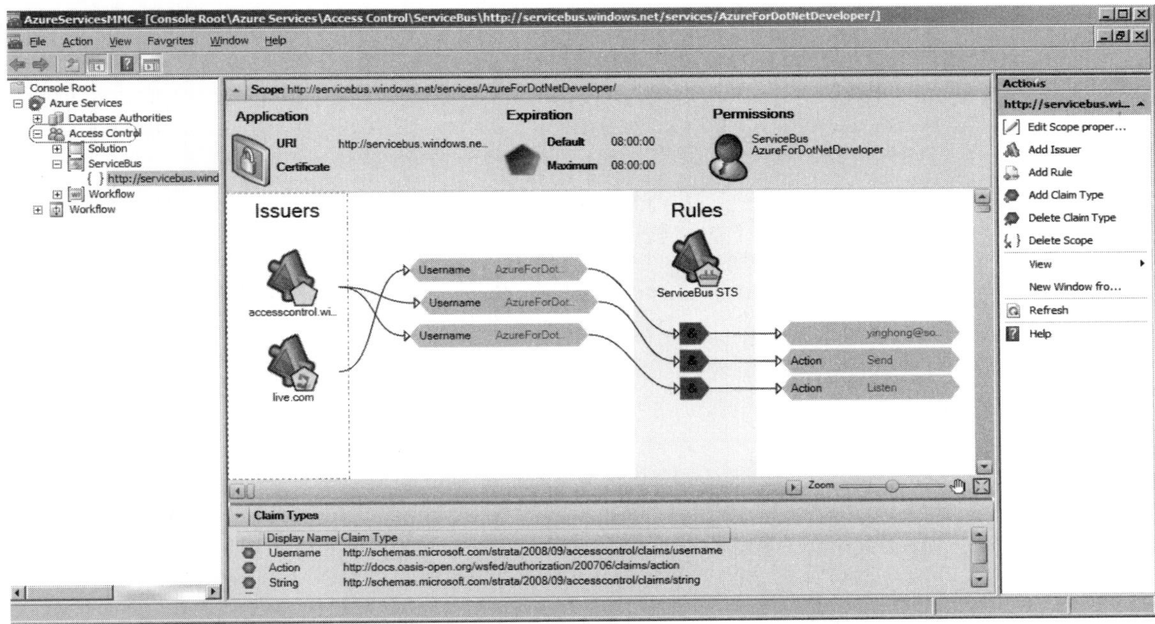

Figure 5-2. Screenshot of the rules currently assigned to my Azure development account using `AzureServiceMMC`

Build Your First Cloud Application Using the .NET Access Control Service

In this exercise, we are going to build a very simple WCF service, which supports duplex communication between server and client, and host it in a Windows console application. Using a local console application is the simplest way to host a service, which we use as our host to prove the concept.

■ **Note** The code for this example is in the Exercise 5-1 bundle from the code download.

---

1. Create a WCF service library project, `WCFServiceLibrary`. For this simple example, there is only one operation contract defined, `PingService`, which accepts a string parameter, which is posted from the client application. The implementation for this operation contract is very straightforward as shown in Listing 5-1; it simply returns the posted message back to the client. (Note that the attribute of the service declaration uses a namespace. A namespace can be given a hierarchical structure, and there is no restriction on the number of levels and name conventions. A `Relay` sublevel has been defined in the namespace in this example for us to reuse when we deal with the relay bindings.)

Listing 5-1. *WCF Service Contract Interface* `IAccountFederationService`

```
using System;
using System.Collections.Generic;
using System.Linq;
using System.Text;
using System.ServiceModel;

namespace AzureForDotNetDeveloper.DotNetService.ServiceBus.WCFServiceLibrary
{
[ServiceContract(Name = "IAccountFederationService",
                 Namespace = "http://SoftnetSolutions.com/ServiceModel/Relay/")]
    public interface IAccountFederationService
    {
        [OperationContract]
        string PingServer(string message);
    }
}

using System;
using System.Collections.Generic;
using System.Linq;
using System.Text;
using System.ServiceModel;
using System.Diagnostics;

namespace AzureForDotNetDeveloper.DotNetService.ServiceBus.WCFServiceLibrary
{
    [ServiceBehavior(Name = "AccountFederationService",
                     Namespace = "http://SoftnetSolutions.com/ServiceModel/Relay/")]
    public class AccountFederationService : IAccountFederationService
    {
        public string PingServer(string message)
        {
            string results =
              string.Format(
                        "---{0}:PingServer, message received from client : {1}{2}",
                        this.ToString(),
                        Environment.NewLine,
                        message
              );
```

```
            Console.WriteLine(results);
            Trace.WriteLine(results);
            return message;
        }

        #region Console Utilities

        static public string ProcessPassword()
        {
            StringBuilder password = new StringBuilder();

            ConsoleKeyInfo info = Console.ReadKey(true);
            while (info.Key != ConsoleKey.Enter)
            {
                if (info.Key == ConsoleKey.Backspace)
                {
                    if (password.Length != 0)
                    {
                        password.Remove(password.Length - 1, 1);
                        Console.Write("\b \b");
                    }
                }
                else if (info.KeyChar >= ' ')
                {
                    password.Append(info.KeyChar);
                    Console.Write("*");
                }
                info = Console.ReadKey(true);
            }

            Console.WriteLine();
            Console.Write(
              string.Format(
                "--- Please sit back and wait for your account to be authenticated
from .Net access service {0}{0}...{0}",
                Environment.NewLine
              )
            );

            return password.ToString();
        }

        #endregion
    }
}
```

2. Define a client communication channel interface `IAccountFederationClientChannel` derived from the interface `System.ServiceModel.IClientChannel` in order to do the duplex communication. The code is shown in Listing 5-2. This listing is for the implementation of the `Main()` function of the host application.

Listing 5-2. WCF Client Channel Service Contract Definition

```
using System;
using System.Collections.Generic;
using System.Linq;
using System.Text;
using System.ServiceModel;

namespace AzureForDotNetDeveloper.DotNetService.ServiceBus.WCFServiceLibrary
{
    public interface IAccountFederationClientChannel :
      IAccountFederationService, IClientChannel { }
}
```

3. Next, we are going to build a console application to host the WCF service. As Listing 5-3 shows, we need to do the following steps to the initialization on the server side.

    1. Create a endpoint URI. The URI address for the .NET Access Control Service is `sb://servicebus.windows.net/services/AzureForDotNetDeveloper/[SolutionName]`.

    2. Define a `TransportClientEndpointBehavior` instance. This instance takes the user credential information. Currently the .NET Access Control Service accepts three types of credential: Solution Password, Windows CardSpace Information Card, and X.509 Certificates. In this example we use the user name and password for credential information. The user name is the solution name used to create a solution in the cloud via the portal. The password is the password to the solution. Follow the steps shown in Listing 5-3 to construct the transport client endpoint behavior instances.

    3. Construct a host instance. The host instance takes the WCF service implementation class type for instantiation. The syntax is as follows and is also shown in Listing 5-3.

```
ServiceHost host = new ServiceHost(typeof(AccountFederationService), address);
```

    4. Add the authentication token, username, and password to the endpoint. Once the host instance has been instantiated, the endpoint needs to be bound to the service behavior.

    5. Start services. When the user credential information has been sent to the .NET Access Control Service for authentication, the process we saw illustrated in Figure 5-1 runs its course. Note that in order to use the URI of the .NET Access Control Service, two namespace declarations—`Microsoft.ServiceBus` and `Microsoft.ServiceBus.Description`—must be inserted into the `using` clause section to distinguish the URI from the WCF `System.ServiceModel` namespace. References to the assembly `Microsoft.ServiceBus.dll` must also be added to the project. This assembly can be found in the Microsoft .NET Services SDK `Assemblies` folder. You call `host.Open()` to start services and `host.Close()` to close up the service when the user presses the key to stop the service.

Listing 5-3. A Console Application Server Host Implementation Used to Host the Authentication WCF Services

```
using System;
using System.ServiceModel;
using System.ServiceModel.Description;
using Microsoft.ServiceBus;
using Microsoft.ServiceBus.Description;
using System.Text;

namespace AzureForDotNetDeveloper.DotNetService.ServiceBus
{
    using AzureForDotNetDeveloper.DotNetService.ServiceBus.WCFServiceLibrary;

    class Program
    {
        static void Main(string[] args)
        {
               Console.Write(
                 string.Format(
                   "--- WCF Service local host --- {0}--- Please enter your Azure Solution
Name:{0}",
                   Environment.NewLine
                 )
               );
               string solutionName = Console.ReadLine();
               Console.Write(string.Format("--- Solution Password: {0}",
                              Environment.NewLine));
               string solutionPassword = AccountFederationService.ProcessPassword();

               Uri address =
                 new Uri(String.Format("sb://{0}/services/{1}/AuthenticationService/",
                         ServiceBusEnvironment.DefaultRelayHostName, solutionName));
               TransportClientEndpointBehavior userNamePasswordServiceBusCredential =
                 new TransportClientEndpointBehavior();
               userNamePasswordServiceBusCredential.CredentialType =
                 TransportClientCredentialType.UserNamePassword;
               userNamePasswordServiceBusCredential.Credentials.UserName.UserName =
                 solutionName;
               userNamePasswordServiceBusCredential.Credentials.UserName.Password =
                 solutionPassword;

               ServiceHost host =
                 new ServiceHost(typeof(AccountFederationService), address);

               //add the Service Bus credentials to all endpoints specified in configuration
               foreach (ServiceEndpoint endpoint in host.Description.Endpoints)
               {
                   endpoint.Behaviors.Add(userNamePasswordServiceBusCredential);
               }

               host.Open();
```

```
                Console.WriteLine(
                  string.Format(
                    "--- Authentication success from .Net access service.{1}Service address:
{1}{0}{1}",
                    address,
                    Environment.NewLine
                  )
                );
                Console.WriteLine(
                  string.Format(
                  "--- Ready to receive message...{0} Press <Enter> to terminate server ---",
                  Environment.NewLine
                  )
                );

                Console.ReadLine();

                host.Close();
            }
        }
}
```

4. Add a configuration file to the project and insert configuration information as Listing 5-4 shows.

Listing 5-4. *Configuration for Service Host*

```
<?xml version="1.0" encoding="utf-8" ?>
<configuration>
  <system.serviceModel>
    <services>
      <service name="AzureForDotNetDeveloper.DotNetService.ServiceBus➥
.WCFServiceLibrary.AccountFederationService">
        <endpoint contract="AzureForDotNetDeveloper.DotNetService.ServiceBus➥
.WCFServiceLibrary.IAccountFederationService"
                  binding="netTcpRelayBinding" />
      </service>
    </services>
  </system.serviceModel>
<configuration>
```

5. Create a new Windows console application to be a test client as Listing 5-5 shows. The implementation URI for the client is the same as the server. We use the `ChannelFactory` class provided by `System.ServiceModel` to instantiate a client channel WCF service instance used to send an acknowledgement message back to the server. As we did for the server host program, the namespace `Microsoft.ServiceBus` and the reference to assembly `Microsoft.ServiceBus.dll` need to be added to the project as well. Note that when creating the client channel factory, the relay

endpoint needs to be specified because the authentication for the client application to use the WCF service endpoint is through the relay from the server endpoint.

Listing 5-5. *Implementation for Client Application*

```
using System;
using System.ServiceModel;
using Microsoft.ServiceBus;

namespace AzureForDotNetDeveloper.DotNetService.ServiceBus
{
    using AzureForDotNetDeveloper.DotNetService.ServiceBus.WCFServiceLibrary;

    class Program
    {
        static void Main(string[] args)
        {
            Console.Write(
              string.Format(
                "--- Test Client--- {0}--- Please enter your Azure Solution Name:{0} ",
                Environment.NewLine
              )
            );
            string solutionName = Console.ReadLine();
            Console.Write(string.Format("--- Solution Password: {0}",
                          Environment.NewLine));
            string solutionPassword = AccountFederationService.ProcessPassword();

            // create the service URI based on the solution name
            Uri serviceUri =
              new Uri(String.Format("sb://{0}/services/{1}/AuthenticationService/",
                      ServiceBusEnvironment.DefaultRelayHostName, solutionName));
            TransportClientEndpointBehavior userNamePasswordServiceBusCredential =
              new TransportClientEndpointBehavior();
            userNamePasswordServiceBusCredential.CredentialType =
              TransportClientCredentialType.UserNamePassword;
            userNamePasswordServiceBusCredential.Credentials.UserName.UserName =
              solutionName;
            userNamePasswordServiceBusCredential.Credentials.UserName.Password =
              solutionPassword;

            //create the channel factory loading the configuration
            ChannelFactory<IAccountFederationClientChannel> channelFactory =
              new ChannelFactory<IAccountFederationClientChannel> ("RelayEndpoint",
                                                                   new
EndpointAddress(serviceUri));

            //apply the Service Bus credentials
            channelFactory.Endpoint.Behaviors.Add(userNamePasswordServiceBusCredential);
```

```
            // create and open the client channel
            IAccountFederationClientChannel channel = channelFactory.CreateChannel();
            channel.Open();

            Console.WriteLine(string.Format("--- Please type message to ping service:{0}",
                              Environment.NewLine));
            string inputMessage = Console.ReadLine();
            while (inputMessage != String.Empty)
            {
                try
                {
                    Console.WriteLine("--- Receive response from Server: {0}",
                                      channel.PingServer(inputMessage));
                }
                catch (Exception e)
                {
                    Console.WriteLine(
                      string.Format("--- Test Client:Program, exception caught :{0}",
                                    e.Message));
                }
                inputMessage = Console.ReadLine();
            }

            channel.Close();
            channelFactory.Close();
        }
    }
}
```

6. Add `App.config` to the client application and input the binding information as Listing 5-6 shows.

Listing 5-6. *Configuration for Client Application*

```
<?xml version="1.0" encoding="utf-8" ?>
<configuration>
  <system.serviceModel>
    <services>
<service name="AzureForDotNetDeveloper.DotNetService.ServiceBus➥
.WCFServiceLibrary.AccountFederationService">
<endpoint contract="AzureForDotNetDeveloper.DotNetService.ServiceBus➥
.WCFServiceLibrary.IAccountFederationService"
        binding="netTcpRelayBinding" />
      </service>
    </services>
  </system.serviceModel>
</configuration>
```

To start the server application, we are going to enter the Azure solution name and password, which will be used to do the authentication by the .NET Access Control Service. When the .NET Access Control Service has finished authenticating the request, the server is running to listen for the message posted to the endpoint.

One thing that needs to be clear is that the custom service we host is running from the local machine, but the access is controlled and established through the endpoints from remote Azure services. This can be verified by the atom feed automatically assigned to every service by Azure services from the Azure portal page. Go to the Azure portal at `http://portal.ex.azure.microsoft.com/` and log on to the .NET Services Bus. Figure 5-3 shows how to access the feed, and Figure 5-4 shows our service as expected.

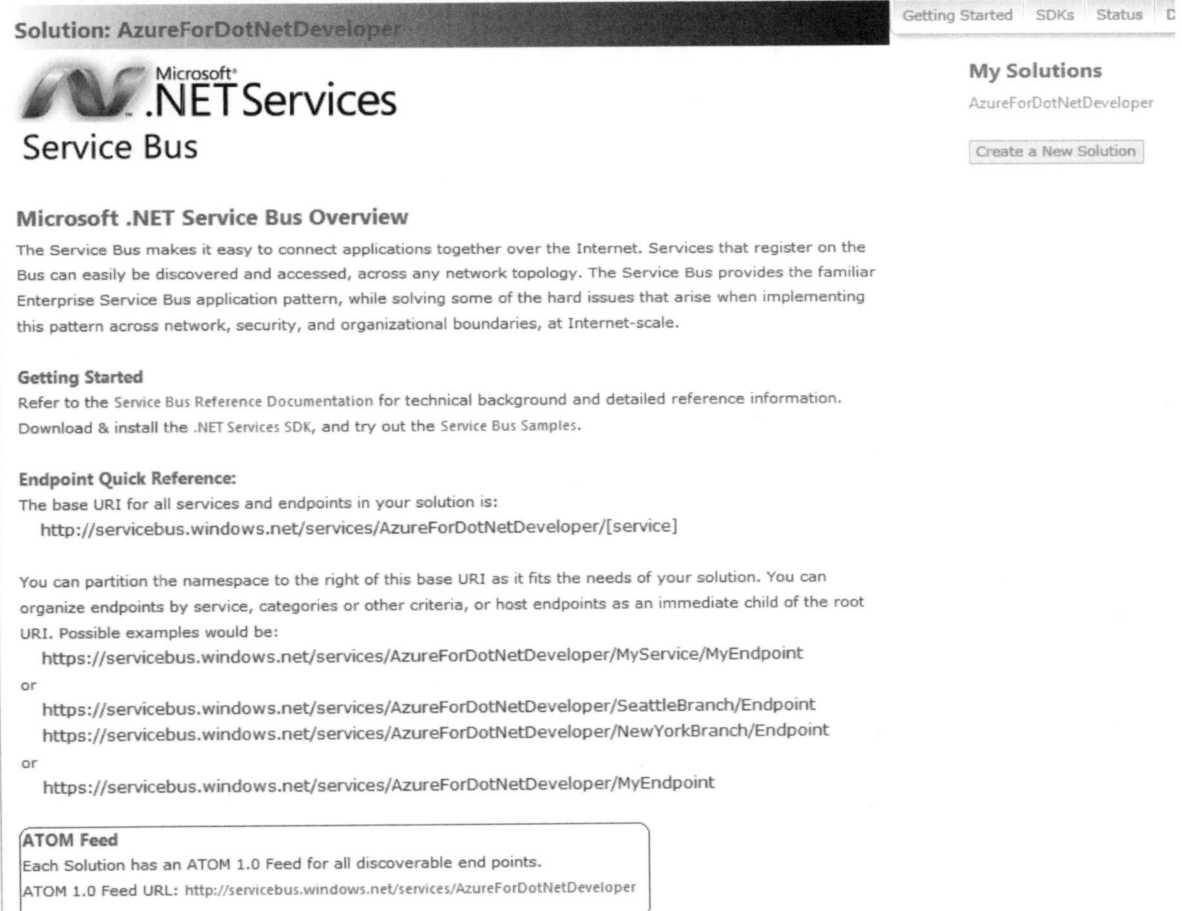

***Figure 5-3.** The Atom feed for our service*

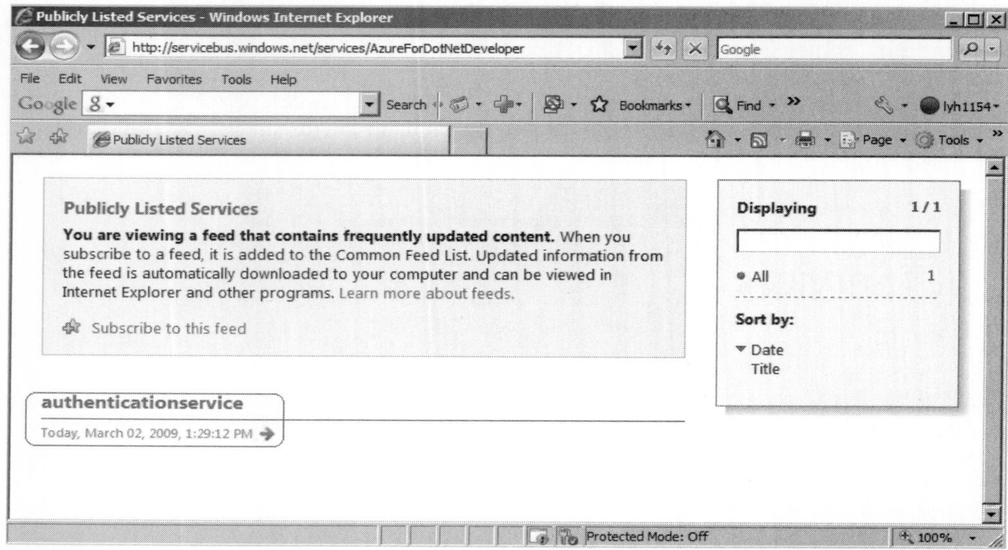

Figure 5-4. Verifying that the WCF service is leveraging .NET Access Control Service

Start the client application and enter the solution name and password. Send a message from the client, and the server sends back acknowledgement information.

Finally, close both client and server applications. Go back to the Azure portal. We can see that the endpoint is also removed from Azure as Figure 5-5 shows.

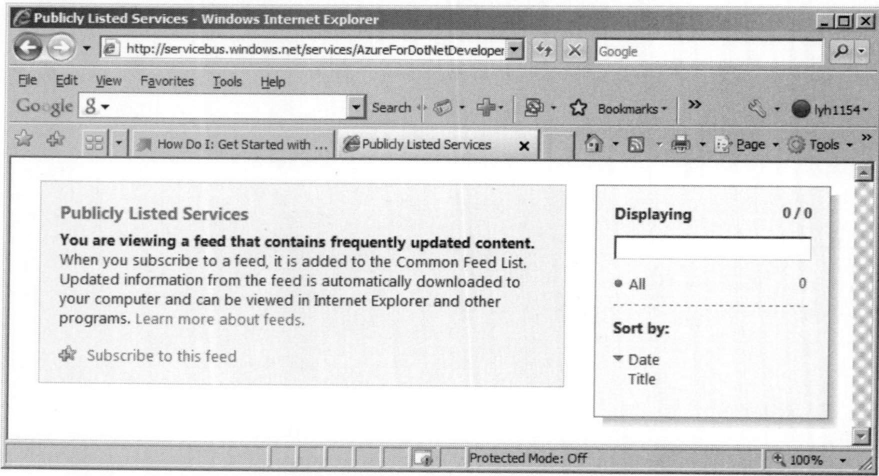

Figure 5-5. The service endpoint has been removed from Azure when the service is closed

This exercise demonstrates how to tremendously simplify authentication by using the .NET Access Control Service from the cloud; all you need to do is deal with the configuration.

The .NET Access Control Service redirected the service call back to the local machine, where the service is also hosted; in so doing, it crossed the Internet and reached behind the local machine's firewall. The client application has not even noticed that it actually invoked a WCF service host. This is really a gift to all .NET developers.

CardSpace .Net Access Control Services

In the previous exercise we used the user name and password as security credentials. This is just an alternate approach to access security. In this exercise we explore the .NET Access Control Service with CardSpace security and learn how the token claim and STS work from the .NET Access Control Service. Be mentally prepared that there is heavy local and remote configuration involved to reach that goal.

This exercise is divided into two sections. The first section is the fundamental step that needs to be done before we move to the second section. The source code for the first section is separated from that for the second section. The file name of the source code is `Exercise_5_2_1.zip`, which can be downloaded from the download site of the book. The source code for the second section is `Exercise_5_2.zip`, which can also be found in the same location as the previous one.

In the first section we are going to create three projects: a WCF services project `AzureForDotNetDeveloperWCFserviceLibrary`, a service host project `Service`, and a client project `Client`. This is a typical WCF client-server solution without using the .NET Access Control Service and security access.

AzureForDotNetDeveloperWCFserviceLibrary

In this project we'll define a simple WCF service contract interface. This interface has three methods declared: `Ping()`, `RegisterUser()`, and `GetRegisteredUser()`. The service is a simulation service to handle user registration to a site. The source code is shown in Listing 5-7, the implementation for this interface is shown Listing 5-8, and the configuration is shown in Listing 5-9. There is nothing special except that the decorated attribute parameter `InstanceContextMode` of `ServiceBehavior` is assigned a value of `Single`, which means using a singleton pattern for service calls because we need to share the service instance in order to return the information of the last registered user.

The attribute values to the `GetRegisteredUser()` operation contract, `Action` and `ReplayAction`, are used by the WCF service to dispatch an input or output message to an appropriate handler method. In this example there is no output handler, so the reply attributes do not trigger any action and can be removed from the code. It won't cause any trouble though if you leave it alone. For more information about `Action` and `ReplayAction` see `http://msdn.microsoft.com/en-us/library/system.servicemodel.operationcontractattribute.replyaction.aspx`.

Listing 5-7. *Service Contact `IAzureForDotNetDeveloper` and Data Contract User*

```
using System;
using System.Runtime.Serialization;
using System.ServiceModel;
using System.ServiceModel.Channels;

namespace AzureForDotNetDeveloper.DotNetService.ServiceBus
```

```
{
[ServiceContract(Name = "UserRegisterService",
                 Namespace = "http://AzureForDotNetDeveloper.DotNetService.ServiceBus")]
    public interface IAzureForDotNetDeveloperWCFservice
    {
        [OperationContract(Action = "Ping", ReplyAction = "PingResponse")]
        string Ping();

        [OperationContract(Action = "RegisterUser", ReplyAction = "AddUserResponse")]
        void RegisterUser(string xmlString);

        [OperationContract(Action = "GetRegisteredUser",
                           ReplyAction = "GetUserListResponse")]
        string GetRegisteredUser();
    }

    [DataContract]
    public class User
    {
        [DataMember]
        public string FirstName;

        [DataMember]
        public string LastName;

        [DataMember]
        public DateTime TimeRegistered;

        [DataMember]
        public string Password;
    }
}
```

Listing 5-8. *Implementations for IAzureForDotNetDeveloperWCFService*

```
using System;
using System.Runtime.Serialization;
using System.ServiceModel;
using System.ServiceModel.Channels;
using System.Collections.Generic;
using System.IO;
using System.Xml;
using System.Xml.Serialization;
using System.Text;

namespace AzureForDotNetDeveloper.DotNetService.ServiceBus
{

    [ServiceBehavior(InstanceContextMode = InstanceContextMode.Single)]
    public class AzureForDotNetDeveloperWCFservice : IAzureForDotNetDeveloperWCFservice
    {
```

```
        private User _registeredUser = null;

        #region IUserRegisterService Members

        public string Ping()
        {
            return string.Format("--- I am here <{0}>", this.ToString());
        }

        public void RegisterUser(string xmlString)
        {
            try
            {
                XmlDocument xmlDoc = new XmlDocument();
                xmlDoc.LoadXml(xmlString);
                XmlSerializer serializer = new XmlSerializer(typeof(User));
                StringReader reader = new StringReader(xmlString);

                _registeredUser = (User)serializer.Deserialize(reader);
            }
            catch (Exception ex)
            {
            }
        }

        public string GetRegisteredUser()
        {
            XmlSerializer serializer = new XmlSerializer(typeof(User));
            StringBuilder sb = new StringBuilder();
            StringWriter writer = new StringWriter(sb);

            serializer.Serialize(writer, _registeredUser);
            return writer.GetStringBuilder().ToString();
        }

        #endregion
    }
}
```

Service Implementations and Configurations

The following is the implementation of the server (Listing 5-9) and its configuration (Listing 5-10).

Listing 5-9. *Implementations for Service Host*

```
using System;
using System.Security.Cryptography.X509Certificates;
using System.ServiceModel;
using System.ServiceModel.Description;
```

```
namespace AzureForDotNetDeveloper.DotNetService.ServiceBus
{
    class Program
    {
        static void Main(string[] args)
        {
            ServiceHost host = new  ServiceHost(typeof(AzureForDotNetDeveloperWCFservice));
            host.Open();

            Console.WriteLine("---UserRegister service is running.");
            Console.WriteLine("---Press <Enter> to terminate server");
            Console.ReadLine();

            host.Close();
        }

        private static string ReadSolutionName()
        {
            Console.Write(
              string.Format(
                "---Please enter your solution name: {0}",
                Environment.NewLine
              )
            );
            return Console.ReadLine();
        }

    }
}
```

Listing 5-10. *Configurations for Service Host*

```
<?xml version="1.0" encoding="utf-8" ?>
<configuration>
  <system.serviceModel>
    <bindings>
      <basicHttpBinding>
        <binding name="basicHttpBinding1" />
      </basicHttpBinding>
    </bindings>
    <services>
      <service behaviorConfiguration="UserRegisterServiceBehavior"
               name="AzureForDotNetDeveloper.DotNetService.ServiceBus➥
.AzureForDotNetDeveloperWCFservice">
        <endpoint address=""
                  binding="basicHttpBinding"
                  bindingConfiguration=""
                  name="UserRegisterEndpoint"
                  contract="AzureForDotNetDeveloper.DotNetService.ServiceBus➥
.IAzureForDotNetDeveloperWCFservice" />
        <endpoint address="mex"
```

```
                binding="mexHttpBinding"
                name="mexEndpoint"
         contract="IMetadataExchange" />
        <host>
          <baseAddresses>
            <add baseAddress="http://localhost/AzureForDotNetDeveloperWCFservice" />
          </baseAddresses>
        </host>
      </service>
    </services>

    <behaviors>
      <serviceBehaviors>
        <behavior name="UserRegisterServiceBehavior">
          <serviceMetadata httpGetEnabled="True"
             httpGetUrl="http://localhost/AzureForDotNetDeveloperWCFservice/wsdl" />
        </behavior>
      </serviceBehaviors>
    </behaviors>
  </system.serviceModel>
</configuration>
```

Client Implementations and Configurations

The client proxy class needs to be generated from Visual Studio. Compile the server and start the server. When the server is running, right-click on the client project References node and select Add Service Reference from the context menu to bring up the Add Service Reference dialog windows. As Figure 5-6 shows, enter the service address `http://localhost/AzureForDotNetDeveloperWCFservice` in the address text box, and the name of the client class in the namespace text box to generate the client proxy class.

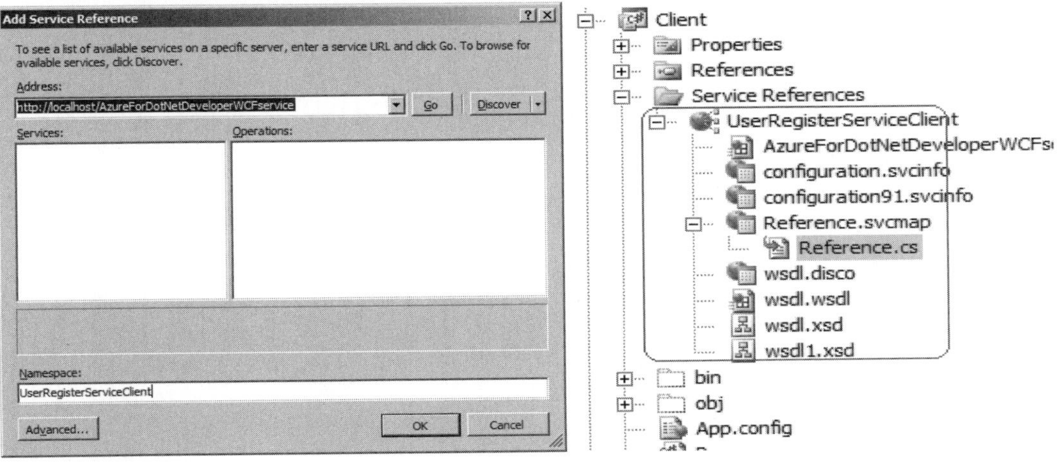

Figure 5-6. *Run server and generate the client proxy class from Visual Studio*

The following is the client implementation using the proxy.

Listing 5-11. Using the Proxy in a Client Implementation

```
static void Main(string[] args)
{
    UserRegisterServiceClient.UserRegisterServiceClient client =
      new UserRegisterServiceClient.UserRegisterServiceClient();

    try
    {
        Console.WriteLine(string.Format("--- Ping server return = <{0}>{1}",
            client.Ping(),
            Environment.NewLine));

        User user = new User();
        user.FirstName = "Henry";
        user.LastName = "Li";
        user.Password = "Hello Azure WCF host";
        user.TimeRegistered = DateTime.Now;
        XmlSerializer serializer = new XmlSerializer(user.GetType());
        StringBuilder sb = new StringBuilder();
        StringWriter writer = new StringWriter(sb);

        serializer.Serialize(writer, user);
        client.RegisterUser(writer.GetStringBuilder().ToString());

        string xmlString = client.GetRegisteredUser();
        XmlSerializer deSerializer = new XmlSerializer(typeof(User));
        StringReader stringReader = new StringReader(xmlString);

        User registeredUser = (User)serializer.Deserialize(stringReader);
        Console.WriteLine(
            string.Format("--- User <{0} {1}> register success @[{2}].{3}",
            registeredUser.FirstName,
            registeredUser.LastName,
            registeredUser.TimeRegistered.ToString(),
            Environment.NewLine));

    }
    catch (Exception e)
    {
        DumpException(e);
    }

    client.Close();

    Console.WriteLine();
    Console.WriteLine("Press <ENTER> to exit client.");
    Console.ReadLine();
}
```

```
static void DumpException(Exception e)
{
    Console.WriteLine(e.Message);
}
```

Test Results for What We Have Built

At this point we have done the first section of development. Let's test what we have so far. Start the server if it is not running yet; in this case we have the server running as `localhost`. Now enter the service address `http://localhost/AzureForDotNetDeveloperWCFservice` in a browser; we should see the results as Figure 5-7 shows. Run the client program, and we should have results as in Figure 5-8.

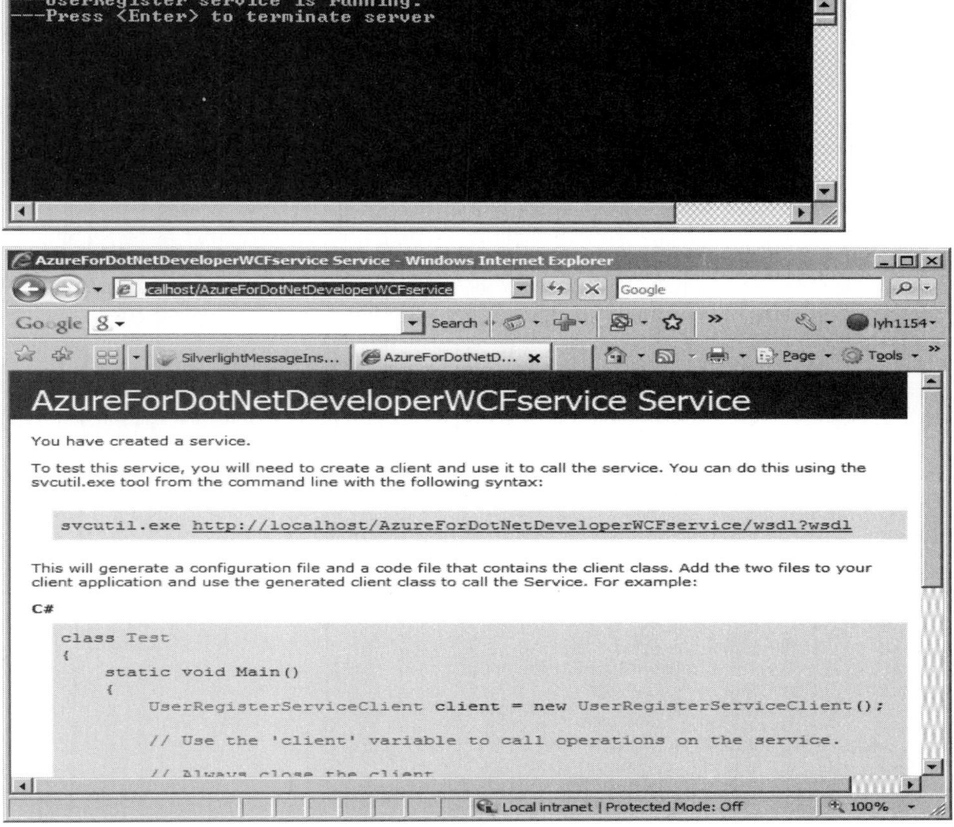

Figure 5-7. Run the server and use Internet Explorer to verify that the service has been created

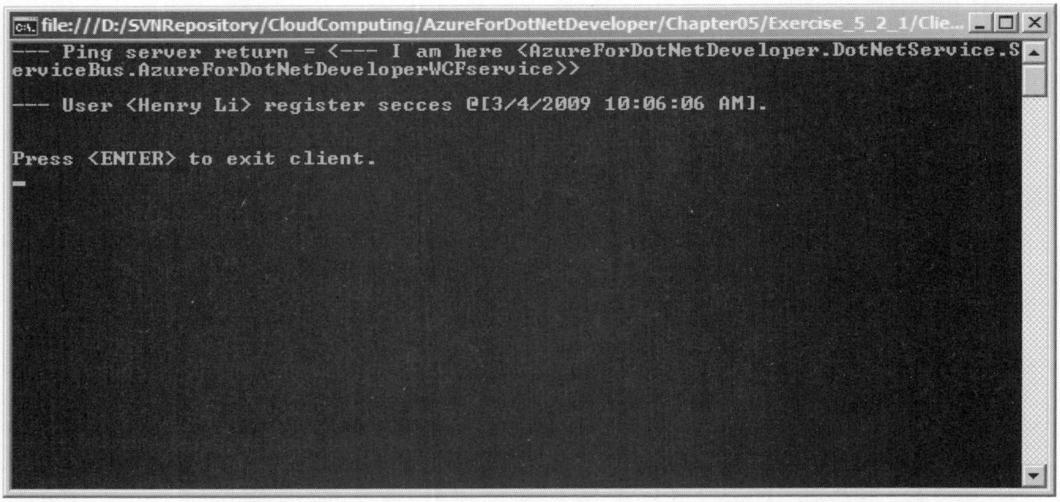

```
file:///D:/SVNRepository/CloudComputing/AzureForDotNetDeveloper/Chapter05/Exercise_5_2_1/Clie...
--- Ping server return = <--- I am here <AzureForDotNetDeveloper.DotNetService.S
erviceBus.AzureForDotNetDeveloperWCFservice>>

--- User <Henry Li> register secces @[3/4/2009 10:06:06 AM].

Press <ENTER> to exit client.
```

Figure 5-8. *Run the client; we have the echo from the server, and a user has been registered successfully*

The Access Control Service can provide authentication interactively using CardSpace. This approach will be covered at the end of this exercise. Alternatively, the authentication can be done using X.509 certification. Both approaches require that the client application preregister client-side information in the Azure cloud environment. Before we move forward to discuss the Access Control Service using X.509 and CardSpace authentication, we have to do some configuration in the local development environment.

Authentication Using X.509 Certification or CardSpace in .NET Access Control Service

Let's start the process by installing the X.509 certificate.

Installing the X.509 Certificate

The source code of this exercise (`Exercise_5_2`) contains a generated certificate file called `localhost.cer`, which can be found in the subfolder `Certificate` after unzipping the source code as Figure 5-9 shows.

■ **Note** To generate a new certificate you need to use the certificate enrollment service. Since Windows Vista/7 and Windows Server 2008 are designed as high-security operating systems, by default this service is disabled from Windows Vista/7 and Windows Server 2008. If the operating system from your local development is either Windows Vista/7 or Windows Server 2008, the easiest workaround to this issue is to request a new certificate from another computer that runs Window XP or Windows Server 2003. (You can reference the following article from The Code Project to request a new certificate using Windows XP or Windows 2003: `http://69.10.233.10/kb/wcf/wcf_certificates.aspx`. For troubleshooting the certificate enrollment, see `http://blogs.msdn.com/windowsvistanow/archive/2008/04/08/troubleshooting-certificate-enrollment.aspx`.)

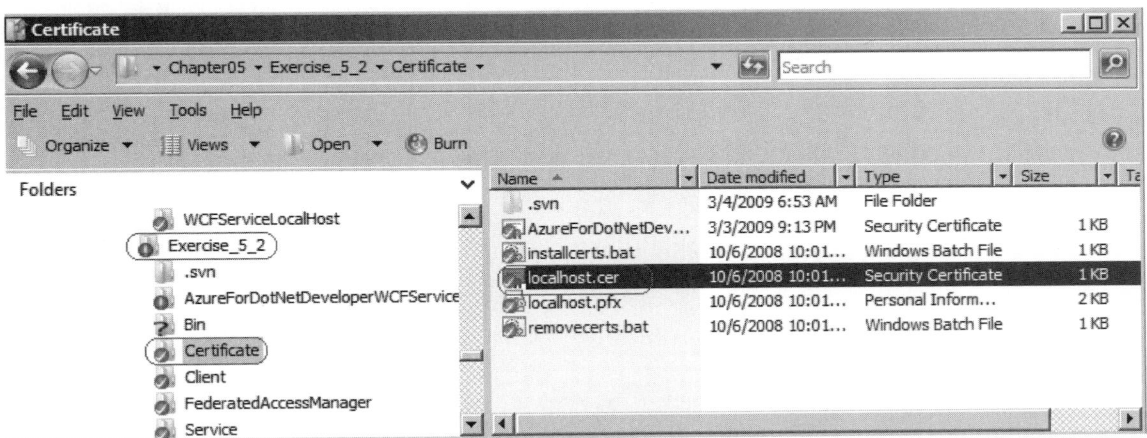

Figure 5-9. *Locate the certificate file that will be associated with the scope of an Azure solution in .NET Access Control Service*

Find that file, right-click it, and select Install Certificate. Follow the steps shown in Figure 5-10 to install the certificate in the Trusted Root Certificate Authorities/Local Computer/Certificates store. The results are shown in Figure 5-11.

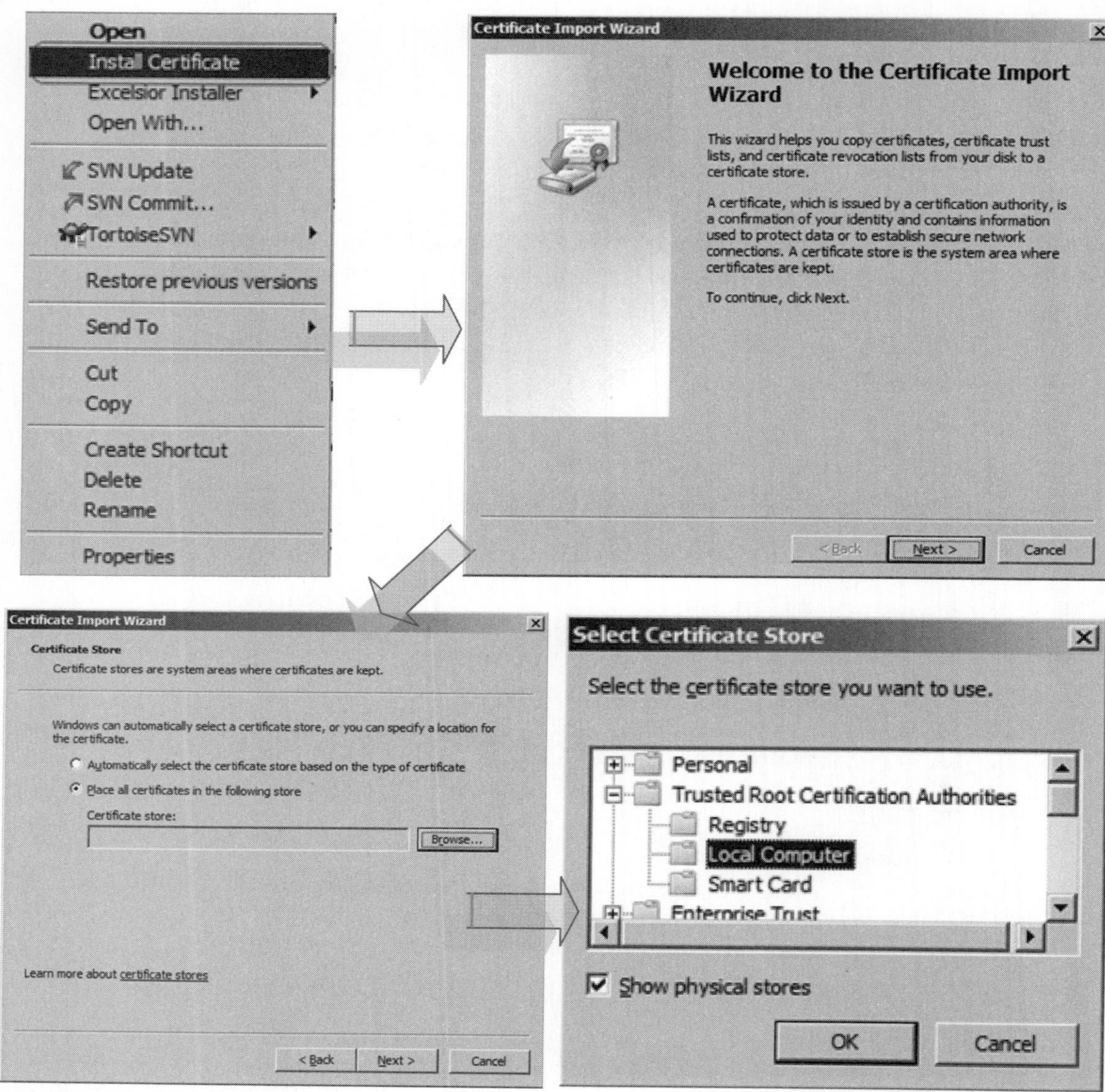

Figure 5-10. Import certificate using `certmgr.exe`

Click the Windows Start button and type “mmc” in the search bar to find the utility program `mmc.exe`, and bring up the snap-in management console. From the File menu, select the `certmgr.msc` certificate management snap-in.

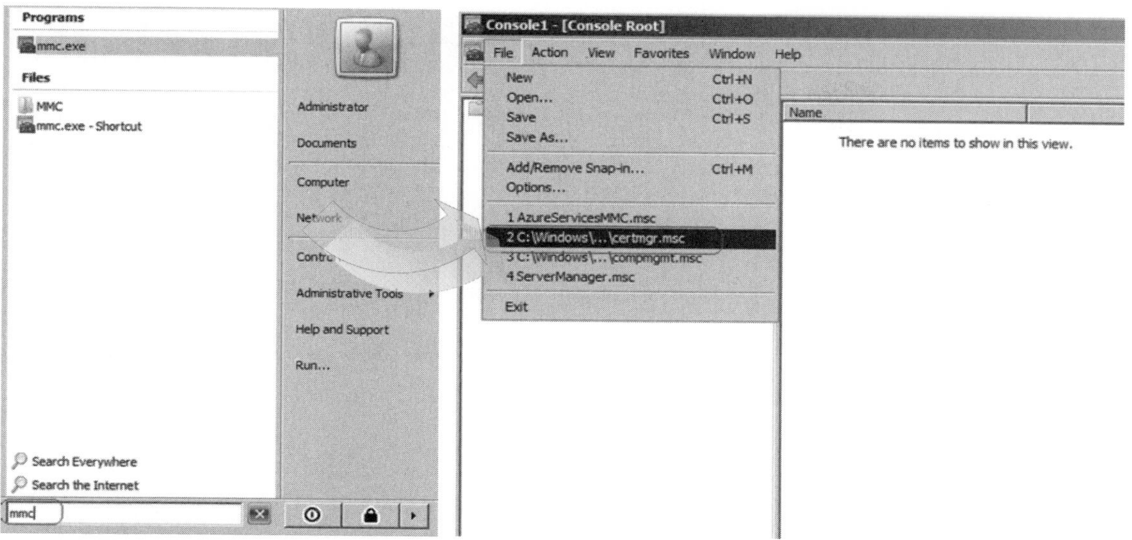

Figure 5-11. Start `certmgr.msc` *Windows snap-in certificate management tool*

Figure 5-12 shows the results after the certificate has been installed successfully. Follow the arrow to get the detailed information of the Thumbprint and copy the data to the "<behavior>" section of the Service project configuration file `App.config` as shown in the boldface lines in Listing 5-12.

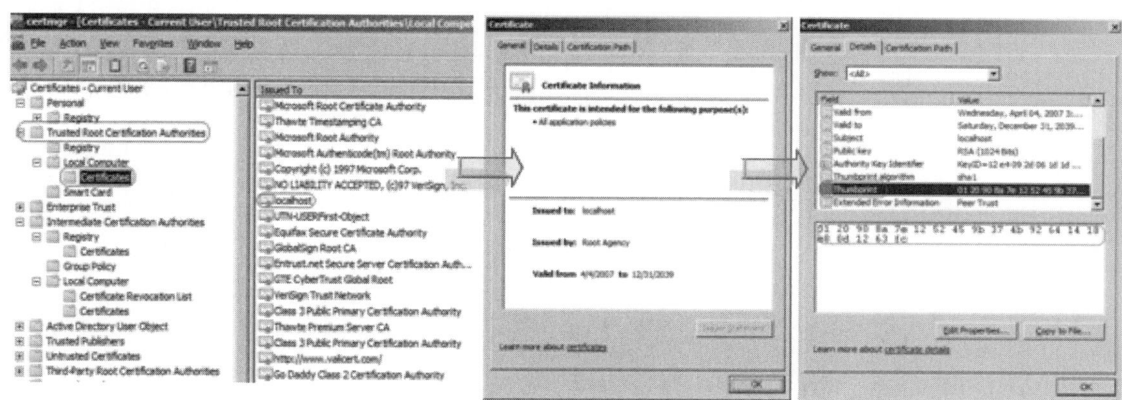

Figure 5-12. Certificate has been installed to Trust Root Certificate Authorities, Local Computer store

Listing 5-12. *Insert the Data of the Installed Certificate Thumbprint Information in the Configuration File* `App.config` *of the Service Project*

```
<behaviors>
  <serviceBehaviors>
    <behavior name="UserRegisterServiceBehavior">
      <serviceMetadata httpGetEnabled="True"
               httpGetUrl="http://localhost/AzureForDotNetDeveloperWCFservice/wsdl" />
      <serviceDebug includeExceptionDetailInFaults="True" />
      <serviceCredentials>
        <clientCertificate>
          <authentication certificateValidationMode="True" />
        </clientCertificate>
        <serviceCertificate storeLocation='LocalMachine'
          storeName='My'
          x509FindType='FindByThumbprint'
          findValue='01 20 90 8a 7e 12 52 45 9b 37 4b 92 64 14 18 e8 0d 12 63 fc' />
      </serviceCredentials>
    </behavior>
  </serviceBehaviors>
</behaviors>
```

Associating the Certificate to the Azure Application URL

To associate an installed X.509 on a client-side machine to the Azure cloud you use the registration process. The installed certification can be exported into a file of the `.pfx` format via the certificate management snap-in tool we used above. The file exported with the extension `.pfx` contains the certificate information and a corresponding private key (for CA-issued certification of a self-signed certificate). This exercise's code also provides the exported `.pfx` certificate file, which can be found in the same folder as the `localhost.cer` file. In the next section I am going to walk you through this procedure step by step.

To associate a certificate with an Azure application:

1. Sign in to the Azure portal and navigate to X.509 Certificates in .NET Access Control and select the Basic configuration as Figure 5-13 shows.
2. On the X.509 Certificates setup page, enter the endpoint address of the WCF services.
3. Uncheck the box labeled "Retrieve certificate from URL (http or https)" and select Browse.

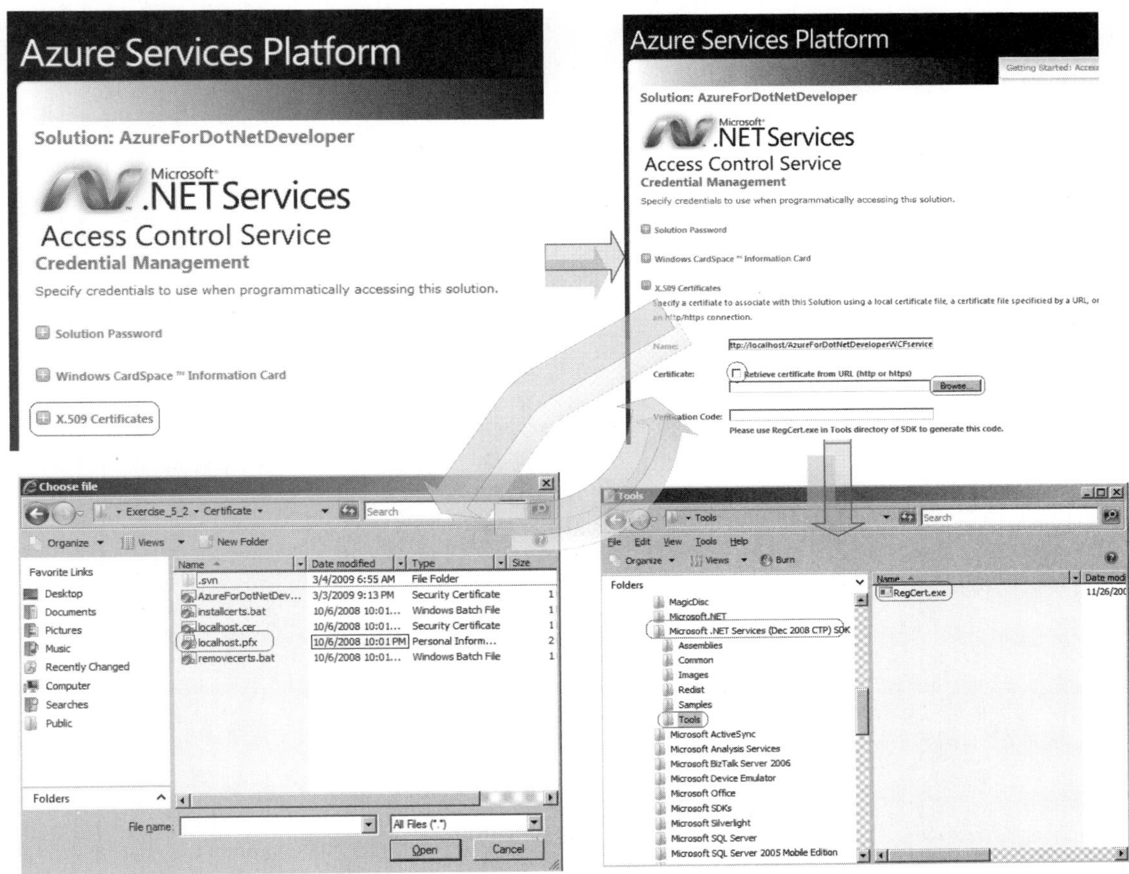

Figure 5-13. On the X.509 certificate setup page enter the endpoint of the service and select Browse to find `Regcert.exe`

4. Navigate to the Microsoft .NET Services SDK `Tools` folder and launch `RegCert.exe` to generate the verification code as Figure 5-14 shows.
5. Copy the generated code and paste to the Verification Code box.
6. Click the Save button to associate the certificate to the WCF services. If there is a certificate already associated with the same URL, there will be an error message, and you need to go back to the previous page and select the Advanced configuration to fix it.

Figure 5-14. *Generate a verification code with* `Regcert.exe` *and copy to the X.509 Certificates setup page*

Using CardSpace in the .NET Access Control Service

Sign in to the Azure Services Platform portal and navigate to the Windows CardSpace Card Setup page. Add a new card if there is no card, as shown in Figure 5-15, to create one and send it to Azure. There is no extra installation needed to generate the CardSpace after the local Azure development has been set up. This CardSpace will be sent to the Access Services at runtime for interactive authentication.

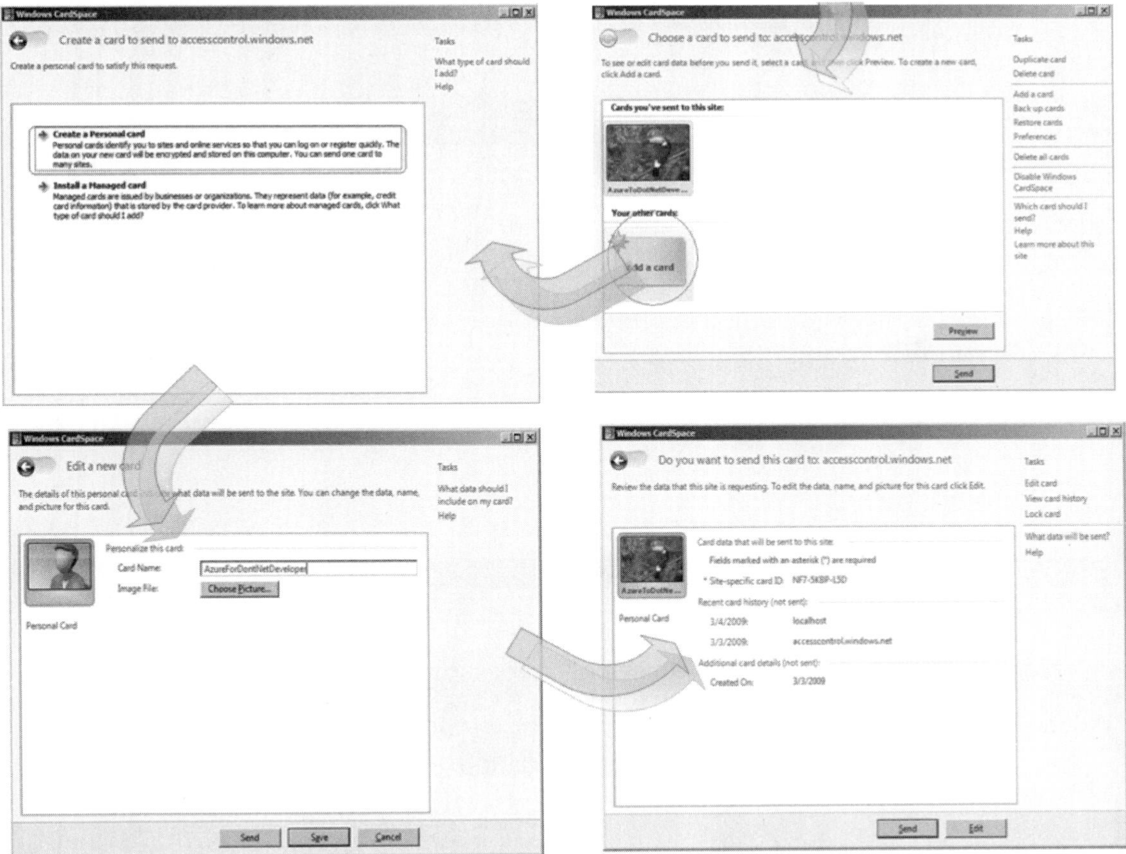

Figure 5-15. *Procedure to send CardSpace from the local computer*

Associating a Card with a Solution

Click the Send button shown in the last step of Figure 5-15 to send the card to Azure for association. The setup will save the file as Figure 5-16 shows. The file name must be unique, and duplication is not allowed.

Figure 5-16. Sending a card to Azure to associate an URL using a unique name

Registering the Generated CardSpace with Azure Access Control

The generated CardSpace needs to be registered before it can be used at runtime for interactive authentication. The screenshot in Figure 5-17 shows how to register the CardSpace from the Azure portal.

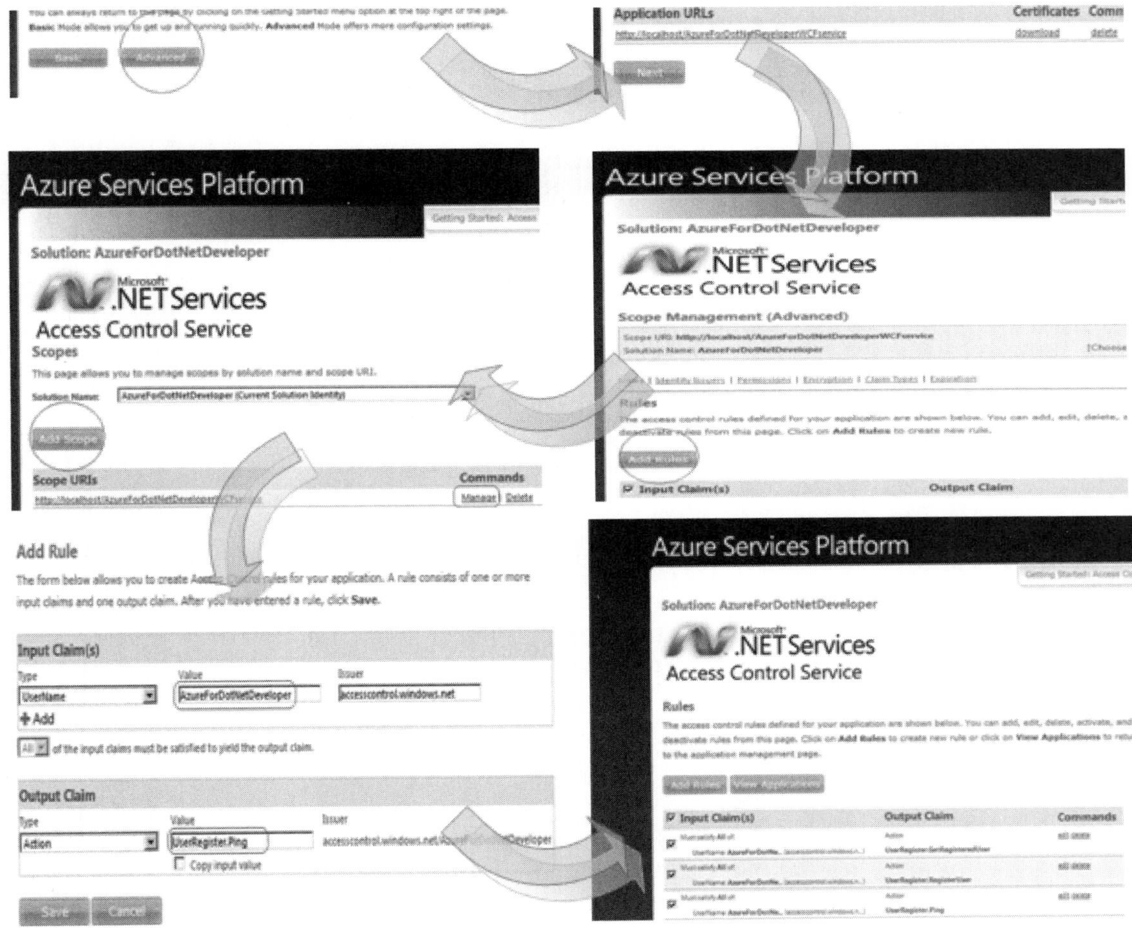

Figure 5-17. Defining the access rules for each operation contract respectively

Modifying the Code to Use the CardSpace .NET Access Control Service

Create a new project FederateAccessManager and add three classes to this project. These three classes are all derived from classes of the System.ServiceModel.Security namespace as Table 5-1 shows. Listing 5-13, Listing 5-14, and Listing 5-15 are the implementation for these classes respectively.

Table 5-1. Class Definition in FederateAccessManager Assembly

Class	Derived From	Override	Input Parameters	Output
UserRegister Service Credentials	ServiceCredentials	CloneCore		
		CreateSecurity TokenManager		SecurityTokenManager
UserRegister Security TokenManager	ServiceCredentials SecurityTokenManager	CreateSecurity TokenAuthenticator	SecurityToken Requirement	SecurityToken Authenticator SecurityTokenResolver
UserRegister Token Authenticator	SamlSecurityToken Authenticator	ValidateTokenCore	SecurityToken	ReadOnlyCollection <IAuthorizationPlicy>

The UserRegisterServiceCredentials class is derived from ServiceCredentials and accepts the name of the corresponding Azure solution and overrides two methods of its base class, CloneCore() and CreateSecurityTokenManager(). At runtime the certificate that has been installed on a local device and registered from Azure Access Control will be assigned to the instance of this class. The type of the ServiceCredentials class must be specified when you instantiate a service host instance, and an instance of the UserRegisterServiceCredentials class needs to be added to the host behaviors collection after the host has been instantiated. The responsibility of the class UserRegisterTokenAuthenticator is to communicate to the Access Control Service to validate the security token for authentication. This class is used by the UserRegisterSecurityTokenManager class.

Listing 5-13. *Implementations for Class UserRegisterServiceCredentials*

```
using System;
using System.IdentityModel.Selectors;
using System.ServiceModel.Description;

namespace AzureForDotNetDeveloper.DotNetService.ServiceBus
{

    public class UserRegisterServiceCredentials : ServiceCredentials
    {
        String solutionName;

        public UserRegisterServiceCredentials(String solutionName)
            : base()
        {
            this.solutionName = solutionName;
        }

        protected override ServiceCredentials CloneCore()
        {
```

```
            return new UserRegisterServiceCredentials(solutionName);
        }

        public override SecurityTokenManager CreateSecurityTokenManager()
        {
            return new UserRegisterSecurityTokenManager(this, solutionName);
        }
    }
}
```

Listing 5-14. Implementations of Class `UserRegisterSecurityTokenManager`

```
using System;
using System.IdentityModel.Selectors;
using System.IdentityModel.Tokens;
using System.ServiceModel.Security;

namespace AzureForDotNetDeveloper.DotNetService.ServiceBus
{

    public class UserRegisterSecurityTokenManager : ServiceCredentialsSecurityTokenManager
    {
        UserRegisterServiceCredentials UserRegisterServiceCredentials;
        String solutionName;

        public UserRegisterSecurityTokenManager(
          UserRegisterServiceCredentials UserRegisterServiceCredentials,
          String solutionName
        )
            : base(UserRegisterServiceCredentials)
        {
            this.UserRegisterServiceCredentials = UserRegisterServiceCredentials;
            this.solutionName = solutionName;
        }

        public override SecurityTokenAuthenticator CreateSecurityTokenAuthenticator(
          SecurityTokenRequirement tokenRequirement,
          out SecurityTokenResolver outOfBandTokenResolver
        )
        {
            if (tokenRequirement.TokenType.Equals(
                  "http://docs.oasis-open.org/wss/oasis-wss-saml-token-profile-1.1#SAMLV1.1",
                  StringComparison.OrdinalIgnoreCase))
            {
                base.CreateSecurityTokenAuthenticator(tokenRequirement,
                                                      out outOfBandTokenResolver);
                return new UserRegisterTokenAuthenticator(
                  new SecurityTokenAuthenticator[] {
                    new X509SecurityTokenAuthenticator(X509CertificateValidator.None),
                    new RsaSecurityTokenAuthenticator()
                  },
```

```
                solutionName
            );
        }
        else
        {
            return base.CreateSecurityTokenAuthenticator(tokenRequirement,
                                                         out outOfBandTokenResolver);
        }
    }
  }
}
```

Listing 5-15. *Implementations of Class* `UserRegisterTokenAuthenticator`

```
using System;
using System.Collections.Generic;
using System.Collections.ObjectModel;
using System.IdentityModel.Claims;
using System.IdentityModel.Policy;
using System.IdentityModel.Selectors;
using System.IdentityModel.Tokens;
using System.ServiceModel;

namespace AzureForDotNetDeveloper.DotNetService.ServiceBus
{

    class UserRegisterTokenAuthenticator : SamlSecurityTokenAuthenticator
    {
        IList<SecurityTokenAuthenticator> supportingAuthenticators;
        SamlSecurityTokenAuthenticator innerSamlSecurityTokenAuthenticator;
        String solutionName;

        public UserRegisterTokenAuthenticator(
          IList<SecurityTokenAuthenticator> supportingAuthenticators, String solutionName)
            : base(supportingAuthenticators)
        {
            this.supportingAuthenticators =
              new List<SecurityTokenAuthenticator>(supportingAuthenticators);
            this.innerSamlSecurityTokenAuthenticator =
              new SamlSecurityTokenAuthenticator(supportingAuthenticators);
            this.solutionName = solutionName;
        }

        public UserRegisterTokenAuthenticator(
          IList<SecurityTokenAuthenticator> supportingAuthenticators, TimeSpan maxClockSkew)
            : base(supportingAuthenticators, maxClockSkew)
        {
            this.supportingAuthenticators =
              new List<SecurityTokenAuthenticator>(supportingAuthenticators);
            this.innerSamlSecurityTokenAuthenticator =
              new SamlSecurityTokenAuthenticator(supportingAuthenticators, maxClockSkew);
```

```
        }

        protected override
          ReadOnlyCollection<IAuthorizationPolicy>ValidateTokenCore(SecurityToken token)
        {
            if (token == null)
            {
                throw new ArgumentNullException("token");
            }

            SamlSecurityToken samlToken = token as SamlSecurityToken;

            if (samlToken == null)
            {
                throw new SecurityTokenException("Not a SamlSecurityToken.");
            }

            if (!samlToken.Assertion.Issuer.Equals(
              String.Format("http://accesscontrol.windows.net/{0}", this.solutionName),
              StringComparison.OrdinalIgnoreCase))
            {
                throw new SecurityTokenException("Not expected issuer.");
            }

            return this.innerSamlSecurityTokenAuthenticator.ValidateToken(token);
        }
    }
}
```

Now insert code on the server to use security credentials as Listing 5-16 shows.

Listing 5-16. *Insert Security Credential Code into Server Implementations*

```
using System;
using System.Security.Cryptography.X509Certificates;
using System.ServiceModel;
using System.ServiceModel.Description;

namespace AzureForDotNetDeveloper.DotNetService.ServiceBus
{
    class Program
    {
        static void Main(string[] args)
        {
            ServiceHost host = new ServiceHost(typeof(AzureForDotNetDeveloperWCFservice));

            String solutionName = ReadSolutionName();
            ServiceCredentials sc = host.Credentials;
            X509Certificate2 cert = sc.ServiceCertificate.Certificate;
            UserRegisterServiceCredentials serviceCredential =
              new UserRegisterServiceCredentials(solutionName);
```

```
            serviceCredential.ServiceCertificate.Certificate = cert;
            host.Description.Behaviors.Remove((typeof(ServiceCredentials)));
            host.Description.Behaviors.Add(serviceCredential);

            host.Open();

            Console.WriteLine("---UserRegister service is running.");
            Console.WriteLine("---Press <Enter> to terminate server");
            Console.ReadLine();

            host.Close();
        }

        private static string ReadSolutionName()
        {
            Console.Write(string.Format("---Please enter your solution name: {0}",
                          Environment.NewLine));
            return Console.ReadLine();
        }

    }
}
```

Add a new class AccessControlHelper to the WCF service project AzureForDotNetDeveloperWCFserviceLibrary. This is a helper class used to validate the claim token string. The string parameters passed in should match those that we defined in the rules when we configured the rule from Azure (see Figure 5-14).

Listing 5-17. *Implementation of Class* `AccessControlHelper`

```
using System;
using System.Collections.Generic;
using System.IdentityModel.Claims;
using System.IdentityModel.Policy;
using System.ServiceModel;

namespace AzureForDotNetDeveloper.DotNetService.ServiceBus
{
    public class AccessControlHelper
    {
        public static void DemandActionClaim(string claimValue)
        {
            foreach (
             ClaimSet claimSet in
             OperationContext.Current.ServiceSecurityContext.AuthorizationContext.ClaimSets
            )
            {
                foreach (Claim claim in claimSet)
                {
                    if (AccessControlHelper.CheckClaim(
                      claim.ClaimType,
```

```
                    claim.Resource.ToString(),
                    "http://docs.oasis-open.org/wsfed/authorization/200706/claims/action",
                    claimValue))
                  {
                    if (AccessControlHelper.IsIssuedByIbn(claimSet))
                    {
                        return;
                    }
                  }
              }
          }

          throw new FaultException("Access denied.");
      }

      static bool IsIssuedByIbn(ClaimSet claimSet)
      {
          foreach (Claim claim in claimSet.Issuer)
          {
              if (AccessControlHelper.CheckClaim(
                    claim.ClaimType,
                    claim.Resource.ToString(),
                    "http://schemas.xmlsoap.org/ws/2005/05/identity/claims/dns",
                    "accesscontrol.windows.net"))
              {
                  return true;
              }
          }

          return false;
      }

      static bool CheckClaim(string claimType, string claimValue,
                             string expectedClaimType, string expectedClaimValue)
      {
          if (
            StringComparer.OrdinalIgnoreCase.Equals(claimType, expectedClaimType) &&
            StringComparer.OrdinalIgnoreCase.Equals(claimValue, expectedClaimValue)
          )
          {
              return true;
          }
          return false;
      }
  }
}
```

Now let's modify the WCF service operation implementation. For all implementations of the operation in the WCF service contract we need to insert the code to demand the claim for the security token by using the previous helper class as Listing 5-18 shows.

Listing 5-18. Implementation of the WCF Service Contract

```
using System;
using System.Runtime.Serialization;
using System.ServiceModel;
using System.ServiceModel.Channels;
using System.Collections.Generic;
using System.IO;
using System.Xml;
using System.Xml.Serialization;
using System.Text;

namespace AzureForDotNetDeveloper.DotNetService.ServiceBus
{

    [ServiceBehavior(InstanceContextMode = InstanceContextMode.Single)]
    public class AzureForDotNetDeveloperWCFservice : IAzureForDotNetDeveloperWCFservice
    {
        private User _registeredUser = null;

        #region IUserRegisterService Members

        public string Ping()
        {
            AccessControlHelper.DemandActionClaim("UserRegister.Ping");
            return string.Format("--- I am here <{0}>", this.ToString());
        }

        public void RegisterUser(string xmlString)
        {
            try
            {

               AccessControlHelper.DemandActionClaim("UserRegister.RegisterUser");
                XmlDocument xmlDoc = new XmlDocument();
                xmlDoc.LoadXml(xmlString);
                XmlSerializer serializer = new XmlSerializer(typeof(User));
                StringReader reader = new StringReader(xmlString);

                _registeredUser = (User)serializer.Deserialize(reader);
            }
            catch (Exception ex)
            {
            }
        }

        public string GetRegisteredUser()
        {
            AccessControlHelper.DemandActionClaim("UserRegister.GetRegisteredUser");
            XmlSerializer serializer = new XmlSerializer(typeof(User));
            StringBuilder sb = new StringBuilder();
```

```
            StringWriter writer = new StringWriter(sb);

            serializer.Serialize(writer, _registeredUser);
            return writer.GetStringBuilder().ToString();
        }

        #endregion
    }
}
```

Finally, update the service reference on the client project. Start running the service, and go to Visual Studio. Right-click on the Service Reference node to update the client proxy class. The `App.config` file is also going to be regenerated by Visual Studio to reflect the security access information with binding type `ws2007FederationHttpBinding` as Listing 5-19 shows.

Listing 5-19. *Generated Client Proxy Configuration with Security Access Claim Token Encoding*

```
      <ws2007FederationHttpBinding>
        <binding name="UserRegisterEndpoint1" closeTimeout="00:01:00"
          openTimeout="00:01:00" receiveTimeout="00:10:00" sendTimeout="00:01:00"
          bypassProxyOnLocal="false" transactionFlow="false"
          hostNameComparisonMode="StrongWildcard"
          maxBufferPoolSize="524288" maxReceivedMessageSize="65536" messageEncoding="Text"
          textEncoding="utf-8" useDefaultWebProxy="true">
          <readerQuotas maxDepth="32" maxStringContentLength="8192" maxArrayLength="16384"
            maxBytesPerRead="4096" maxNameTableCharCount="16384" />
          <reliableSession ordered="true" inactivityTimeout="00:10:00"
            enabled="false" />
          <security mode="Message">
            <message algorithmSuite="Default" issuedKeyType="SymmetricKey"
  issuedTokenType="http://docs.oasis-open.org/wss/oasis-wss-saml-token-profile-1.1#SAMLV1.1"
              negotiateServiceCredential="false">
              <issuer
                address=
     "http://accesscontrol.windows.net/sts/replacewithsolutionname/issued_for_certificate"
                binding="customBinding"
                bindingConfiguration=
    "http://accesscontrol.windows.net/sts/replacewithsolutionname/issued_for_certificate">
                <identity>
                  <certificate
             encodedValue="AwAAAAEAAAAUAAAAQW5vpdmCsJaTH79CxKPc1giFbJUgAAAAAQAAADMGAAAwggYvM
IIFF6ADAgECAgowSxUCAAUAAN+/MAOGCSqGSIb3DQEBBQUAMIGLMRMwEQYKCZImiZPyLGQBGRYDY29tMRkwFwYKCZImi
ZPyLGQBGRYJbWljcm9zb2ZOMRQwEgYKCZImiZPyLGQBGRYEY29ycDEXMBUGCgmSJomT8ixkARkWB3JlZG1vbmQxKjAoB
gNVBAMTIU1pY3Jvc29mdCBTZWN1cmUgU2VydmVyIEF1dGhvcml0eTAeFw0wODA5MDQyMDExMDJaFw0wOTA5MDQyMDExM
DJaMHOxCzAJBgNVBAYTAlVTMQswCQYDVQQIEwJXQTEQMA4GA1UEBxMHUmVkbW9uZDESMBAGA1UEChMJTWljcm9zb2ZOM
RcwFQYDVQQLEw5Qcm9qZWNoIFp1cmljaDEiMCAGA1UEAxMZYWNjZXNzY29udHJvbC53aW5kb3dzLm5ldDCBnzANBgkqh
kiG9w0BAQEFAAOBjQAwgYkCgYEAreESUDU/HSaVXHmBHfBdUZW7yLlvFRiB+GX/gIEz94H6HW85Doo+OgT8GEORtite+
oREcom6euSUYarP3Rt/1rIvtJAU/+GhcupKvICZAavx9vPLrfjxgayHuSCc8QbAOnpn44f/LE37q+Y22g8uqOg3aQE7J
```

```
Olb0wW//+2yXScCAwEAAaOCAyQwggMgMAsGA1UdDwQEAwIEsDAdBgNVHSUEFjAUBggrBgEFBQcDAgYIKwYBBQUHAwEwe
AYJKoZIhvcNAQkPBGswaTAOBggqhkiG9w0DAgICAIAwDgYIKoZIhvcNAwQCAgCAMAsGCWCGSAFlAwQBKjALBglghkgBZ
QMEAS0wCwYJYIZIAWUDBAECMAsGCWCGSAFlAwQBBTAHBgUrDgMCBzAKBggqhkiG9w0DBzAdBgNVHQ4EFgQUaqPI5cP+U
HaMNfk5i8kWU3mza84wHwYDVR0jBBgwFoAUFFXEOeA9LtFVLkiWsNh+FCIGk7wwggEKBgNVHR8EggEBMIH+MIH7oIH4o
IH1hlhodHRwOi8vbXNjcmwubWljcm9zb2Z0LmNvbS9wa2kvbXNjb3JwL2NybC9NaWNyb3NvZnQlMjBTZWN1cmUlMjBTZ
XJ2ZXIlMjBBdXRob3JpdHkoNSkuY3JshlZodHRwOi8vY3JsLm1pY3Jvc29mdC5jb20vcGtpL21zY29ycC9jcmwvTWljc
m9zb2Z0JTIwU2VjdXJlJTIwU2VydmVyJTIwQXV0aG9yaXR5KDUpLmNybIZBaHR0cDovL2NvcnBwa2kvY3JsL01pY3Jvc
29mdCUyMFNlY3VyZSUyMFNlcnZlciUyMEF1dGhvcml0eSg1KS5jcmwwgb8GCCsGAQUFBwEBBIGyMIGvMF4GCCsGAQUFB
zAChlJodHRwOi8vd3d3Lm1pY3Jvc29mdC5jb20vcGtpL21zY29ycC9NaWNyb3NvZnQlMjBTZWN1cmUlMjBTZXJ2ZXIlM
jBBdXRob3JpdHkoNSkuY3J0MEOGCCsGAQUFBzAChkFodHRwOi8vY29ycHBraS9haWEvTWljcm9zb2Z0JTIwU2VjdXJlJ
TIwU2VydmVyJTIwQXV0aG9yaXR5KDUpLmNydDA/BgkrBgEEAYI3FQcEMjAwBigrBgEEAYI3FQiDz4lNrfIChaGfDIL6y
n2B4ftOgU+Dwu2FCI6pOoVjAgFkAgEGMCcGCSsGAQQBgjcVCgQaMBgwCgYIKwYBBQUHAwIwCgYIKwYBBQUHAwEwDQYJK
oZIhvcNAQEFBQADggEBAB3JqyYxQ8OPLVFMRoE2chNO+QlA8oijsPNkEz0ycysiyQQ3zpDgJxqa2IgULzFvuKB7C1FlD
SM5U6tWQcKKeJQ2sqAreR1mYec1JIpJQZG6KZDAQHqe2Rvhg54kD8MZeJCbd7Rkxl2E5ivekhbxZhKoNnsCOpEN2rEoQ
urCSkzDQ1eTNp3PaiHds+6iVNsg+u8aIXkWqn7/mj9x6UJQeOvXGhy/h/tBJLrCXzBl8gDdG7ie5VNC1LzW6gjukQEJf
mlEZTWW/EnMhj7cubG7/VHjk/2rvjbJS2pjxojRwyqLwyRHfSMpTP92pJ7REu91d1jReylDFdn58PfA3eYOoik=" />
          </identity>
        </issuer>
        <issuerMetadata
           address="http://accesscontrol.windows.net/sts/replacewithsolutionname/mex">
          <identity>
            <dns value="accesscontrol.windows.net" />
          </identity>
        </issuerMetadata>
        <tokenRequestParameters>
          <trust:SecondaryParameters
              xmlns:trust="http://docs.oasis-open.org/ws-sx/ws-trust/200512">
            <trust:TokenType
                xmlns:trust="http://docs.oasis-open.org/ws-sx/ws-trust/200512">
              http://docs.oasis-open.org/wss/oasis-wss-saml-token-profile-1.1#SAMLV1.1
            </trust:TokenType>
            <trust:KeyType
                xmlns:trust="http://docs.oasis-open.org/ws-sx/ws-trust/200512">
              http://docs.oasis-open.org/ws-sx/ws-trust/200512/SymmetricKey
            </trust:KeyType>
            <trust:KeySize
                xmlns:trust="http://docs.oasis-open.org/ws-sx/ws-trust/200512">
              256
            </trust:KeySize>
            <trust:Claims Dialect="http://schemas.xmlsoap.org/ws/2005/05/identity"
              xmlns:trust="http://docs.oasis-open.org/ws-sx/ws-trust/200512">
              <wsid:ClaimType
             Uri="http://docs.oasis-open.org/wsfed/authorization/200706/claims/action"
             xmlns:wsid="http://schemas.xmlsoap.org/ws/2005/05/identity" />
            </trust:Claims>
            <trust:KeyWrapAlgorithm
                xmlns:trust="http://docs.oasis-open.org/ws-sx/ws-trust/200512">
              http://www.w3.org/2001/04/xmlenc#rsa-oaep-mgf1p
            </trust:KeyWrapAlgorithm>
            <trust:EncryptWith
                xmlns:trust="http://docs.oasis-open.org/ws-sx/ws-trust/200512">
```

```
              http://www.w3.org/2001/04/xmlenc#aes256-cbc
            </trust:EncryptWith>
            <trust:SignWith
                xmlns:trust="http://docs.oasis-open.org/ws-sx/ws-trust/200512">
              http://www.w3.org/2000/09/xmldsig#hmac-sha1
            </trust:SignWith>
            <trust:CanonicalizationAlgorithm
                xmlns:trust="http://docs.oasis-open.org/ws-sx/ws-trust/200512">
              http://www.w3.org/2001/10/xml-exc-c14n#
            </trust:CanonicalizationAlgorithm>
            <trust:EncryptionAlgorithm
                xmlns:trust="http://docs.oasis-open.org/ws-sx/ws-trust/200512">
              http://www.w3.org/2001/04/xmlenc#aes256-cbc
            </trust:EncryptionAlgorithm>
          </trust:SecondaryParameters>
        </tokenRequestParameters>
      </message>
    </security>
  </binding>
</ws2007FederationHttpBinding>
    </bindings>
    <client>
      <endpoint address="http://localhost/AzureForDotNetDeveloperWCFservice"
        binding="basicHttpBinding" bindingConfiguration="UserRegisterEndpoint"
        contract="UserRegister" name="UserRegisterEndpoint" />
      <endpoint address="http://localhost/AzureForDotNetDeveloperWCFservice"
        binding="ws2007FederationHttpBinding" bindingConfiguration="UserRegisterEndpoint1"
        contract="UserRegisterService.UserRegisterService" name="UserRegisterEndpoint1">
        <identity>
          <certificate encodedValue="AwAAAAEAAAAUAAAAASCQin4SUkWbNOuSZBQY6AOSY/wgAAAAAQAAALU
BAAAwggGxMIIBX6ADAgECAhDvE+ZAuwIqhU9cQqsE44DOMAkGBSsOAwIdBQAwFjEUMBIGA1UEAxMLUm9vdCBBZ2VuY3k
wHhcNMDcwNDA0MjMyMTAxWhcNMzkxMjMxMjM1OTU5WjAUMRIwEAYDVQQDEwlsb2NhbGhvc3QwgZ8wDQYJKoZIhvcNAQE
BBQADgYOAMIGJAoGBAK3fOF9Q789iQiEs5FpNTOLOnraBTcoNMxK+jFasM+S8FMLSqPGRgrKearjGwAum3diRBKOngDj
bJ+Vp8TxtgvhEhed9JBuWh5hg6nkOjVS7emHjwkBoacULtYTo4QC2/Bav/eK6ibO/kSknnVG45v7kNWG2gyJh+/HCJIc
xQ3oFAgMBAAGjSzBJMEcGA1UdAQRAMD6AEBLkCSOGHR1PAI1hIdwWZGOhGDAWMRQwEgYDVQQDEwtSb29OIEFnZW5jeYI
QBjdsAKoAZIoRz7jUqlw19DAJBgUrDgMCHQUAA0EAdZ/POLONGuxU3kAoTsbSPdvi3k5PhAYLYbIL2RRHxjcV5lPHqK9
BP2QoctoRFt1Kqb3OZSrGXH5oaq3B/Vdpdg==" />
        </identity>
      </endpoint>
    </client>
  </system.serviceModel>
</configuration>
```

Start the server and enter the Azure solution name. The server will retrieve the certificate information from the system as Figure 5-18 shows.

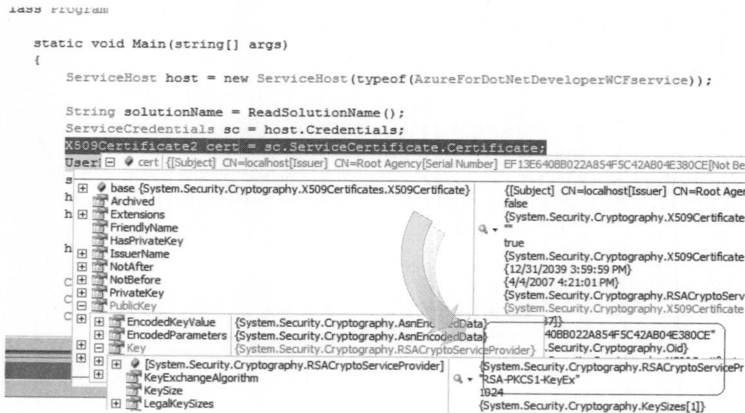

Figure 5-18. The certificate information retrieved when server is starting

Run the client application. You are asked to send the card every single time to invoke the WCF service action via .NET Access Control Service to claim the security tokens. As Figure 5-19 shows, there is an interactive model involved for this activity. The desktop is grayed out, and the CardSpace card is selected and sent. The action will not be processed until the security token has been claimed and validated successfully.

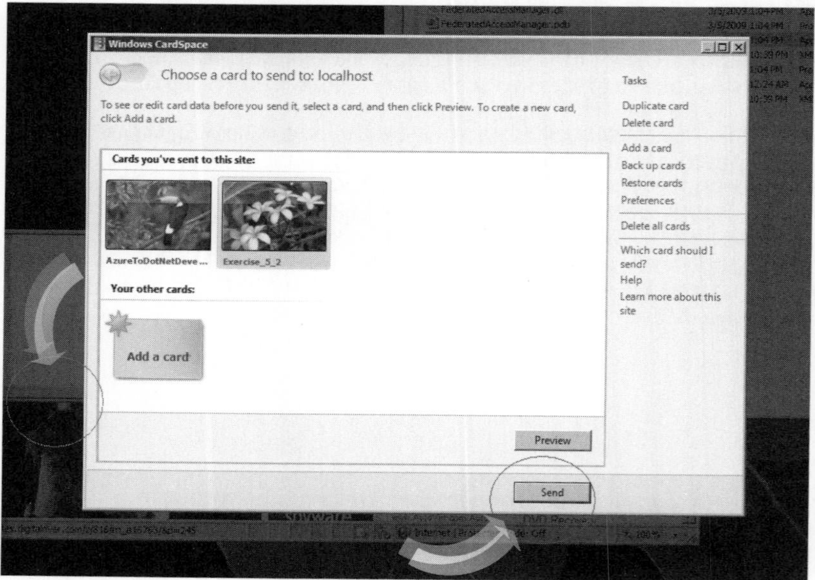

Figure 5-19. The CardSpace card must be sent to the .NET Access Control Service to claim the security access token on each WCF action

If a problem is caught, the error information can be viewed from the EventViewer as Figure 5-20 shows.

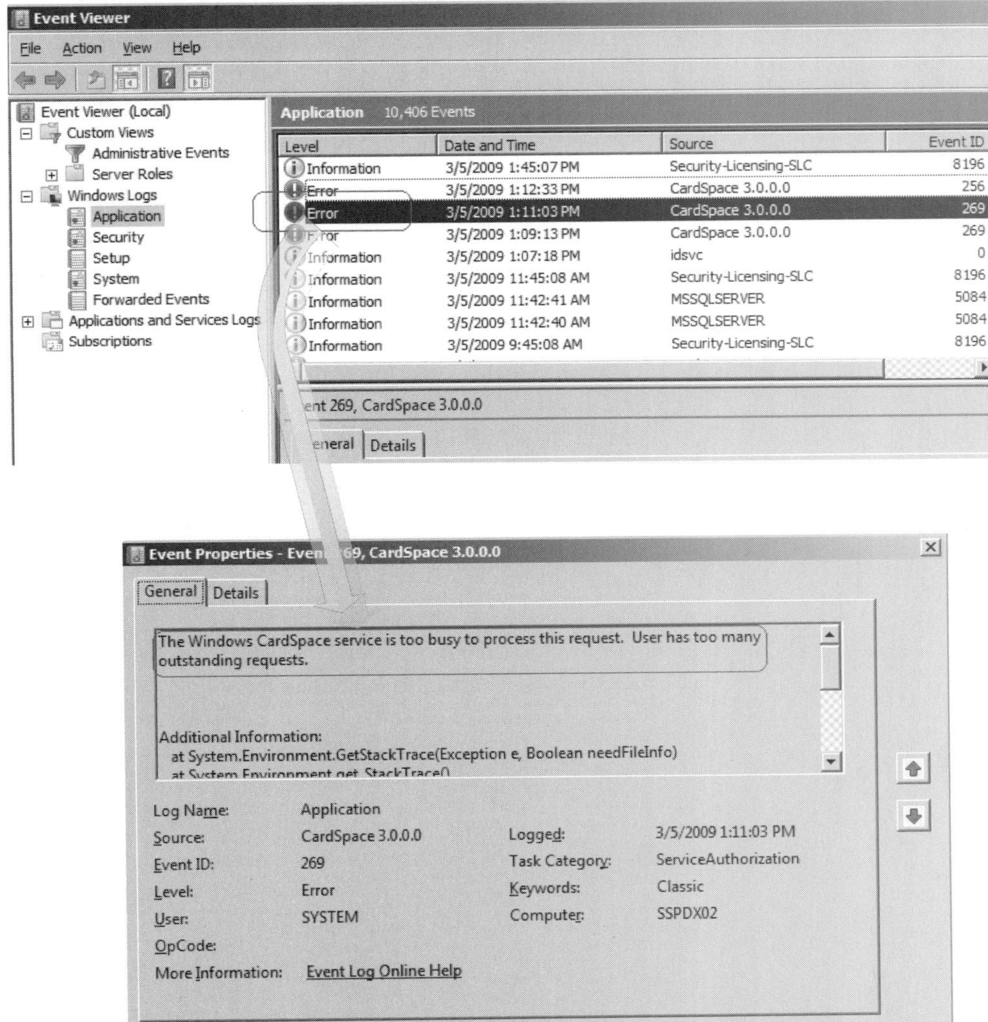

Figure 5-20. Using EventViewer for troubleshooting

Summary

This chapter forms the foundation for the next two, as it describes the underlying authentication mechanism used for all the Azure Services. In it I took you through authentication in Azure, using the .NET Access Control Service. I started by describing the underlying mechanisms, before showing an example of a cloud-based application that used authentication.

The second part of the chapter covered CardSpace and X.509 certificates. We saw how to use these security mechanisms in an Azure application, so that you have more options when writing your own.

CHAPTER 6

■ ■ ■

Azure .NET Services—Service Bus

.NET Service Bus solves the following two problems to help connect applications:

- How to get service requests through a firewall
- How to discover service endpoints

Currently the most popular solutions to these two problems are web services. Web services are based on SOAP communication protocols. Application clients use WSDL as the metadata to generate proxy classes to find the endpoints and reach the services provided by applications behind firewalls. .NET Framework 3.0 introduced the Windows Communication Foundation (WCF), which provides a powerful tool to solve these problems. It uses all web-based communication protocols, including SOAP. However, the challenge these two approaches need to face is not how to request a service behind a firewall but how to locate the service endpoint IP address, since an application frequently does not have a fixed IP address to expose externally.

Today existing workarounds to this challenge take two approaches. The first approach is used for small network environments. The approach used to solve the firewall and the NAT (network address translation) issue is to selectively allow applications to open inbound ports on the local and network router firewalls, such as the familiar DHCP (Dynamic Host Configuration Protocol) or Dynamic DNS technology. The limit of this approach is the scalability. It realistically only works for small networks, and security is a big concern. The second approach, which a large organization usually uses, is to use relay services. A relay service stands between firewalls and client applications as a bridge to route the messages. The challenge with relay services is that they are extremely hard to build to meet Internet scalability requirements, routing between thousands or millions of connections, with acceptable costs and effort. The data traffic exponentially increases and turns the connection into a bottleneck.

In this chapter you are going to see how Windows Azure solves these two problems nicely via .NET Service Bus and how you can leverage this building block to construct cloud-based distributed applications.

Connecting to Remote Applications with the Service Bus

The .NET Service Bus addresses these challenges based upon the concept shown in Figure 6-1. Applications that need to communicate via .NET Service Bus must register with the .NET Service Bus registry. When an application requests a service from a source behind a firewall, it needs to simply find the endpoint of the target service via .NET Service Bus and to establish the communication channel for services. In other words, the services are provided by service applications run behind the firewall, and the connection endpoints are provided by .NET Service Bus. The reason .NET Service Bus makes communication easier is that all its clients now see only an IP address provided by it instead of one directly exposed by organizations. It also improves service access security because it is designed to collaborate with .NET Service Access Control, which applies user-defined rules to ensure security when an application claims tokens via the STS service provided by .NET Service Access Control.

In practice, an application that intends to expose its service via .NET Service Bus implements the services based upon WCF, but it does not have to. As long as the calling application can make the request via SOAP or REST, there is no restriction for which technology the target application uses to implement the service interfaces.

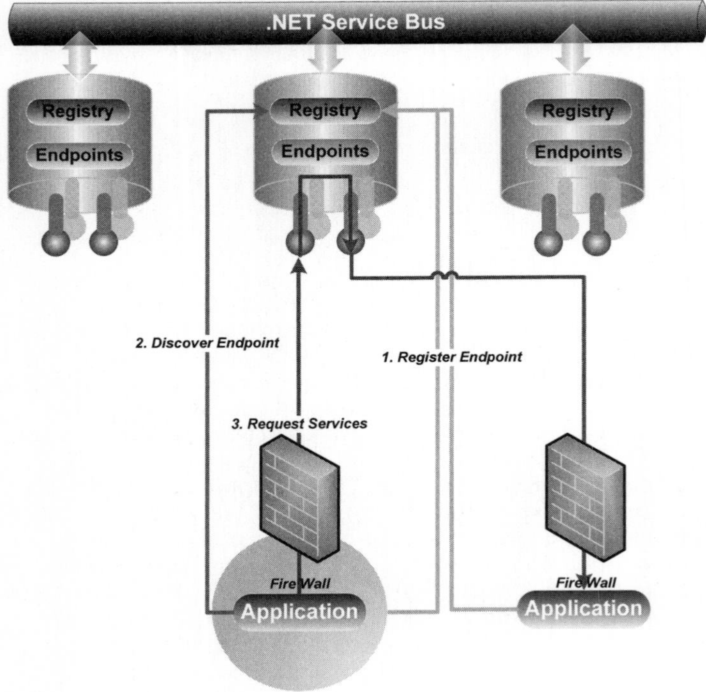

Figure 6-1. *.NET Service Bus concept*

The core and essential part of .NET Service Bus uses globally addressable Internet access based on REST or SOAP. All endpoints, resources, and applications provide a URI for access. The Internet services provided by .NET Service Bus cover the following three major categories:

- Service name hierarchy system
- Service registry and publishing
- Endpoint relay connectivity

Let's look at each of these in turn.

Service Name Hierarchy System

.NET Service Bus is built upon WCF. All interactions with the application are URI-addressable. The URI address uses a hierarchical structure. In principle this name hierarchy system in .NET Service Bus is a forest and can go infinitely deep. There is no need for applications to explicitly perform name system housekeeping. The name system is a virtual logic system. When an application's registration is deleted or removed from the system, all names under that application are automatically deleted.

.NET Service Bus maintains the name system based upon the Azure solution created from the cloud. In other words, the Azure solution name is the first level in the URI hierarchy structure. It is an application's call how to organize its name hierarchy system starting from the application root (the registered solution name from Azure), as long as the solution's name makes sense to the application. An application associated with .NET Service Bus can have multiple instances. The solution name is to allow .NET Service Bus to manage and distinguish the applications. On the client or user side, there is no limit to how many applications can be registered or how many instances can be associated to an application.

Service Registry and Publishing

The service registry is where we publish service endpoint references to the .NET Service Bus name system by sending an HTTP PUT request; we send an HTTP DELETE request to remove the registration from the name system. We can discover a service by traversing the name hierarchy tree.

Endpoint Relay Connectivity

The core part of .NET Service Bus is the relay service that supports connection-oriented bidirectional communication. Relay services listen for HTTP requests from the cloud instead of from a local source. The connection usually starts with a listener, either local or remote. To establish the bidirectional communication, the approach is to simply pair up two connections and reverse the listener and sender roles. The advantage of using relay services is obvious. An application can use the relay service as a filter to block the traffic it is not interested in and hides all detailed information about network locations to reduce security threats. The relay services can also provide access control to request application authentication before establishing the connection.

Using WCF with the Service Bus

The key difference between a standard WCF binding and its counterpart relay binding is where the service establishes the listener. The standard WCF application establishes the listeners locally, whereas the relay binding does so from the cloud. .NET Service Bus allows applications to connect across platforms since it is based on open Internet standards. Those applications using the WCF communication framework to switch to .NET Service Bus services just need to modify the configuration file to change the regular WCF binding types to relay binding types. For example, the `WebHttpBinding` has a corresponding `WebHttpRelayBinding`, the `BasicHttpBinding` has a corresponding `BasicHttpRelayBinding`, and so forth. The significant difference after switching to the relay service is that the application is listening for the HTTP request from the cloud instead of locally. All relay connections must connect to the .NET Service Bus. That is the essential difference between using relay connections and regular WCF connections. The .NET Service Bus also supports all regular WCF features, such as reliable message delivery, message security, and transport security. However, the transaction delivery between clients and servers is not supported by .NET Service Bus. Highlights of the technical features are shown in Table 6-1.

Using the Microsoft .NET Service Bus in conjunction with WCF is the easiest way to build a connected distributed system.

Table 6-1. *Highlights of Technical Features for Available .NET Service Bus Connection Modes*

.NET Service Bus Relay Binding Types and Connection Mode		Technical Specification Highlight	Open Port Required
`netEventRelayBinding` `netOnewayRelayBinding`		Provide lightweight event-distribution mechanisms to deliver events to all participating parties via relay services from the cloud. Do not support duplex or call back. Do not support event filtering.	n/a
`netTcpRelayBinding` `netTcpRelayContextBinding`	Relayed	`Relayed` mode is the default mode of `TcpRelayConnection` when configuring the connection bindings using the TCP relay binding.	808 or 828 for operation transport security bindings, 818 for data channel
	Direct	In `Direct` mode, a typical scenario is two parties residing in the same intranet, and the service tries to promote the connection to direct. If the connection cannot be established, the initialization will fail.	
	Hybrid	For the `Hybrid` connection mode, the relay service uses the `Relayed` mode to establish the connection and switches the connection to `Direct` connection.	
`wsHttpRelayBinding` `wsHttpRelayContextBinding`		Web services relay binding, like regular WCF WS binding, sends and receives interoperable messages, which can be consumed using HTTP or HTTPS.	There is no special port opening required; these binding types use the regular IIS ports, such as 80 for HTTP and 443 for HTTPS.
`basicHttpRelayBinding` `basicHttpRelayContextBinding`		Similar to regular WCF `basicHttpBinding`. The `basicHttpRelayBinding` creates a publicly discoverable HTTP endpoint listening to the cloud-based Service Bus application.	80 and 443 for HTTP and HTTPS respectively For the SSL protected.

The TCP relay binding offers the best performance and throughput. That supports request-response operation, one-way operation, and event duplex callback.

Post a Net Event Using Relay Connection

This exercise uses a very simple Windows console application to demonstrate how to post a net message event through .NET Service Bus. The connection model used in this exercise is the relay hub connection as shown in Figure 6-2. All participating parties are hooked up as a publisher as well as a subscriber. Any message posted to the hub will be delivered to all participating parties, which use the same endpoint address to bind to the WCF services. The type of binding used for this relay hub connection is `netEventRelayBinding`, which does not support two-way communication. It is good enough for this demo, since we just need to listen for events. All service operation contracts must be marked as `OperationContract(IsOneWay = true)` as the boldface lines show in Listing 6-1.

■ **Note** The code for this example is in the Exercise 6-1 bundle from the code download.

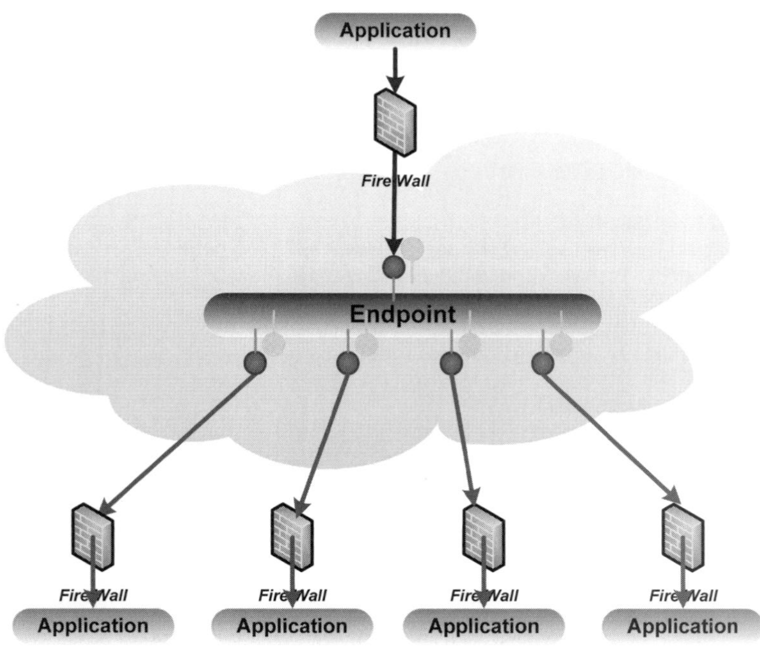

Figure 6-2. *.NET Service Bus event hub*

Let's implement this now.

1. Create a WCF service. Listing 6-1 shows the service contract definition for the WCF service `IPublishEventService`. This interface exposes only one method, `PostMessage()`.

Listing 6-1. Service Contract and Data Contract Definition for WCF Service `IPublishEventService`

```
using System;
using System.ServiceModel;

namespace SoftnetSolutions.RelayService.PublishChannel
{
[ServiceContract(
  Name = "IPublishEventService", Namespace = "http://SoftnetSolutions.RelayService/")]
    public interface IPublishEventService
    {
       [OperationContract(IsOneWay = true)]
       void PostMessage(PostData postData);
    }

public interface IRelayPublishEventService : IPublishEventService, IClientChannel {
}


using System;
using System.ServiceModel;
using System.Runtime.Serialization;
using System.Text;

namespace SoftnetSolutions.RelayService.PublishChannel
{
    [ServiceBehavior(Name = "PublishEventService",
                     Namespace = "http://SoftnetSolutions.RelayService/",
                     InstanceContextMode = InstanceContextMode.Single)]
    public class PublishEventService : IPublishEventService
    {
        private StringBuilder _messageBuffer = new StringBuilder();

        public void PostMessage(PostData postData)
        {
            _messageBuffer.Append(string.Format("[{0}]:received message - {1}{2}",
                DateTime.Now.ToString(),
                postData.Message,
                Environment.NewLine));
            Console.Write(_messageBuffer.ToString());
        }
    }

    [DataContract]
    public class PostData
```

```
    {
        [DataMember]
        public string Message;
    }
}
```

2. Now create the configuration for this service as shown in Listing 6-2, where the default binding `netEventRelayBinding` is used. This type of binding only supports one-way communication.

Listing 6-2. *Configuration for* `IPublishEventService` *WCF Service Using* `netRelayEvent` *Bindings*

```
<?xml version="1.0" encoding="utf-8" ?>
<configuration>
  <appSettings>
    <add key="Topic" value="Pheonix"/>
    <add key="Solution" value="SoftnetSolutionsServiceBus"/>
    <add key="password" value="My password"/>
  </appSettings>
  <system.serviceModel>

    <bindings>

      <netEventRelayBinding>
        <binding name="default" />
      </netEventRelayBinding>
    </bindings>

    <client>
      <endpoint name="RelayEndpoint"
                contract="SoftnetSolutions.RelayService.PublishChannel.IPublishEventService"
                binding="netEventRelayBinding"
                bindingConfiguration="default"
                address="" />
    </client>

    <services>

      <service name="SoftnetSolutions.RelayService.PublishChannel.PublishEventService">
        <endpoint name="RelayEndpoint"
                contract="SoftnetSolutions.RelayService.PublishChannel.IPublishEventService"
                binding="netEventRelayBinding"
                bindingConfiguration="default"
                address="" />
      </service>
    </services>

  </system.serviceModel>
</configuration>
```

3. Create a service host class. The format to compose an address of .NET Service Bus is the following, where, [ ] = optional, < > = required.

```
<[sb][http][https]>://<solution>.servicebus.windows.net[/service topic][/sub topic]
```

   The endpoint address to be used in this exercise is

```
sb://softnetsolutionsservicebus.servicebus.windows.net/Pheonix/RelayService/
```

4. Listing 6-3 shows the implementation for the host class. This class declares two constructors. The second constructor takes the endpoint URI as a parameter. This allows the host to be able to accept different endpoints in order to support multiple modes for the .NET relay connection. As you can see, we use a username and password to authenticate in this example. The class constructor of the service host accepts four parameters that will be passed in when the host instance is instantiated. The first parameter is a generic type parameter of the WCF service implementation class (not the service contract interface type), and the other three parameters are account-related parameters: `solutionName`, `password`, and `topic`. The `topic` parameter is used to construct the URI address as a lower-level hierarchy in case there are multiple service hosts registered under the same solution, and we can get all URI addresses that are globally unique. The remaining part of the host implementation is pretty straightforward. We use the URI address to instantiate a `ChannelFactory` instance (the `ChannelFactory` class can accept the WCF interface type `IRelayPublishEventService`, which is derived from both the custom-defined WCF service interface and the `IClientChannel` interface defined from the `System.ServiceModel` namespace). We then call the `CreateChannel()` and `Open()` methods sequentially to start the service request listener on the host side from the cloud.

Listing 6-3. *Implementation of the Host Class*

```
using System;
using System.Collections.Generic;
using System.Linq;
using System.Text;
using System.Security.Cryptography;
using System.ServiceModel;

namespace SoftnetSolutions.RelayService.PublishChannel
{
    using Microsoft.ServiceBus;
    using Microsoft.ServiceBus.Description;
    public class RelayPublishEventHost <T> where T : class
    {
        protected ChannelFactory<IRelayPublishEventService> _channelFactory = null;
        public string ServiceTitle { get; set; }
        public IRelayPublishEventService Channel { get; set; }

        public RelayPublishEventHost(T serviceImpl,
                                     string topic,
                                     string solutionName,
                                     string password)
        {
```

```
            ServiceBusEnvironment.SystemConnectivity.Mode = ConnectivityMode.AutoDetect;
            TransportClientEndpointBehavior relayCredentials =
              new TransportClientEndpointBehavior();
            relayCredentials.CredentialType =
              TransportClientCredentialType.UserNamePassword;
            relayCredentials.Credentials.UserName.UserName = solutionName;
            relayCredentials.Credentials.UserName.Password = password;
            ServiceTitle = topic;

            Uri serviceAddress =
              ServiceBusEnvironment.CreateServiceUri("sb", solutionName,
                  String.Format("{0}/RelayService/", ServiceTitle));
            ServiceHost host = new ServiceHost(serviceImpl.GetType(), serviceAddress);
            host.Description.Endpoints[0].Behaviors.Add(relayCredentials);
            host.Open();

            _channelFactory =
              new ChannelFactory<IRelayPublishEventService>("RelayEndpoint",
                new EndpointAddress(serviceAddress));
            _channelFactory.Endpoint.Behaviors.Add(relayCredentials);
            Channel = _channelFactory.CreateChannel();
            Channel.Open();
        }

        public RelayPublishEventHost(T serviceImpl,
                                     Uri serviceAddress,
                                     TransportClientEndpointBehavior relayCredentials)
        {
            ServiceHost host = new ServiceHost(serviceImpl.GetType(), serviceAddress
            host.Description.Endpoints[0].Behaviors.Add(relayCredentials);
            host.Open();

            _channelFactory =
              new ChannelFactory<IRelayPublishEventService>("RelayEndpoint",
                new EndpointAddress(serviceAddress));
            _channelFactory.Endpoint.Behaviors.Add(relayCredentials);
            Channel = _channelFactory.CreateChannel();
            Channel.Open();
        }
    }
}
```

5. Create a Windows console application, as shown in Listing 6-4. This class reads the password and solution name from the configuration file and creates an instance of the host class. A user can type any text message and post to the hub. All parties hooked to the hub will be notified when the event happens. The credential authentication is against a .NET Service Bus instead of the local Windows system. Therefore the event can be delivered to applications behind a firewall.

Listing 6-4. *Implementation for Windows Console Application*

```
using System;
using System.Collections.Generic;
using System.Text;
using System.Security.Cryptography;
using System.ServiceModel;
using Microsoft.ServiceBus.Description;
using System.Configuration;

namespace SoftnetSolutions.RelayService.PublishChannel
{
    using Microsoft.ServiceBus;

    class Program
    {
        private Program(string[] args)
        {
        }

        static void Main(string[] args)
        {
            Program programInstance = new Program(args);
            programInstance.Run();
        }

        private void Run()
        {
            string subject = ConfigurationManager.AppSettings["Topic"];
            string solutionName = ConfigurationManager.AppSettings["Solution"];
            string password = ConfigurationManager.AppSettings["password"];

            PublishEventService service = new PublishEventService();
            RelayPublishEventHost<PublishEventService> _host =
              new RelayPublishEventHost<PublishEventService>(service,
            subject,
            solutionName,
            password);

            Console.WriteLine(string.Format(
              "{0}--- Connecting success, Press <Enter> to exit ---{0}",
              Environment.NewLine));

            string input = Console.ReadLine();
            while (input != String.Empty)
            {

                PostData postData = new PostData();
                postData.Message = input;
                _host.Channel.PostMessage(postData);
```

```
                input = Console.ReadLine();
            }

            _host.Channel.Close();
        }
    }
}
```

6. Set up CardSpace .NET Service Bus Relay Authentication. To use the CardSpace runtime authentication mode, the following steps need to be done.

    1. Add a card to the solution in the cloud via the .NET Service Bus management portal page. Log in to the .NET Services and SQL Azure portal at `http://portal.ex.azure.microsoft.com/default.aspx`. (Note that this portal page is a different portal page from the Windows Azure portal page and the Azure Services Developer Portal.) Then follow the instructions to submit the card shown in Figure 6-3.

    2. Modify the code of the host implementation from Listing 6-3 as shown in Listing 6-5.

Authentication Modes

.NET Service Bus supports runtime authentication with six modes:

1. `UserNamePassword`
2. `CardSpace`
3. `X509Certificate`
4. `Unauthenticated`
5. `FederationViaCardSpace`
6. `AutomaticRenewal`

Discussion of all these modes is beyond the scope of this book. We are going to investigate two of these supported modes as an example. The `UserNamePassword` mode is the most frequently used runtime authentication mode. That is also used in this exercise as the boldface lines show in Listing 6-3.

Listing 6-5. *Use the CardSpace for .NET Service Bus Connection Authentication*

```
relayCredentials.CredentialType = TransportClientCredentialType.CardSpace;
```

Figure 6-3. Submit a CardSpace to .NET Services

7. Send the card interactively at runtime. Now, when you run the application, you are asked to submit the same card for authentication as Figure 6-4 shows.

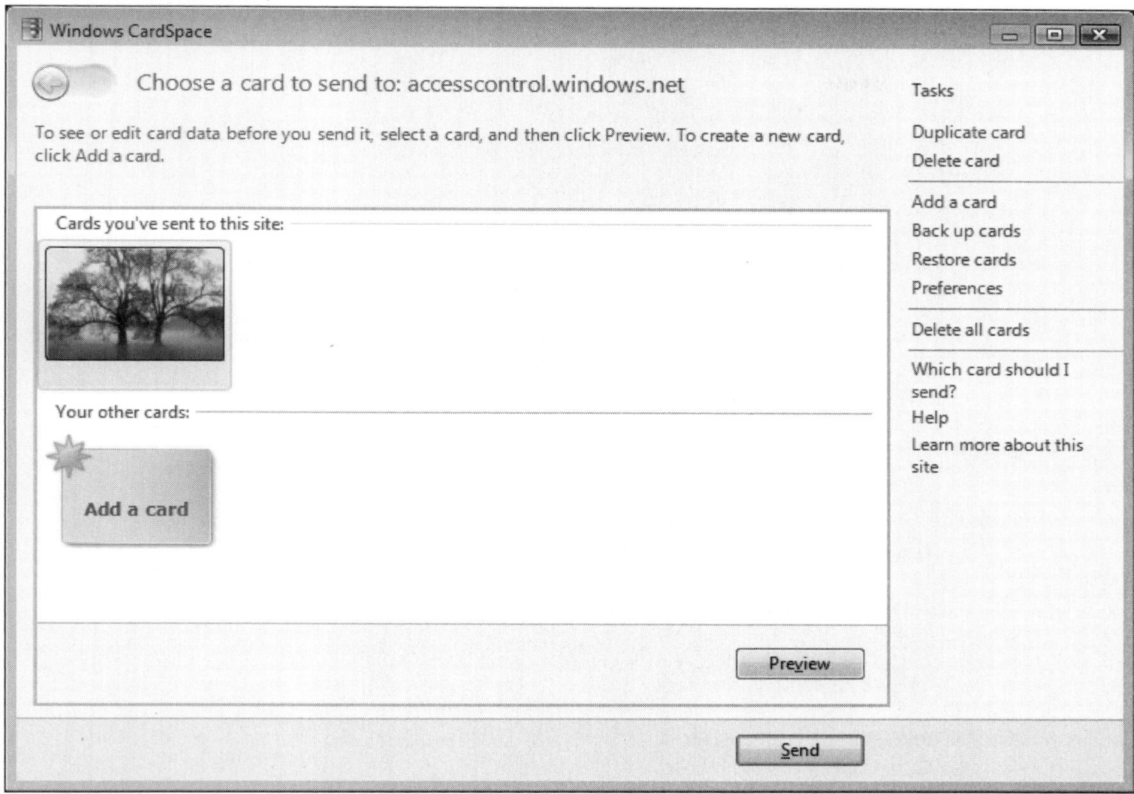

Figure 6-4. *A correct card must be sent to .NET Service Bus for authentication in order to establish a connection for the relay services*

Test results are shown in Figure 6-5, which demonstrates how a message (event) is posted from an application and how all participating parties are notified via relay services.

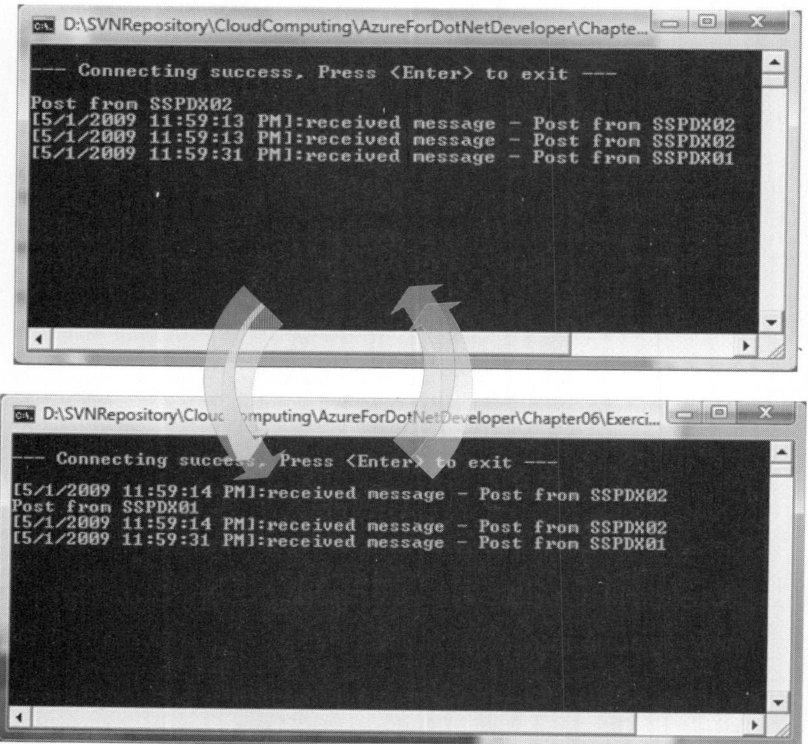

Figure 6-5. *Test results*

One thing you need to bear in mind that whenever an event happens all clients hooked up to the event hub will be notified whether they are interested or not. In practice, a peer-to-peer connected distributed system is a very useful system that enables the message flow to be controlled nicely. Before Azure, the technogy used by the .NET Framework to build such a system is .NET Remoting. The challenge in .NET Remoting is how to connect applications run behind firewalls. .NET Service Bus makes this goal very easy to achieve. Next we are going to look at how to build a non-connected system using the .NET Service Bus.

Simple Direct Connected System Using Hybrid Relay Connection Mode

As I mentioned before, the .NET Service Bus can be used to build distributed connection systems. Figure 6-6 presents the concept of how to use the WCF relay and Hybrid connection mode to establish a direct connection between two applications residing behind firewalls. The process includes two steps.

1. A client application negotiates the connectivity to a service application through the cloud using a relay connection.
2. When the endpoint has been found and the relay connection has been established, .NET Service Bus automatically promotes the connection from a relay connection to a direct connection.

The connection mode used in this approach is the `Hybrid` connection mode, and the binding type of the WCF service is the `netTcpRelayBinding`. This can be done by modifying the `App.config` file of the previous exercise to the code shown in Listing 6-6.

■ **Note** The code for this example is in the Exercise 6-2 bundle from the code download.

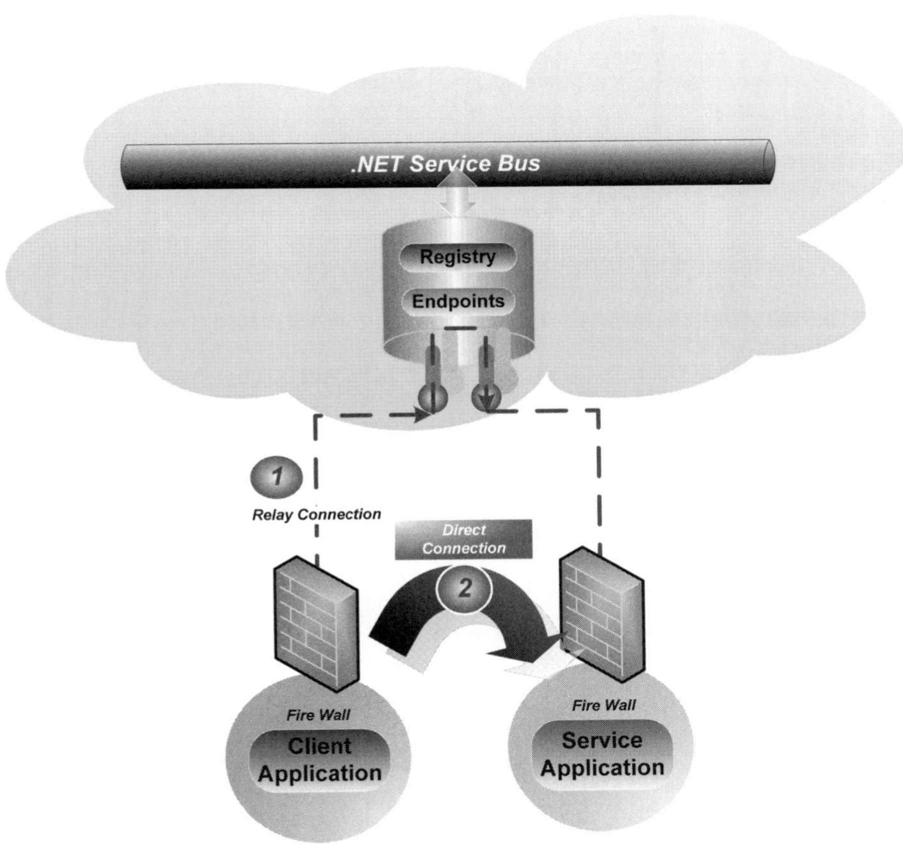

Figure 6-6. *Use the .NET Service Bus to Create a Direct Connection Distributed Application System*

Listing 6-6. WCF Service Configuration Using `netTcpRelayBinding` *with Hybrid Connection Mode*

```
<?xml version="1.0" encoding="utf-8" ?>
<configuration>
  <appSettings>
    <add key="Topic" value="Pheonix"/>
    <add key="Solution" value="SoftnetSolutionsServiceBus"/>
    <add key="password" value="9j!Ns$R8%7"/>
  </appSettings>
  <system.serviceModel>

    <bindings>

      <netEventRelayBinding>
        <binding name="default"  connectionMode="Hybrid"/>
          <security mode="None" />
        </netEventRelayBinding>
    </bindings>

    <client>
      <endpoint name="RelayEndpoint"
contract="SoftnetSolutions.RelayService.PublishChannel.IPublishEventService"
                binding="netTcpRelayBinding"
                bindingConfiguration="default"
                address="" />
    </client>

    <services>
      <service name="SoftnetSolutions.RelayService.PublishChannel.PublishEventService">
        <endpoint name="RelayEndpoint"
                contract="SoftnetSolutions.RelayService.PublishChannel.IPublishEventService"
                binding="netTcpRelayBinding"
                bindingConfiguration="default"
                address="" />
      </service>
    </services>

  </system.serviceModel>
</configuration>
```

The data contract we use for this exercise is the same as defined in Listing 6-1. Listing 6-7 shows the implementation for creating a communication channel used to post the messages. There is not much difference from the implementation compared to the same part of the last exercise except for the interface type passed to the channel factory.

Listing 6-7. Implementation of `HybridPublishService`

```
using System;
using System.ServiceModel;
using System.ServiceModel.Description;
using Microsoft.ServiceBus;
```

```
using System.Text;
using System.Configuration;

namespace SoftnetSolutions.RelayService.ServiceContract
{
    public class HybridPublishService
    {
        public IPublishEventServiceChannel ClientChannel { get; set; }

        private ChannelFactory<IPublishEventServiceChannel> _channelFactory = null;

        public HybridPublishService(string endpoint)
        {
            string subject = ConfigurationManager.AppSettings["Topic"];
            string solutionName = ConfigurationManager.AppSettings["Solution"];
            string password = ConfigurationManager.AppSettings["password"];

            TransportClientEndpointBehavior relayCredentials =
              new TransportClientEndpointBehavior();
            relayCredentials.CredentialType =
              TransportClientCredentialType.UserNamePassword;
            relayCredentials.Credentials.UserName.UserName = solutionName;
            relayCredentials.Credentials.UserName.Password = password;

            Uri serviceUri = ServiceBusEnvironment.CreateServiceUri("sb",
                                                                     solutionName,
                                                                     subject);
            _channelFactory =
              new ChannelFactory<IPublishEventServiceChannel>(
                endpoint, new EndpointAddress(serviceUri));
            _channelFactory.Endpoint.Behaviors.Add(relayCredentials);
            ClientChannel = _channelFactory.CreateChannel();
            ClientChannel.Open();
        }

        public void Dispose()
        {
            ClientChannel.Close();
            _channelFactory.Close();
        }
    }
}
```

Listing 6-8 shows how to instantiate the communication with relay service and register the connection status change event. The status change event will be triggered when the connection type switches from relay connection to direct connection. Compared to the same part from the last exercise, as the boldface lines in Listing 6-7 show, an event handler function, `ConnectionStateChanged()`, has to be defined and registered to the service instance. The event handler in this exercise is used to monitor the connection status change. You can insert any business logic into the event handler in your application, but in this exercise we only output trace information to acknowledge the status change. The connection status is initially set to relay binding and will be automatically switched to direct binding a few seconds after the connection has been established.

Listing 6-8. *Implementation of Console Application Instantiates a Connection Starting with Relay Service*

```
using System;
using System.ServiceModel;
using Microsoft.ServiceBus;
using System.Text;
using System.Configuration;

namespace SoftnetSolutions.RelayService.PublishChannel
{
    using SoftnetSolutions.RelayService.ServiceContract;

    class Program
    {
        static void Main(string[] args)
        {

            PublishEventService service = new PublishEventService();
            string endpoint = "RelayEndpoint";
            HybridPublishService hybridPublishService = new HybridPublishService(endpoint);
            Console.WriteLine(
              string.Format(
                "---Relay connection has been established ----{0}", Environment.NewLine
              )
            );

            IHybridConnectionStatus hybridConnectionStatus =
              hybridPublishService.ClientChannel.GetProperty<IHybridConnectionStatus>();

            hybridConnectionStatus.ConnectionStateChanged +=
              new EventHandler<HybridConnectionStateChangedArgs>(
                hybridConnectionStatus_ConnectionStateChanged
              );

            Console.WriteLine(
              string.Format("---Press <Enter> to exit publishing----{0}",
                            Environment.NewLine));

            string input = Console.ReadLine();
            while (input != String.Empty)
            {

                PostData postData = new PostData();
                postData.Message =
                  string.Format("[{0}]:{1}", DateTime.Now.ToString(), input);
                (hybridPublishService.ClientChannel as IPublishEventService)
                  .PostMessage(postData);
```

```
                input = Console.ReadLine();
            }

            hybridPublishService.ClientChannel.Dispose();
        }

        static private void hybridConnectionStatus_ConnectionStateChanged(
          object sender, HybridConnectionStateChangedArgs args)
        {
            Console.WriteLine(
              string.Format(
                "---Connection has been switched from relay to direct connection ---{0}",
                Environment.NewLine
              )
            );
        }
    }
}
```

The screenshot of Figure 6-7 caught at the breakpoint from Visual Studio shows that the connection type is relayed when the connection is established. Figure 6-8 shows that the connection has been automatically switched to direct a few seconds later and that a notification event has been raised and caught by the console application.

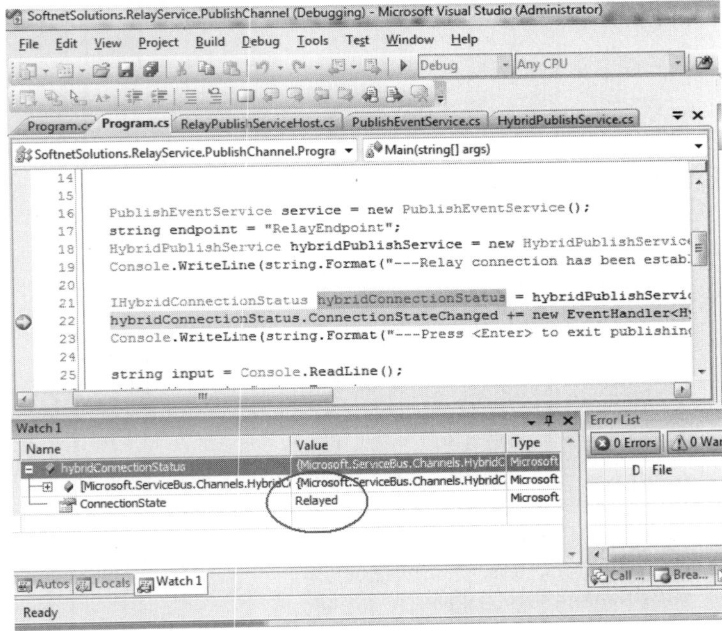

Figure 6-7. When the connection has been established the type of connection is relayed

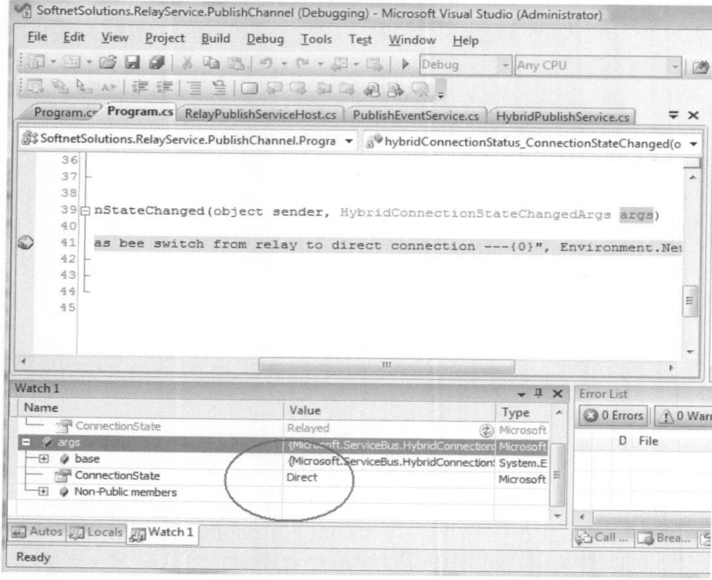

Figure 6-8. The relay service switches the connection from relayed to direct a few seconds later

Test results of the exercise are shown in Figure 6-9, which demonstrates how a connection switches from relayed to direct and the messages are delivered from publisher to listener.

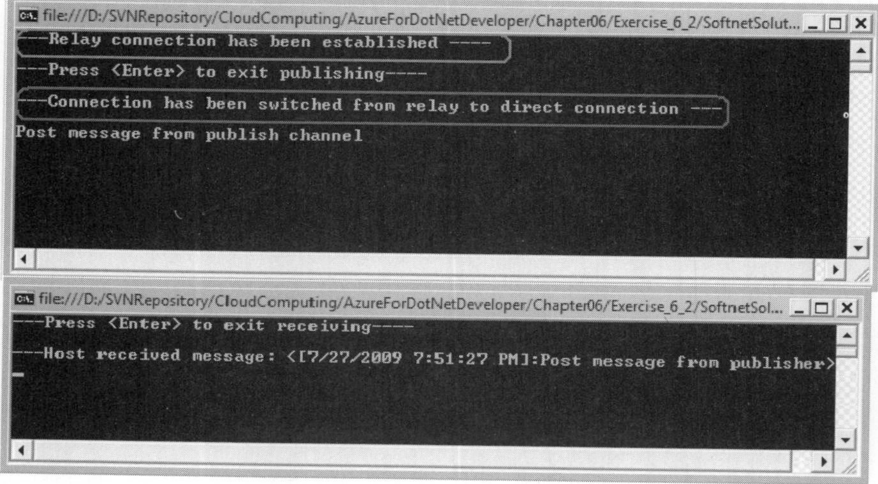

Figure 6-9. Runtime screenshots from the results of Exercise 6-2

Using .NET Service Bus to Build a Distributed Connected Windows Application

The building blocks we built in the last exercise can be used to build a direct connected Windows application system leveraging the .NET Service Bus. As Figure 6-10 shows, this system contains two Windows applications. The Draw Shape application draws shapes using random colors, sizes, and positions. The Shape Controller application picks the types of shape to draw and sends a notification to the Draw Shape application via a .NET TCP connection using WCF services. The binding mode is also the `Hybrid` type. The communication is initialized using the .NET Service Bus relay connection and automatically switches to direct bindings.

■ **Note** The code for this example is in the Exercise 6-3 bundle from the code download.

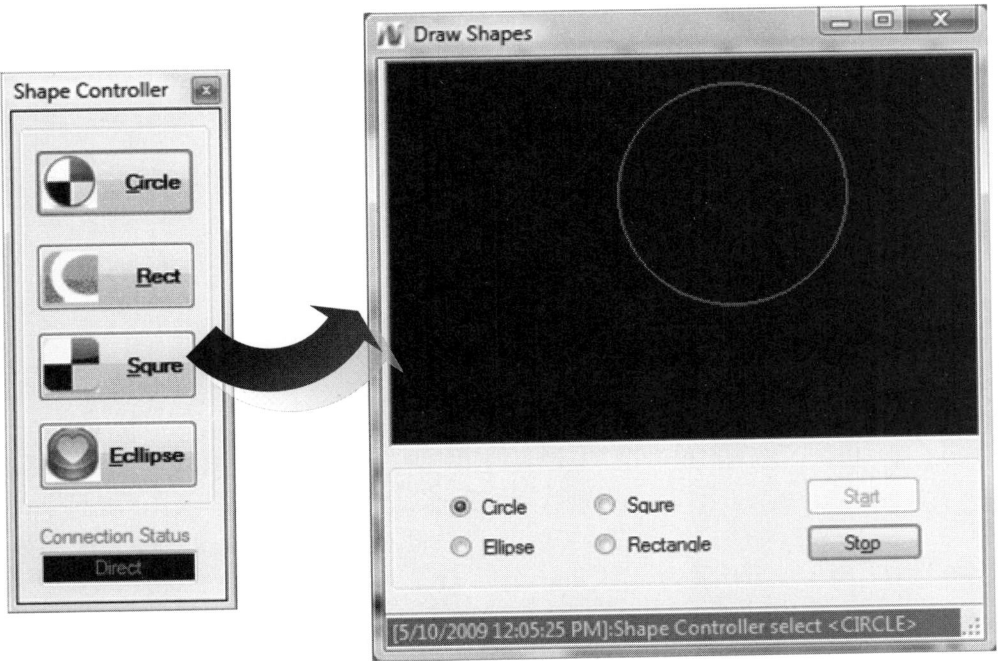

Figure 6-10. Distributed direct-connected Windows application system

The entire solution contains five C# projects.

- Two projects, SoftnetSolutions.IShape and SoftnetSolutions.Shape, are used to handle the shape drawing.
- SoftnetSolutions.RelayService.ServiceContract defines a WCF service contact.
- The final two projects, SoftnetSolutions.RelayService.ShapeController and SoftnetSolutions.Shape.Draw, are Windows client-server applications.

SoftnetSolutions.IShape

This project defines an IShape interface, which contains one read-only property Map and one method Draw() as Listing 6-9 shows. All classes used to handle the shape drawing implement this interface.

Listing 6-9. *Interface Definition for IShape*

```
using System;
using System.Drawing;

namespace SoftnetSolutions.Shape
{
    public enum SHAPE_TYPE { CIRCLE, ELLIPSE, SQUARE, RECTANGLE, NOT_SUPPORTED_TYPE };

        public interface IShape
        {
                void Draw();
                Bitmap Map{ get; }
        }
}
```

SoftnetSolutions.Shape

The implementation for base class Shape is shown in Listing 6-10. The constructor for this class accepts one parameter with type of windows Panel, which is used as the shape-drawing surface. The base class implements shared methods for all derived subclasses, such as those that generate random color and drawing sizes.

Listing 6-10. *Implementation for Base Class Shape*

```
using System;
using System.Drawing;
using System.Drawing.Imaging;
using System.Windows.Forms;

namespace SoftnetSolutions.Shape
{
    abstract public class Shape : IShape
    {
```

```
const PixelFormat PIXELFORMAT = PixelFormat.Format24bppRgb;
protected Bitmap _bitmap = null;
protected Random _random = null;
protected Graphics _graphics = null;
protected int _shapeWidth = 0;
protected int _shapeHeight = 0;
protected int _drawAreaWidth = 0;
protected int _drawAreaHeight = 0;


public Shape(Panel drawArea)
{
    if (null == drawArea
        || drawArea.Width <= 0
        || drawArea.Height <= 0)
    {
        throw new ArgumentException(
          "The draw area must be specified and valid", drawArea.ToString());
    }

    _random = new Random((int)DateTime.Now.Ticks);
    _bitmap = new Bitmap(drawArea.ClientRectangle.Width,
                         drawArea.ClientRectangle.Height,
                         PIXELFORMAT);
    _graphics = Graphics.FromImage(_bitmap);
    _drawAreaWidth = drawArea.Width;

public Bitmap Map
{
    get { return _bitmap; }
}

public int ShapeWidth
{
    get { return _shapeWidth; }
}

public int ShapeHeight
{
    get { return _shapeHeight; }
}

protected int _RandomWidth
{
    get
    {
        _shapeWidth = _random.Next(0, _drawAreaWidth);
        return _shapeWidth;
    }
}
```

```
        protected int _RandomHeight
        {
            get
            {
                _shapeHeight = _random.Next(0, _drawAreaHeight);
                return _shapeHeight;
            }
        }

        protected Pen _RandomColorPen
        {
            get
            {
                return new Pen(Color.FromArgb(_random.Next(0, 255),
                    _random.Next(0, 255),
                    _random.Next(0, 255)));
            }
        }

        #endregion

        #region Protected Method

        protected void _Reset()
        {
            if (null != _bitmap)
            {
                Graphics.FromImage(this._bitmap).Clear(Color.Black);
            }
        }

        #endregion

        abstract public void Draw();
    }
}
```

A class derived from this base class is responsible for drawing a specific shape. Listing 6-11 shows how to draw a `Circle` bitmap programmatically on the panel surface. A protected function, `_Reset()`, is called before drawing. This function clears the previously drawn bitmap and sets the bitmap to the background color. When an application needs to draw different shapes on the same panel surface, it just needs to dynamically construct a drawing class and pass in the panel object instance. The implementation will be presented later in this exercise.

Listing 6-11. Derived `Drawing` *Class Used to Draw a Circle Bitmap on a Panel Surface*

```
using System;
using System.Drawing;
using System.Drawing.Imaging;
using System.Windows.Forms;
```

```
namespace SoftnetSolutions.Shape
{

        public class Circle : Shape, IShape
        {
                public Circle(Panel drawArea) : base(drawArea)
                {
                }

                override public void Draw()
                {
                        int width = base._RandomWidth;
                        int height = base._RandomHeight;
                        int radius = width / 2;

                        base._Reset();
                        base._graphics.DrawEllipse( base._RandomColorPen,
                                width - radius,//convert to bounding rectangle
                                height - radius,//convert to bounding rectangle
                                radius,
                                radius);
                }
        }
}
```

SoftnetSolutions.RelayService.ServiceContract

The WCF service contract stays the same as the one we defined in the last exercise except for adding an operation contract, as Listing 6-12 shows.

Listing 6-12. *Adding an Operation Contact* `OnShapeSelecChanged` *to the Service Contract* `IPublishEventService`

```
using System;
using System.ServiceModel;

namespace SoftnetSolutions.RelayService.ServiceContract
{
    [ServiceContract(Name = "IPublishEventService",
        Namespace = "http://SoftnetSolutions.RelayService/")]
    public interface IPublishEventService
    {
        [OperationContract(IsOneWay = true)]
        void PostMessage(PostData postData);

        [OperationContract(IsOneWay = true)]
        void OnShapeSelectChanged(PostData shapeData);
    }
```

```
    public interface IPublishEventServiceChannel : IPublishEventService, IClientChannel { }
}
```

```
using System;
using System.Collections.Generic;
using System.Linq;
using System.Text;
using System.Runtime.Serialization;
using System.Reflection;

namespace SoftnetSolutions.RelayService.ServiceContract
{
    using SoftnetSolutions.Shape;

    [DataContract]
    public class PostData : IComparable
    {
        [DataMember]
        public string Message;

        [DataMember]
        public SHAPE_TYPE shape { get; set; }

        public int CompareTo(object obj)
        {
            if (obj is PostData)
            {
                PostData temp = (PostData)obj;

                return shape.CompareTo(temp.shape);
            }
            throw new ArgumentException(
              string.Format("object is not a <{0}> type", this.GetType().Name));
        }
    }
}
```

SoftnetSolutions.Shape.Draw

SoftnetSolutions.Shape.Draw is a Windows application that has two responsibilities:

1. Listen to the event published by the ShapeController and update the UI. This is done by implementing the WCF service contract IPublishEventService as the class declaration shows in Listing 6-13.

Listing 6-13. *The* `FormDrawShape` *Implements the WCF Service Contract* `IPublishEventService`

```
[ServiceBehavior(Name = "PublishEventService",
    Namespace = "http://SoftnetSolutions.RelayService/",
    InstanceContextMode = InstanceContextMode.Single)]
public partial class FormDrawShape : Form, IPublishEventService
{
}
```

2. Draw a shape according to the selected shape type. This is done by using a factory method design pattern in conjunction with a reflection class to dynamically load a drawing object into memory as shown in Listing 6-14. Bitmap drawing is done by implementing the `drawPanel_Paint()` method and associating the bitmap to the background image of the drawing panel as shown in Listing 6-15.

Listing 6-14. *Use Factory Method Design Pattern and Reflection Class to Dynamically Create a Shape Object as a Type of IShape*

```
private IShape _ClassFactory()
{
    string assemblyName = "SoftnetSolutions.Shape";
    string className = string.Format("{0}.{1}",
                                     assemblyName,
                                     SHAPE_NAME[(int)this._shapeType]);
    Assembly assembly = Assembly.Load(assemblyName);
    Type classType = assembly.GetType(className);
    IShape shapeClass =
      (IShape)Activator.CreateInstance(
        classType, new object[] {this.drawingPanel});

    return shapeClass;
}
```

Listing 6-15. *Implement the* `drawingPanel_Paint` *Method to Associate the Bitmap Instance to the Background Image of the Drawing Panel*

```
private void drawingPanel_Paint(object sender, System.Windows.Forms.PaintEventArgs e)
{
    if (null == _shape)
    {
        return;
    }

    drawingPanel.BackgroundImage = this._shape.Map;
}
```

SoftnetSolutions.RelayService.ShapeController

The Draw Shape Controller is another part of this system. The responsibility of this Windows-based application is to select a drawing shape type and publish a message with the type of PostData that contains a string description and the enumeration value for the selected drawing shape. The data contract PostData is defined in Listing 6-12 and implements the IComparable interface to allow the service application to check for selected drawing shape changes from the client drawing controller application. The implementation of this class is straightforward as Listing 6-16 shows. When a button is clicked, a different drawing shape is selected and a new PostData object is created and sent out as part of the publishing message sent from the drawing controller to the shape-drawing application. The component that we use to create out the communication channel is the HybridPublishService we created in the last exercise.

Listing 6-16. *Implementation of* `ShapeController`

```
using System;
using System.Collections.Generic;
using System.ComponentModel;
using System.Data;
using System.Drawing;
using System.Linq;
using System.Text;
using System.Windows.Forms;
using System.ServiceModel;
using Microsoft.ServiceBus;

namespace SoftnetSolutions.RelayService.ShapeController
{
    using SoftnetSolutions.RelayService.ServiceContract;
    using SoftnetSolutions.Shape;
    using SoftnetSolutions.Shape.Draw;
       public partial class FormController : Form
       {
        private IPublishEventService _publishEventService = null;
        private HybridPublishService _hybridPublishService = null;
        private string _connectionStatus = "Disconnected";

        public FormController()
        {
            InitializeComponent();
        }

        public FormController(IPublishEventService publishEventService)
        {
            InitializeComponent();

            _publishEventService = publishEventService;
            string endpoint = "RelayEndpoint";
            _hybridPublishService = new HybridPublishService(endpoint);
```

```
    IHybridConnectionStatus hybridConnectionStatus =
      _hybridPublishService.ClientChannel.GetProperty<IHybridConnectionStatus>();
    _connectionStatus = hybridConnectionStatus.ConnectionState.ToString();

    hybridConnectionStatus.ConnectionStateChanged +=
      new EventHandler<HybridConnectionStateChangedArgs>(
        hybridConnectionStatus_ConnectionStateChanged);

    (_publishEventService as FormDrawShape).Show();
}

private void btnCircle_Click(object sender, EventArgs e)
{
    PostData shapeData = new PostData();
    shapeData.shape = SHAPE_TYPE.CIRCLE;
    _PostMessage(shapeData);
}

private void btnRectangle_Click(object sender, EventArgs e)
{
    PostData shapeData = new PostData();
    shapeData.shape = SHAPE_TYPE.RECTANGLE;
    _PostMessage(shapeData);
}

private void btnSqure_Click(object sender, EventArgs e)
{
    PostData shapeData = new PostData();
    shapeData.shape = SHAPE_TYPE.SQUARE;
    _PostMessage(shapeData);
}

private void btnEcllipse_Click(object sender, EventArgs e)
{
    PostData shapeData = new PostData();
    shapeData.shape = SHAPE_TYPE.ELLIPSE;
    _PostMessage(shapeData);
}

private void hybridConnectionStatus_ConnectionStateChanged(
  object sender, HybridConnectionStateChangedArgs args)
{
    System.Diagnostics.Trace.WriteLine(
      string.Format(
        "---Connection has been switched from relay to direct connection ---{0}",
        Environment.NewLine));
    _connectionStatus = args.ConnectionState.ToString();
}
```

```
        private void _PostMessage(PostData postData)
        {
            postData.Message =
              string.Format("[{0}]:Shape Controller select <{1}>", DateTime.Now.ToString(),
                postData.shape);
            _publishEventService.OnShapeSelectChanged(postData);
            _publishEventService.PostMessage(postData);
        }

        private void timer1_Tick(object sender, EventArgs e)
        {
            textBoxConnectinStatus.Text = _connectionStatus;

            switch (_connectionStatus)
            {
                case "Relayed":
                    textBoxConnectinStatus.ForeColor = Color.Red;
                    break;
                case "Direct":
                    textBoxConnectinStatus.ForeColor = Color.Lime;
                    break;

            }
        }

    }
}
```

Before going any further, we should look at port forwarding when using `netTcpRelayBinding` with `Hybrid` mode. This may or may not be a potential issue depending upon the Internet service provider behind the system infrastructure, especially if you are working from a small LAN system or from home.

Port Forwarding

If the DHCP connection type is used by the local gateway system, port forwarding usually needs to be configured in order that the communication from .NET Service Bus can be routed to the application correctly. How to configure port forwarding depends on the Internet provider your organization has. Port forwarding should be configured to allow Internet access to port 80 using HTTP and port 808 using TCP. Figure 6-11 shows how to configure port forwarding based on the Verizon FIOS gateway.

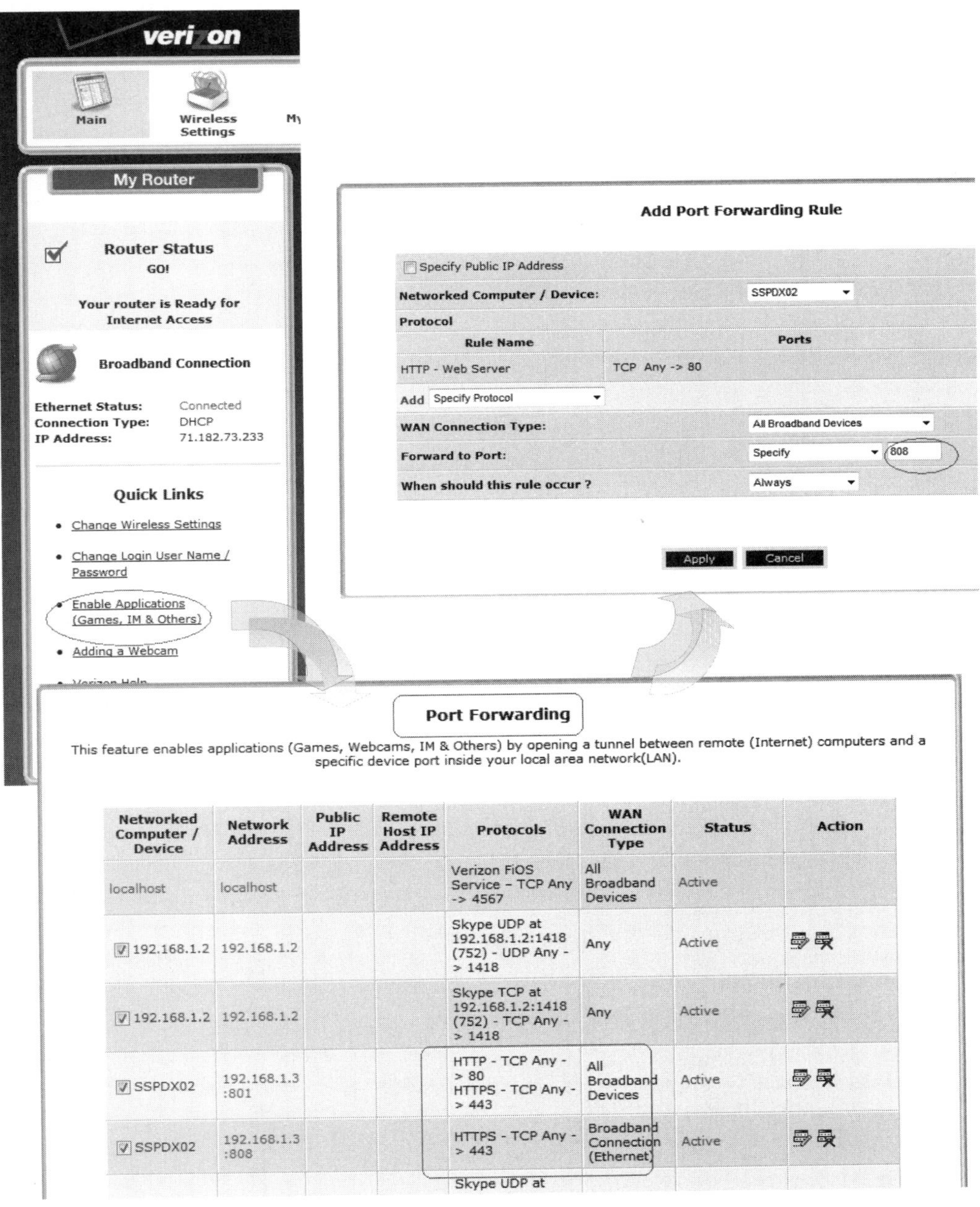

Figure 6-11. An example of port forwarding configuration using Verizon FIOS gateway

Change Credential Type

To modify the access federation type, modify the configuration file `App.config` for `ShapeController`. The boldface lines in Listing 6-17 and Listing 6-18 show how to use the `CardSpace` and `AutomaticRenewal` credentials respectively. The most frequently used options of federation are

- `CardSpace`
- `UserNamePassword`
- `X509Certificate`
- `AutomaticRenewal`

Listing 6-17. *Change the Credential Type to CardSpace in the Configuration File `App.config` of `ShapeController`*

```
<?xml version="1.0" encoding="utf-8" ?>
<configuration>
  <appSettings>
    <add key="Topic" value="PublishEventService"/>
    <add key="Solution" value="SoftnetSolutionsServiceBus"/>
    <add key="password" value="9j!Ns$R8%7"/>
  </appSettings>
  <system.serviceModel>

    <bindings>
      <netTcpRelayBinding>
        <binding name="default" connectionMode="Hybrid">
          <security mode="None" />
        </binding>
      </netTcpRelayBinding>
    </bindings>

    <behaviors>
      <endpointBehaviors>
        <behavior name="CardSpaceBehavior">
          <transportClientEndpointBehavior credentialType="CardSpace">
            <clientCredentials>
              <userNamePassword
                userName="SoftnetSolutionsServiceBus"
                password="9j!Ns$R8%7" />
              <federationViaCardSpace>
                <issuer address="http://idp.sts.microsoft.com" />
                <claimTypeRequirements>
                  <add claimType=http://schemas.xmlsoap.org/claims/Group
                       isOptional="false" />
                </claimTypeRequirements>
              </federationViaCardSpace>
            </clientCredentials>
          </transportClientEndpointBehavior>
```

```
        </behavior>
      </endpointBehaviors>
    </behaviors>

    <client>
      <endpoint name="RelayEndpoint"
                contract="SoftnetSolutions.RelayService.ServiceContract.IPublishEventService"
                binding="netTcpRelayBinding"
                bindingConfiguration="default"
                behaviorConfiguration="CardSpaceBehavior"
                address="http://AddressToBeReplacedInCode/" />
    </client>
    <services>
      <service name="SoftnetSolutions.Shape.Draw.FormDrawShape">
        <endpoint name="RelayEndpoint"
                contract="SoftnetSolutions.RelayService.ServiceContract.IPublishEventService"
                binding="netTcpRelayBinding"
                bindingConfiguration="default"
                behaviorConfiguration="CardSpaceBehavior"
                address="" />
      </service>
    </services>
  </system.serviceModel>
</configuration>
```

Listing 6-18. *Change the Credential Type to* `automaticRenewalClientCredentials` *in the Configuration File* `App.config` *of* `ShapeController`

```
<?xml version="1.0" encoding="utf-8" ?>
<configuration>
  <appSettings>
    <add key="Topic" value="PublishEventService"/>
    <add key="Solution" value="SoftnetSolutionsServiceBus"/>
    <add key="password" value="9j!Ns$R8%7"/>
  </appSettings>
  <system.serviceModel>

    <bindings>
      <netTcpRelayBinding>
        <binding name="default" connectionMode="Hybrid">
          <security mode="None" />
        </binding>
      </netTcpRelayBinding>
    </bindings>

    <behaviors>
      <endpointBehaviors>
        <behavior name="automaticRenewalClientCredentials">
          <transportClientEndpointBehavior credentialType="AutomaticRenewal" />
        </behavior>
```

```
      </endpointBehaviors>
    </behaviors>

    <client>
      <endpoint name="RelayEndpoint"
              contract="SoftnetSolutions.RelayService.ServiceContract.IPublishEventService"
              binding="netTcpRelayBinding"
              bindingConfiguration="default"
              behaviorConfiguration="automaticRenewalClientCredentials"
              address="http://AddressToBeReplacedInCode/" />
    </client>
    <services>
      <service name="SoftnetSolutions.Shape.Draw.FormDrawShape">
        <endpoint name="RelayEndpoint"
              contract="SoftnetSolutions.RelayService.ServiceContract.IPublishEventService"
              binding="netTcpRelayBinding"
              bindingConfiguration="default"
              behaviorConfiguration="automaticRenewalClientCredentials"
              address="" />
      </service>
    </services>
  </system.serviceModel>
</configuration>
```

In Chapter 3 we discussed Azure Queue storage, which is one of the three basic storage types used as part of the Azure framework. .NET Service Bus also provides application-level queue storage, called .NET Service Bus Queue, that tremendously simplifies the message delivery between applications run behind a firewall. In the next exercise we are going to refactor this exercise to use .NET Service Bus Queue and let you get hands-on experience with .NET Service Bus Queue. You'll be able to reuse the libraries from the project in your future development.

.NET Service Bus Queue Client Facade

The .NET Service Bus Queue leverages every Internet communication protocol to allow message delivery through the cloud. The .NET Services SDK provides rich .NET Service Bus Queue examples and covers all its features in detail. This book does not intend to duplicate these examples but build a facade `QueueClientFactory` component allowing you to easily integrate the .NET Service Bus Queue into applications run from either a cloud or on-premises environment. You should be able to easily find a lot of blogs and technical articles, such as `http://vasters.com/clemensv/PermaLink,guid,0f64f592-7239-42fc-aed2-f0993701c5f6.aspx`.

Before we move on, let us cover some background information that may be useful in future development. As you know from Chapter 3, the Azure Queue service runs from local or cloud fabric. In contrast, .NET Service Bus Queue exists on the Internet and is URI addressable using the address format list shown in the following bullet points. The URI addresses should contain the phrase `servicebus.windows.net`.

There is no limitation to the format for the .NET Service Bus queue, so the queue message can carry user-defined data types. The .NET Service Bus uses the URI for the name or address of a queue.

The format of a queue address is:

- `sb://solution.servicebus.windows.net/QueueName`
- `http://solution.servicebus.windows.net/QueueName`
- `https://solution.servicebus.windows.net/QueueName`

The queue name can be in any format. In other words, the .NET Service Bus queues can be addressed by subject in the hierarchical structure. This makes the .NET Service Bus Queue a good candidate to be used in an event-driven distributed system.

This exercise refactors the .NET Services SDK example `TypedMessages`. The original source code and document can be found at `[install drive]:\Program Files\Microsoft .NET Services SDK\Samples\ServiceBus\ExploringFeatures\Queues\TypedMessages`.

■ **Note** The code for this example is in the Exercise 6-4 bundle from the code download.

To use the .NET Service Bus Queue it is essential to create an instance of the `QueueClient` class. The core class is the `QueueClientFactory`, which accepts a generic type `T` as a parameter since the core member variable in this class, `_queueMessage` (of type of `QueueMessage`), does. The steps to create a .NET Service Bus `QueueClient` are straightforward.

1. Create a service URI by calling a static method `CreateServiceUri()` from the class `ServiceBusEnvironment` in the `Microsoft.ServiceBus.dll` assembly. (This assembly can be found in the `Assemblies` folder of the .NET Services SDK path.)
2. Create a `QueuePolicy`. The simplest way, which this exercise uses, is to create the queue policy using the .NET Services SDK's `Microsoft.ServiceBus.QueuePolicy` class. The `QueueClient` instances cannot be created directly but must be created via the `QueueManagementClient`.
3. Create the `QueueClientFactory` class to wrap up the methods from the SDK's `TypedMessages` example. This class can be used for both client-side and server-side applications. If this factory class is used for a server-side application, the application can register an update callback notification when a new queue message is detected.

The implementation of the `QueueClientFactory` is shown in Listing 6-19. In order to process the update callback notification, the data entity object needs to implement the `IComparable` interface allowing the caller object to detect the value change of the internal custom-defined data types (in this example the custom data is the enumerator type). This all applies where a WCF data contract type class is used (since under the hood `QueueClient` uses the WCF service for communication).

The `QueueClientFactory` class has two member variables, `_queueMessage` and `_lastQueueMessage`, with the type of `QueueMessage` defined in the `Microsoft.Samples.ServiceBus` namespace. Unlike the Azure Queue we explored in Chapter 3, this class dose not fire the callback event when a new message is put into the queue. Therefore our wrapper class has to actively poll the queue periodically to get the new message. This is done from the timer tick handler `PollingQueueData`. If the internal data value of the message is different from that of the last message, the factory wrapper class fires a notification event and persists the message instance to the member variable `_lastQueueMessage`. This is the reason why the data contract class must implement the IComparable interface if the embedded data is a custom-defined type. Another difference between the Azure Queue storage and .NET Service Bus Queue is that the queue message is not persisted in the QueueMessage class. As I mentioned at the beginning of this exercise, the .NET Service Bus Queue is an application-level queue available through the Internet. Therefore, it would make sense to expect it to have a permanent persistence storage space. This also explains why the Azure Queue does not actively remove the message from queue storage until the client explicitly calls a service to delete it, while the .NET Service Bus Queue does actively remove messages.

Listing 6-19. *Implementation of QueueClientFactory*

```
using System;
using System.ServiceModel;
using System.ServiceModel.Description;
using Microsoft.ServiceBus;
using Microsoft.ServiceBus.Description;
using System.Text;
using System.ServiceModel.Channels;
using System.Configuration;

namespace SoftnetSolutions.ServiceBus.QueueFacade
{
    using Microsoft.Samples.ServiceBus;
    using SoftnetSolutions.AzureSolutionCredential;
    using CSharpBuildingBlocks.EventsHelper;

    public class QueueClientFactory<T> where T: class
    {
        protected System.Timers.Timer _timer = null;
        protected QueueClientFactory<T> _queueClientFactory = null;
        protected QueueMessage<T> _queueMessage = null;
        protected QueueMessage<T> _lastQueueMessage = null;
        protected event EventNotificationHandler _dataUpdateEvent = null;

        public QueueClient<T> QueueClient { get; set; }
        public QueueClientFactory()
        {
            _Initialization();
            _StartQueuePollingTimer();
        }

        public event EventNotificationHandler DataUpdateEvent
        {
            add
            {
                _dataUpdateEvent += value;
                _StartQueuePollingTimer();
            }
            remove { _dataUpdateEvent -= value; }
        }

        private void _StartQueuePollingTimer()
```

```
{
    _timer = new System.Timers.Timer(1000);
    _timer.Elapsed += new System.Timers.ElapsedEventHandler(PollingQueueData);
    _timer.AutoReset = true;

    _timer.Enabled = true;

    _timer.Start();
}

private void _Initialization()
{
    string solutionName = ConfigurationManager.AppSettings["Solution"];
    string queueName = ConfigurationManager.AppSettings["QueueName"];

    AzureSolutionCredential azureSolutionCredential =
      new AzureSolutionCredential(solutionName);
    Uri queueUri =
      ServiceBusEnvironment.CreateServiceUri("sb", solutionName,
        string.Format("/{0}/", queueName));

    TransportClientEndpointBehavior userNamePasswordServiceBusCredential =
      new TransportClientEndpointBehavior();
    userNamePasswordServiceBusCredential.CredentialType =
      TransportClientCredentialType.UserNamePassword;
    userNamePasswordServiceBusCredential.Credentials.UserName.UserName =
      solutionName;
    userNamePasswordServiceBusCredential.Credentials.UserName.Password =
      azureSolutionCredential.Password;

    QueuePolicy queuePolicy = new QueuePolicy();
    queuePolicy.ExpirationInstant = DateTime.UtcNow + TimeSpan.FromHours(1);
    QueueClient = QueueRenewalHelper<T>.GetOrCreateQueue<T>(
      userNamePasswordServiceBusCredential, queueUri, ref queuePolicy);
}

protected void PollingQueueData(object source, System.Timers.ElapsedEventArgs e)
{
    if (null != QueueClient)
    {
        try
        {
            _queueMessage = QueueClient.Retrieve();
        }
        catch { }
        if (null != _queueMessage)
        {
            T queueData = _queueMessage.Value as T;
```

```
                        if (queueData is IComparable)
                        {
                            if (null == _lastQueueMessage ||
                             (queueData as IComparable).CompareTo(_lastQueueMessage.Value) != 0)
                            {
                                _lastQueueMessage = _queueMessage;
                                if (null != _dataUpdateEvent)
                                {
                                    _dataUpdateEvent(this, new

                                    QueueDataUpdateArgs<T>(_queueMessage.Value));
                                }
                            }
                        }
                        else
                        {
                            throw new ArgumentException(
                              "The data object must implement IComparable interface!",
                              queueData.GetType().Name);
                        }
                    }
                }
            }
        }
    }
```

4. Add a new class, QueueDataUpdateArgs<T>, to the project SoftnetSolutions.ServiceBus.QueueFacade. This class is derived from the EventArgs class and accepts a generic type class as the embedded object for the queue message class. The implementation is shown in Listing 6-20.

Listing 6-20*. Implementation of QueueDataUpdateArgs<T> Class*

```
using System;
using System.Collections.Generic;
using System.Linq;
using System.Text;

namespace SoftnetSolutions.ServiceBus.QueueFacade
{
    using CSharpBuildingBlocks.EventsHelper;

    public class QueueDataUpdateArgs<T> :EventHelperArgs
    {
        public T QueueData { get; set; }
        public QueueDataUpdateArgs() { }
        public QueueDataUpdateArgs(T queueData)
        {
            QueueData = queueData;
        }
```

```
        public override string ToString()
        {
            return string.Empty;
        }
    }
}
```

Adapting the QueueFacade class to the applications created in the previous exercise, we have the same results as that from the previous exercise but using the .NET Service Bus Queue.

Summary

In this chapter we saw how .NET Service Bus solves two major problems:

- How to get service requests through a firewall
- How to discover service endpoints

We started by examining the .NET Service Bus in detail, including how its service name hierarchy worked and how we register and discover applications with its service registry.

The rest of the chapter contained examples of using the .NET Service Bus to connect applications. We wrote a message hub that clients subscribed to. It was fairly simple but demonstrated the simplicity of .NET Service Bus. The next two examples were distibuted connected systems, one of which demonstrated a loosely coupled distributed drawing application.

Our final example used the .NET Service Bus Queue and demonstrated the difference between the .NET Service Bus Queue and the Queue storage we saw in Chapter 3.

CHAPTER 7

■ ■ ■

Azure .NET Services—Workflows

The .NET Workflow Service provides a highly scalable host for running workflows in the cloud. Workflows can be designed and constructed using Visual Studio's Workflow Designer. A workflow is a set of activities working together to reach the goal of controlling the logic flow and managing the status of an application, as Figure 7-1 shows. Each activity performs a predefined action, for example, sending or receiving a message, implementing the logic of an `if`-match, or controlling a `while` loop. In practice, the set of activities is implemented in a separate .NET assembly library to be reused by different applications.

Two types of Windows workflows are available in .NET 3.0 or later: sequential workflows and state machine workflows. At the time of this writing, only one type of workflow template is available for a cloud application, the sequential workflow template. To deploy a state machine workflow to the cloud, the dependent .NET assemblies for the workflow item must be deployed to the cloud fabric, which is not supported by Microsoft yet. (All custom-defined machine workflows, where an activity is derived from the base activity class, are not supported either, because you have to deploy the base activity assembly together with the application. I will provide reasons in detail during the exercise project later in the chapter.) An alternate way to support a state machine workflow from a cloud application is using `HttpWebRequest` and `HttpWebResponse` instead of using the template from the workflow designer. In this chapter I'll provide a sample solution to address this issue. We are going to see a .NET Workflow Service example limited to the `CloudSequential` workflow and provide an example of a work-around for a state machine workflow running in the cloud using `HttpWebRequest`.

Note Windows Workflow Foundation (WF) uses a SQL Server database to persist its status. However, this database is not installed by the .NET Framework. This database needs to be manually set up before working with WF. Follow the steps at `http://msdn.microsoft.com/en-us/library/aa349366(VS.85).aspx` to set up the database in your local development environment.

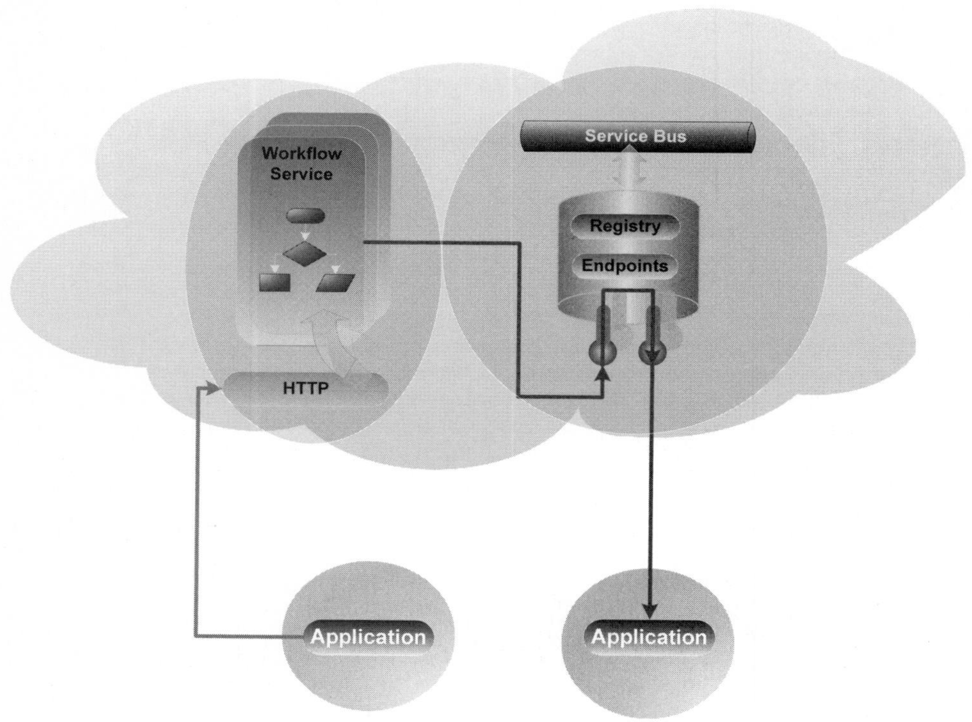

Figure 7-1. Concept of Microsoft .NET workflow services

Hosting a Workflow Service in an Azure Cloud Environment

In this exercise we are going to create a very simple cloud workflow service and deploy it to Azure data centers. To build a cloud-based workflow is very similar to building a Windows-based workflow except there is no code-behind allowed.

■ **Note** The code for this example is in the Exercise 7-1 bundle from the code download.

---

1. Create a WCF DLL library project in order to get services from WCF and .NET Service Bus, as Listing 7-1 shows. This WCF service has only one method, called `Ping()`. Set the contact attribute to `[OperationContract(IsOneWay = true)]`, otherwise it causes an error at runtime because the default value is `false`, which is not supported yet. Hopefully it will be supported in future releases.

Listing 7-1. ShoppingCart WCF Service Library

```
using System;
using System.Collections.Generic;
using System.Linq;
using System.Text;
using System.Runtime.Serialization;
using System.ServiceModel;

namespace CloudWorkflowServiceLibrary
{
    [ServiceContract]
    public interface IShoppingCartService
    {
       [OperationContract(IsOneWay = true)]
        void Ping();
    }

    [DataContract]
    public class ShoppingCartItem
    {
        [DataMember]
        public string SKU;

        [DataMember]
        public string ProductName;

        [DataMember]
        public DateTime AddTime;

        [DataMember]
        public int ItemCount;
    }
}

using System;
using System.Collections.Generic;
using System.Linq;
using System.Text;
using System.Runtime.Serialization;
using System.ServiceModel;
using System.Diagnostics;

namespace CloudWorkflowServiceLibrary
{
    [ServiceBehavior(InstanceContextMode = InstanceContextMode.Single)]
    public class ShoppingCartService : IShoppingCartService
    {
        public void Ping()
        {
            string message =
```

```
                string.Format("---{0}:Ping, {1}", DateTime.Now.ToString(), this.ToString());
            Trace.WriteLine(message);
            Console.WriteLine(message);
        }

        #endregion
    }
}
```

2. Create a console application project to host the WCF service that we have just created. Name the project `ShoppingCartServiceHost`. Add a reference to `System.ServiceModel.dll` and `Microsoft.ServiceBus.dll`. (This assembly can be found in `C:\Program Files\Microsoft .NET Services SDK\Assemblies`.) Insert a few lines of code into the `Main()` method body as Listing 7-2 shows. The setting options `NetEventRelayBinding`, `TransportClientEndpointBehavior`, and `UserNamePassword` credentials to authenticate to the .NET Service Bus are needed here because the workflow will be calling the service. There is not much difference from the `Main()` methods we have seen in previous chapters: the security authentication type can be switched from the user name and password to other types such as CardSpace or X.509 certificate.

Listing 7-2. *Local WCF Service Host `ShoppingCartServiceHost`*

```
using System;
using System.Collections.Generic;
using System.Linq;
using System.Text;
using System.ServiceModel;
using System.ServiceModel.Description;

namespace ShoppingCartServiceHost
{
    using Microsoft.ServiceBus;
    using CloudWorkflowServiceLibrary;

    class Program
    {
        static void Main(string[] args)
        {
            ServiceHost host = new ServiceHost(typeof(ShoppingCartService));

            ServiceEndpoint endpoint =
              host.AddServiceEndpoint("CloudWorkflowServiceLibrary.IShoppingCartService",
                  new NetEventRelayBinding(),
                  "sb://servicebus.windows.net/services/SoftnetSolutions_113/ShoppingCart");
            TransportClientEndpointBehavior transportEndpointBehavior =
              new TransportClientEndpointBehavior();
            transportEndpointBehavior.CredentialType =
              TransportClientCredentialType.UserNamePassword;
            transportEndpointBehavior.Credentials.UserName.UserName = "[your user name]";
```

```
            transportEndpointBehavior.Credentials.UserName.Password =
              "[your solution password]";

            endpoint.Behaviors.Add(transportEndpointBehavior);

            try
            {
                host.Open();
                Console.WriteLine("Host is running");
                Console.ReadLine();
                host.Close();
            }
            catch (Exception ex)
            {
                Console.WriteLine(
                  string.Format("---ShoppingCartServiceHost:Main, exception caught {0}",
                                ex.Message));
            }
        }
    }
}
```

3. Create a cloud sequential workflow project from Visual Studio as shown in Figure 7-2 and call it `CloudSequentialShoppingCartWorkflow`.

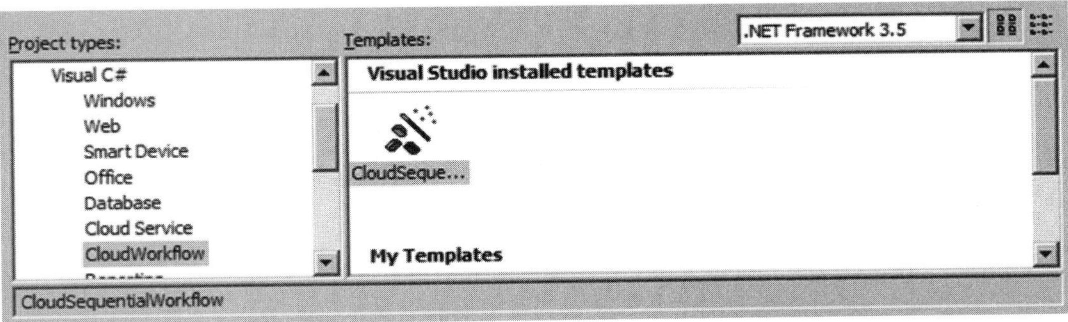

Figure 7-2. Create a cloud sequential workflow project

4. Drag a `CloudXPathUpdate` from the toolbox and drop it on the workflow design surface, as Figure 7-3 shows. Call it `CreateShoppingCartServiceBusMessage`.

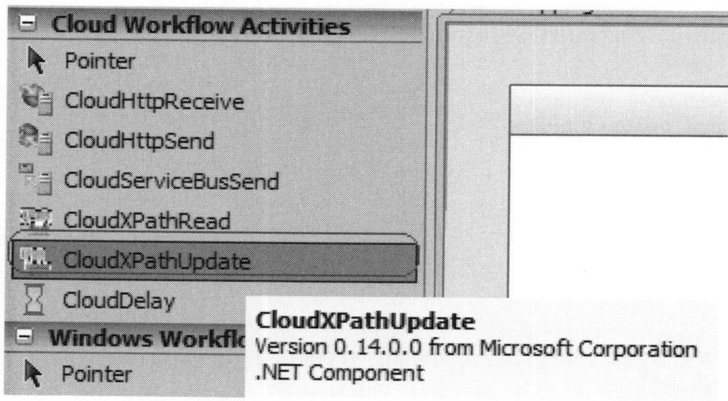

Figure 7-3. *Add a `CloudXPathUpdate` activity to the design surface*

5. Enter the binding information into the Properties dialog box as shown following. At runtime, the input information (`InNewValue`) will be populated into the `<input></input>` node using the XPath expression as the search string.

```
InNewValue = "Hello from ShoppingCart Workflow"
InXml = "<Ping><input></input></Ping>"
InXPathExpresssion ="/Ping/input"
```

6. Add a `CloudServiceBusSend` activity below the `CloudXPathUpdate` activity on the workflow design surface and call it `SendShoppingCartInfo`.

7. Make sure the binding information is as following.

```
Action = "urn:IShoppingCartService/Ping"
Body Name = "CreateShoppingCartServiceBusMessage"
Body Path = "OutXml"
ConnectionMode = "Multicast"
URL = "sb://servicebus.windows.net/services/SoftnetSolutions_113/ShoppingCart"
```

8. Now we have all the necessary information for the workflow design and are ready to deploy to the Microsoft data center. Right-click on the workflow design surface to bring up the Workflow Cloud Deployment dialog box, and enter your credential information.

9. Go to `https://workflow.ex.azure.microsoft.com/WorkflowManagement.asp` and verify that the workflow has been successfully deployed to Microsoft as shown in Figure 7-4.

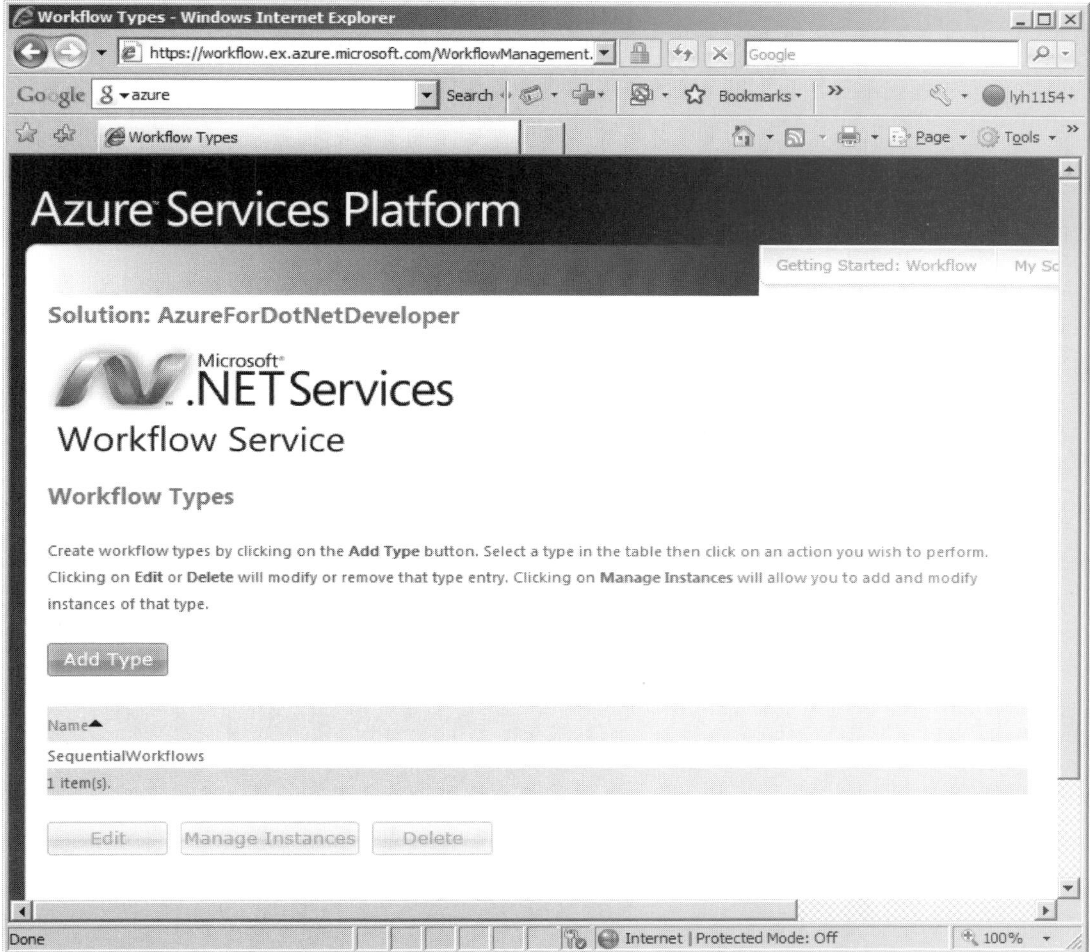

Figure 7-4. *Verifying that the service has been deployed using Azure Portal*

Before we finish our development let's shift the topic a little bit to discuss the limitations of using cloud state machine workflows with the current .NET Workflow Service. In order to understand what is going to happen at runtime if we deploy a state machine workflow to the cloud, let us deploy a workflow with state machine type or with a custom-defined activity to the cloud. For example, let's switch back to our project and define a custom workflow activity as Listing 7-3 and Listing 7-4 show. This is a very simple custom activity used to send an e-mail notification when a WCF service call is received. If we host this workflow activity in a worker role like in Listing 7-2, we get a security exception, saying that the worker role failed to start because an assembly call cannot be loaded from a partially trusted assembly, as Figure 7-5 shows. Actually, the assembly related to the exception is `System.Workflow.Activities` as highlighted in Listing 7-3; we have to reference this assembly from the project, but it has not been officially signed by Microsoft yet. (If you use Red Gate's .NET reflector to load the assembly, you will see that it has no strong name key assigned by Microsoft.) If the state machine workflow is required from a cloud application the only way to work around this issue is using `HttpWebRequest` to generate a REST call via HTTP. That is the topic we are going to focus on in the next exercise, which provides an example of a work-around to address the issue.

Listing 7-3. *Define a Custom Workflow Activity to Send a Notification E-mail When a WCF Call Is Received*

```
using System;
using System.Collections.Generic;
using System.Linq;
using System.Text;
using System.Workflow.ComponentModel;
using System.Workflow.Activities;
using System.Net.Mail;
using System.Diagnostics;

namespace ActivityClassLibrary
{
    public class EmailNotificationActivity : Activity
    {
        public string To { get; set; }
        public string From { get; set; }
        public string Subject { get; set; }
        public string MessageBody { get; set; }

    protected override ActivityExecutionStatus Execute(
      ActivityExecutionContext executionContext)
        {
            SmtpClient smtpClient = new SmtpClient();
            smtpClient.Host = "smtp.1and1.com";
            smtpClient.EnableSsl = false;
            smtpClient.UseDefaultCredentials = true;
            MailMessage message = new MailMessage(From,
                                                  To,
                                                  Subject,
                                                  MessageBody);
            try
            {
                Trace.WriteLine(
                  string.Format("---{0}:Execute, send notification to :{1}",
                                this.ToString(), To));
                smtpClient.Send(message);
            }
            catch (Exception ex)
            {
                Trace.WriteLine(
                  string.Format("---{0}:Execute, exception caught:{1}",
                                this.ToString(), ex.Message));
```

```
            }

            return (ActivityExecutionStatus)ActivityExecutionResult.Succeeded;
        }
    }
}
```

Listing 7-4. Host the Workflow with the Custom-Defined Activity from a Worker Role

```
using System;
using System.Collections.Generic;
using System.Threading;
using System.Linq;
using System.Text;
using Microsoft.ServiceHosting.ServiceRuntime;
using System.ServiceModel;
using System.Workflow.Runtime;
using System.Workflow.ComponentModel;

namespace Workflow_WorkerRole
{
    using CustomerRegisterNotification;
    public class WorkerRole : RoleEntryPoint
    {
        public override void Start()
        {
            RoleManager.WriteToLog("Information", "Worker Process entry point called");

            using (WorkflowRuntime workflowRuntime = new WorkflowRuntime())
            {
                AutoResetEvent waitHandle = new AutoResetEvent(false);
                workflowRuntime.WorkflowCompleted +=
                  delegate(object sender, WorkflowCompletedEventArgs e) {
                    waitHandle.Set();
                  };
                workflowRuntime.WorkflowTerminated +=
                  delegate(object sender, WorkflowTerminatedEventArgs e) {
                    Console.WriteLine(e.Exception.Message);
                    waitHandle.Set();
                  };

                WorkflowInstance instance =
                  workflowRuntime.CreateWorkflow(
                    typeof(CustomerRegisterNotificationWorkflow)
                  );
                instance.Start();

                waitHandle.WaitOne();
            }

            while (true)
```

```
                {
                    Thread.Sleep(10000);
                    RoleManager.WriteToLog("Information", "Working");
                }
            }

            public override RoleStatus GetHealthStatus()
            {
                // This is a sample worker implementation. Replace with your logic.
                return RoleStatus.Healthy;
            }
        }
    }
```

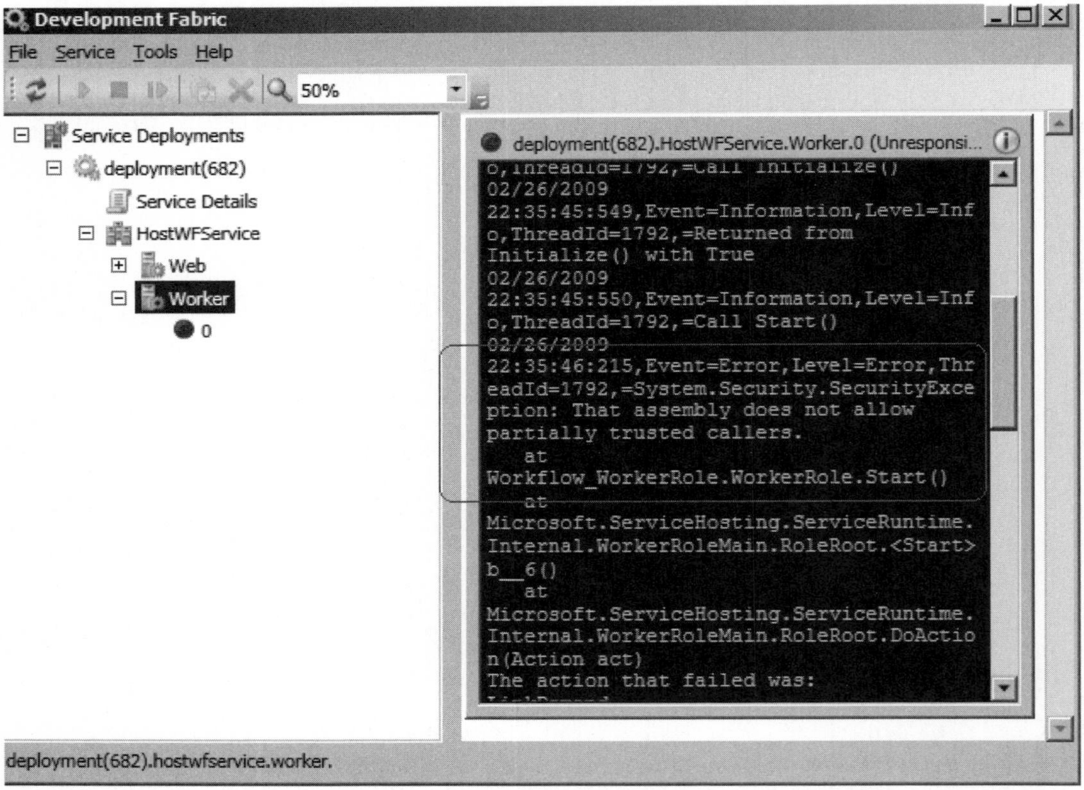

Figure 7-5. A custom-defined workflow activity caused the worker role to fail

Coordinating WF Services Using HttpWebRequest

The .NET Framework provides two classes, `HttpWebRequest` and `HttpWebResponse`, which are designed to handle communication using HTTP for URIs beginning with `http`, `https`, `ftp`, and `file`. These two classes with WCF REST support allow us to coordinate WF service applications running in the cloud. In this exercise we use `HttpWebRequest` to communicate with applications running in the cloud and implement WCF services to support REST queries and drive the activities of a WF service. To do so, we implement custom WF activities that must be derived from a `System.Workflow.Activities` base class (`StateMachineWorkflowActivity`). With this exercise, we will learn

- How to compose a WF state machine
- How to implement a WCF service to support a REST query
- How to drive the WF state machine using `HttpWebRequest` and `HttpWebResponse`

■ **Note** The code for this example is in the Exercise 7-2 bundle from the code download.

The concept of this solution is shown in Figure 7-6. Since the entire Azure framework is based on the HTTP paradigm, if WCF client services are hosted in Azure and support `HttpWebRequest`, then both on-premises applications and cloud applications can post an HTTP message via `HttpWebRequest` to invoke the WCF service running in the cloud; WCF will also drive the workflows through `HttpWebRequest`.

Figure 7-6. Using WCF services hosted in Azure to drive WF workflows via `HttpWebRequest` and `HttpWebResponse`

Having understood the big picture, let's get started building a WCF state machine workflow that supports HttpWebRequest. In order to be consistent, we use the shopping cart example we used in the previous exercise.

■ **Note** A library WebHttpContext is required for this exercise. This library is defined in the Microsoft.ServiceModel.Samples namespace. The source code for this library comes with the source code package of this exercise.

---

1. Create a State Machine Workflow Library project called ShoppingCartWorkflow from Visual Studio (as Figure 7-7 shows) and add a reference to the System.ServiceModel and System.ServiceModel.Web assemblies.

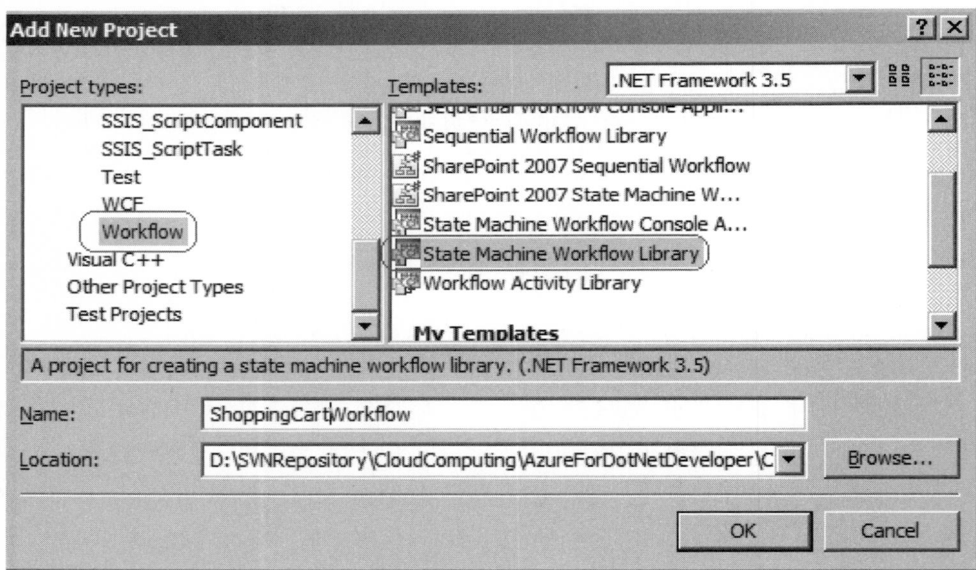

Figure 7-7. *Create a state machine workflow library project ShoppingCartWorkflow from Visual Studio*

2. Add an interface, IShoppingCartService, to the project. This interface is the WCF service contract definition as shown in Listing 7-5. You may notice that the attributes of the operation contracts in the service interface definition are slightly different from those we have used in past chapters. The WebInvoke attribute has been attached to each operation contract in order to support HttpWebRequest. There are two parameters

passed into the WebInvoke attribute, Method and UriTemplate. The value for Method could be either POST or PUT. The value of POST is used for inserting or deleting data, and the value of PUT is used for updating data. There are four methods defined in this interface:

- PlaceShoppingCartItem()
- UpdateShoppingCartItem()
- DeleteShoppingCartItem()
- PayShoppingCartItem()

Listing 7-5. *WCF Service Contract Interface Definition of IShoppingCartService*

```
using System;
using System.Collections.Generic;
using System.Linq;
using System.Text;
using System.ServiceModel;
using System.ServiceModel.Web;
using ShoppingCartServiceLibrary;

namespace ShoopingCartWorkflows
{
        [ServiceContract]
        public interface IShoppingCartService
        {
                [OperationContract]
                [WebInvoke(Method="POST", UriTemplate="ShoppingCartItem")]
                ShoppingCartItem PlaceShoppingCartItem(ShoppingCartItem ShoppingCartItem);

                [OperationContract]
                [WebInvoke(Method = "PUT", UriTemplate = "ShoppingCartItem/{id}")]
                ShoppingCartItem
                  UpdateShoppingCartItem(string id, ShoppingCartItem ShoppingCartItem);

                [OperationContract]
                [WebInvoke(Method = "POST", UriTemplate = "ShoppingCartItem/{id}")]
                ShoppingCartItem
                  DeleteShoppingCartItem(string id, ShoppingCartItem ShoppingCartItem);

                [OperationContract]
                [WebInvoke(Method="PUT",
                           UriTemplate="CreditCardPayment/ShoppingCartItem/{id}")]
                void PayShoppingCartItem(string id, CreditCardPayment CreditCardPayment);
        }
}
```

3. Add a C# library project ShoppingCartServiceLibrary to implement the IShoppingCartService service contract and data contract as shown in Listing 7-6 and Listing 7-7. Listing 7-6 is the implementation for the service interface, and Listing 7-7 is the data contract used to hold the shopping card property data.

Listing 7-6. *WCF IShoppingCartService Service Contract Implementation*

```
using System;
using System.Collections.Generic;
using System.Linq;
using System.Text;
using System.Runtime.Serialization;

namespace ShoppingCartServiceLibrary
{
        [Serializable]
         [DataContract(Name="ShoppingCartItem",
                       Namespace="http://costco.com/OnlineShopping")]
        public class ShoppingCartItem
        {
                static public string ENDPOINT_CREDITCARD_PAYMENT =
                  "http://costco.com/OnlineShopping/CreditCardPayment/";
                static public string ENDPOINT_ITEM_UPDATE =
                  "http://costco.com/OnlineShopping/ShoppingCartItem/update/";
                static public string ENDPOINT_ITEM_DELETE =
                  "http://costco.com/OnlineShopping/ShoppingCartItem/delete/";
                static public string CREDIT_CARD_PAYMENT_URI =
                  "http://localhost:8000/CreditCardPayment/ShoppingCartItem/";
                static public string SHOPPING_CART_URI =
                  "http://localhost:8000/ShoppingCartItem/";

                public string ShoppingCartItemId { get; set; }

                [DataMember(Name="ItemName")]
                public string ItemName { get; set; }

                [DataMember(Name="Price")]
                public decimal? Price { get; set; }

                [DataMember(Name="NextItem")]
                public NextItem[] NextItem { get; set; }
        }

        [Serializable]
        [DataContract(Name="NextItem", Namespace="http://costco.com/OnlineShopping")]
        public class NextItem
```

```
        {
                [DataMember(Name="Relative")]
                public string Relative { get; set; }

                [DataMember(Name="uri")]
                public string Uri { get; set; }

                [DataMember(Name="type")]
                public string Type { get; set; }

                public NextItem()
                {
                        Type = "application/xml";
                }
        }
}
```

Listing 7-7. *WCF IShoppingCartService Service Data Contract Implementations*

```
using System;
using System.Collections.Generic;
using System.Linq;
using System.Text;
using System.Runtime.Serialization;

namespace ShoppingCartServiceLibrary
{
        [Serializable]
        [DataContract(Name = "CreditCardPayment",
                      Namespace = "http://costco.com/OnlineShopping")]
        public class CreditCardPayment
        {
                public string ShoppingCartItemId { get; set; }

                [DataMember(Name = "CardNumber")]
                public string CardNumber { get; set; }

                [DataMember(Name = "ExpiresDate")]
                public string ExpiresDate { get; set; }

                [DataMember(Name = "CardHolerName")]
                public string CardHolerName { get; set; }

                [DataMember(Name = "amount")]
                public decimal ChargedAmount { get; set; }
        }
}
```

4. Go back to the State Machine Workflow design surface and drag and drop four state artifacts onto the design surface and name them `WaitingForShoppingCartItem`, `ShoppingCartItemPlaced`, `ItemCheckOut`, and `CartClosed`, as shown in Figure 7-8. The process to work out the logic of state transaction is the same as the process to work on the standard WF state machine. Please see `http://msdn.microsoft.com/en-us/netframework/aa663328.aspx` to understand Microsoft Windows Workflow Foundation and how to work on the WF state machine design in Visual Studio.

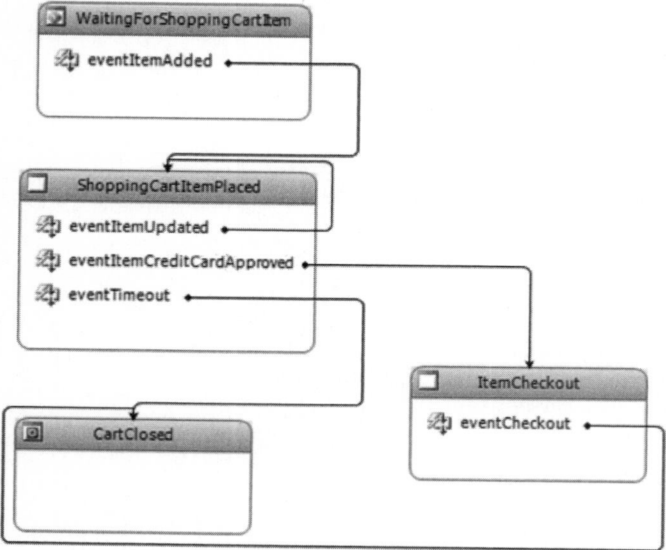

Figure 7-8. *States defined in `ShoppingCartWorkflow` state machine*

5. Now let's build up the state machine used to handle a shopping cart service. Implement a code-behind for the `ShoppingCartItemWorkflow` state machine as shown in Listing 7-8. The event handler functions in the code-behind will be bound to events in the state machine during the next state machine design. This shopping cart example has four state transaction handlers from the code-behind. These handlers are generated from the WF design surface; insert the code from the listing into the handlers' bodies. (Right-click the design surface and select View Code, or press F7, to get into the state transaction handler body.) There is an array called `NextItem` defined in each handler, which is the data contract of the WCF services in this example. The member items in the array also have the type of `NextItem` that is used to simulate the business activities, such as shopping cart data insert, update, or delete. The state will be transacted depending on the activities in the handler.

Listing 7-8. Code-behind for ShoppingCartWorkflow

```
using System;
using System.ComponentModel;
using System.ComponentModel.Design;
using System.Collections;
using System.Drawing;
using System.Linq;
using System.Workflow.ComponentModel.Compiler;
using System.Workflow.ComponentModel.Serialization;
using System.Workflow.ComponentModel;
using System.Workflow.ComponentModel.Design;
using System.Workflow.Runtime;
using System.Workflow.Activities;
using System.Workflow.Activities.Rules;
using System.ServiceModel.Web;
using ShoppingCartServiceLibrary;
using System.ServiceModel;

namespace ShoppingCartWorkflows
{
    using ShoppingCartServiceLibrary;

    public sealed partial class ShoppingCartItemWorkflow : StateMachineWorkflowActivity
    {
        public ShoppingCartItem receivedShoppingCartItem;
        public string receivedId;
        public ShoppingCartItem currentShoppingCartItem;
        public CreditCardPayment ShoppingCartItemCreditCardPayment;

        public ShoppingCartItemWorkflow()
        {
            InitializeComponent();
        }

        private void OnShoppingCartItemPlacedCode_ExecuteCode(object sender, EventArgs  e)
        {
            var id = WorkflowEnvironment.WorkflowInstanceId.ToString();

            currentShoppingCartItem = new ShoppingCartItem();
            currentShoppingCartItem.ShoppingCartItemId = id;
            currentShoppingCartItem.Price = receivedShoppingCartItem.Price;
            currentShoppingCartItem.ItemName = receivedShoppingCartItem.ItemName;

            currentShoppingCartItem.NextItem = new NextItem[]
            {
                new NextItem {
                    Relative = ShoppingCartItem.ENDPOINT_CREDITCARD_PAYMENT,
                    Uri = string.Format("{0}{1}",
                      ShoppingCartItem.CREDIT_CARD_PAYMENT_URI,
                      WorkflowEnvironment.WorkflowInstanceId.ToString()),
```

```
            },
            new NextItem {
                Relative = ShoppingCartItem.ENDPOINT_ITEM_UPDATE,
                Uri = string.Format("{0}{1}",
                  WorkflowEnvironment.WorkflowInstanceId.ToString())
            },
            new NextItem {
                ShoppingCartItem.SHOPPING_CART_URI,
                Relative = ShoppingCartItem.ENDPOINT_ITEM_DELETE,
                Uri = string.Format("{0}{1}",
                  ShoppingCartItem.SHOPPING_CART_URI,
                  WorkflowEnvironment.WorkflowInstanceId.ToString())
            }
        };

        WebOperationContext.Current.OutgoingResponse.StatusCode =
          System.Net.HttpStatusCode.Created;
    }

    private void codeUpdateShoppingCartItem_ExecuteCode(object sender, EventArgs e)
    {
        var id = WorkflowEnvironment.WorkflowInstanceId.ToString();

        currentShoppingCartItem.ShoppingCartItemId = receivedId;
        currentShoppingCartItem.ItemName = receivedShoppingCartItem.ItemName;
        currentShoppingCartItem.Price = receivedShoppingCartItem.Price;
        currentShoppingCartItem.NextItem = new NextItem[]
        {
            new NextItem
            {
                Relative = ShoppingCartItem.ENDPOINT_CREDITCARD_PAYMENT,
                Uri = string.Format("{0}{1}",
                  ShoppingCartItem.CREDIT_CARD_PAYMENT_URI,
                  id.ToString()),
            },
            new NextItem
            {
                Relative = ShoppingCartItem.ENDPOINT_ITEM_UPDATE,
                Uri = string.Format("{0}{1}",
                  ShoppingCartItem.SHOPPING_CART_URI,
                  id.ToString()),
            },
            new NextItem
            {
                Relative = ShoppingCartItem.ENDPOINT_ITEM_DELETE,
                Uri = string.Format("{0}{1}",
                  ShoppingCartItem.SHOPPING_CART_URI,
                  id.ToString()),
            }
        };
```

```
            WebOperationContext.Current.OutgoingResponse.StatusCode =
              System.Net.HttpStatusCode.OK;
        }

        private void codePayShoppingCartItem_ExecuteCode(object sender, EventArgs e)
        {
            var id = WorkflowEnvironment.WorkflowInstanceId.ToString();

            currentShoppingCartItem.ShoppingCartItemId = receivedId;
            currentShoppingCartItem.ItemName = receivedShoppingCartItem.ItemName;
            currentShoppingCartItem.Price = receivedShoppingCartItem.Price;
            currentShoppingCartItem.NextItem = new NextItem[]
            {
                new NextItem
                {
                    Relative = ShoppingCartItem.ENDPOINT_CREDITCARD_PAYMENT,
                    Uri = string.Format("{0}{1}",
                      ShoppingCartItem.CREDIT_CARD_PAYMENT_URI,
                      id.ToString()),
                },
                new NextItem
                {
                    Relative = ShoppingCartItem.ENDPOINT_ITEM_UPDATE,
                    Uri = string.Format("{0}{1}",
                      ShoppingCartItem.SHOPPING_CART_URI,
                      id.ToString()),
                },
                new NextItem
                {
                    Relative = ShoppingCartItem.ENDPOINT_ITEM_DELETE,
                    Uri = string.Format("{0}{1}",
                      ShoppingCartItem.SHOPPING_CART_URI,
                      id.ToString()),
                }
            };
            WebOperationContext.Current.OutgoingResponse.StatusCode =
              System.Net.HttpStatusCode.Created;
        }

        private void codeCheckOutShoppingCartItem_ExecuteCode(object sender, EventArgs e)
        {
            WebOperationContext.Current.OutgoingResponse.StatusCode =
              System.Net.HttpStatusCode.Created;
        }
    }
}
```

6. Now we need to bind the state machine workflow item properties to the corresponding handler. Figure 7-9 shows the bindings for `WaitingForShoppingCartItem:eventItemAdded`.

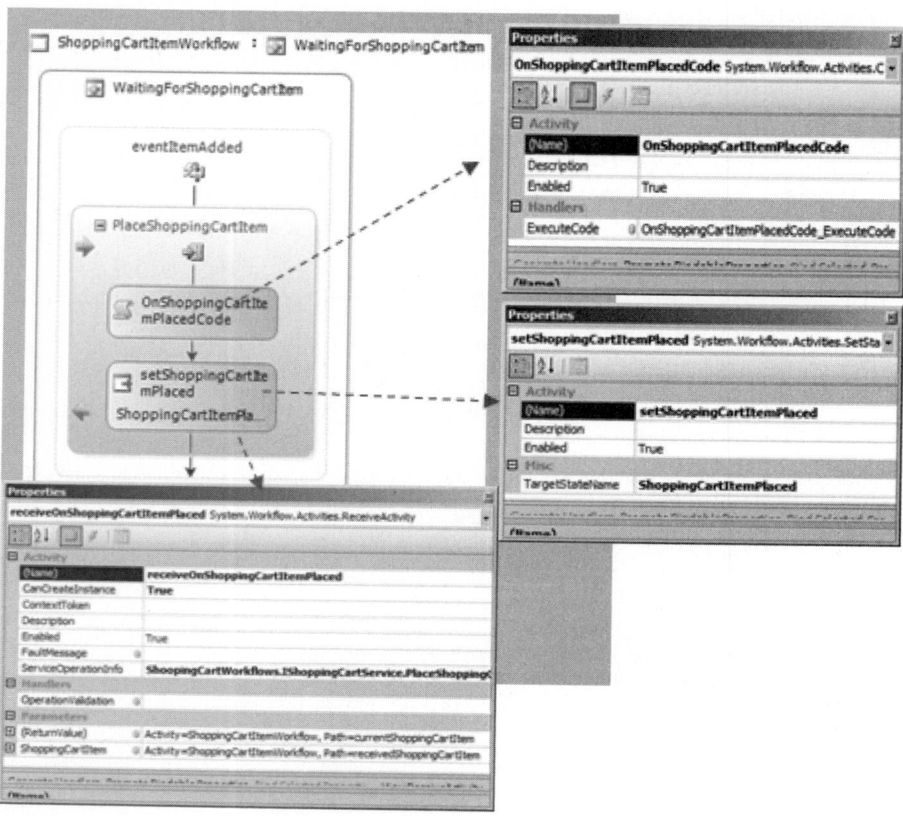

Figure 7-9. Bindings for `WaitingForShoppingCartItem:eventItemAdded`

7. The bindings for `ShoppingCartItemPlaced:eventItemUpdated` are shown in Figure 7-10.

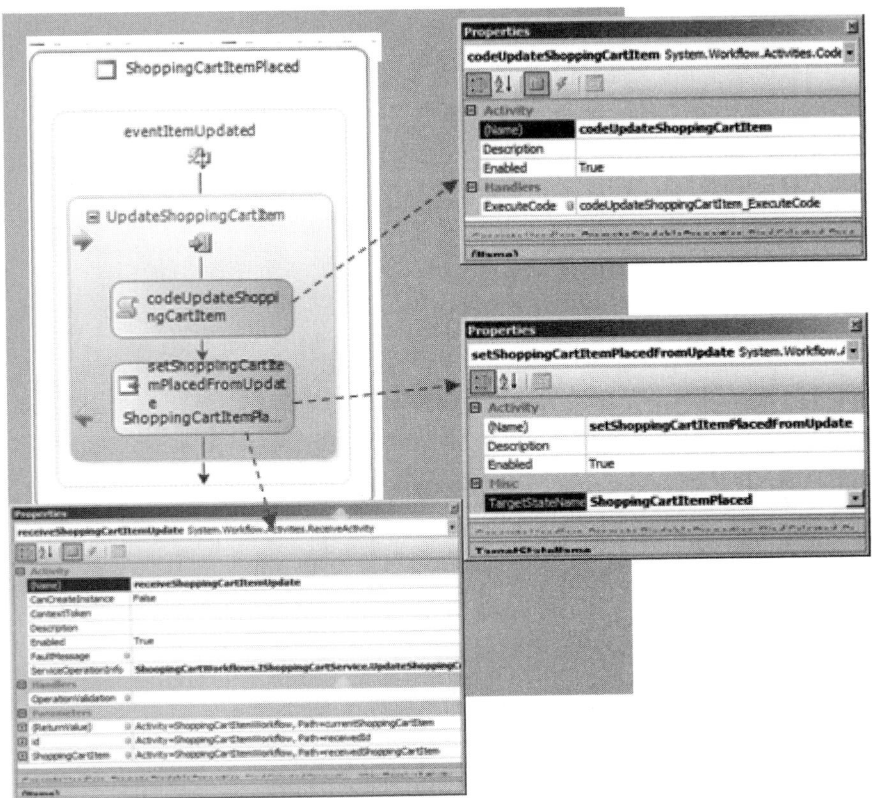

Figure 7-10. Bindings for `ForShoppingCartItem:eventItemUpdated`

8. Bindings for `ShoppingCartItemWorkflow:ShoppingCartItemPlaced` are shown in Figure 7-11.

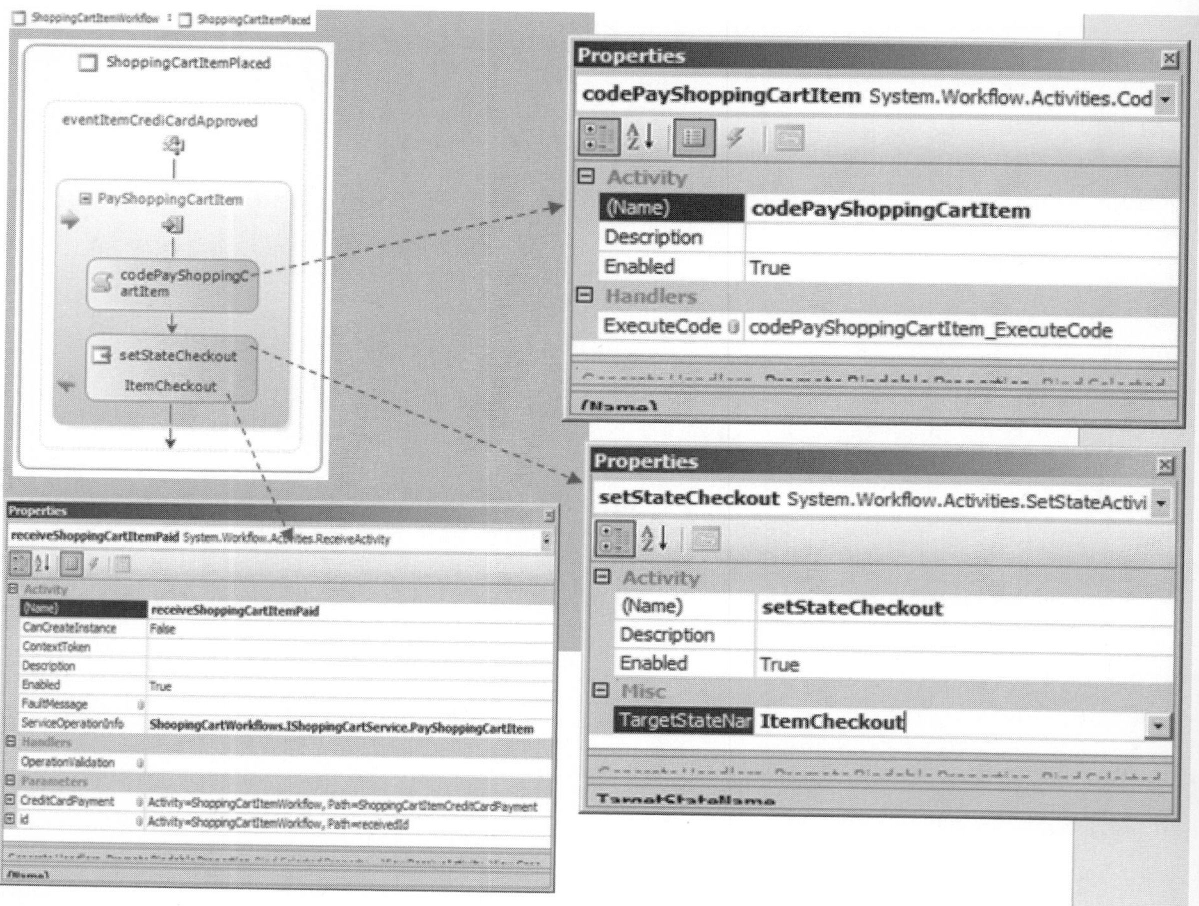

Figure 7-11. Bindings for `ShoppingCartItemWorkflow:ShoppingCartItemPlaced`

9. Bindings for `ShoppingCartItemWorkflow:StateCheckout` are shown in Figure 7-12.

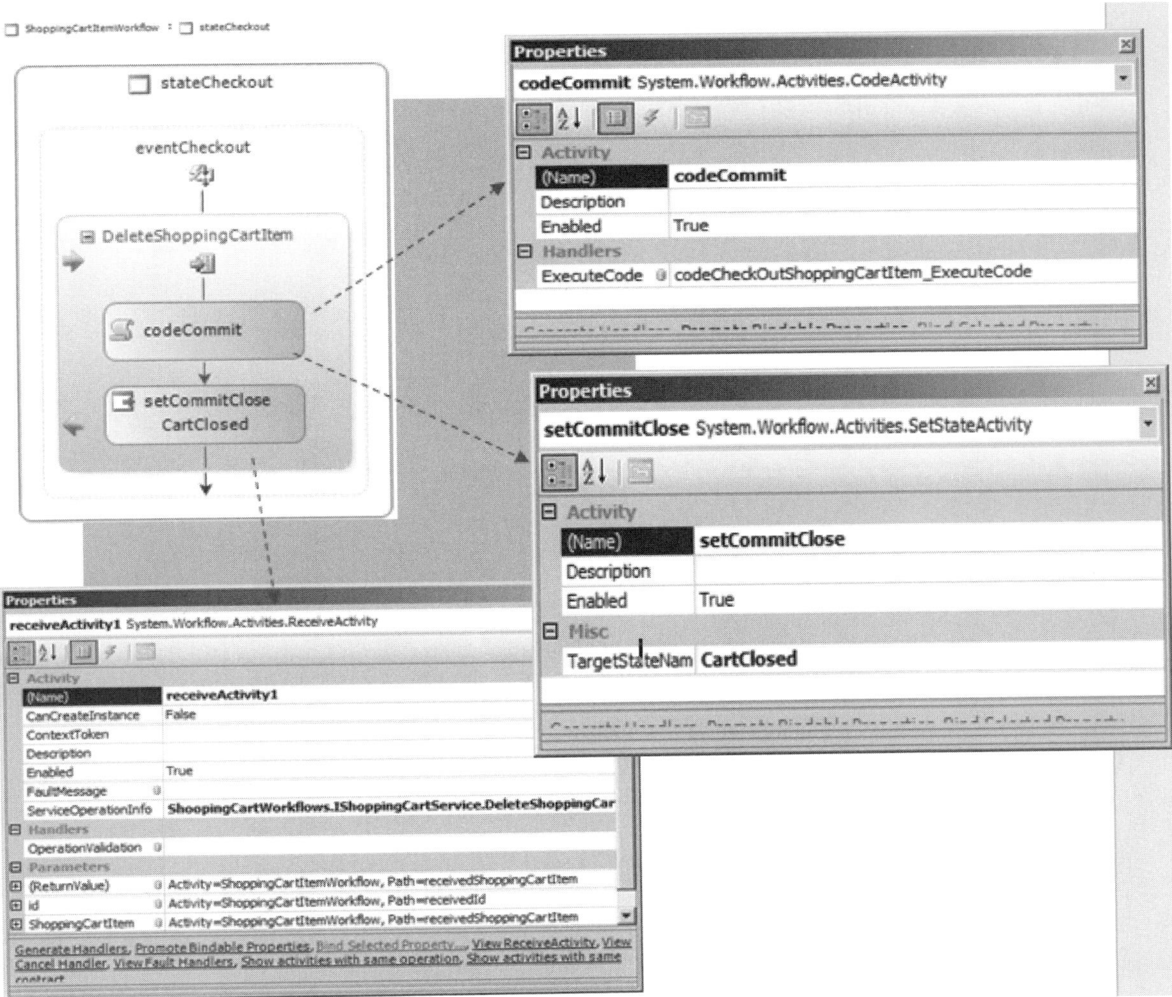

Figure 7-12. Bindings for `ShoppingCartItemWorkflow:StateCheckout`

10. Bindings for `ShoppingCartItemWorkFlow:Timeout` are shown in Figure 7-13.

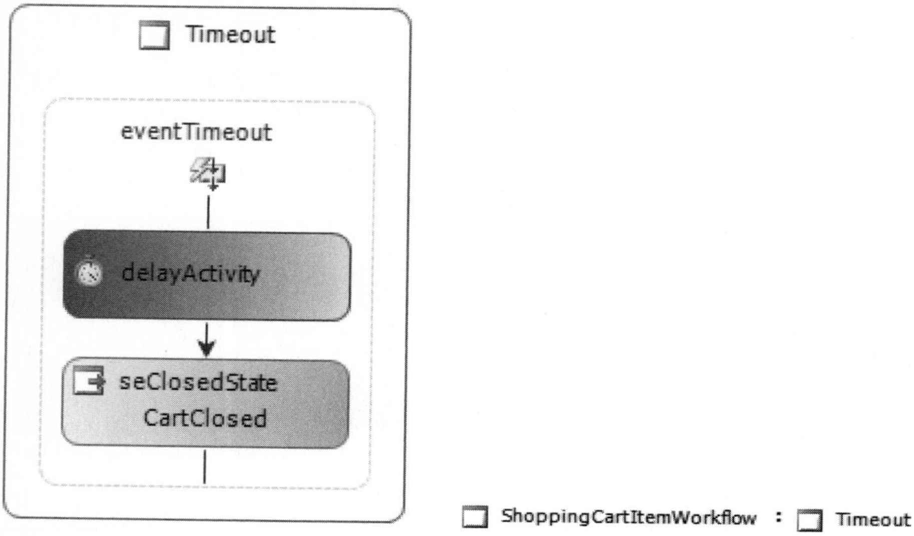

Figure 7-13. *Bindings for* `ShoppingCartItemWorkFlow:Timeout`

11. Create a host project, `ShoppingCartWorkflowServiceHost`, as Listing 7-9 shows. There are three callback delegates created in the `Main()` method. The first two are used to output trace information regarding the state transaction, and the third one is used to bind the persistence service for the workflow, so we can persist the workflow state.

Listing 7-9. *Create a Host Project* `ShoppingCartWorkflowServiceHost` *to Run the Workflow as a Service*

```
using System;
using System.Collections.Generic;
using System.Linq;
using System.Text;
using System.Threading;
using System.Workflow.Runtime;
using System.Workflow.Runtime.Hosting;
using System.ServiceModel;
using System.ServiceModel.Description;
```

```
namespace ShoppingCartWorkflowServiceHost
{
    using ShoopingCartWorkflows;

    class Program
    {
        static void Main(string[] args)
        {
            Uri baseAddress = new Uri("http://localhost:8000");

            WorkflowServiceHost host =
              new WorkflowServiceHost(typeof(ShoppingCartItemWorkflow), baseAddress);
            host.Description.Behaviors
              .Find<WorkflowRuntimeBehavior>().WorkflowRuntime.WorkflowTerminated +=
                delegate(object sender, WorkflowTerminatedEventArgs e) {
                    Console.WriteLine("WorkflowTerminated: " + e.Exception.Message);
                };
            host.Description.Behaviors
              .Find<WorkflowRuntimeBehavior>().WorkflowRuntime.WorkflowCompleted +=
                delegate(object sender, WorkflowCompletedEventArgs e) {
                    Console.WriteLine("WorkflowCompleted.");
                };

            host.Description.Behaviors
              .Find<WorkflowRuntimeBehavior>().WorkflowRuntime.AddService(
                new SqlWorkflowPersistenceService(
                  "Initial Catalog=WorkflowPersistenceStore;Data Source=localhost ➥
\\SQLEXPRESS;Integrated Security=SSPI;",
                true,
                TimeSpan.FromHours(1.0),
                TimeSpan.FromSeconds(5.0)
            ));
            host.Open();

            Console.WriteLine("---- Press <enter> key to exit ----");

            Console.ResetColor();
            Console.ReadLine();

            host.Close();
        }
    }
}
```

12. In order to use HttpWebRequest and HttpWebResponse, add an App.config file to the project and insert the configuration for the host as shown in Listing 7-10. This host creates a Windows console application. When the host application starts, it instantiates a WorkflowServiceHost instance. Two parameters need to pass into the constructor to instantiate the host instance. The first one is the type of the workflow, which in our case is ShoppingCartItemWorkflow, and the second one is the URI of the base address that the host is going to listen to for HTTP messages. The host is going to look for the service contract from the workflow instance. This is why we have to keep the service contract interface definition IShoppingCartService in the same assembly as the host and the implementation stays in a separate assembly ShoppingCartServiceLibrary; this assembly is also referenced by a client application.

Listing 7-10. Configurations for the Service Host Program

```
<?xml version="1.0" encoding="utf-8" ?>
<configuration>
    <system.serviceModel>
      <serviceHostingEnvironment aspNetCompatibilityEnabled="true" />
      <services>
        <service name="ShoopingCartWorkflows.ShoppingCartItemWorkflow">
                 contract="ShoopingCartWorkflows.IShoppingCartService" />
        </service>
      </services>
      <bindings>
        <webHttpContext>
          <binding name="myServiceBinding" contextMode="UriTemplate">
            <uriTemplates>
              <add name="ShoppingCartItems value="ShoppingCartItem/{instanceId}"></add>
              <add name="CreditCardPayments
                   value="CreditCardPayment/ShoppingCartItem/{instanceId}"></add>
            </uriTemplates>
          </binding>
        </webHttpContext>
      </bindings>
      <behaviors>
        <endpointBehaviors>
          <behavior name="MyServiceBehavior"><webHttp /></behavior>
        </endpointBehaviors>
      </behaviors>
      <extensions>
        <bindingExtensions>
          <add name="webHttpContext"
               type="Microsoft.ServiceModel.Samples.WebHttpContextBindingCollectionElement,
                     WebHttpContext, Version=1.0.0.0, Culture=neutral,
                     PublicKeyToken=null" />
        </bindingExtensions>
      </extensions>
```

```
    <diagnostics>
      <messageLogging logMalformedMessages="true"
                      logMessagesAtServiceLevel="true"
                      logEntireMessage="true"
                      logMessagesAtTransportLevel="true" />
    </diagnostics>
  </system.serviceModel>
  <system.diagnostics>
    <sources>
      <source name="System.ServiceModel.MessageLogging"
              switchValue="Information, ActivityTracing">
        <listeners>
          <add name="ServiceModelMessageLoggingListener" />
        </listeners>
      </source>
      <source name="System.ServiceModel" switchValue="Verbose, ActivityTracing"
              propagateActivity="true">
        <listeners>
          <add name="ServiceModelTraceListener" />
        </listeners>
      </source>
    </sources>
    <sharedListeners>
      <add initializeData="messages.svclog"
           type="System.Diagnostics.XmlWriterTraceListener, System, Version=2.0.0.0,
                 Culture=neutral, PublicKeyToken=b77a5c561934e089"
           name="ServiceModelMessageLoggingListener" traceOutputOptions="Timestamp">
      </add>
      <add initializeData="tracelog.svclog"
           type="System.Diagnostics.XmlWriterTraceListener, System, Version=2.0.0.0,
                 Culture=neutral, PublicKeyToken=b77a5c561934e089"
           name="ServiceModelTraceListener" traceOutputOptions="Timestamp">
      </add>
    </sharedListeners>
    <trace autoflush="true" />
  </system.diagnostics>
</configuration>
```

In order to test the results locally we need to set up a SQL Server database. The WF workflow state machine runtime needs SQL Server database support to persist runtime transaction data. This database can be set up using a SQL script. The SQL scripting file used to create this database can be found in `C:\Windows\Microsoft.NET\Framework\v3.0\Windows Workflow Foundation\SQL\EN`, as Figure 7-14 shows. Before running the script from SQL Server Management Studio, manually create a new database `WorkflowPersistenceStore` from SQL Server Management Studio or run `CREATE TABLE WorkflowPersistenceStore`.

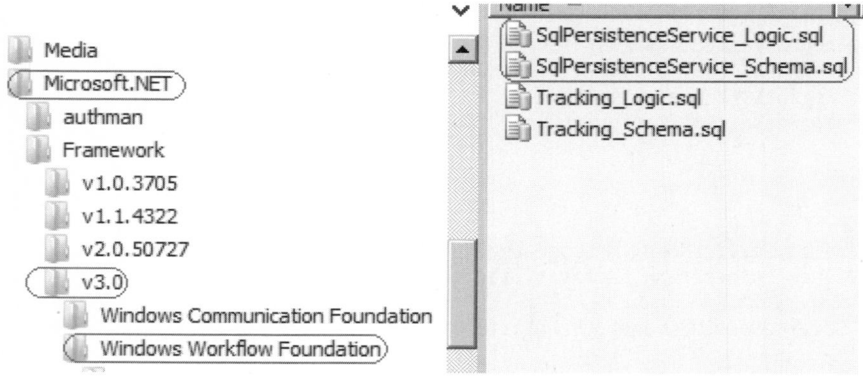

Figure 7-14. *Use the SQL scripts provided by the .NET 3.0 Windows Workflow Foundation to set up the persistent SQL data table from the local development environment*

Create a console application as a test client for testing. This test application instantiates a unit test library class `InvokeWorkflows` and calls `InvokeHttpWebRequest`. In this test client, we use `HttpWebRequest` to post or put a message via HTTP with the following steps to trigger the workflow state machine transaction from one state to another. Note that the client does not need to reference the `System.Workflow.Activities` assembly at all. That is why we can deploy an application that uses this approach to the cloud without dealing with authentication security trust issues. The sample client code is shown in Listing 7-11, and the following steps are the actions to simulate a shopping cart business flow.

1. Create a `ShoppingCartItem` object and call `HttpWebRequest` to post data to the workflow server. This should advance the workflow state machine from the initial state of waiting for shopping cart item state to shopping cart item place state.
2. Update the contents of the `ShoppingCartItem` and call `HttpWebRequest` to update the data in the shopping cart. The state in this activity should loop back to the same state by design, and the workflow state machine continues to wait for the next event.
3. Create a credit card payment object and call HttpWebRequest to trigger the state machine to move to the check out state. The workflow state machine should finish at the shopping card closed state.

Listing 7-11. *Client Code Using* `HttpWebRequest` *to Invoke the State Machine Workflow*

```
using System;
using System.Collections.Generic;
using System.Linq;
using System.Text;
using System.Net;
using System.IO;
using System.Runtime.Serialization;
using System.ServiceModel;
```

```
using System.ServiceModel.Channels;
using System.ServiceModel.Web;

namespace ClientApplication
{
    using ShoppingCartServiceLibrary;

    class Program
    {
        static void Main(string[] args)
        {
            //Create a new ShoppingCartItem
            ShoppingCartItem shoppingCartItem =
              new ShoppingCartItem {
                ItemName = "Nikon Camera", Price = (decimal)1000.0
              };
            HttpWebRequest createShoppingCartItemRequest =
              CreateRequest(new Uri("http://localhost:8000/ShoppingCartItem"), "POST",
                            shoppingCartItem);
            shoppingCartItem =
              InvokeHttpWebRequest<ShoppingCartItem>(
                createShoppingCartItemRequest.GetResponse()
              );

            Console.WriteLine("ShoppingCartItem Price {0}", shoppingCartItem.Price);
            foreach (NextItem NextItem in shoppingCartItem.NextItem)
            {
                Console.WriteLine("Check NextItem {0}", NextItem.Uri);
            }

            //Update
            shoppingCartItem.ItemName = "Dell latiture D620";
            shoppingCartItem.Price = (decimal)710.0;

            Uri updateShoppingCartItemUri =
              new Uri(shoppingCartItem.NextItem.Where(
                n => n.Relative == ShoppingCartItem.ENDPOINT_ITEM_UPDATE).Single().Uri);

            HttpWebRequest updateShoppingCartItemRequest =
              CreateRequest(updateShoppingCartItemUri, "PUT", shoppingCartItem);
            ShoppingCartItem updatedShoppingCartItem =
              InvokeHttpWebRequest<ShoppingCartItem>(
                updateShoppingCartItemRequest.GetResponse()
              );

            Console.WriteLine("ShoppingCartItem Price {0}", updatedShoppingCartItem.Price);
            foreach (NextItem NextItem in updatedShoppingCartItem.NextItem)
            {
                Console.WriteLine("Process NextItem {0}", NextItem.Uri);
            }
```

```
            //Pay
            CreditCardPayment CreditCardPayment =
              new CreditCardPayment {
                CardHolerName = "David Smith",
                CardNumber = "1234567,
                ExpiresDate = "10/10",
                ChargedAmount = updatedShoppingCartItem.Price.GetValueOrDefault()
              };

            Uri payShoppingCartItemUri = new Uri(shoppingCartItem.NextItem.Where(
             n => n.Relative == ShoppingCartItem.ENDPOINT_CREDITCARD_PAYMENT).Single().Uri);
            HttpWebRequest payShoppingCartItemRequest =
              CreateRequest(payShoppingCartItemUri, "PUT", CreditCardPayment);

            int statusCode = Execute(payShoppingCartItemRequest.GetResponse());

            if (statusCode == 201)
                Console.WriteLine("Transaction success!");
            else
                Console.WriteLine("Failed to process the CreditCardPayment");

            //Checkout
            Uri deleteShoppingCartItemUri =
              new Uri(shoppingCartItem.NextItem.Where(
                n => n.Relative == ShoppingCartItem.ENDPOINT_ITEM_DELETE).Single().Uri);

            HttpWebRequest deletehoppingCartItemRequest =
              CreateRequest(deleteShoppingCartItemUri, "POST", shoppingCartItem);

            ShoppingCartItem deletedShoppingCartItem =
              InvokeHttpWebRequest<ShoppingCartItem>(
                deletehoppingCartItemRequest.GetResponse()
              );
        }

        static HttpWebRequest CreateRequest(Uri address, string method, object contract)
        {
            HttpWebRequest webRequest = (HttpWebRequest)WebRequest.Create(address);
            webRequest.ContentType = "application/xml";
            webRequest.Timeout = 20000;
            webRequest.Method = method;

            DataContractSerializer serializer =
              new DataContractSerializer(contract.GetType());
            using (Stream stream = webRequest.GetRequestStream())
            {
                serializer.WriteObject(stream, contract);
                stream.Flush();
            }
```

```
            return webRequest;
        }

        static T InvokeHttpWebRequest<T>(WebResponse response)
        {
            DataContractSerializer serializer = new DataContractSerializer(typeof(T));
            using (Stream stream = response.GetResponseStream())
            {
                return (T)serializer.ReadObject(stream);
            }
        }

        static int InvokeHttpWebRequest (WebResponse response)
        {
            using (Stream stream = response.GetResponseStream()) { };
            return (int)((HttpWebResponse)response).StatusCode;
        }
    }
}
```

Start the host service to listen to the HTTP web request. When the service host starts, it listens to the HTTP web request.

```
---- Press <enter> key to exit ----
```

Run the test client project. The test results show that the workflow state machine goes through all states, ending with the shopping cart state:

```
---- Press <enter> key to exit ----

WorkflowCompleted.
```

Create a cloud service `HostWCFServiceInCloud` with a `WorkflowsClient_WorkerRole` and invoke the state machine workflows from the local cloud fabric. We have the same results as previously. This demonstrates that with the help of `HttpWebRequest` we can invoke the state machine workflows from the cloud to work around the limitation from the current Azure .NET service state machine workflow. The code for the worker role is shown in Listing 7-12.

Listing 7-12. *Invoke State Machine Workflows from the Cloud Using Worker Role*

```
using System;
using System.Collections.Generic;
using System.Threading;
using System.Linq;
using System.Text;
using Microsoft.ServiceHosting.ServiceRuntime;
using System.Runtime.Serialization;
```

```
using System.ServiceModel;
using System.ServiceModel.Channels;
using System.ServiceModel.Web;
using System.Net;
using System.IO;

namespace WorkflowsClient_WorkerRole
{
    using ClientUnitestibrary;

    public class WorkerRole : RoleEntryPoint
    {
        public override void Start()
        {
            RoleManager.WriteToLog("Information", "Worker Process entry point called");

            InvokeWorkflows invokeWorkflows = new InvokeWorkflows();
            invokeWorkflows.HttWebRequestInvokeWorkflows();

            while (true)
            {
                Thread.Sleep(10000);
                RoleManager.WriteToLog("Information", "Working");
            }
        }

        public override RoleStatus GetHealthStatus()
        {
            return RoleStatus.Healthy;
        }
    }
}
```

Summary

In this chapter we covered workflows and how to host them in the cloud. We started with an example of a sequential workflow service and saw how easy it was to use in Azure. The workflow service was essentially the same as regular .NET workflow, with the exception that we could not use any code-behind files.

Our second example provided a work-around to a limitation in the .NET Workflow service: namely that we can't deploy state machine or custom workflows to the cloud. Our example used `HttpWebRequest` to switch the states of a state machine workflow to demonstrate the work-around.f

CHAPTER 8

SQL Azure

At the end of July 2009 Microsoft announced SQL Azure community technology preview (CTP) and aimed to go live in November 2009 for SQL Azure and to phase out SQL Data Services (SDS). SQL Azure and SDS are both cloud-based services but are built using different data models. With the introduction of SQL Azure, Azure has reached a breakthrough point, leaving this new platform in a good position to be accepted by the enterprise and for winning marking share, since:

- SQL Azure is the first cloud service completely supporting the relational database model.
- SQL Azure is fully committed to supporting T-SQL, SQL query, stored procedures, data views, and so on.
- SQL Azure supports the traditional Windows user/password security model.
- The first release of SQL Azure is almost fully compatible with all existing relational development tools and IDEs, such as SQL Server Management Studio (SSMS) and Visual Studio.
- SQL Azure allows all SQL developers and IT staff to seamlessly migrate from an on-premises environment to a cloud environment with almost no learning curve. All knowledge and skills for SQL developers and IT staff can be applied to SQL Azure. This should remove a big concern from when the Azure framework was announced in October 2008 regarding potential job losses for the IT industry (worries brought on because the infrastructure and data storage hardware for an organization no longer need to exist in the organization).
- SQL Azure supports PHP, which makes SQL Azure more friendly to Internet applications.

The most important thing is that SQL Azure is the first platform supporting the rational database model and database as a service running in the cloud. The major changes are not in the physical domain but in the logical virtual domain.

Since SQL Server and T-SQL have been in the market for decades, there is a lot of information that can be found on them. This chapter does not cover SQL or T-SQL based upon the assumption that you know SQL. Instead, this chapter covers the fundamentals, including how to register to set up your SQL Azure account and how to connect to a cloud database from SSMS.

Create a Virtual Server for SQL Azure

The first step to using SQL Azure is to create a SQL service. For a CTP account user, redeem your invitation code from Microsoft and create a SQL service. You will see the results when a SQL service has been created in the cloud as Figure 8-1 shows.

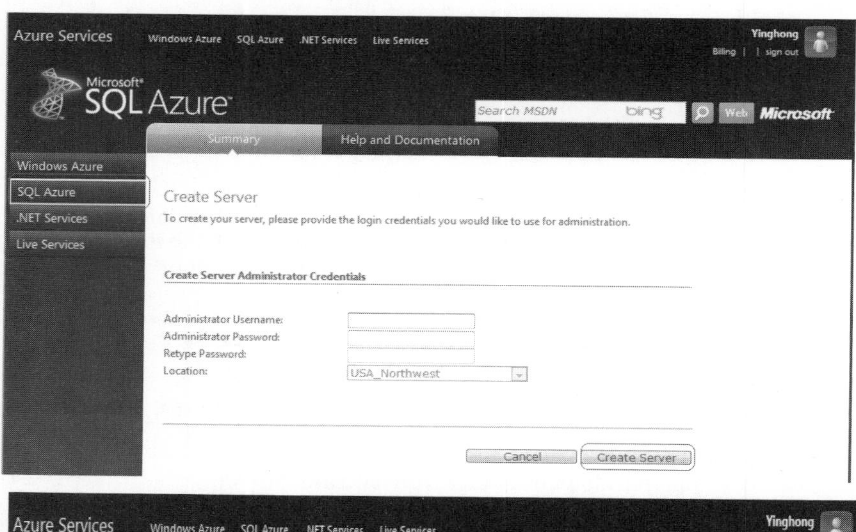

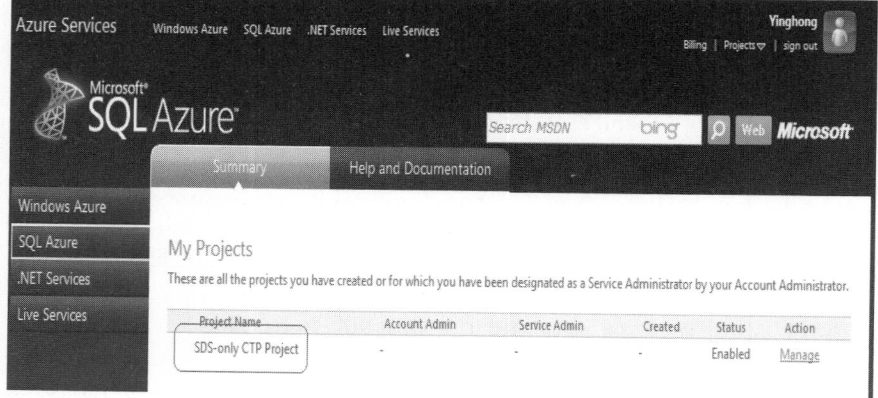

Figure 8-1. *The results of creating a SQL Azure server from the cloud*

Click the Manage link, and you will be redirected to the management page where you can see that a default database, `master`, has been created in the SQL Azure server you have just created. Click the Connection Strings button, and you get the connection strings for ADO.NET, ODBC, and OLE DB as shown in Figure 8-2. You can use them to access this database using SQL access clients. You will also be able to see that the server name is assigned to the SQL Azure server that you have just created.

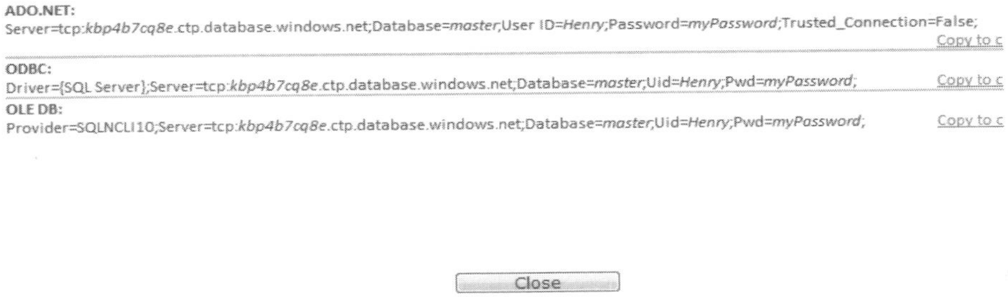

ADO.NET:
Server=tcp:*kbp4b7cq8e*.ctp.database.windows.net;Database=*master*;User ID=*Henry*;Password=*myPassword*;Trusted_Connection=False;
Copy to c

ODBC:
Driver={SQL Server};Server=tcp:*kbp4b7cq8e*.ctp.database.windows.net;Database=*master*;Uid=*Henry*;Pwd=*myPassword*; Copy to c

OLE DB:
Provider=SQLNCLI10;Server=tcp:*kbp4b7cq8e*.ctp.database.windows.net;Database=*master*;Uid=*Henry*;Pwd=*myPassword*; Copy to c

Close

Figure 8-2. *The connection strings used to access SQL Azure using ADO.NET, ODBC, or OLE DB*

You can easily create a new database by clicking the Create Database button in the management page. An example of the results of creating a custom database is shown in Figure 8-3.

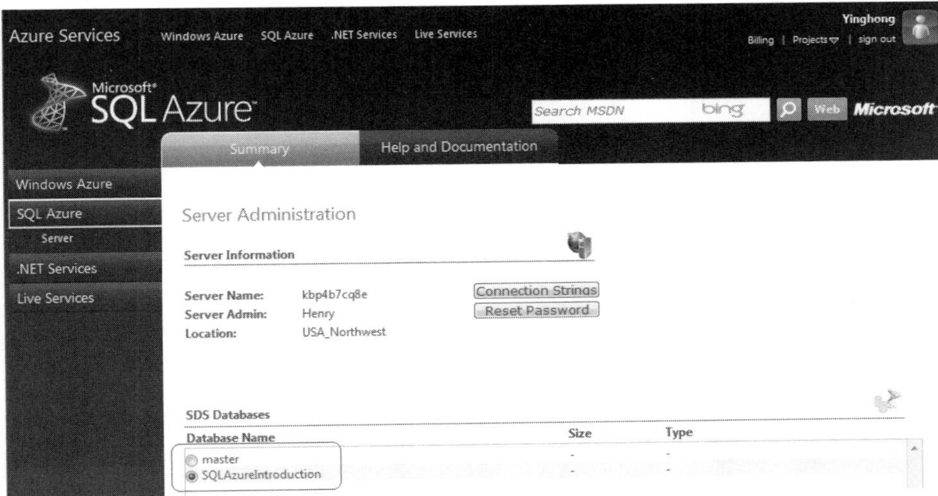

Figure 8-3. *Create a custom SQL Azure database* `SQLAzureIntroduction`

Connect to a SQL Azure Database Using SQL Server Management Studio

Please bear in mind that SQL Azure does not support object browsing from SQL Server Management Studio. To connect to the SQL Azure database in the cloud using SQL Server Management Studio, launch SQL Server Management Studio. Close the Connect to Server dialog box and click the ribbon button New Query as Figure 8-4 shows. This will lead you back to the Connect to Server dialog box again. By clicking the Options button and selecting the Connection Properties tab, you can specify the target custom database you created in the cloud. The correct server name must be filled in as Figure 8-4 shows. The format of the server name is:

```
[Data server name assigned by SQL Azure].ctp.database.windows.net
```

The authentication type that should be selected is SQL Server Authentication. The login name and password are the same as the ones you used to redeem your invitation code. After the connection succeeds you may get an error message box as Figure 8-5 shows. This is a known issue in the current SQL Azure release, but it will not prevent you moving forward.

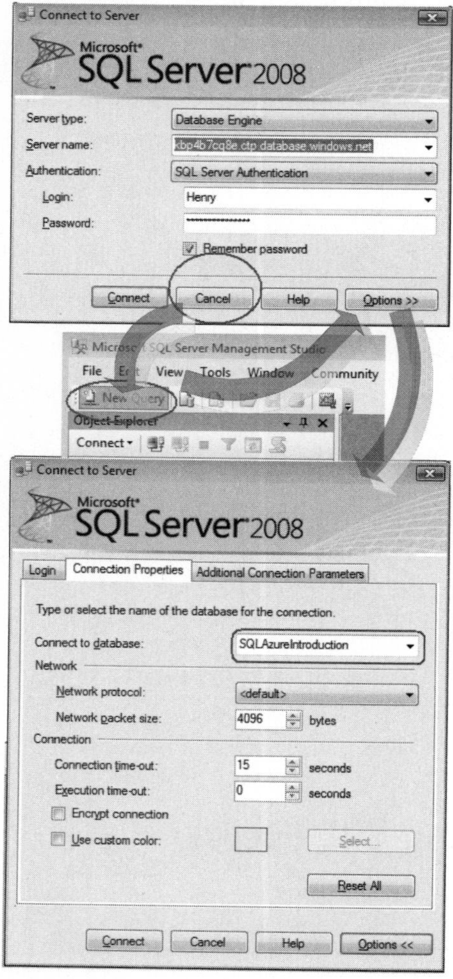

Figure 8-4. To connect to SQL Azure database, click the ribbon button New Query

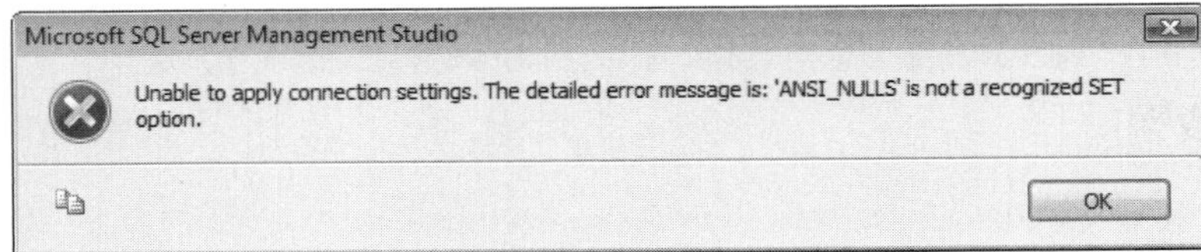

Figure 8-5. A known issue in the current SQL Azure release when connecting to the SQL Azure database using SQL Server Management Studio

A quick way to verify the creation of the database from the cloud is to execute the following T-SQL query:

```
SELECT * FROM sys.databases
```

The returned message should show that the database exists in the current virtual SQL Azure server as Figure 8-6 shows.

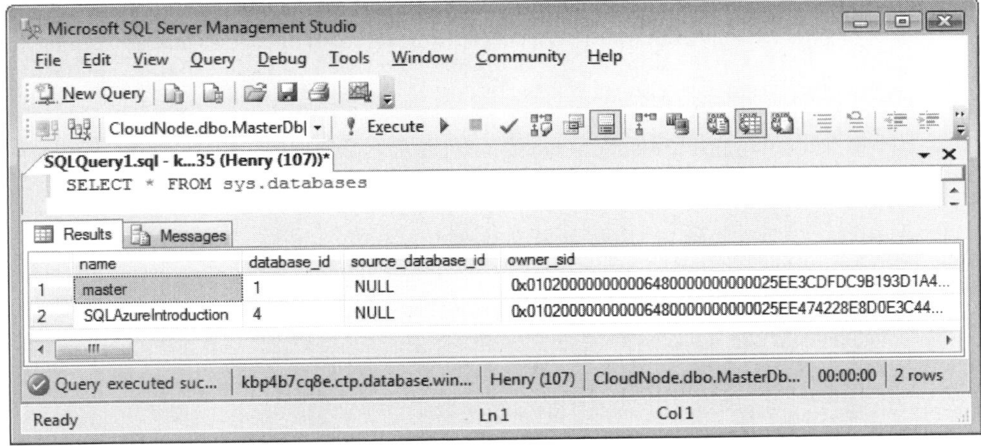

Figure 8-6. *Using* `SELECT * FROM sys.databases` *to query information of existing databases from the virtual data server*

SQL Azure Timeout

The connection to SQL Azure will be automatically deactivated if there is no activity detected by SQL Azure. The error message will be thrown as below, and you just need to reconnect to the service by clicking on the button shown in Figure 8-7 from SQL Server Management Studio.

```
Msg 10053, Level 20, State 0, Line 0
A transport-level error has occurred when sending the request to the server. (provider:
```

```
TCP Provider, error: 0 - An established connection was aborted by the software in your
host machine.)
```

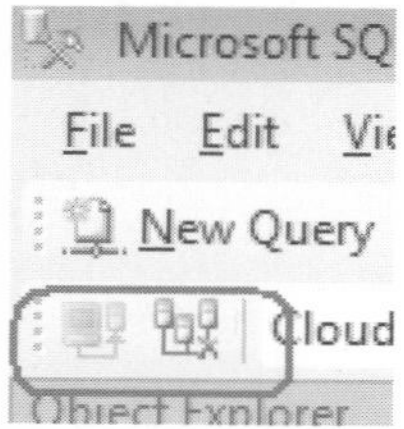

Figure 8-7. The connection can be resumed by clicking the Change Connection button from SQL Management Studio if the connection has been interrupted

Create a Data Table Using SQL Server Management Studio

A custom table can be created in the SQL Azure cloud database by using SQL Server Management Studio in a way that is pretty similar to creating a database on a server running in an on-premises environment. One difference, for example, is that the USE statement is not supported when using SQL Azure since we have used New Query to connect to the specific database already. If you need to access a different database, you can start a new query by clicking the New Query button. To find more guidelines and limitations to using SQL Azure, see http://msdn.microsoft.com/en-us/library/ee336245.aspx.

Run the script in Listing 8-1 to create a data table called UserTable. The results are shown in Figure 8-8.

Listing 8-1. SQL Script Used to Create a Data Table in SQL Azure

```
CREATE TABLE [dbo].[UserTable](
        [UserID] [int] IDENTITY(1,1)NOT NULL PRIMARY KEY CLUSTERED,
        [Password] [nvarchar](100) NULL,
        FirstName [nvarchar](100) NOT NULL,
        LastName [nvarchar](100) NOT NULL,
        [Timestamp] [timestamp] NOT NULL
)
GO
INSERT INTO UserTable
([Password],
 FirstName,
 LastName)
 Values(
 'password',
 'Henry',
 'Li'
 )
 GO
SELECT COUNT(*) FROM UserTable
SELECT * FROM UserTable
```

Results | Messages

	(No column name)
1	1

	UserID	Password	FirstName	LastName	Timestamp
1	1	password	Henry	Li	0x00000000002A25AB

__Figure 8-8.__ Query results from Listing 8-1

Simple Benchmark Testing Results

Results of a simple benchmark test for SQL Azure access are shown in Table 8-1. (The scripts for the test follow.) It may satisfy your curiosity as to the performance of the database in the cloud (I certainly was curious). Figure 8-9 shows the Internet access bandwidth used to get the results of Table 8-1. (A free speed-testing tool Speakeasy (`www.speakeasy.net/speedtest`) can be used to determine your broadband speed.)

__Table 8-1.__ Results of a Simple Benchmark Test for SQL Azure Database Access

Number of Rows	1,000,000	10,000	100
`INSERT`	19 min, 46 sec	12 sec	< 1 sec
`SELECT`	4 min, 39 sec	7 sec	< 1sec
`UPDATE`	20 min, 11 sec	12 sec	1 sec
`DELETE`	20 min, 47 sec	13 sec	< 1 sec

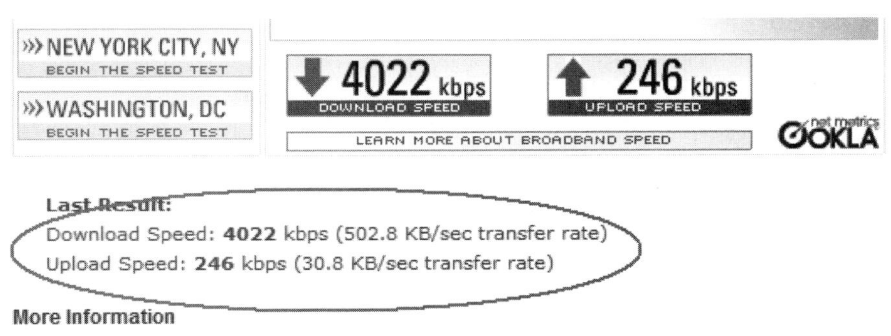

__Figure 8-9.__ Broadband speed of the network used to get the benchmark testing results of Table 8-1

To get benchmark testing results you need to create an index table using the script shown in Listing 8-2.

Listing 8-2. SQL Script Used to Create an Index Table Using `FirstName` *as Index Key*

```
CREATE INDEX IX_UserTable_FirstName
ON [UserTable](FirstName)
Go
```

The SQL script used to do this benchmark testing is shown in Listing 8-3.

Listing 8-3. SQL Scripts Used for Benchmark Testing to Get the Results of Table 8-1

```
CREATE PROCEDURE BatchInsert
@rows int
AS
DECLARE @index int
SELECT @index = 1
WHILE (@index < @rows)
BEGIN
        INSERT INTO UserTable
        ([Password],
         FirstName,
         LastName)
        VALUES
        ('password',
          'Henry' + CAST(@index as nvarchar),
         'Li')
    SELECT @index = @index + 1
END
go

CREATE PROCEDURE BatchUpdate
@rows int
AS
DECLARE @index int
SELECT @index = 1
WHILE (@index < @rows)
BEGIN
        UPDATE UserTable
        SET
        [Password] = 'passworduPDATE',
         FirstName = 'Henry' + CAST(@index as nvarchar),
         LastName = 'Li'
         WHERE [UserID] = @index
    SELECT @index = @index + 1
END
go

CREATE PROCEDURE BatchDelete
```

```
@rows int
AS
DECLARE @index int
SELECT @index = 1
WHILE (@index < @rows)
BEGIN
        DELETE UserTable
        WHERE [UserID] = @index
    SELECT @index = @index + 1
END
go


--truncate table UserTable
DECLARE @NUMBER_OF_TEST_ROWS INT
SET @NUMBER_OF_TEST_ROWS = 100000
EXEC BatchInsert @NUMBER_OF_TEST_ROWS
select * from UserTable where FirstName like 'Henry%'
EXEC BatchUpdate @NUMBER_OF_TEST_ROWS
EXEC BatchDelete @NUMBER_OF_TEST_ROWS
```

Verifying That SQL Azure Supports Relational Data Tables

Run the SQL script in Listing 8-4 against the SQL Azure cloud database described previously to create two relational data tables. The diagram of the table structure and relationships is shown in Figure 8-10. In the Address table the field UserID is a foreign key, which references UserID in UserTable. The script to create the foreign key is shown in the boldface lines in Listing 8-4.

Listing 8-4. *SQL Script Used to Create Relational Data Tables*

```
DROP TABLE [UserTable]
GO

CREATE TABLE [dbo].[UserTable](
        [UserID] [int] IDENTITY(1,1)NOT NULL,
        [Password] [nvarchar](100) NULL,
        FirstName [nvarchar](100) NOT NULL,
        LastName [nvarchar](100) NOT NULL,
        [Timestamp] [timestamp] NOT NULL
)
GO

ALTER TABLE [UserTable]
ADD CONSTRAINT UserID_PK PRIMARY KEY (UserID)
GO

CREATE TABLE [dbo].[Address](
        AddressID [int] IDENTITY(1,1)NOT NULL,
        [UserID] [int] NOT NULL,
```

```
        Address1 [nvarchar](100) NULL,
        Address2 [nvarchar](100) NULL,
        City [nvarchar](100) NULL,
        State [nvarchar](100) NULL,
        Zip [nvarchar](9) NULL,
        County [nvarchar](50) NULL,
        Email1 [nvarchar](100) NOT NULL,
        Email2 [nvarchar](100) NULL
)
GO

ALTER TABLE [Address]
ADD CONSTRAINT AddressID_PK PRIMARY KEY (AddressID)
GO

ALTER TABLE [dbo].[Address]  WITH CHECK ADD  CONSTRAINT [FK_Address_UserTable]
 FOREIGN KEY([UserID])
REFERENCES [dbo].[UserTable] ([UserID])
GO
ALTER TABLE [dbo].[Address] CHECK CONSTRAINT [FK_Address_UserTable]
GO
```

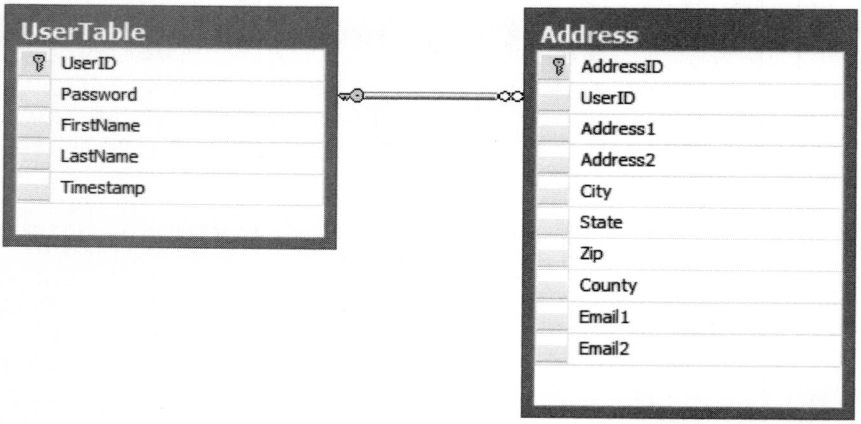

Figure 8-10. Table structure and relationship between `UserTable` *and* `Address` *tables*

■ **Note** Since SQL Azure does not support object browsing from SQL Server Management Studio, this database diagram is generated from a local SQL database. The script used to create this database table is exported and executed against the SQL Azure server. We are going to cover data table migration later in this chapter.

Run the SQL script in Listing 8-5 to insert data into these two tables and run the script in Listing 8-6. You will see that the correct data is returned.

Listing 8-5. *Sample Data to Insert into the Tables Created Previously*

```
INSERT INTO UserTable
([Password],
 FirstName,
 LastName)
VALUES
('password',
 'Henry',
 'Li')
 GO

 INSERT INTO UserTable
([Password],
 FirstName,
 LastName)
VALUES
('password',
 'Emma',
 'Li')
 GO

 INSERT INTO UserTable
([Password],
 FirstName,
 LastName)
VALUES
('password',
 'David',
 'Kruger')
GO

INSERT INTO Address(
        UserID,
        Address1,
        City,
        [State],
        Zip,
        County,
        Email1,
        Email2
        )
VALUES(
        1,
        '12 King Street',
        'Salem',
        'OR',
        '97304',
```

```
            'Polk',
            'yinghong@softnetsolution.net',
            'henry@softnetsolution.net')
    GO
    INSERT INTO Address(
            UserID,
            Address1,
            City,
            [State],
            Zip,
            County,
            Email1,
            Email2
            )
    VALUES(
            3,
            '99 Universal Park',
            'Denver',
            'CO',
            '80201',
            'Denver',
            'david.kruger@example.com',
            ' ')
    GO

    INSERT INTO Address(
            UserID,
            Address1,
            City,
            [State],
            Zip,
            County,
            Email1,
            Email2
            )
    VALUES(
            2,
            '19 West Ave',
            'Aberdeen',
            'WA',
            '98520',
            'Grays Harbor',
            'emma@example.com',
            ' ')
    GO
```

Listing 8-6. Query Data with Joined Tables

```
SELECT U.FirstName, U.LastName, A.Address1, A.City, A.Email1 FROM UserTable U
JOIN Address A
ON A.UserID =U.UserID
WHERE U.LastName = 'Li'
GO

SELECT * FROM UserTable
SELECT * FROM [Address]
GO
```

Now try to delete a record from `UserTable` using the highlighted code in Figure 8-11. An expected SQL exception will be thrown because the record is referenced by `Address`. This demonstrates that SQL Azure is truly a relational database service.

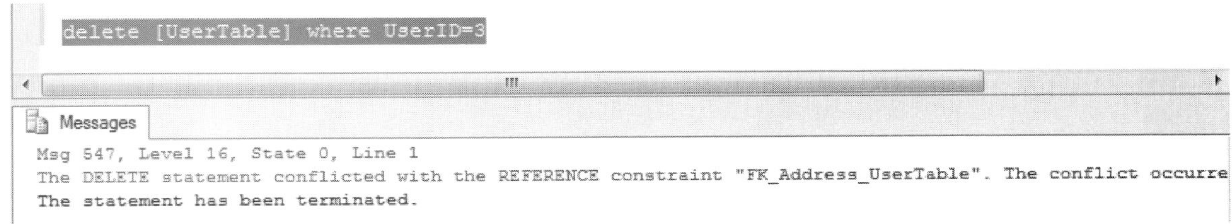

Figure 8-11. An expected SQL exception is thrown when trying to delete a record from a referenced table

Connect to a SQL Azure Database Using ADO.NET

To connect to SQL Azure using ADO.NET is very similar to connecting to a traditional database. The difference is the connection string format. Let's take an example where there are two identical databases, with one from SQL Azure and the other from the local workstation. Listing 8-7 shows the difference between the two connection strings used to connect to these two databases.

Listing 8-7. Comparison of Connection Strings Between SQL Azure and Local SQL Database

```
"Server=tcp:{SQL Azure Server Name}.ctp.database.windows.net;Database={SQL Azure
Database};User ID={my user ID};Password={my password};Trusted_Connection=False;"

"Data Source={Local Database Workstation};Initial Catalog={Database Name};Integrated
Security=True;"
```

An example of how to connect to SQL Azure from C# code will be presented in a SQL Azure access tool, `SQLAzureConnect`, developed later in this chapter.

Migrate Existing Databases from an On-Premises System to SQL Azure

Existing on-premises databases can easily migrate to SQL Azure. In the first release of SQL Azure, the scripts generated by SQL Server Management Studio need some extra cleanup. This can be avoided in future SQL Azure releases.

In this section we are going to use SQL Server Management Studio to generate SQL scripts and migrate an existing database from a local database to a SQL Azure database. The database we'll use is `SQLAzure`, which you can create on a local workstation using Listing 8-1 and Listing 8-3. The steps are as follows.

1. Open SQL Server Management Studio, right-click on the database node `SQLAzure` in the object browser pane, and select Tasks ➤ Generate Script.
2. Select the database `SQLAzure` (as Figure 8-12 shows) and check all objects from the dialog boxes.

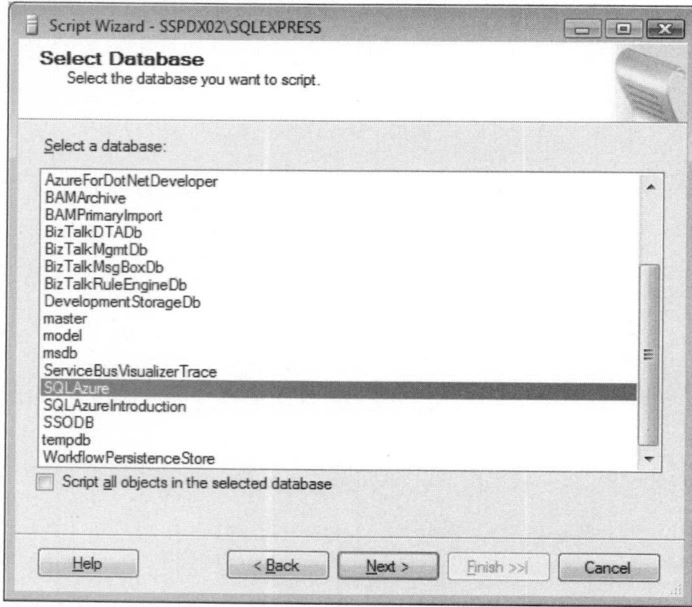

Figure 8-12. Select database `SQLAzure`

3. Before moving forward, some options need to be set correctly as Figure 8-13 shows.

    - **Convert UDDTs to Base Type:** This option needs to be set to true since SQL Azure does not support user-defined types. They need to be converted into underlying SQL Azure portable types.

- **Script extended properties:** This option needs to be set to false since SQL Azure does not support extended properties.
- **Script USE DATABASE:** This option needs to be set to false since SQL Azure does not support the USE statement.
- **Script Data:** This option needs to be set to false since we do not care about the data at this moment.

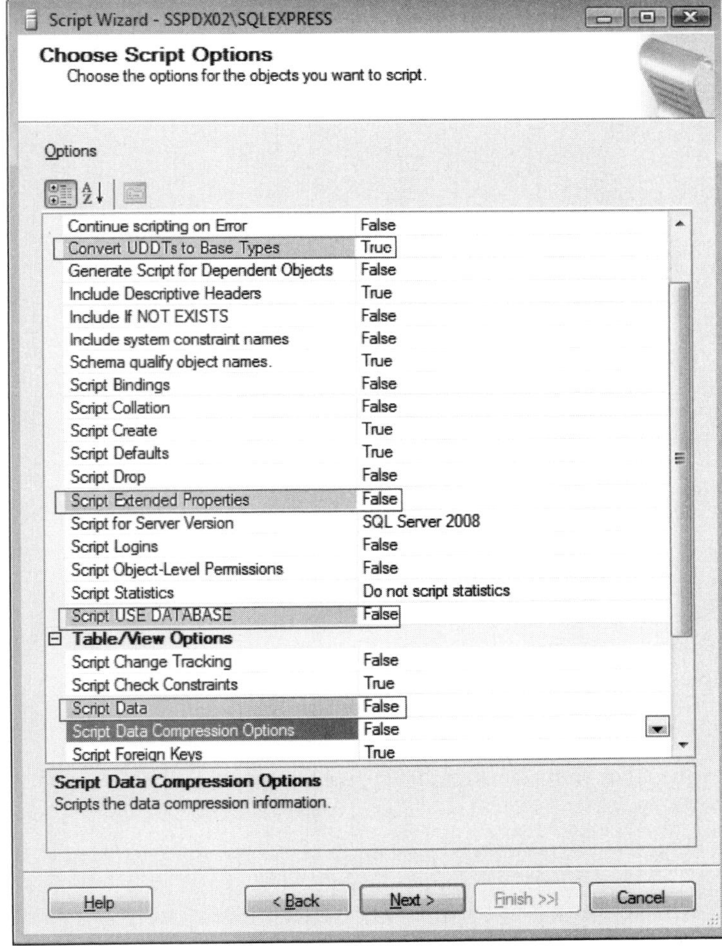

Figure 8-13. Set the values to false for those options that SQL Azure does not support

4. Click Next. SQL Server Management Studio will generate the scripts in a new SQL script edit window. Figure 8-14 shows a successful generation.

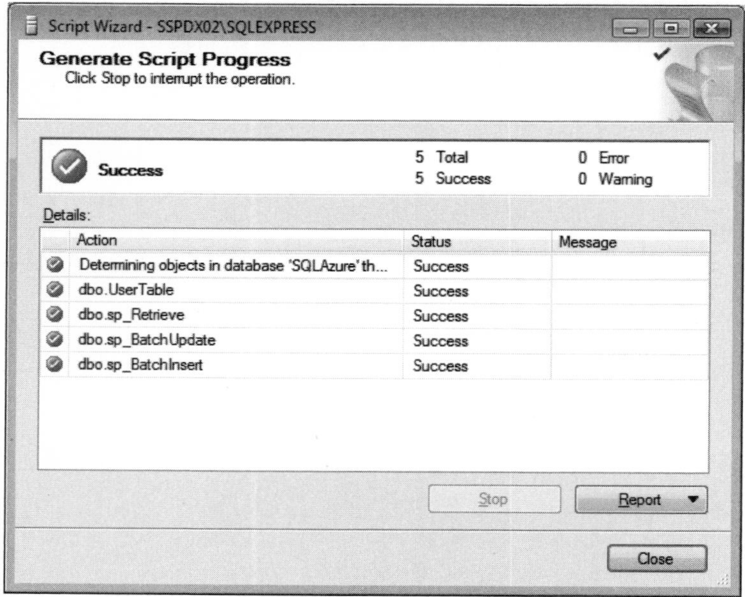

Figure 8-14. *The scripts were successfully generated*

5. Log in to the Azure platform portal at `https://lx.azure.microsoft.com/` and create a database `AzureForDotNetDeveloper` from SQL Azure in the cloud (recall that the screenshot shown in Figure 8-3 shows the created database).

6. Copy the previously generated script to the clipboard or save it into a file. Close SQL Server Management Studio and reopen it by following the steps shown in Figure 8-4 to establish a connection to the `AzureForDotNetDeveloper` database in the cloud.

7. If you run the generated script without any modification, then you will get an error message as Listing 8-8 shows.

Listing 8-8. *Error Message from Running Scripts Generated by SQL Server Management Studio Against SQL Azure Without Modification*

```
Msg 195, Level 15, State 5, Line 2
'ANSI_NULLS' is not a recognized SET option.
Msg 40512, Level 16, State 1, Procedure InsertInstanceState, Line 3
Deprecated feature 'Data types: text ntext or image' is not supported in this➥
 version of SQL Server.
Msg 195, Level 15, State 5, Line 2
```

```
'ANSI_NULLS' is not a recognized SET option.
Msg 40512, Level 16, State 1, Procedure InsertCompletedScope, Line 5
Deprecated feature 'Data types: text ntext or image' is not supported in this➥
 version of SQL Server.
Msg 195, Level 15, State 5, Line 2
'ANSI_NULLS' is not a recognized SET option.
Msg 195, Level 15, State 5, Line 2
'ANSI_NULLS' is not a recognized SET option.
Msg 40517, Level 16, State 1, Line 16
    Option 'pad_index' is not supported in this version of SQL Server.
```

8. Modify the output script as follows.

   a. Delete all:

```
SET ANSI_NULLS ON
GO
```

   b. Delete all:

```
PAD_INDEX  = OFF,
```

   c. Delete all:

```
ALLOW_ROW_LOCKS  = ON, ALLOW_PAGE_LOCKS  = ON
```

   d. And, replace it with the following:

```
ALLOW_ROW_LOCKS  = OFF, ALLOW_PAGE_LOCKS  = OFF
```

   e. Delete:

```
SORT_IN_TEMPDB = OFF
```

   f. The first release of SQL Azure does not support partitions. The KEY constraint statement for all table-creation scripts needs to be removed and replaced with a separate script. For example, the original script for creating a data table generated by SQL Server Management Studio should look like Listing 8-9. The highlighted parts need to be removed and replaced with a separate KEY constraint statement as Listing 8-10 shows:

***Listing 8-9.** Table-creating Script Generated by SQL Management Studio*

```
CREATE TABLE [dbo].[UserTable](
        [UserID] [int] IDENTITY(1,1) NOT NULL,
        [Password] [nvarchar](100) NULL,
        [FirstName] [nvarchar](100) NOT NULL,
        [LastName] [nvarchar](100) NOT NULL,
        [Timestamp] [timestamp] NOT NULL,
PRIMARY KEY CLUSTERED
(
[UserID] ASC
)WITH (STATISTICS_NORECOMPUTE  = OFF, IGNORE_DUP_KEY = OFF) ON [PRIMARY]
) ON [PRIMARY]
    GO
```

Listing 8-10. Replace the KEY Constraint Statement from Listing 8-9 with a Separate ALTER TABLE Script to Assign a Key to a Table

```
ALTER TABLE [UserTable]
ADD CONSTRAINT ID_PK PRIMARY KEY (UserID)
```

g. Remove the boldface lines in the `CREATE NONCLUSTERED INDEX` scripts generated by SQL Server Management Studio as shown in Listing 8-11.

Listing 8-11. Remove Code from All Index-creating Scripts

```
CREATE NONCLUSTERED INDEX [IX_UserTable_FirstName] ON [dbo].[UserTable]
(
        [FirstName] ASC
)WITH (STATISTICS_NORECOMPUTE  = OFF, IGNORE_DUP_KEY = OFF, DROP_EXISTING = OFF,↵
 ONLINE = OFF) ON [PRIMARY]
GO
```

9. Try to resolve all issues if there are other complaints from executing the generated scripts, and you will successfully run the script against the SQL Azure cloud database. You can run a query to verify that the expected tables have been created as shown in Figure 8-6.

```
SELECT * FROM sys.databases
```

SQL Azure Application Developing Tool: SQLAzureConnect

In this section I am going to present a Windows application designed and developed for .NET developers to access SQL Azure services. This project will show you how to use ADO.NET to create a connection to SQL Azure services to execute SQL queries and stored procedures just as you do from SQL Server Management Studio. The major added value provided by this tool are detailed below. They make this application a very handy tool for SQL Azure or on-premises SQL application development. It provides:

- A quick way to switch back and forth between SQL Azure cloud services and traditional on-premises SQL Server environments.
- A SQL data access component class that can be used for both SQL Azure and on-premises SQL application development.
- XML data-driven SQL query and stored procedure composition, editing, and executing, and UI dynamic factoring. A `SQLAccessHelper` class makes SQL query and stored procedure execution from C# extremely easy. All scripts and parameters needed for a stored procedure can be put into an XML data file or added on the fly and executed using this tool.

Functions of SQLAzureConnect

A screenshot of `SQLAzureConnect` is shown in Figure 8-15. Two radio buttons can be found to the left of the button Test Connection, which allows users to quickly switch the connection back and forth between the SQL Azure cloud service and on-premises SQL workstation environments. A new SQL service can be added by clicking the Add Service button. The script box is below the text box Description.

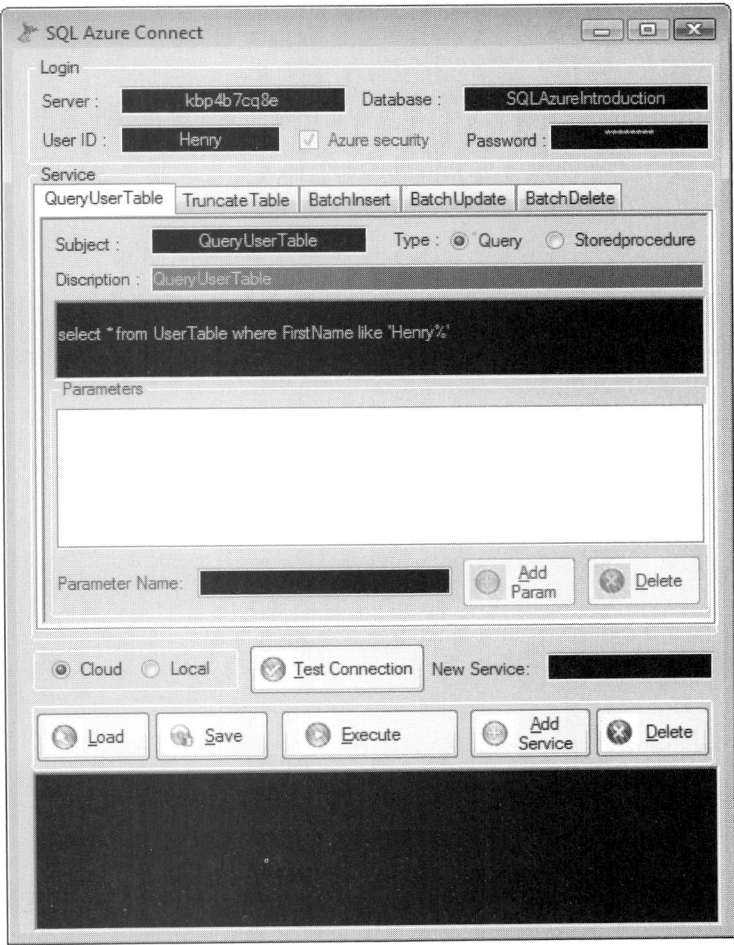

Figure 8-15. *Screenshot of* `SQLAzureConnect`

There are two ways to execute a script. One way is to click the Execute button, and the other way is to select and highlight the text and press F5. If there is a script selected, the caption of the Execute button turns to Execute Selected, and the background color of the button changes, as Figure 8-16 shows.

Figure 8-16. The caption of the Execute button turns to Execute Selected, and the background color turns to gold

There are two SQL execution options selected from a pair of radio buttons, Query and Storedprocedure. When Storedprocedure is selected, you can add and delete parameters required by a stored procedure. A specific SQL Azure service execution can be navigated using the tabs of the tab control in the window. The results of executing the SQL service are displayed in the bottom window, along with the error report. Figure 8-17 shows the results of the connection test.

All the newly created service configuration data can be saved as an XML data file and played back later. (You also can manually create an XML data file and load it into this tool to execute.) Next we are going to go over the XML schema and data file that are the driving force of this tool.

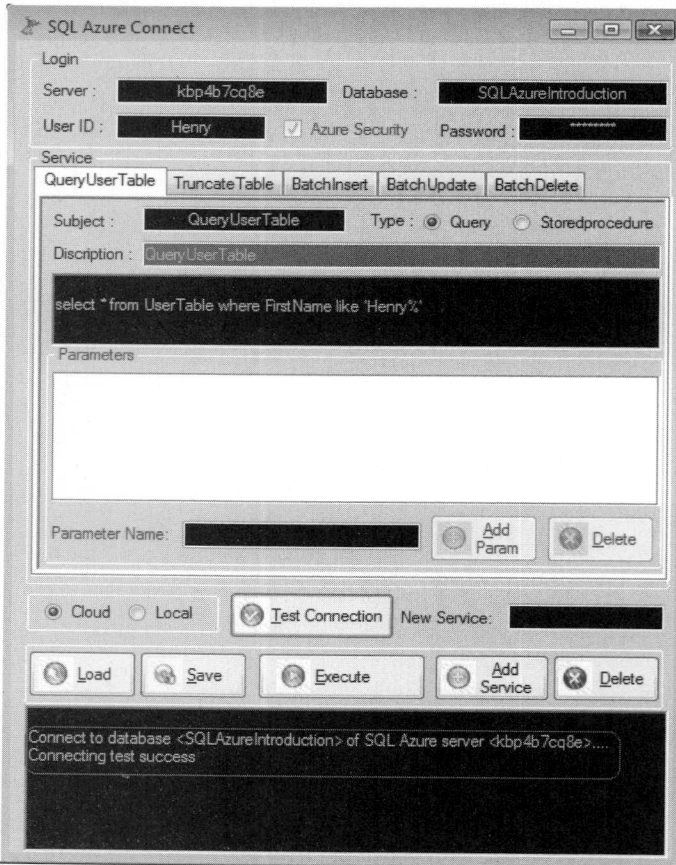

Figure 8-17. Connect to SQL Azure test results

■ **Note** Use `SQLAzureConnect` to connect to the local on-premises SQL server. If this tool is used for on-premises SQL development and database security requires local administrator access privileges, then you may need to run this application with Windows administrator privileges, since by design Windows integration security is going to be applied when this tool is used for an on-premises system, and SQL security is used for SQL Azure cloud services. What you need to do is to create a shortcut on your desktop and right-click on the shortcut icon to launch the Shortcut Properties dialog box. In the Advanced pane, check the box "Run as administrator" as Figure 8-18 shows.

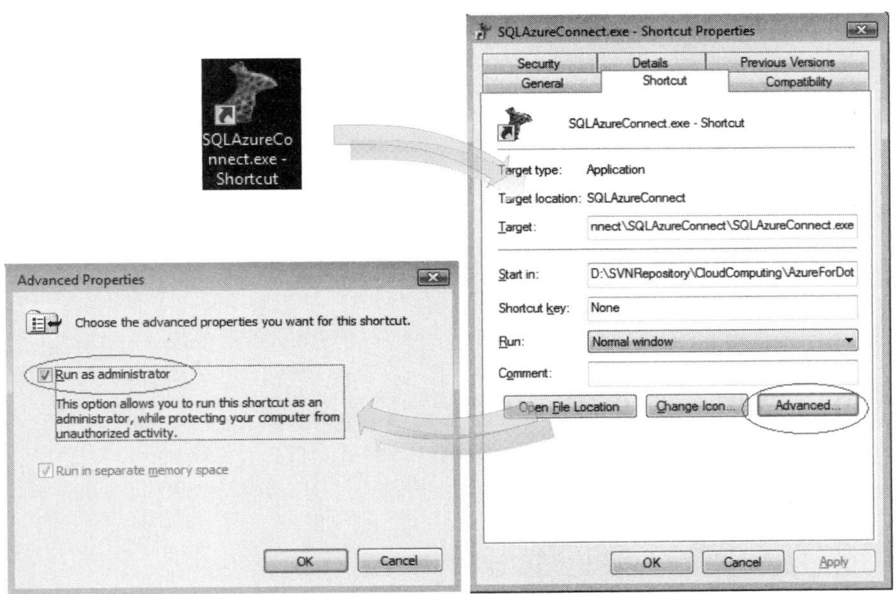

Figure 8-18. *Run* `SQLAzureConnect` *as local administrator when using this tool in an on-premises environment*

Using XML Data to Define UI Components Dynamically

Using XML data as the driving force for SQL Azure and on-premises SQL application service execution is an essential design concept for the `SQLAzureConnect` tool. Another essential design concept is to define user interface components dynamically. The binding source component from Visual Studio is also introduced to this tool to allow data bindings and data updating dynamically. The data domain of the binding source component is the XML data behind data objects.

The hierarchical structure of the schema definition is shown in Figure 8-19. The schema `SQLDataAccess` has two record nodes, `ServiceConnection` and `SqlDataService`. `SqlDataService` is unbounded, which means that this node is a collection node and is a group record of `SqlDataService` records. Each `SqlDataService` has one attribute Subject and one element Description and a child collection node Command. The Command node has an imported schema SQLParameter, which also is a group collection of the Parameter record. The SQLParameter schema defines the attribute Direction, with optional values In, Out, InOut, and ReturnValue, and four elements Name, Type, Value, and Size, that are required for specifying a SQL parameter. An example of an XML data file matching this schema is shown in Listing 8-12.

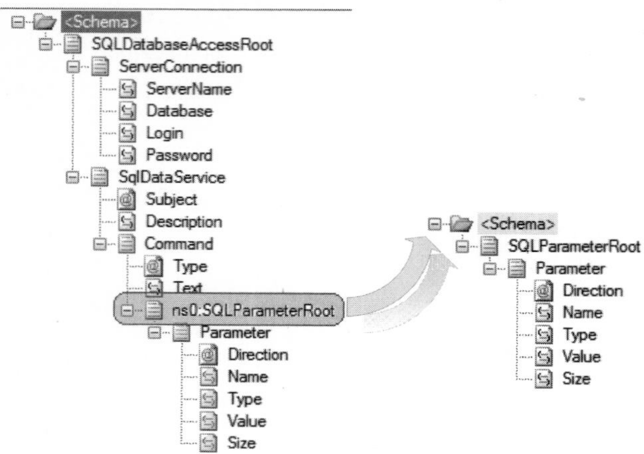

Figure 8-19. *XML schema definition for the XML data source used as the driving force of* SQLAzureConnect

Listing 8-12. *An Example of an XML Data File Used for SQL Azure Service*

```
<ns0:SQLDatabaseAccessRoot xmlns:ns0="http://SQLAzureConnect.Schema.SQLDatabaseAccess">
  <ServerConnection>
    <ServerName>kbp4b7cq8e</ServerName>
    <Database>SQLAzureIntroduction</Database>
    <Login>Henry</Login>
    <Password>mypassword</Password>
  </ServerConnection>
  <SqlDataService Subject="QueryUserTable">
    <Description>QueryUserTable</Description>
    <Command Type="Query">
      <Text>
        <![CDATA[
select * from UserTable where FirstName like 'Henry%'
        ]]>
      </Text>
    </Command>
  </SqlDataService>
  <SqlDataService Subject="TruncateTable">
    <Description>TruncateTable</Description>
    <Command Type="Query">
      <Text>
        <![CDATA[
```

```
TRUNCATE TABLE UserTable
        ]]>
      </Text>
    </Command>
  </SqlDataService>
  <SqlDataService Subject="BatchInsert">
    <Description>BatchInsert</Description>
    <Command Type="Storedprocedure">
      <Text>sp_BatchInsert</Text>
      <ns1:SQLParameterRoot xmlns:ns1="http://SQLAzureConnect.Schema.SQLParameter">
        <Parameter Direction="In">
          <Name>rows</Name>
          <Type>INT</Type>
          <Value>100</Value>
          <Size>4</Size>
        </Parameter>
      </ns1:SQLParameterRoot>
    </Command>
  </SqlDataService>
  <SqlDataService Subject="BatchUpdate">
    <Description>BatchUpdate</Description>
    <Command Type="Storedprocedure">
      <Text>sp_BatchUpdate</Text>
      <ns1:SQLParameterRoot xmlns:ns1="http://SQLAzureConnect.Schema.SQLParameter">
        <Parameter Direction="In">
          <Name>rows</Name>
          <Type>INT</Type>
          <Value>100</Value>
          <Size>4</Size>
        </Parameter>
      </ns1:SQLParameterRoot>
    </Command>
  </SqlDataService>
  <SqlDataService Subject="BatchDelete">
    <Description>BatchDelete</Description>
    <Command Type="Storedprocedure">
      <Text>sp_BatchDelete</Text>
      <ns1:SQLParameterRoot xmlns:ns1="http://SQLAzureConnect.Schema.SQLParameter">
        <Parameter Direction="In">
          <Name>rows</Name>
          <Type>INT</Type>
          <Value>100</Value>
          <Size>4</Size>
        </Parameter>
      </ns1:SQLParameterRoot>
    </Command>
  </SqlDataService>
</ns0:SQLDatabaseAccessRoot>
```

SQLDataAccessComponent Class

The SQLDataAccessComponent class encapsulates the client-side functions for SQL database access, including database connection handling using ADO.NET, transaction handling, and all basic SQL client-access actions that should be familiar to all SQL developers and ADO.NET users. It includes the following methods:

- ExecuteNonQuery()
- ExecuteScalar()
- GetDataReader()
- ExecuteDataSet()
- ExecuteDataTable()

All those methods accept SqlCommand as a parameter. The code is shown in Listing 8-13. A parameterized constructor has been defined besides the default constructor, which accepts the connection string as a parameter. The three public methods defined in this class, BeginTrans(), CommitTrans(), and RollbackTrans(), are used for applications to force invoking a transaction manually. The connection will time out in two seconds to avoid the calling thread been stacked if there is a connection difficulty.

Listing 8-13. *Implementation for Class SQLDataAccessComponent*

```
using System;
using System.Configuration;
using System.Data;
using System.Data.SqlClient;
using System.Globalization;
using System.Collections;
using System.ComponentModel;
using System.Text;

namespace SQLAzureConnect
{
    public class SQLDataAccessComponent : IDisposable
    {
        #region Private Fields

        static protected SqlConnection _connection = null;
        private const Int32 COMMAND_TIMEOUT = 60;
        private SqlTransaction _transaction;
        protected string _SQL_CONNECTION_STRING = string.Empty;

        #endregion

        #region Constructors/Destructors

        /// <summary>
        /// Default Contstructor
```

```
/// </summary>
public SQLDataAccessComponent()
{
    _transaction = null;
    _connection = new SqlConnection(_SQL_CONNECTION_STRING);
}

public SQLDataAccessComponent(String connectionString)
{
    _transaction = null;
    _connection = new SqlConnection(connectionString);
    _SQL_CONNECTION_STRING = connectionString;

}

public void Dispose()
{
    CloseConn();
    _transaction = null;
    _connection = null;
}


#endregion

#region Public Properties

public bool IsInTransaction
{
    get
    {
        return _transaction != null;
    }
}

#endregion

#region Private Methods

private void OpenConn()
{
    Dispose();

    if (_connection == null)
    {
        _connection = new SqlConnection(_SQL_CONNECTION_STRING);
    }

    _connection.Open();

    TimeSpan timeOutSetting = new TimeSpan(0, 0, 2);//2 sec
```

```
        DateTime connectingStart = DateTime.Now;
        int timeout = 0;
        while (_connection.State == ConnectionState.Connecting && timeout <= 1)
        {
            DateTime timeNow = DateTime.Now;
            TimeSpan timespanElapsed =
              new TimeSpan(timeNow.Hour - connectingStart.Hour,
                           timeNow.Minute - connectingStart.Minute,
                           timeNow.Second - connectingStart.Second);
            timeout = TimeSpan.Compare(timespanElapsed, timeOutSetting);
        }
    }

    private void CloseConn()
    {
        lock (_connection)
        {
            while (null != _connection && _connection.State != ConnectionState.Broken
                  && _connection.State == ConnectionState.Open)
            {
                _connection.Close();
            }
        }
    }

    #endregion

    #region Public Methods

    public void BeginTrans()
    {
        if (_connection.State != ConnectionState.Closed &&
            _connection.State != ConnectionState.Broken)
        {
            CloseConn();
        }
        OpenConn();
        _transaction = _connection.BeginTransaction();
    }

    public void CommitTrans()
    {
        if (null != _transaction)
        {
            _transaction.Commit();
        }
        CloseConn();
        _transaction = null;
    }

    public void RollBackTrans()
```

```
{
    if (null != _transaction)
    {
        _transaction.Rollback();
    }
    CloseConn();
    _transaction = null;
}

public SqlDataReader GetDataReader(SqlCommand command)
{
    try
    {
        OpenConn();
        command.Connection = _connection;
        command.Transaction = _transaction;
        command.CommandTimeout = COMMAND_TIMEOUT;

        return command.ExecuteReader(CommandBehavior.CloseConnection);

    }
    finally
    {
        if (_transaction != null)
        {
            RollBackTrans();
        }
        command.Dispose();
    }
}

public Object ExecuteNonQuery(SqlCommand command)
{

    OpenConn();
    command.Connection = _connection;
    command.Transaction = _transaction;
    command.CommandTimeout = COMMAND_TIMEOUT;

    try
    {
        int rowsAffected = command.ExecuteNonQuery();

        return
           (command.Parameters.Contains("@ReturnValue")) ?
          Convert.ToInt32(command.Parameters["@ReturnValue"].Value) : rowsAffected;

    }
    finally
    {
        if (_transaction != null)
```

```
            {
                RollBackTrans();
            }
            command.Dispose();
        }
    }

    public string ExecuteScalar(SqlCommand command)
    {
        try
        {
            OpenConn();
            command.Connection = _connection;
            command.Transaction = _transaction;
            command.CommandTimeout = COMMAND_TIMEOUT;
            return command.ExecuteScalar().ToString();
        }
        finally
        {
            if (_transaction != null)
            {
                RollBackTrans();
            }
            command.Dispose();
        }
    }

    public DataSet ExecuteDataSet(SqlCommand command)
    {
        DataSet oDataSet = new DataSet();
        try
        {
            SqlDataAdapter da;
            oDataSet.Locale = CultureInfo.InvariantCulture;

            OpenConn();
            command.Connection = _connection;
            command.Transaction = _transaction;
            command.CommandTimeout = COMMAND_TIMEOUT;

            da = new SqlDataAdapter(command);

            da.Fill(oDataSet);
        }
        finally
        {
            command.Dispose();
        }
        return oDataSet;
    }
```

```
        public int ExecuteDataTable(SqlCommand command, ref DataTable datatable)
        {
            int rowAffected = 0;
            try
            {
                SqlDataAdapter da;
                datatable.Locale = CultureInfo.InvariantCulture;

                OpenConn();
                command.Connection = _connection;
                command.Transaction = _transaction;
                command.CommandTimeout = COMMAND_TIMEOUT;

                da = new SqlDataAdapter(command);
                rowAffected = da.Fill(datatable);
            }
            finally
            {
                command.Dispose();
            }
            return rowAffected;
        }

        #endregion


    }
}
```

SQLDataAccessHelper Class

A helper class `SQLDataAccessHelper` is designed to help applications use `SQLDataAccessComponent` based on the XML service configuration data in a simple and agile way. The responsibilities of this class are to:

- Extract the SQL data-access-configuration data by using the service name as the key from the deserialized XML data classes.
- Invoke a SQL query to execute a stored procedure depending on the type of command. If the service request is a SQL stored procedure, populate the parameter with the corresponding SQL data type and assign values to the parameter.
- Invoke a SQL query to execute the selected script text.
- Compose the return results as the display message for UI updating.
- Handle errors.
- Serialize and deserialize XML.

This class has two parameterized constructors. Both constructors take the deserialized XML data object as an input parameter. There are five public access methods that have been exposed from this helper class.

- `XmlRetrive()` and `XmlPersist()`, used to deserialize and serialize XML data files and data objects.
- `Execute()`, used to execute a SQL query or stored procedure predefined in the XML data file. The application just needs to pass the subject name of the SQL service and a reference to an object that will hold a possible return object from the SQL services. This method will invoke either a SQL query or execute a stored procedure from the `SQLAccessComponent` according to the command type specified from the data file. This makes the code extremely concise and lean for a SQL Azure or on-premises SQL application.
- `ExecuteSelected()`, used to execute a SQL query script text block selected by a user on the fly. This function can be invoked by a user using the F5 shortcut key after the user selected a block of script text.
- `CreateStoredProcedure()`, which has not been integrated into the user interface of `SQLAzureConnect` yet. It is ready for any other client application to invoke. With the current `SQLAzureConnect` this function can be mimicked by using the `ExecuteSelected()` feature.

Compose a connection string using the XML data. The connection string will come up in two distinct formats, SQL Azure cloud connection string format and on-premises connection string format to allow this tool to support both cloud SQL services and on-premises SQL server access.

Listing 8-14 is the source code of the class `SQLDataAccessHelper`. We have explained all member methods and their responsibilities. The other member methods, such as `_PopulateParameters()` and `_PopulateStoredProcedureParameters()`, are fairly straightforward.

Listing 8-14. *Implementation for Class `SQLDataAccessHelper`*

```
using System;
using System.Collections.Generic;
using System.Linq;
using System.Text;
using System.Data;
using System.Data.Sql;
using System.Data.SqlClient;
using System.Xml;
using System.Xml.Serialization;
using System.IO;
using Microsoft.SqlServer.Management.Smo;
using Microsoft.SqlServer.Management.Common;
using System.Text.RegularExpressions;

namespace SQLAzureConnect
{
    using SQLAzureConnect.Schema.SQLDatabaseAccess;
    using SQLAzureConnect.Schema.SQLParameter;
```

```
public class SQLDataAccessHelper
{
    protected SQLDatabaseAccessRoot _sqlDatabaseAccessRoot = null;

    #region Constructors

    public SQLDataAccessHelper(SQLDatabaseAccessRoot sqlDatabaseAccessRoot)
    {
        _sqlDatabaseAccessRoot = sqlDatabaseAccessRoot;
    }

    public SQLDataAccessHelper(SQLDatabaseAccessRoot sqlDatabaseAccessRoot,
                               string connectionString) : this(sqlDatabaseAccessRoot)
    {
        ConnectionString = connectionString;
    }

    #endregion

    #region Properties

    public string ConnectionString { get; set; }
    public string ConnectedDatabase
    {
        get
        {
            string database = string.Empty;
            string[] split = ConnectionString.StartsWith("Server")?
                  Regex.Split(ConnectionString, "Server=")
                 :Regex.Split(ConnectionString, "Data Source=");
            if (null != split && split.Length > 1)
            {
                string strValue = split[split.Length - 1];
                int indexEnd = strValue.IndexOf(';');
                try
                {
                    database = strValue.Substring(0, indexEnd);
                }
                catch { }
            }

            return database;
        }
    }

    #endregion

    #region Public Methods

    public StringBuilder Execute(string subject, ref Object results)
```

```
{
    StringBuilder sb = null;
    if (null != _sqlDatabaseAccessRoot)
    {
        SQLDatabaseAccessRootSqlDataService dataService =
          this._sqlDatabaseAccessRoot.SqlDataService
            .FirstOrDefault<SQLDatabaseAccessRootSqlDataService>(
              x => x.Subject == subject);
        if (null != dataService)
        {
            if (dataService.Command.Type ==
                SQLDatabaseAccessRootSqlDataServiceCommandType.Query)
            {
                sb = _ExecuteQuery(dataService.Command.Text);
            }
            else if (dataService.Command.Type ==
                     SQLDatabaseAccessRootSqlDataServiceCommandType.Storedprocedure)
            {
                sb = _ExecuteStoredProcedure(dataService);
            }
        }
    }
    else
    {
        throw new ApplicationException(
          string.Format("---SqlDatabaseService:Query,  Subject = <{0}>,
                      SqlDatabaseService is not initialized correctly.", subject));
    }

    return sb;
}

public StringBuilder ExecuteSelected(string selectedText)
{
    return _ExecuteQuery(selectedText);
}

public bool CreateStoredProcedure(string storedProcedureName,
                         string storedProcedureBody,
                         SQLDatabaseAccessRootSqlDataServiceCommand serviceCommand)
{
    bool success = false;
    StoredProcedure strordProcedure = null;
    if (null != storedProcedureName
        && null != storedProcedureBody
        && null != serviceCommand
        && string.Empty != storedProcedureName
        && string.Empty != storedProcedureBody)
    {
        try
        {
```

```
            SqlConnection _connection = new SqlConnection(ConnectionString);
            if (null != _connection)
            {
                _connection.Open();

                Server server = new Server(new ServerConnection(_connection));
                Database db = server.Databases[ConnectedDatabase];
                stroredProcedure = new StoredProcedure(db, storedProcedureName);
                stroredProcedure.TextMode = false;
                stroredProcedure.AnsiNullsStatus = false;
                stroredProcedure.QuotedIdentifierStatus = false;

                stroredProcedure.TextBody = storedProcedureBody;

                if (null != serviceCommand)
                {
                    this._PopulateStoredProcedureParameters(ref stroredProcedure,
                                                            serviceCommand);
                }
                stroredProcedure.Create();
                success = stroredProcedure == null ? false : true;
            }
        }
        catch (Exception ex)
        {
            string msg = string.Empty;
            if (null != ex.InnerException)
            {
                msg = ex.InnerException.Message;
                if (ex.InnerException.InnerException != null)
                {
                    msg = ex.InnerException.InnerException.Message;
                    if (
                      msg.Equals(
                        string.Format(
                          "There is already an object named '{0}' in the database.",
                          storedProcedureName
                        )
                      )
                    )
                    {
                        success = true;
                    }
                }
            }
            else
            {
                msg = ex.Message;
            }
        }
    }
```

```
        return success;
    }

    static public object XmlRetrive(Type type, XmlDocument xmlDoc)
    {
        object o = null;

        if (null != xmlDoc && null != xmlDoc.DocumentElement)
        {
            XmlSerializer serializer = new XmlSerializer(type);
            StringReader reader = new StringReader(xmlDoc.OuterXml);

            try
            {
                o = serializer.Deserialize(reader);
            }
            catch (Exception e)
            {
                System.Diagnostics.Trace.WriteLine(e.Message);
                System.Diagnostics.Trace.WriteLine(e.StackTrace);
                throw e;
            }
        }

        return o;
    }

    static public StringBuilder XmlPersist(object o, Type type)
    {
        XmlSerializer serializer = new XmlSerializer(type);
        StringBuilder sb = new StringBuilder();
        StringWriter writer = new StringWriter(sb);

        try
        {
            serializer.Serialize(writer, o);
        }
        catch (Exception e)
        {
            System.Diagnostics.Trace.WriteLine(e.Message);
            System.Diagnostics.Trace.WriteLine(e.StackTrace);
            throw e;
        }

        return writer.GetStringBuilder();
    }
    #endregion

    #region Private Methods
```

```
protected StringBuilder _ExecuteQuery(string commandText)
{
    int rowAffected = 0;
    DataTable datatable = new DataTable();
    StringBuilder sb = new StringBuilder();

    SQLDataAccessComponent dac = null;
    SqlCommand Command = null;

    try
    {
        dac = new SQLDataAccessComponent(this.ConnectionString);
        Command = new SqlCommand(commandText, new SqlConnection());
        dac.BeginTrans();
        rowAffected = dac.ExecuteDataTable(Command, ref datatable);
        dac.CommitTrans();
        if (datatable.Rows.Count > 0)
        {
            foreach (DataRow dataRow in datatable.Rows)
            {
                StringBuilder rowBuilder = new StringBuilder();
                foreach (object obj in dataRow.ItemArray)
                {
                    if (!(obj is DBNull || (obj is System.Byte[])))
                    {
                        rowBuilder.Append(string.Format("{0}  ", obj.ToString()));
                    }
                }
                sb.Append(string.Format("{0}{1}", rowBuilder.ToString(),
                          Environment.NewLine));
            }
        }
        sb.Append(
          string.Format("------ SQL execute success, row affected : {0} ------{1}",
                        rowAffected, Environment.NewLine));
        sb.Append(Environment.NewLine);
    }
    catch (Exception ex)
    {
        throw new ApplicationException(
          string.Format("------ SQL execute failed, error message: {0}",
                        ex.Message, Environment.NewLine));
    }
    finally
    {
        if (null != Command)
        {
            Command.Dispose();
        }
        if (null != dac)
        {
```

```
                dac.Dispose();
            }
        }

        return sb;
    }

    protected StringBuilder _ExecuteStoredProcedure(
      SQLDatabaseAccessRootSqlDataService dataService)
    {
        StringBuilder sb = new StringBuilder();
        int rowAffected = 0;
        SQLDataAccessComponent dac = null;
        SqlCommand Command = null;

        try
        {
            SQLDatabaseAccessRootSqlDataServiceCommand serviceCommand =
              dataService.Command;
            string storedProcedure = serviceCommand.Text;
            dac = new SQLDataAccessComponent(this.ConnectionString);
            Command = new SqlCommand(storedProcedure, new SqlConnection());
            Command.CommandType = CommandType.StoredProcedure;

            bool output = this._PopulateParameters(serviceCommand, ref Command);
            dac.BeginTrans();
            rowAffected = (int)dac.ExecuteNonQuery(Command);
            dac.CommitTrans();
            if (output)
            {
                foreach (SqlParameter parameter in Command.Parameters)
                {
                    if (parameter.Direction == ParameterDirection.Output)
                    {
                        sb.Append(parameter.Value.ToString());
                        sb.Append(Environment.NewLine);
                    }
                }
            }
            sb.Append(
              string.Format(
                "------ SQL execute success, row affected : {0} ------{1}",
                rowAffected, Environment.NewLine
              )
            );
            sb.Append(Environment.NewLine);
        }
        finally
        {
            if (null != Command)
            {
```

```
                Command.Dispose();
            }
            if (null != dac)
            {
                dac.Dispose();
            }
        }

        return sb;
    }

    private bool _PopulateParameters(
      SQLDatabaseAccessRootSqlDataServiceCommand serviceCommand,
      ref SqlCommand Command)
    {
        bool output = false;
        string direction = string.Empty;

        try
        {
            Command.Parameters.Clear();
            foreach (SQLParameterRoot parameterRoot in serviceCommand.SQLParameterRoot)
            {
                direction =
                  parameterRoot.Parameter.Direction.ToString().Trim().ToUpper();
                output |= direction == "OUT" || direction == "INOUT" ? true : false;
                if (parameterRoot.Parameter.Type.ToUpper().StartsWith("NCHAR"))
                {
                    int length = 0;
                    length = Convert.ToInt32(parameterRoot.Parameter.Size);
                    Command.Parameters.Add(
                      string.Format("@{0}", parameterRoot.Parameter.Name),
                                    SqlDbType.NChar,
                                    length).Value = parameterRoot.Parameter.Value;
                }
                else if (parameterRoot.Parameter.Type.ToUpper().StartsWith("VARCHAR"))
                {
                    int length = Convert.ToInt32(parameterRoot.Parameter.Size);
                    Command.Parameters.Add(
                      string.Format("@{0}", parameterRoot.Parameter.Name),
                      SqlDbType.VarChar, length).Value = parameterRoot.Parameter.Value;
                }
                else if (parameterRoot.Parameter.Type.ToUpper().StartsWith("NVARCHAR"))
                {
                    int length = Convert.ToInt32(parameterRoot.Parameter.Size);
                    Command.Parameters.Add(
                      string.Format("@{0}", parameterRoot.Parameter.Name),
                      SqlDbType.NVarChar,
                      length).Value = parameterRoot.Parameter.Value;
                }
                else if (parameterRoot.Parameter.Type.ToUpper().StartsWith("INT"))
```

```
                    {
                        Command.Parameters.Add(
                          string.Format("@{0}", parameterRoot.Parameter.Name),
                          SqlDbType.Int, 4).Value =
                            Convert.ToInt32(parameterRoot.Parameter.Value);
                    }
                    else if (parameterRoot.Parameter.Type.ToUpper().StartsWith("UNIQUE"))
                    {
                        Command.Parameters.Add(
                          string.Format("@{0}", parameterRoot.Parameter.Name),
                          SqlDbType.UniqueIdentifier, 32).Value =
                            new Guid(parameterRoot.Parameter.Value);
                    }
                    else if (parameterRoot.Parameter.Type.ToUpper().StartsWith("XML"))
                    {
                        Command.Parameters.Add(
                          string.Format("@{0}", parameterRoot.Parameter.Name),
                          SqlDbType.Xml, 0).Value = parameterRoot.Parameter.Value;
                    }
                    else if (parameterRoot.Parameter.Type.ToUpper().StartsWith("TIMSTAMP"))
                    {
                        Command.Parameters.Add(
                          string.Format("@{0}", parameterRoot.Parameter.Name),
                          SqlDbType.Timestamp, 0).Value = parameterRoot.Parameter.Value;
                    }
                    else if (parameterRoot.Parameter.Type.ToUpper().StartsWith("DATETIME"))
                    {
                        DateTime dt = DateTime.Now;
                        if (parameterRoot.Parameter.Value != string.Empty)
                        {
                            dt = DateTime.Parse(parameterRoot.Parameter.Value);
                        }
                        Command.Parameters.Add(
                          string.Format("@{0}", parameterRoot.Parameter.Name),
                          SqlDbType.DateTime,
                          0).Value = dt;
                    }
                }
            }
            finally
            {
                if (null != Command)
                {
                    Command.Dispose();
                }
            }

            return output;
        }

        private bool _PopulateStoredProcedureParameters(ref StoredProcedure storedProcedure,
```

```
                SQLDatabaseAccessRootSqlDataServiceCommand serviceCommand)
{
    bool success = false;
    try
    {
        foreach (SQLParameterRoot parameterRoot in serviceCommand.SQLParameterRoot)
        {
            StoredProcedureParameter param = null;
            if (parameterRoot.Parameter.Type.ToUpper().StartsWith("NCHAR"))
            {
                param = new StoredProcedureParameter(storedProcedure,
                  string.Format("@{0}", parameterRoot.Parameter.Name),
                  DataType.NVarCharMax);
            }
            else if (parameterRoot.Parameter.Type.ToUpper().StartsWith("VARCHAR"))
            {
                param = new StoredProcedureParameter(storedProcedure,
                  string.Format("@{0}", parameterRoot.Parameter.Name),
                  DataType.VarCharMax);
            }
            else if (parameterRoot.Parameter.Type.ToUpper().StartsWith("NVARCHAR"))
            {
                param = new StoredProcedureParameter(storedProcedure,
                  string.Format("@{0}", parameterRoot.Parameter.Name),
                  DataType.NVarCharMax);
            }
            else if (parameterRoot.Parameter.Type.ToUpper().StartsWith("INT"))
            {
                param = new StoredProcedureParameter(storedProcedure,
                  string.Format("@{0}", parameterRoot.Parameter.Name),
                  DataType.Int);
            }
            else if (parameterRoot.Parameter.Type.ToUpper().StartsWith("UNIQUE"))
            {
                param = new StoredProcedureParameter(storedProcedure,
                  string.Format("@{0}", parameterRoot.Parameter.Name),
                  DataType.UniqueIdentifier);
            }
            else if (parameterRoot.Parameter.Type.ToUpper().StartsWith("XML"))
            {
                param = new StoredProcedureParameter(storedProcedure,
                  string.Format("@{0}", parameterRoot.Parameter.Name),
                  DataType.NVarCharMax);
            }
            else if (parameterRoot.Parameter.Type.ToUpper().StartsWith("TIMSTAMP"))
            {
                param = new StoredProcedureParameter(storedProcedure,
                  string.Format("@{0}", parameterRoot.Parameter.Name),
                  DataType.Timestamp);
            }
            else if (parameterRoot.Parameter.Type.ToUpper().StartsWith("DATETIME"))
```

```
                        {
                            DateTime dt = DateTime.Now;
                            if (parameterRoot.Parameter.Value != string.Empty)
                            {
                                dt = DateTime.Parse(parameterRoot.Parameter.Value);
                            }
                            param = new StoredProcedureParameter(storedProcedure,
                              string.Format("@{0}", parameterRoot.Parameter.Name),
                              DataType.DateTime);
                        }

                        if (null != parameterRoot.Parameter)
                        {
                            storedProcedure.Parameters.Add(param);
                        }
                    }

                    success = true;
                }
                catch (Exception ex)
                {
                    string msg = string.Empty;
                    if (null != ex.InnerException)
                    {
                        msg = ex.InnerException.Message;
                    }
                    else
                    {
                        msg = ex.Message;
                    }
                }

                return success;
            }
            #endregion
        }
    }
```

Component Design and Implementation

The concept of using XML data as a driving force can also be applied to user interface design and implementation. Usually user interface implementation is a tedious job. Using XML data to design and implement the user interface will tremendously reduce the lines of code and make the UI design more componentized and more object-oriented. The user interface for `SQLAzureConnect` is composed of two user controls and a Windows form. The core concept to identify the UI user control is very straightforward. A user control should naturally reflect the XML schema. When the XML schema is defined, all C# data objects and all UI user controls are actually defined. Since we use the UI user controls and Windows form as the front end for presenting the XML data, the instance of the XML data object will be bound to the underlying data source object.

As I mentioned, there are two XML schemas that have been defined, `SQLParameter.xsd` and `SQLDatabaseAccess.xsd`, therefore we have corresponding UI components identified as `ParameterControl` and `SQLDataServiceControl`. Now let us have a close look at how this approach tremendously simplified the UI design and development for an application such as `SQLAzureConnect`.

ParameterControl

The UI layout of the `ParameterControl` is shown in Figure 8-20, and the implementation is shown in Listing 8-15. A parameterized constructor has been added to this user control. The parameterized constructor accepts the XML data object `SQLParameterRoot` (marked as a reference type) and the instance of the parent form (used to display the message back to the parent form). A `BindingSource` component is defined in this control and has been bound to the instance of the XML data object with the type of XML schema `SQLParameter` in the constructor of the user control as shown in the Listing 8-15.

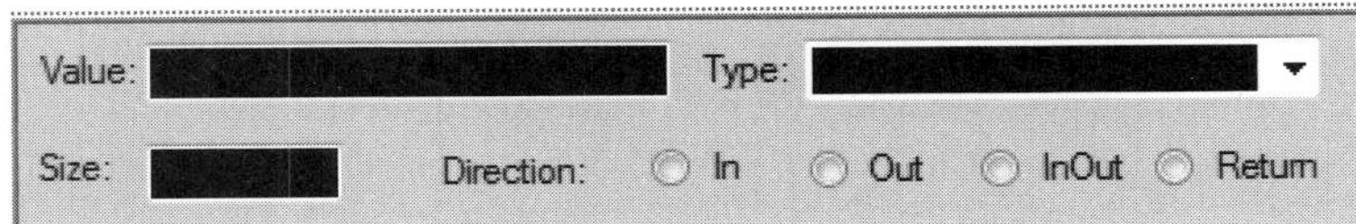

Figure 8-20. *UI layout of the user control* `ParameterControl`

Listing 8-15. *Implementations for* `ParameterControl`

```
using System;
using System.Collections.Generic;
using System.ComponentModel;
using System.Drawing;
using System.Data;
using System.Linq;
using System.Text;
using System.Windows.Forms;

namespace SQLAzureConnect
{
    using SQLAzureConnect.Schema.SQLParameter;

    public partial class ParameterControl : UserControl
    {
        private FormSQLAzureConnect _parentForm = null;
        public SQLParameterRoot _sqlParameter = null;

        public ParameterControl()
        {
            InitializeComponent();
        }

        public ParameterControl(ref SQLParameterRoot sqlParameter,
                                FormSQLAzureConnect parentForm)
```

```
{
    InitializeComponent();
    this.bindingSource.DataSource = _sqlParameter = sqlParameter;
    _parentForm = parentForm;
    _UpdateUI();
}

public void Add(SQLParameterRoot sqlParameter)
{
    this.bindingSource.Add(sqlParameter);
}

public void DoDataExchange()
{
    _sqlParameter.Parameter.Value = this.txtValue.Text.Trim();
    _sqlParameter.Parameter.Size = this.txtSize.Text;
    _sqlParameter.Parameter.Type = this.comboBoxType.SelectedItem.ToString();
    if (radioButtonIn.Checked)
    {
        _sqlParameter.Parameter.Direction = SQLParameterRootParameterDirection.In;
    }
    else if (radioButtonOut.Checked)
    {
        _sqlParameter.Parameter.Direction = SQLParameterRootParameterDirection.Out;
    }
    else if (radioButtonInOut.Checked)
    {
        _sqlParameter.Parameter.Direction =
          SQLParameterRootParameterDirection.InOut;
    }
    else if (radioButtonReturn.Checked)
    {
        _sqlParameter.Parameter.Direction =
          SQLParameterRootParameterDirection.ReturnValue;
    }
}

private void _UpdateUI()
{
    if (null != _sqlParameter)
    {
        this.txtValue.Text = _sqlParameter.Parameter.Value;
        this.txtSize.Text = _sqlParameter.Parameter.Size;
        this.comboBoxType.SelectedIndex =
          comboBoxType.Items.IndexOf(_sqlParameter.Parameter.Type);
        switch (_sqlParameter.Parameter.Direction)
        {
            case SQLParameterRootParameterDirection.Out:
                this.radioButtonOut.Select();
                break;
            case SQLParameterRootParameterDirection.InOut:
```

```
                    this.radioButtonInOut.Select();
                    break;
                case SQLParameterRootParameterDirection.ReturnValue:
                    this.radioButtonReturn.Select();
                    break;
                case SQLParameterRootParameterDirection.In:
                default:
                    this.radioButtonIn.Select();
                    break;
            }
        }
    }

    private void ParameterControl_Leave(object sender, EventArgs e)
    {
        DoDataExchange();
    }
  }
}
```

For this user control and all other user controls following we use a `BindingSource` control to bind and synchronize the data object with the data that was edited by the user. This component comes with Visual Studio and can be found from the Toolbox pane under the Data category as Figure 8-21 shows. Figure 8-22 shows how to set up the property of the component after dragging it from the toolbox onto the user control design surface.

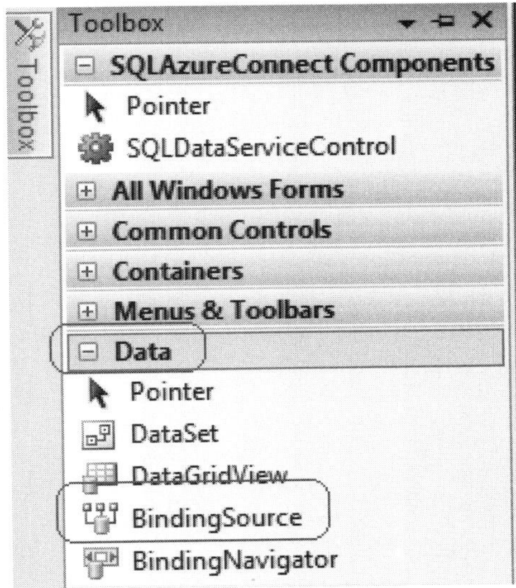

Figure 8-21. Drag and drop the `BindingSource` *component from Visual Studio Toolbox data pane to the* `ParameterControl` *design surface*

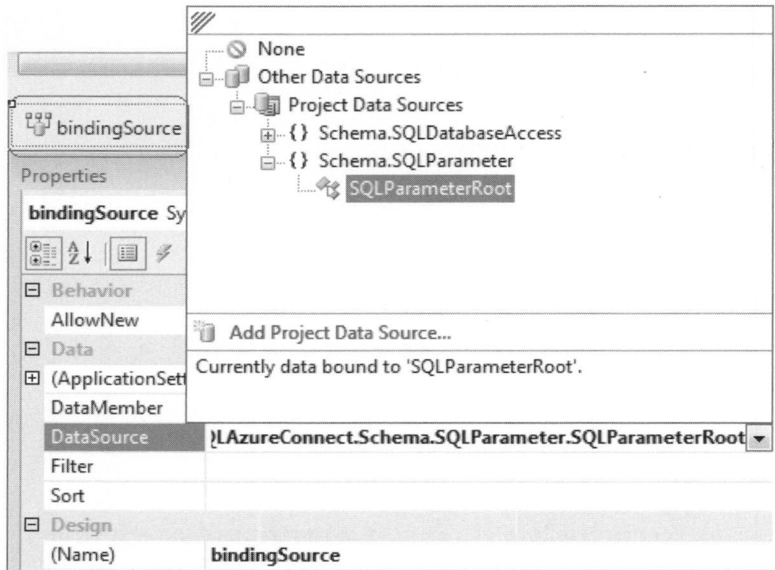

***Figure 8-22.** A `BindingSource` of `ParameterControl` is defined to bind the data source to the data object instance's XML `SQLParameterRoot`*

When the instance of `SQLParameterRoot` has been accepted, the values of the element and attribute will be updated to the UI component via the private method call to `_UpdateUI()`. When the control loses focus, the updated value modified by the user will be synchronized back to the XML data object via the method `DoDataExchange()`. The access to `DoDataExchange()` method is marked as `public` so that the parent host control can force a data refresh if necessary.

SQLDataServiceControl

The UI layout of the user control `SQLDataServiceControl` is shown in Figure 8-23, and the data binding source is defined to bind the data to the `SQLDatabaseAccessRootSqlDataService` as shown in Figure 8-24. The implementation of this user control is similar to that of `ParameterControl`. As with `ParameterControl` there are two methods, `_UpdateUI()` and `DoDataExchange()`, defined in this class that are used to handle UI updating and data synchronization. Since this control is the host control of `Parameter` controls, this control is responsible for handling the adding and deleting of the underlying `Parameter` controls and forcing data synchronization when this control loses focus or when a data synchronization request is received from the parent form. These tasks are handled in the methods `_AddPage()` and `btnAddParameter_Click()`. Listing 8-16 shows the implementation for the user control `SQLDatabaseAccess`.

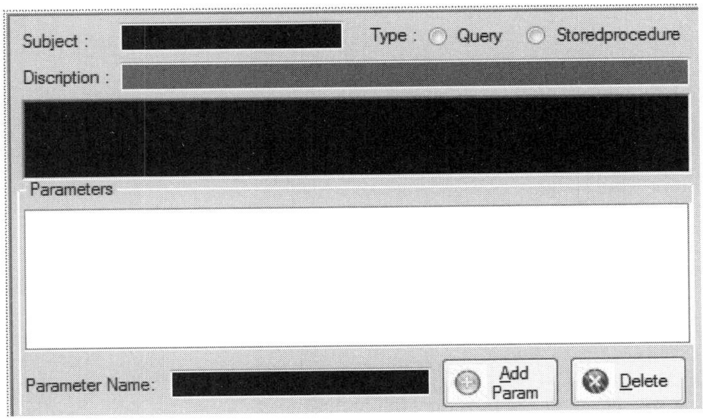

Figure 8-23. UI layout of the user control `SQLDataServiceControl`

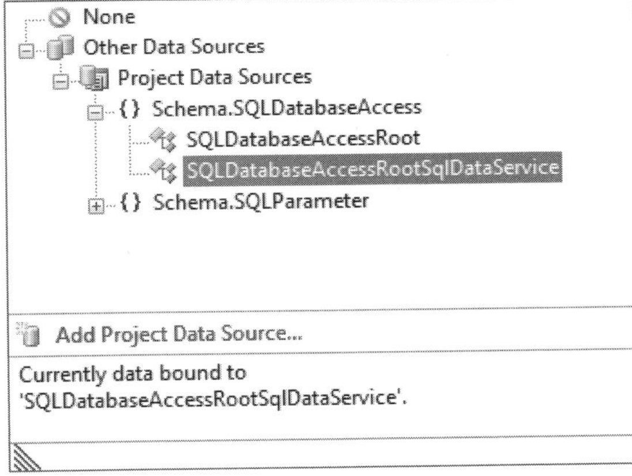

Figure 8-24. A `BindingSource` *of* `SQLDataServiceControl` *is defined to bind the data source to the data object instance's XML* `SQLDatabaseAccessRootSqlDataServiceRoot`

Listing 8-16. Implementation for `SQLDatabaseAccessControl`

```
using System;
using System.Collections.Generic;
using System.ComponentModel;
using System.Drawing;
using System.Data;
using System.Linq;
using System.Text;
using System.Windows.Forms;
```

```
namespace SQLAzureConnect
{
    using SQLAzureConnect.Schema.SQLDatabaseAccess;
    using SQLAzureConnect.Schema.SQLParameter;

    public partial class SQLDataServiceControl : UserControl
    {
        public SQLDatabaseAccessRootSqlDataService _sqlDatabaseAccessService = null;
        private FormSQLAzureConnect _parentForm = null;
        private TabPage _currentSelectedPage = null;
        public string SelectedText {
          get { return this.richTextBoxCommandText.SelectedText.Trim(); }
        }

        public event EventNotificationHandler eventSelectedTextChanged;
        public event EventBubblePreviewKeyDownHandler eventBubblePreviewKeyDown;

        public SQLDataServiceControl()
        {
            InitializeComponent();
        }

        public SQLDataServiceControl(ref SQLDatabaseAccessRootSqlDataService
          sqlDatabaseAccessRoot,
          FormSQLAzureConnect parentForm)
        {
            InitializeComponent();
            this.bindingSourceService.DataSource =
              _sqlDatabaseAccessService = sqlDatabaseAccessRoot;
            _parentForm = parentForm;
            _UpdateUI();
            this.richTextBoxCommandText.PreviewKeyDown +=
              new PreviewKeyDownEventHandler(richTextBoxCommandText_PreviewKeyDown);
        }

        public void DoDataExchange()
        {
            _sqlDatabaseAccessService.Subject = this.txtSubject.Text.Trim();
            _sqlDatabaseAccessService.Description = this.txtDescription.Text.Trim();
            _sqlDatabaseAccessService.Command.Text =
              this.richTextBoxCommandText.Text.Trim();

            if (this.radioButtonQuery.Checked)
            {
                _sqlDatabaseAccessService.Command.Type =
                  SQLDatabaseAccessRootSqlDataServiceCommandType.Query;
            }
            else if (this.radioButtonStoredProcedure.Checked)
            {
                _sqlDatabaseAccessService.Command.Type =
```

```
                SQLDatabaseAccessRootSqlDataServiceCommandType.Storedprocedure;
        }

        foreach (TabPage page in this.tabParameter.TabPages)
        {
            (page.Controls[0] as ParameterControl).DoDataExchange();
        }
    }

    private void _UpdateUI()
    {
        if (null != _sqlDatabaseAccessService)
        {
            this.txtSubject.Text = _sqlDatabaseAccessService.Subject;
            this.txtDescription.Text = _sqlDatabaseAccessService.Description;

            switch (_sqlDatabaseAccessService.Command.Type)
            {
                case SQLDatabaseAccessRootSqlDataServiceCommandType.Storedprocedure:
                    this.radioButtonStoredProcedure.Select();
                    break;
                case SQLDatabaseAccessRootSqlDataServiceCommandType.Query:
                default:
                    this.radioButtonQuery.Select();
                    break;
            }

            this.richTextBoxCommandText.Clear();
            this.richTextBoxCommandText.AppendText(
              _sqlDatabaseAccessService.Command.Text
            );
            if (null != _sqlDatabaseAccessService.Command &&
                null != _sqlDatabaseAccessService.Command.SQLParameterRoot)
            {
                for (int i = 0; i <
                     _sqlDatabaseAccessService.Command.SQLParameterRoot.Length; ++i )
                {
                    _AddPage(ref _sqlDatabaseAccessService.Command.SQLParameterRoot[i]);
                }
            }
            if (this.tabParameter.TabPages.Count > 0)
            {
                tabParameter.SelectedTab = this.tabParameter.TabPages[0];
            }
        }
    }

    private void tabParameter_SelectedIndexChanged(object sender, EventArgs e)
    {
        _currentSelectedPage = this.tabParameter.SelectedTab;
```

```
}

private void btnAddParameter_Click(object sender, EventArgs e)
{
    if (null != _parentForm)
    {
        _parentForm.DisplayMessage(string.Empty, false);
    }

    this.txtParameter.Focus();

    if (string.Empty == this.txtParameter.Text)
    {
        if (null != _parentForm)
        {
            _parentForm.DisplayMessage("Please enter parameter name!", true);
        }

        return;
    }
    SQLParameterRoot sqlParameterRoot = new SQLParameterRoot();
    sqlParameterRoot.Parameter = new SQLParameterRootParameter();
    sqlParameterRoot.Parameter.Name = this.txtParameter.Text.Trim();

    sqlParameterRoot.Parameter.Type = "INT";
    sqlParameterRoot.Parameter.Size = "4";
    TabPage page = _AddPage(ref sqlParameterRoot);
    if (null != page)
    {
        this.tabParameter.SelectedTab = page;
    }

    int parameterCount = 0;
    _sqlDatabaseAccessService.Command.SQLParameterRoot =
      new SQLParameterRoot[parameterCount + 1];

    if (null != _sqlDatabaseAccessService.Command.SQLParameterRoot)
    {
        parameterCount = _sqlDatabaseAccessService.Command.SQLParameterRoot.Length;
        List<SQLParameterRoot> currentParameterList =
          new List<SQLParameterRoot>(
            _sqlDatabaseAccessService.Command.SQLParameterRoot
          );
        currentParameterList.CopyTo(
          _sqlDatabaseAccessService.Command.SQLParameterRoot
        );
    }
    else
    {
        parameterCount = 1;
    }
```

```
    _sqlDatabaseAccessService.Command.SQLParameterRoot[parameterCount - 1] =
      sqlParameterRoot;
}

private TabPage _AddPage(ref SQLParameterRoot sqlParameterRoot)
{
    TabPage page = null;
    if (null != sqlParameterRoot && null != sqlParameterRoot.Parameter)
    {
        if (String.IsNullOrEmpty(sqlParameterRoot.Parameter.Name))
        {
            if (null != _parentForm)
            {
                _parentForm.DisplayMessage(
                  "Please enter parameter name to add", true
                );
                return null;
            }
        }

        if (FormSQLAzureConnect.IsPageExisted(sqlParameterRoot.Parameter.Name,
            this.tabParameter))
        {
            if (null != _parentForm)
            {
                _parentForm.DisplayMessage(
                  string.Format("The name <{0}> of parameter already exists",
                                sqlParameterRoot.Parameter.Name), true);
            }
            return null;
        }

        page = new TabPage(sqlParameterRoot.Parameter.Name);
        ParameterControl parameterControl =
          new ParameterControl(ref sqlParameterRoot, _parentForm);
        page.Controls.Add(parameterControl);
        parameterControl.Dock = DockStyle.Fill;
        this.tabParameter.TabPages.Add(page);
    }
    return page;
}

private void btnDelete_Click(object sender, EventArgs e)
{
    if (null != _parentForm)
    {
        _parentForm.DisplayMessage(string.Empty, false);
    }

    this.txtParameter.Focus();
```

```
if (string.Empty == this.txtParameter.Text)
{
    if (null != _parentForm)
    {
        _parentForm.DisplayMessage(
          "Please enter parameter name for deleting", true
        );
    }

    return;
}

TabPage page = null;
foreach (TabPage p in tabParameter.TabPages)
{
    if (p.Text == txtParameter.Text.Trim())
    {
        page = p;
        break;
    }
}

if (null != page)
{
    int parameterCount =
      _sqlDatabaseAccessService.Command.SQLParameterRoot.Length;
    if (null != _sqlDatabaseAccessService.Command.SQLParameterRoot &&
        parameterCount  > 0)
    {
        List<SQLParameterRoot> parameterList = new List<SQLParameterRoot>();

        foreach (SQLParameterRoot param in
                 _sqlDatabaseAccessService.Command.SQLParameterRoot)
        {
            if (String.Compare(param.Parameter.Name, page.Text, true) != 0)
            {
                parameterList.Add(param);
            }
        }

        _sqlDatabaseAccessService.Command.SQLParameterRoot =
          new SQLParameterRoot[parameterList.Count];
        if (parameterList.Count > 0)
        {
            parameterList.CopyTo(
              _sqlDatabaseAccessService.Command.SQLParameterRoot
            );
        }
        this.tabParameter.TabPages.Remove(page);
    }
}
```

```
            else if (null != this._parentForm)
            {
                this._parentForm.DisplayMessage(
                  string.Format("Can not find the parameter <{0}>", txtParameter.Text),
                  true
                );
            }
        }

        private void radioButtonQuery_CheckedChanged(object sender, EventArgs e)
        {
            this.groupParameter.Enabled = false;
        }

        private void radioButtonStoredProcedure_CheckedChanged(object sender, EventArgs e)
        {
            this.groupParameter.Enabled = true;
        }

        private void richTextBoxCommandText_MouseUp(object sender, MouseEventArgs e)
        {
            if (null != eventSelectedTextChanged)
            {
                try
                {
                    eventSelectedTextChanged(
                      this,
                      new SelectedTextArgs(String.IsNullOrEmpty(SelectedText)?null:this)
                    );
                }
                catch { }
            }
        }

        void richTextBoxCommandText_PreviewKeyDown(object sender, PreviewKeyDownEventArgs e)
        {
            if (null != eventBubblePreviewKeyDown)
            {
                eventBubblePreviewKeyDown(this, e);
            }
        }

        private void SQLDataServiceControl_Leave(object sender, EventArgs e)
        {
            this.richTextBoxCommandText.Clear();
            this.richTextBoxCommandText.Text = _sqlDatabaseAccessService.Command.Text;
            richTextBoxCommandText_MouseUp(this, null);
        }

    }
}
```

FormSQLAzureConnect

The main window of SQLAzureConnect also has a binding source object defined to bind the data source to the data object instance's XML SQLDatabaseAccessRoot as Figure 8-25 shows.

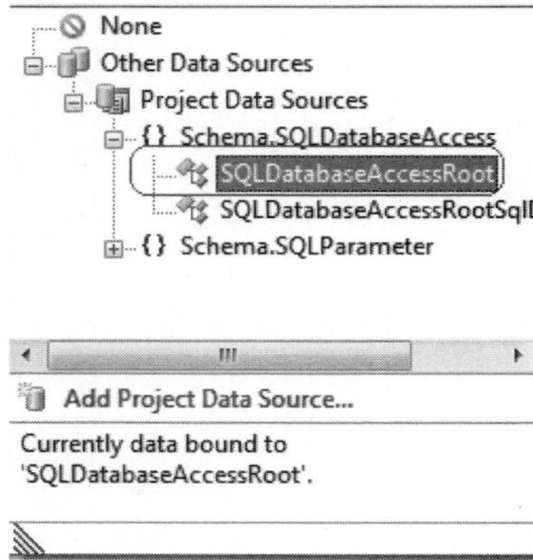

Figure 8-25. *A BindingSource of the FormSQLAzureConnect is defined to bind the data source to the data object instance's XML SQLDatabaseAccessRoot*

When an XML data file is loaded, the data will be deserialized into a data object and assigned to the member variable _sqlDataAccessRoot, and a member method _UpdateUI() is called. This method loops through all the predefined services, factors out the SQLDataServiceControls, and calls the _AddPage() method to assign each control to a tab page. Each SQLDatabaseControl has an underlying ParameterControl if the SQL command type is a stored procedure and requires parameters as Listing 8-12 shows. When a tab page has been created, it registers two events from the underlying SQLDataAccessControls, eventSelectedTextChanged and eventBubblePreviewKeyDown, triggered when the script text is selected by the user, and the F5 shortcut key is pressed to invoke the SQL script. These two events have been handled in two anonymous methods. These two anonymous methods are implemented in the method _AddPage() and shown in Listing 8-17.

Listing 8-17. *The Main Form Formsqlazureconnect Uses the Data Objects Deserialized from an XML Data File to Factor Out the UI Tab Pages and Underline SQLServiceControls*

```
private void _UpdateUI()
{
    if (null != _sqlDataAccessRoot)
    {
       this.txtServer.Text = _sqlDataAccessRoot.ServerConnection.ServerName;
       this.txtDatabase.Text = _sqlDataAccessRoot.ServerConnection.Database;
       this.txtUserID.Text = _sqlDataAccessRoot.ServerConnection.Login;
       this.txtPassword.Text = _sqlDataAccessRoot.ServerConnection.Password;

        for (int i = 0; i < _sqlDataAccessRoot.SqlDataService.Length; ++i)
```

```
        {
            this._AddPage(_sqlDataAccessRoot.SqlDataService[i].Subject,
                          ref _sqlDataAccessRoot.SqlDataService[i]);
        }
        this.tabControlServices.SelectedIndex = 0;
    }
}

private TabPage _AddPage(string pageKey,
                    ref SQLDatabaseAccessRootSqlDataService sqlDatabaseAccessRoot)
{
    TabPage page = null;
    if (IsPageExisted(pageKey, this.tabControlServices))
    {
        DisplayMessage(
          string.Format("The name <{0}> of service already exists",
          pageKey),
          true
        );
        return null;
    }

    page = new TabPage(pageKey);
    page.ForeColor = Color.Navy;
    SQLDataServiceControl serviceCotnrol =
      new SQLDataServiceControl(ref sqlDatabaseAccessRoot, this);
    serviceCotnrol.eventSelectedTextChanged += (s, e) =>
    {
      this.btnExecute.Text = null ==
        (e as SelectedTextArgs).ServiceControl?  "&Execute" : "&Execute Select";
      this.btnExecute.BackColor = null ==
        (e as SelectedTextArgs).ServiceControl ? Color.WhiteSmoke : Color.Goldenrod;
      this._TextSelected = null ==
        (e as SelectedTextArgs).ServiceControl ? null :
          ((e as SelectedTextArgs).ServiceControl as
            SQLDataServiceControl).SelectedText;
    };
    serviceCotnrol.eventBubblePreviewKeyDown += (s, e) =>
    {
        if (e.KeyCode == Keys.F5)
        {
            this.btnExecute_Click(this, null);
        }
    };
    page.Controls.Add(serviceCotnrol);
    serviceCotnrol.Dock = DockStyle.Fill;
    this.tabControlServices.TabPages.Add(page);
    this.tabControlServices.SelectedTab = page;

    return page;
}
```

`SQLAzureConnect` also allows the user to create a new service and underlying parameters manually and edit or delete existing services. The data can be saved and played back. The rest of the implementation for the UI is fairly straightforward, and the total number of code lines is just around 300, thanks to the XML data-driven dynamic factory approach. You can download the source code from the bundled project ZIP file. Feel free to use it directly or to add more functions.

Summary

In this chapter I covered the newly minted SQL Azure features that replaced SQL Data Services. SQL Azure is an exciting innovation, as it is the first relational model cloud database, and it has many advantages. One of the main advantages is that it provides a familiar environment for most developers, which means existing applications can easily be migrated from existing databases.

During the course of this chapter I took you through the fundamentals of SQL Azure to show you its basic features. We created tables, inserted data, and queried the database using SQL Server Management Studio. The main example in the chapter is a tool for working with SQL Azure, and on-premises SQL Server installations, which allows you to unify all your relational database testing and debugging.

CHAPTER 9

■ ■ ■

Deploy Applications and Production Maintenance

In this chapter I am going to provide examples of how to deploy Azure Storage and applications to the cloud. The process of deployment is fairly straightforward and intuitive. The steps are as follows, each of which I'll touch on in this chapter:

1. Prepare the application package and configuration package for deployment.
2. Deploy table storage.
3. Deploy the cloud application.

I'll also cover the maintenance of a deployed cloud application.

Preparing the Application Package and Configuration Package for Deployment

The application and associated configuration need to be packed up before they can be deployed to the cloud. These packages can be generated from Visual Studio as Figure 9-1 shows. This example can be found in `Exercise_4-3` from the download. Select Publish from the context menu by right-clicking on the cloud application solution's node in Solution Explorer.

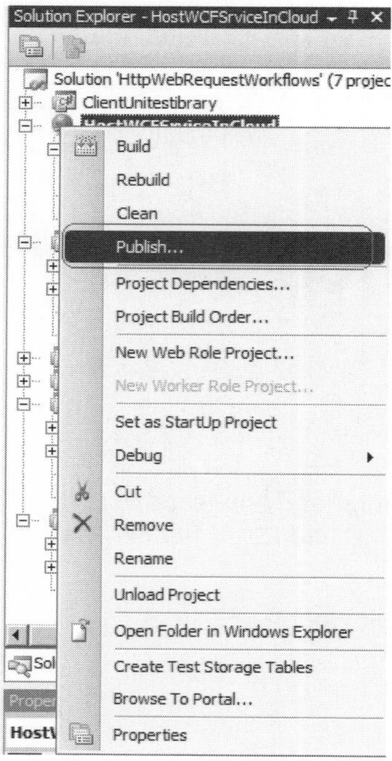

Figure 9-1. Generate the application package and configuration package from Visual Studio

The packages will be generated by Visual Studio, and a new folder called Publish will be created to hold the package files. The path of the folder is under the project node of the specific compiler setting. For example, if the compiler setting is Debug, the folder is located under the Debug folder as Figure 9-2 shows.

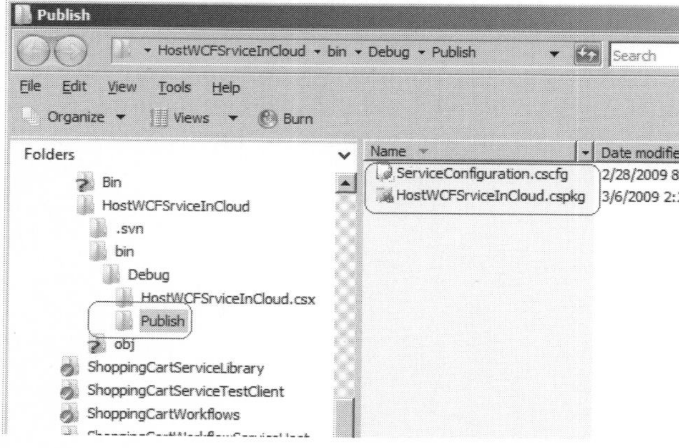

Figure 9-2. The generated package can be found in the folder `Publish` *under the project tree in Windows Explorer*

Deploying Table Storage

We are going to use the table storage we created in Exercise 2-2 as an example to illustrate how to deploy table storage to the cloud.

1. From Internet Explorer, enter the Azure portal address and sign in with your Live ID. Select New Project ➤ Storage Account as Figure 9-3 shows.

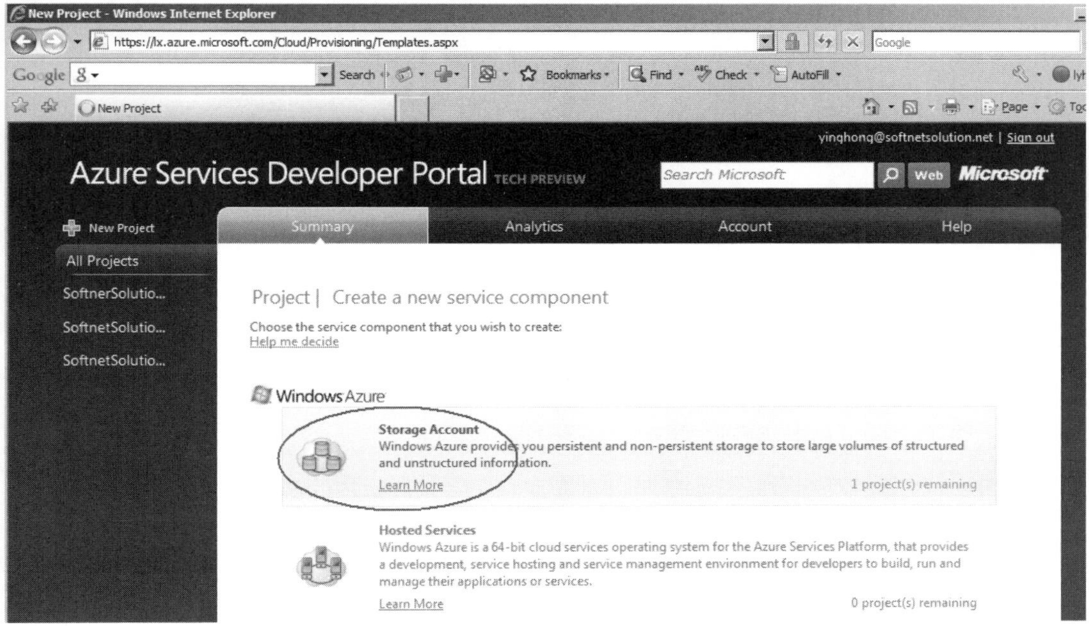

Figure 9-3. Create a new storage account from the Azure portal page

2. Check the availability of the account as Figure 9-4 shows. The name must be in lowercase.

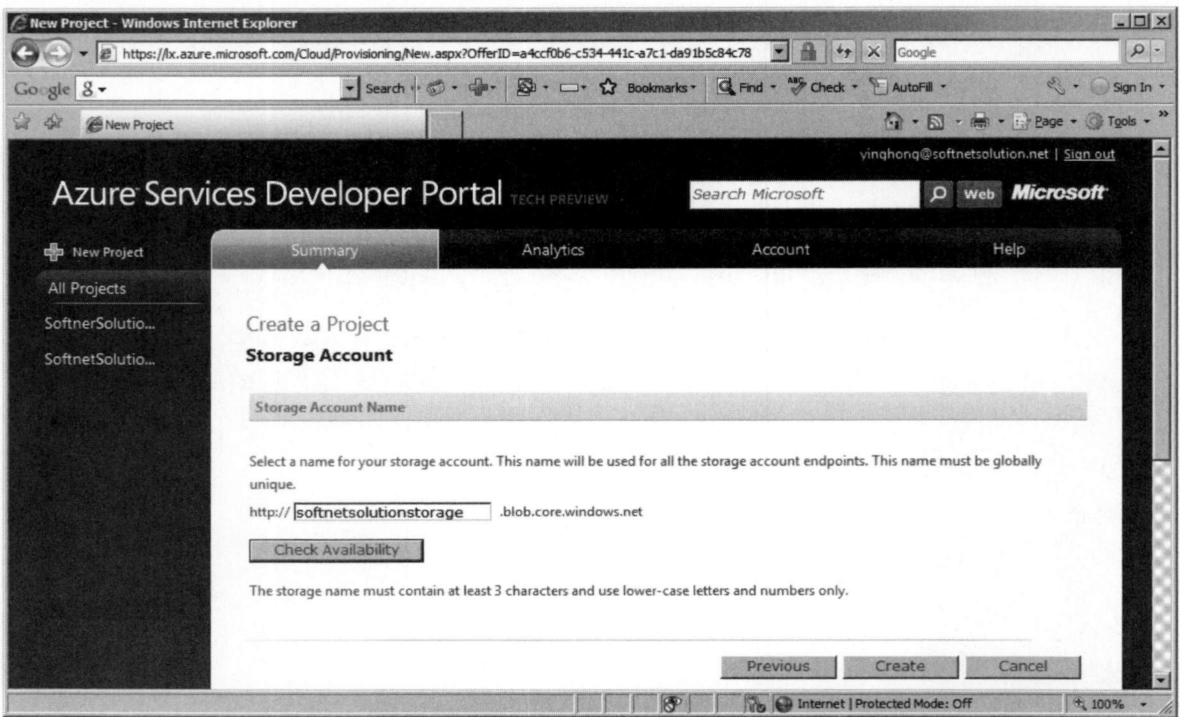

Figure 9-4. Create a new storage account from Azure portal page

3. When the storage account is created from the cloud, the endpoint for blob, table, and queue storage will be displayed, and a new account shared key will be assigned to that account as Figure 9-5 shows.

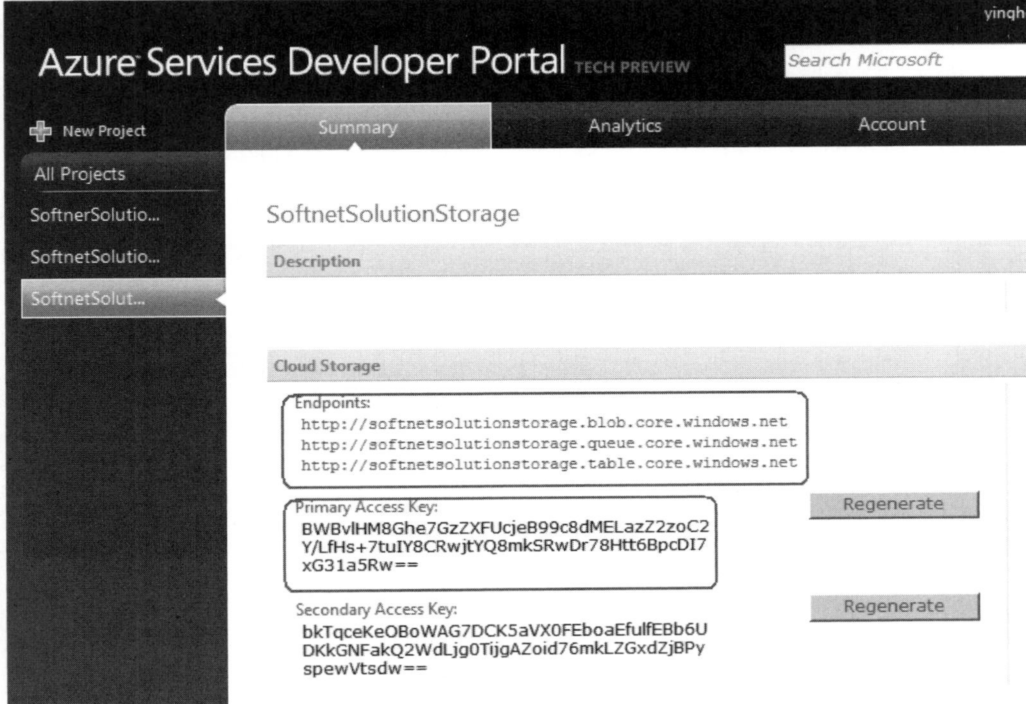

Figure 9-5. Account shared key and the endpoint will be assigned to this newly created account

4. Modify the configuration using the assigned secretary key as Listing 9-1 shows.

Listing 9-1. Updated Configurations for Exercise 2-2

```
<?xml version="1.0"?>
<ServiceConfiguration serviceName="CloudTableStorageService"
         xmlns="http://schemas.microsoft.com/ServiceHosting/2008/10/ServiceConfiguration">
  <Role name="WebRole">
    <Instances count="1"/>
    <ConfigurationSettings>
      <!--Local Development-->
      <!--Setting name="AccountName" value="devstoreaccount1"/>
      <Setting name="AccountSharedKey" value="<SHARED_KEY"/>
      <Setting name="TableStorageEndpoint" value="http://127.0.0.1:10002/"/-->
      <!--Production Environment-->
      <Setting name="AccountName" value="softnetsolutionstorage"/>
```

```
      <Setting name="AccountSharedKey" value="<ACCOUNT_SHARED_KEY>"/>
      <Setting name="TableStorageEndpoint" value="http://table.core.windows.net/"/>
    </ConfigurationSettings>
  </Role>
</ServiceConfiguration>
```

Host an Application from the Cloud

Follow the steps illustrated in the next section to deploy the application that contains the table storage access web role. The results of a successful deployment are shown in Figure 9-6. Test the application after deployment and you can have the same results as in Exercise 2-2.

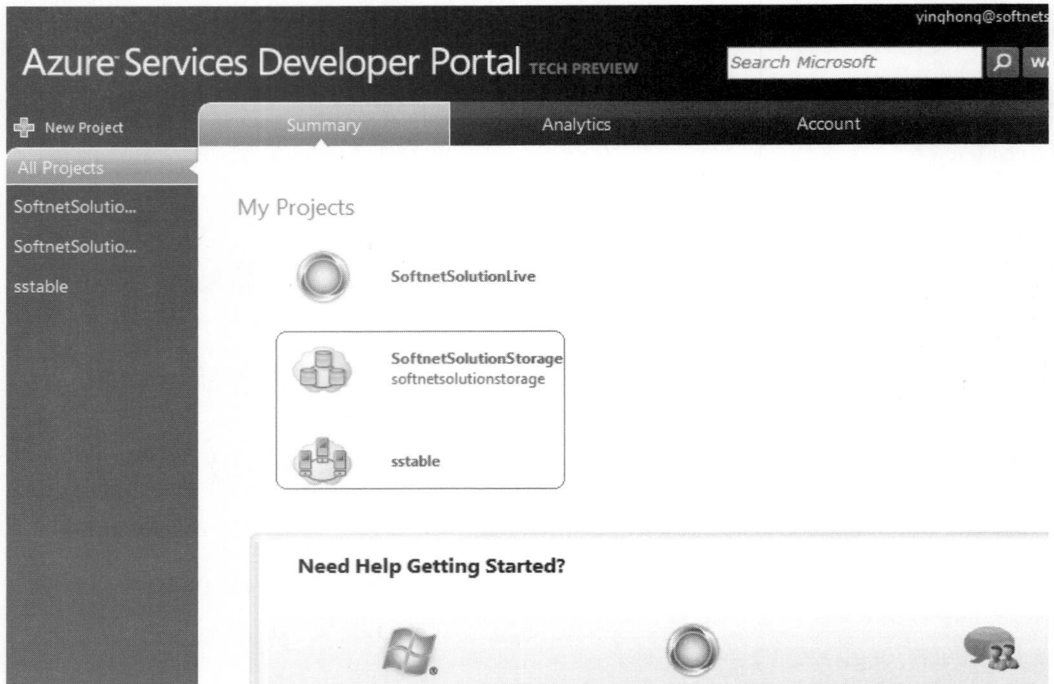

Figure 9-6. Both the table storage and the application used to access the table storage need to be deployed to the cloud

Deploying Cloud Applications

Now let's see how to deploy a cloud application.

1. Select Hosted Services after you have signed in from the Azure portal, as Figure 9-7 shows.

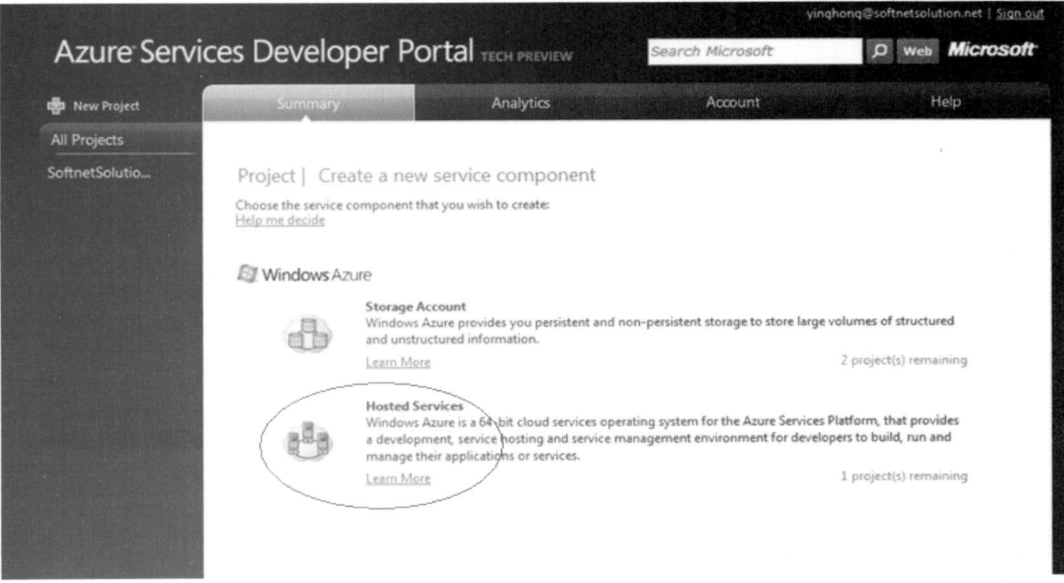

Figure 9-7. Select the Hosted Services from the portal to deploy an application to the cloud

2. Enter a name for the application that will be hosted from the cloud. The maximum length of the name that can be entered is 20 characters, and the name should be unique, as Figure 9-8 shows.

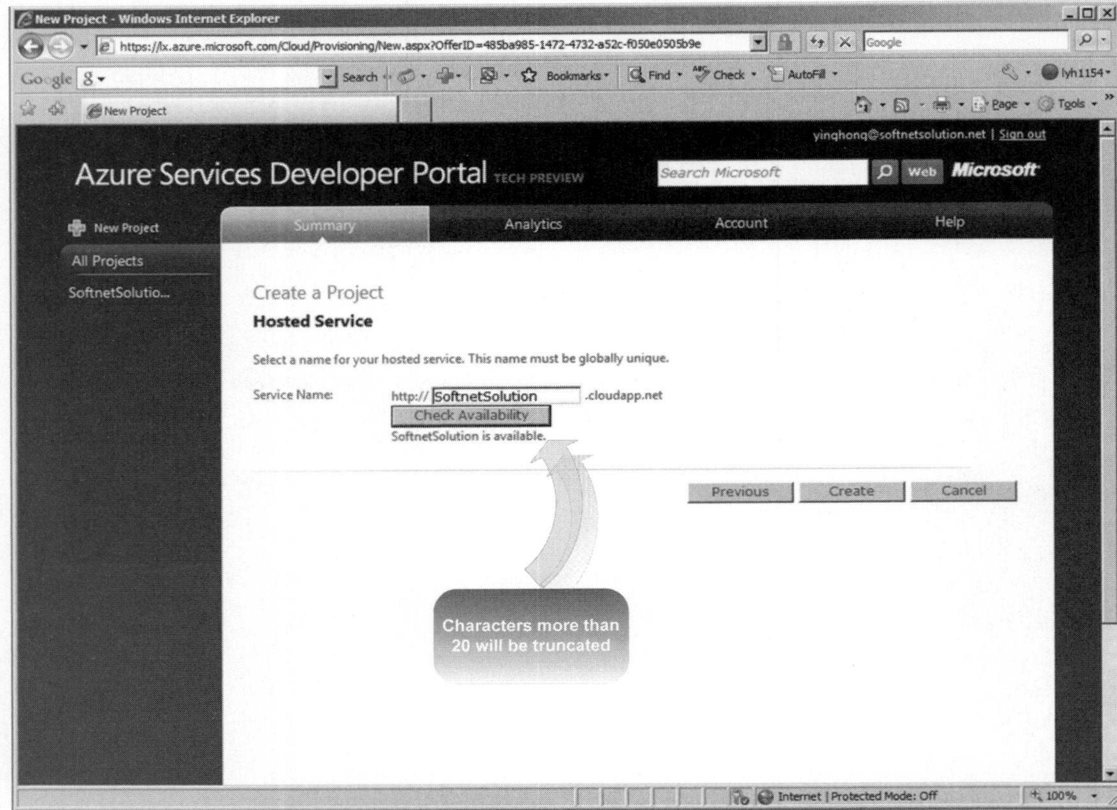

Figure 9-8. *Verify the available name for the application name*

Staging Deployment

Staging deployment (shown in Figure 9-9) is the step where an application runs in pre-production. In this status the application should be fully functional. This provides an opportunity for you to do testing and final tuning in the remote cloud environment. If the application has never been deployed before, then when the Deploy button is pressed the application will be given Staging status and should be fully functional. Revisit this page after testing and deploy the application from Staging to Production as Figure 9-13 shows.

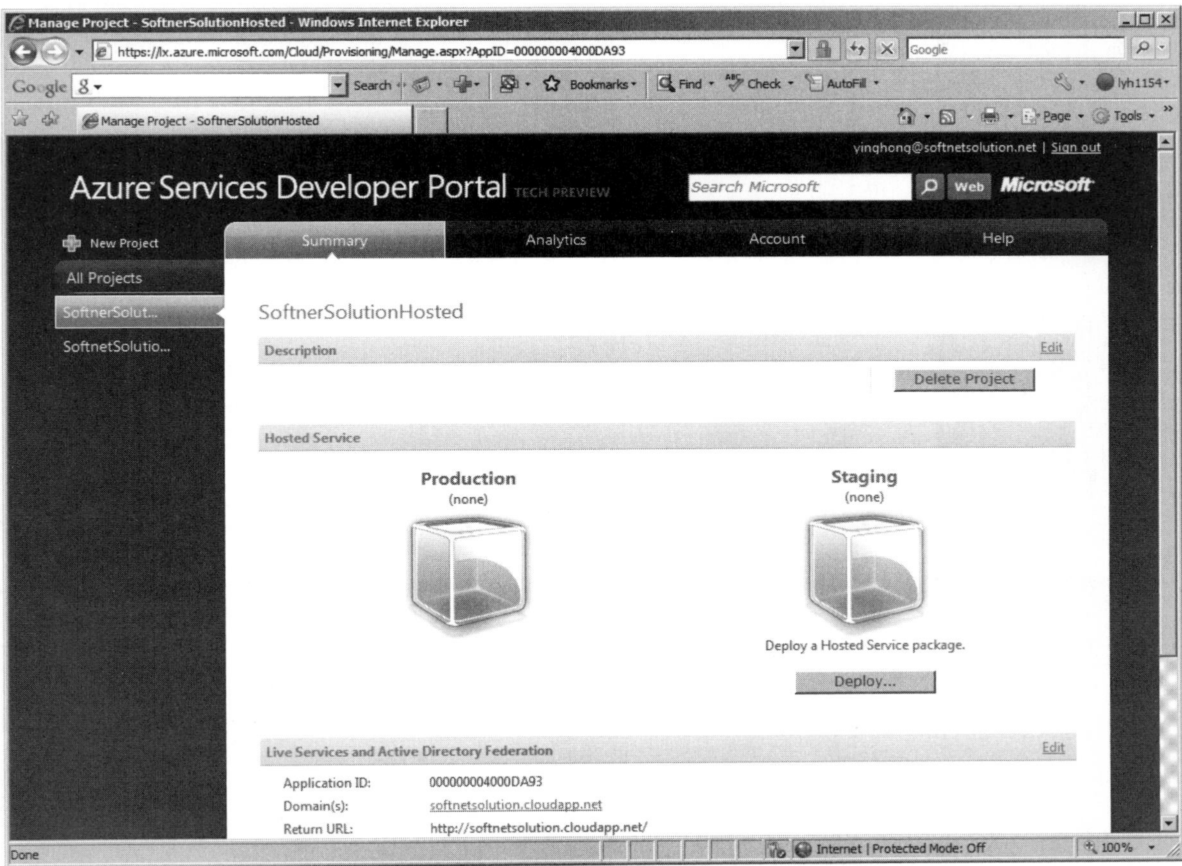

Figure 9-9. *Staging deployment is one step before an application is hosted in production*

Select the Application Package and Configuration Package

At this step you need to provide the path for both the compiled package file and the configuration package file, as Figure 9-10 shows.

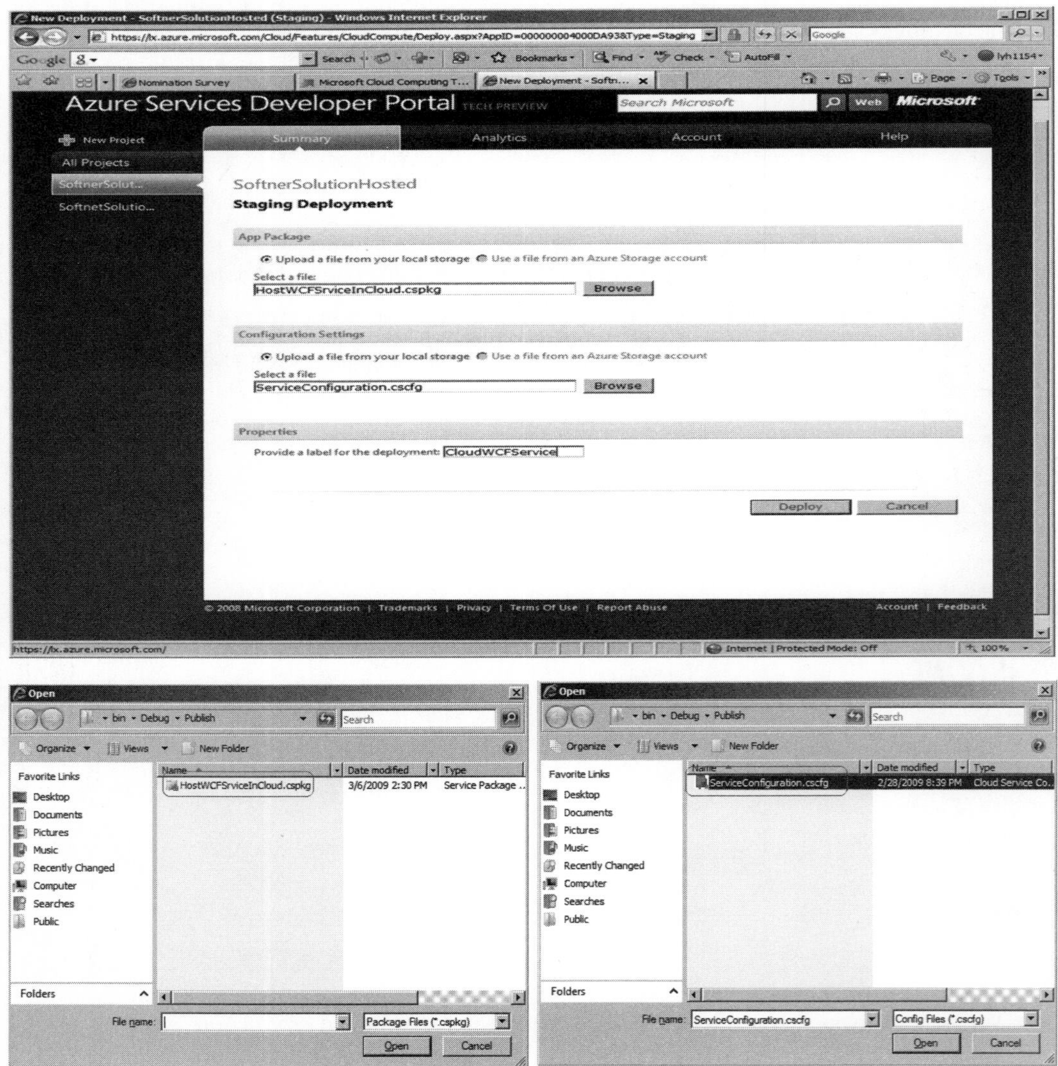

Figure 9-10. Select the application package and configuration package file for deployment

Running a Hosted Application

Figure 9-11 shows that a web role is running from the cloud. Double-click on the URL to access the service provided by that web role.

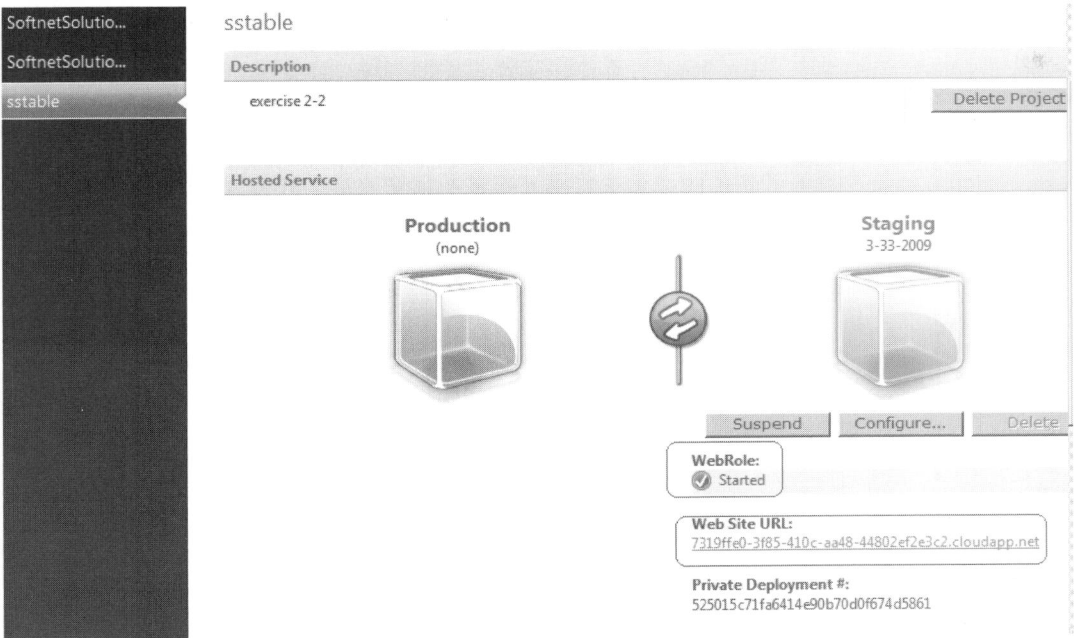

Figure 9-11. An example of a web role hosted and run from the cloud

Figure 9-12 shows a worker role that has been hosted in the cloud.

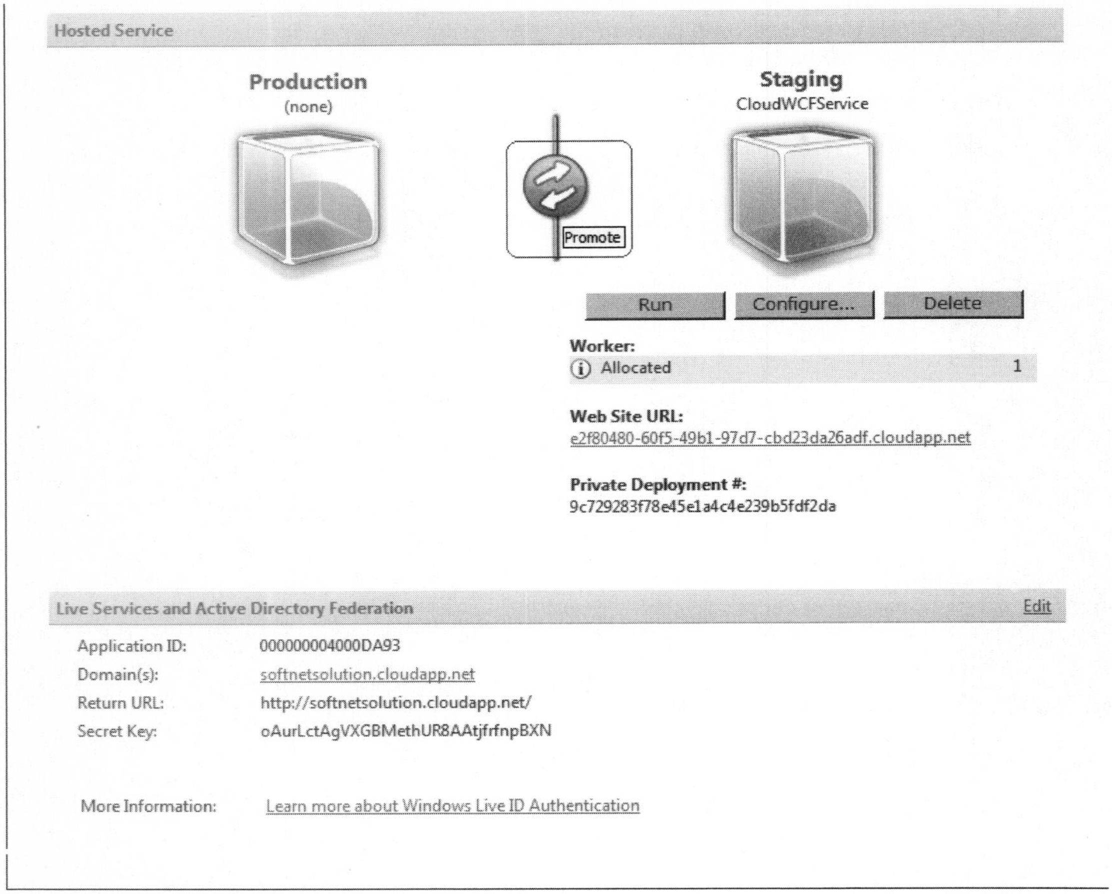

Figure 9-12. *An example of a worker role hosted and run from the cloud*

Click on the Promote button, and the application will be promoted from Staging to Production status as Figure 9-13 shows.

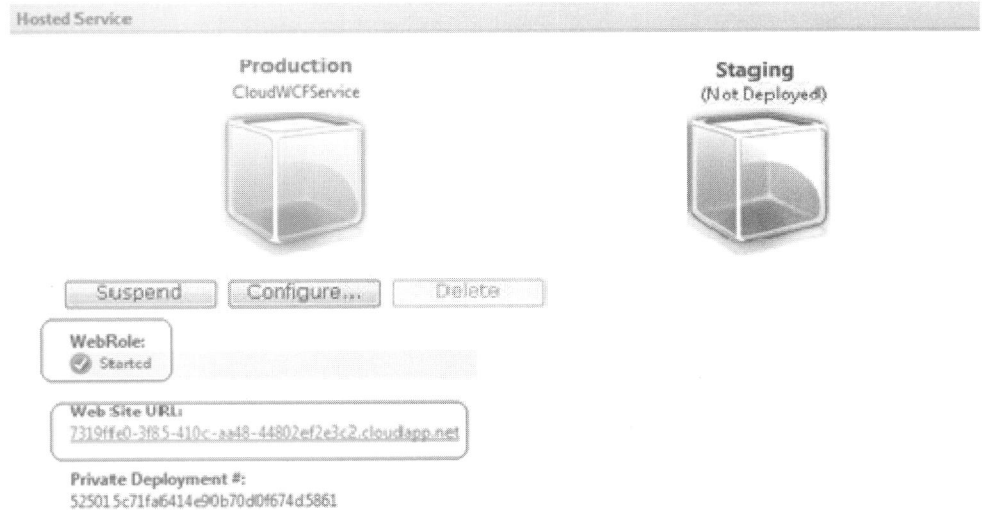

Figure 9-13. *An example of an application that has been deployed to the cloud*

Maintenance of a Cloud Application

In principle, cloud storage, resources, and applications are maintenance-free for users. There is very limited work left for end users to do. Let's have a quick look at some of the tasks you may have to carry out.

Increase or Decrease the Number of Instances

The number of cloud application instances can be changed directly from the Azure portal page without redeployment by selecting the application and clicking on the Configure button as Figure 9-14 shows.

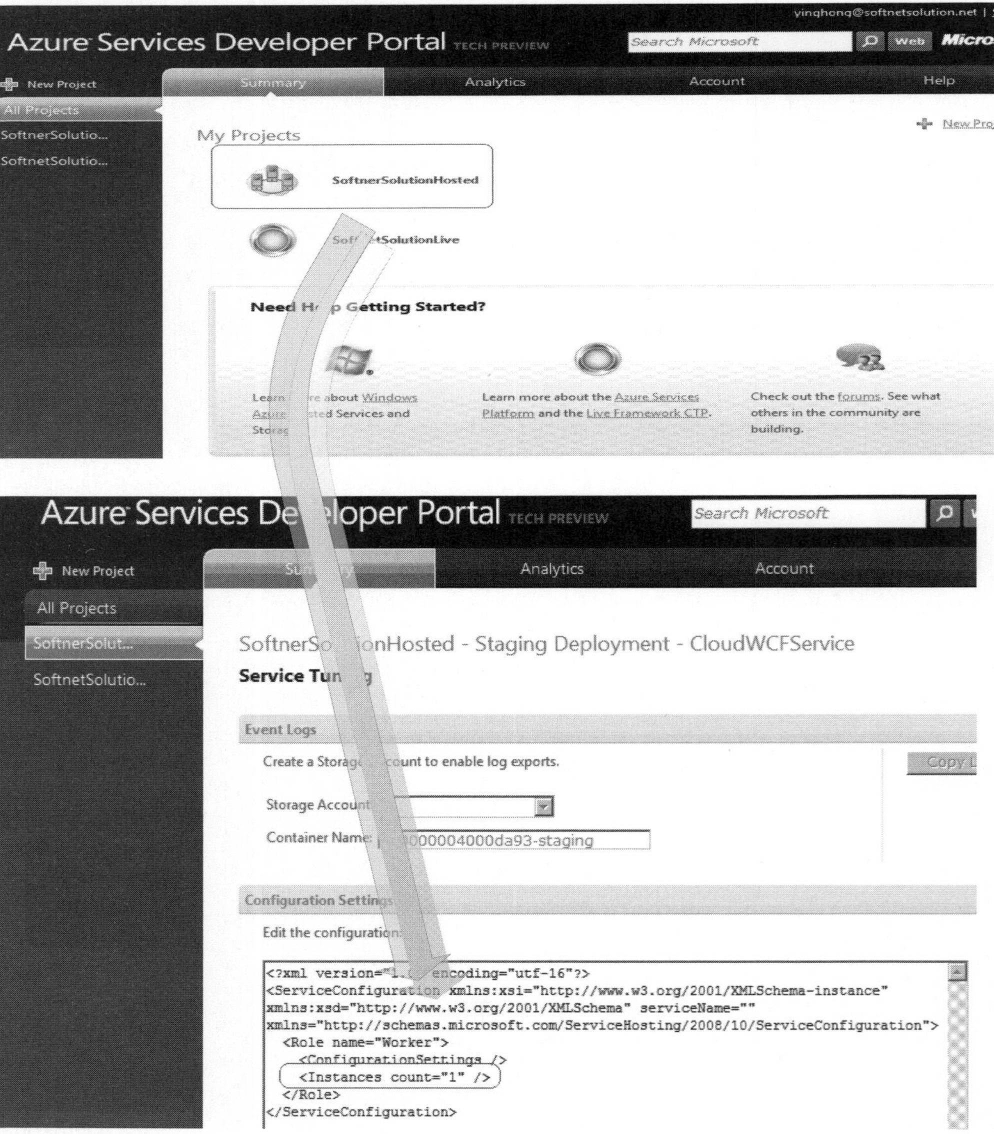

Figure 9-14. Change the number of instances of a cloud application directly from the Azure portal

Override the Configuration

Click the Browse button and upload a new version of the configuration file. This action will cause the application to restart.

Redeploy an Application with a New Version

Delete the application and deploy a new version.

Summary

This chapter was short and sweet compared to the rest of the book, as befits a chapter on cloud application deployment and maintenance. Once your application has been deployed, there is very little for you to worry about; maintenance is largely taken care of.

We started by seeing how to prepare an application for deployment and set up cloud table storage. We then looked at how to deploy the application, including how to use application staging. The final section covered some quick tips on how to configure your application.

APPENDIX

Table A-1. Specifications for Windows Azure Blob Storage

Specification	Tables	Queues	Blobs
ID			• Block ID, b4 byte/block • Blob metadata, 8 KB/blob • Blocks, 4 MB each
Container Name			• Valid DNS resolvable name • 3-63 characters • Letters, numbers and dash • Every dash must be immediately preceded and followed by a letter or number.
Name	• Alphanumeric characters only • Case-insensitive • 3-63 characters • Up to 255 entity properties (including `PartitionKey`, `RowKey`, and `Timestamp`)	• Valid DNS resolvable • Must be in lowercase • 3-63 characters • Begin with a letter or number • First and last letter must be alphanumeric. • Letters, numbers and dashes are accepted. • Dash may not be the first or last letter	• 1,024 characters • Reserved URL characters must be properly escaped. • Blob storage is not hierarchical; specify a delimiter within a blob name to create a virtual hierarchy endpoint address.
Property	• Case-sensitive		Must be unique

Specification	Tables	Queues	Blobs
Name	• Alphanumeric characters only • Maximum 255 characters • Must starting with a letter		
Capacities	< 1 MB	• < 8 KB/message • FIFO (First In First Out) • Infinite number of messages	• Public blob, 64 MB • Public block/public list, 50 GB each

Azure Service Management Tools

Azure Service Management Tools can be downloaded from `http://code.msdn.microsoft.com/AzureManagementTools`. Follow the instructions to install on your local development system. When you first start this Windows snap-in, you need to enter your Azure solution name as the user name as Figure A-1 shows.

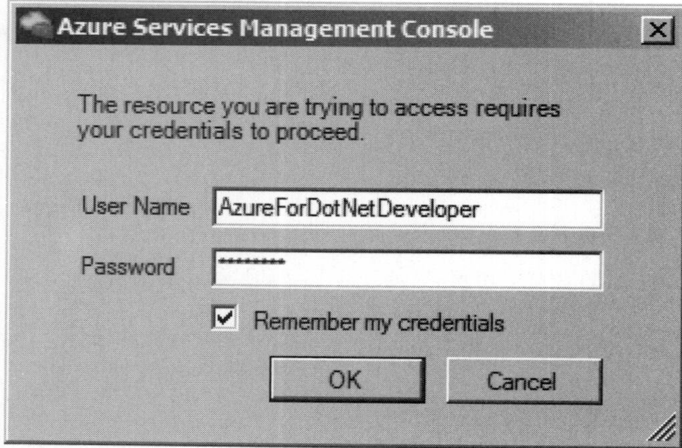

Figure A-1. The Azure solution name should be entered as User Name for Azure Services

Index

D

O

P

Q

R

S

X, Y, Z

eBookshop

Apress®
THE EXPERT'S VOICE™